D0673166

THE GREATEST HOAX ON EARTH?
REFUTING DAWKINS ON EVOLUTION

JONATHAN SARFATI, PH.D., F.M.

First edition: March 2010
Second edition: March 2014

ISBN: 978-1-921643-06-4

Cover Design: Rik Hilverts

Layout: Jessica Spykerman

Please visit our website for further information on the Christian worldview and the creation/evolution issue.

CREATION.com

For information regarding author interviews, please contact the publicity department at (770) 439-9130.

CREATION
BOOK PUBLISHERS

Atlanta, Georgia, USA
www.creationbookpublishers.com

THE GREATEST HOAX ON EARTH?

REFUTING DAWKINS ON EVOLUTION

JONATHAN SARFATI, PH.D., F.M.

A RESPONSE TO RICHARD DAWKINS'

THE GREATEST SHOW ON EARTH
THE EVIDENCE FOR EVOLUTION

ABOUT THE AUTHOR

Jonathan D. Sarfati, Ph.D, F.M., was born in Ararat, Australia, in 1964. He moved to New Zealand as a child, where he later studied mathematics, geology, physics, and chemistry at Victoria University in Wellington. He obtained honours level in physical and inorganic chemistry, as well as in condensed matter physics and nuclear physics.

Dr Sarfati received his Ph.D. in physical chemistry from the same institution in 1995 on the topic of spectroscopy, especially vibrational. He has co-authored various technical papers on such things as high temperature superconductors and sulfur- and selenium-containing ring and cage molecules.

As well as being very interested in formal logic and philosophy, Dr Sarfati is a keen chess player. He represented New Zealand in three Chess Olympiads and is a former New Zealand national chess champion. In 1988, F.I.D.E., the International Chess Federation, awarded him the title of F.I.D.E. Master (F.M.). He is well-known at major creation conferences for successfully playing, while blindfolded, up to 12 sighted challengers simultaneously.

A Christian since 1984, he was for some years on the editorial committee of *Apologia*, the journal of the Wellington Christian Apologetics Society, of which he was a co-founder.

Dr Sarfati has since 1996 worked full-time for *Creation Ministries International* (CMI), a non-profit ministry grouping, as a research scientist, speaker and editorial consultant for *Creation* magazine and the associated *Journal of Creation*, and has written many articles for both. For most of this time, he was based in the CMI office in Brisbane, Australia, until transferring to the CMI-US office in Atlanta, Georgia, in early 2010 with his American-born wife, Sherry.

Jonathan has authored the books *Refuting Evolution* (the biggest selling creation book of all time), *Refuting Evolution 2, Refuting Compromise* (a comprehensive theological and scientific defense of straightforward Genesis) and *By Design: The evidence for nature's intelligent designer, the God of the Bible*. In addition, he has co-authored several other books, including the popular *Creation Answers Book*.

He also contributes specialist information to CMI's multi-country website **creation.com**.

Acknowledgments

I am very grateful to all who helped with the content of this work, by reviewing either specific sections related to their areas of speciality, or the entire manuscript. Their many helpful comments and proofreading pickups greatly improved the final product.

These were (in alphabetical surname order): Don Batten, John Baumgardner, David Catchpoole, Lita Cosner, Russell Grigg, Walter ReMine, John Sanford, Tas Walker, Carl Wieland. Of course, any deficiencies that remain would be my responsibility.

I am also grateful to my dear wife Sherry for her patience and support throughout.

Jonathan Sarfati

CONTENTS

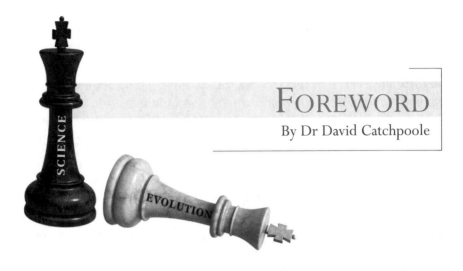

Clash of the titans: Sarfati vs Dawkins

Richard Dawkins is the world's best-known champion of both atheism and its intellectual underpinning, particles-to-people evolution. His latest book, *The Greatest Show on Earth: the evidence for evolution* is touted as an unanswerable challenge to those who believe in divine creation. In the past, he says, he has *assumed* evolution; this time he has set out to present in one major book the *evidence* for evolution (and its corollary, vast geological ages).

Now scientist, chessmaster and logician Jonathan Sarfati Ph.D., F.M. goes head to head with Dawkins in this full-on rebuttal, *The Greatest Hoax on Earth? Refuting Dawkins on evolution*. Sarfati is no lightweight opponent; his *Refuting Evolution* (over 500,000 in print) is the biggest-selling creationist book ever. In his crisp, readable style trademarked by sheer competence, Sarfati calmly but relentlessly erodes each of Dawkins' claims. In the process, he repeatedly exposes logical fallacies—even dubious tactics—employed in Dawkins' ideologically driven crusade.

However, rather than pretending that the science of origins is some ideology-free zone, Sarfati openly declares his own axioms as a committed Bible-believing Christian. He fearlessly grasps the nettle in areas such as geology and dating methods—often downplayed by anti-evolutionists, but recognized by Dawkins as crucial components of this debate.

Those familiar with Dawkins' previous (and, it must be said, elegantly written) works know of his uncompromising commitment to his materialistic/reductionist axioms. One suspects that, while wincing at the body-blows his arguments receive in these pages, he will at least secretly admire Sarfati's similarly consistent commitment—a commitment free of the slippery inconsistency of many who seek to eat their cake and still have it, by claiming that God really used the godless process of evolution, and pretending that the Bible allows this.

It's precisely those who feel smug in the belief that all the intellectual firepower is on the side of evolution who most need to read Sarfati's book—if only to understand better why it is that there are thousands of scientists and intellectuals today who are convinced that in a fair science showdown, stripped bare of rhetoric and ideological 'noise' by comparing each position within its own axioms, biblical creation outguns evolution.

At the very least, fair-minded readers of this book will need to concede that they have been largely fed caricatures of the creationist position, exemplified in spades in *Greatest Show*. If reason, science and rationality were all that were at stake, Sarfati's exposé of what should be the best that evolution has on offer should make it increasingly difficult to exclude creation from a full seat at the table of rational debate. One would hope that his efforts will inspire a whole new generation of qualified believers to put in the hard work and apply their own intellectual horsepower to further loosen the stranglehold of mega-evolutionary thinking on our culture in general.

David Catchpoole, Ph.D.
Scientist, lecturer and writer,
Creation Ministries International (Australia)

Who is Richard Dawkins?

Clinton Richard Dawkins is probably the most famous evolutionist, anticreationist and atheist today, and a staunch admirer of Charles Robert Darwin (1809–1882).

Dawkins was born in Nairobi, part of the then British colony of Kenya, in 1941, and moved to England aged 8. He gained his degree in Zoology at the Balliol College, Oxford, in 1962. There he was tutored by Nikolaas Tinbergen (1907–1988), who shared the 1973 Nobel Prize in Physiology or Medicine for his discoveries about instinct, learning and choice in animals. Dawkins continued to study under Tinbergen, at the University of Oxford, receiving his M.A. and D.Phil. (the Oxford equivalent of Ph.D.) degrees in 1966.

After this, Dawkins took a position of assistant professor of zoology at the University of California, Berkeley, before returning to Oxford as a lecturer in 1970. In this time, he researched animal decision-making. Since the 1970s, he has concentrated on writing for popular audiences, for which he is far more famous than for his scientific research on animal behaviour.

Evolution advocate

Dawkins' first book, *The Selfish Gene* (1976), advocated a gene-centred view of evolution. That is, life first began from a 'replicator' that could make approximate copies of itself, therefore would predominate in a primordial soup. Those copies that could make machines to help them copy better would reproduce more. Dawkins claims that these replicators are basically our genes, and our bodies are just 'gigantic lumbering robots' which are their 'survival machines'. This book also independently introduced the idea of the 'meme', a set of ideas that is replicated in other minds.

Dawkins regards his second book, *The Extended Phenotype* (1982), as his most important contribution to evolutionary biology. This is a kind of sequel and defence of *The Selfish Gene*; whereas in his first book, Dawkins argues that the organism is the gene's survival machine, in his second he extends the genes' influence to the environment modified by the organism's behaviour. If this behaviour helps the organism's survival, then the genes 'for' that behaviour will reproduce best. His examples include beaver dams and termite mounds, as well as animal behaviour that benefits a parasite afflicting it, hence the genes of that parasite.

Anti-creationist

In 1986, Dawkins wrote *The Blind Watchmaker*, an attack on the argument that design in the living world demonstrates an intelligent Designer; rather, the apparent design is the result of evolution by natural selection. He regards that as a vital argument for his own atheistic faith:

> "An atheist before Darwin could have said, following Hume: 'I have no explanation for complex biological design. All I know is that God isn't a good explanation, so we must wait and hope that somebody comes up with a better one.' I can't help feeling that such a position, though logically sound, would have left one feeling pretty unsatisfied, and that although atheism might have been *logically* tenable before Darwin, Darwin made it possible to be an intellectually fulfilled atheist." (*BW*, p.6)

Earlier that year, on Valentine's Day, Dawkins participated in the Huxley Memorial Debate at the Oxford Union, opposing the proposition, "That the doctrine of creation is more valid than the theory of evolution." With him was the leading English evolutionist John Maynard Smith (1920–2004), and opposed were two biblical creationist scientists: triple doctorate organic chemist and pharmacologist A. E. Wilder-Smith (1915–1995) and Edgar Andrews (1932–), then Professor[1] of Materials at the University of London. The audience vote of Oxford students was a modest win for the evolution side, 198–115. Yet Dawkins was not happy—in his closing comments, he had

---

1.   N.B., in the UK and in many Commonwealth countries, "Professor" is a title given only to the highest ranking university academics.

"implored" the audience (his word) not to give a single vote to the creationist side, since every such vote "would be a blot on the escutcheon of the ancient University of Oxford."[2] (Alternatively, it would be a return to Oxford's roots, since it was founded by creationists.) After that, he is on record refusing to debate any biblical creationist.

Simonyi "Chair of Atheism" for "Darwin's Rottweiler"

In 1995, he was appointed the Simonyi Professor for the Public Understanding of Science at Oxford. This was an endowment by leading Microsoft software designer and billionaire Charles Simonyi (b. Simonyi Károly, 1948) explicitly for Dawkins. One report said:

"Evolution's first great advocate, 1860s biologist Thomas Henry Huxley, earned the nickname 'Darwin's bulldog' from his fellow Victorians. In our own less decorous day, Dawkins deserves an even stronger epithet: 'Darwin's Rottweiler, perhaps,' Simonyi suggests."[3]

Dawkins retired from this post in September 2008. I am unable to find any example from this period of Dawkins aiding the public understanding of such *real* science as physics or chemistry, or even of the history or philosophy of science. But during this professorship, Dawkins wrote seven books on evolution/atheism. It's not surprising that British author Paul Johnson called it "Oxford's first Chair of Atheism."[4]

Prolific evolutionary author

For example, *Climbing Mount Improbable* (1996), one of Dawkins' own favourites among his books, aimed to defend slow and gradual evolution. The title is a parable: many structures in living organisms are so complex that there is a vanishingly small probability of producing them in a single step— this corresponds to leaping the high Mt Improbable in a single step. But, says Dawkins, this mountain has a gently upward-sloping terrain on the other side, where a climber can ascend gradually, constantly progressing to the top. This corresponds to the neo-Darwinian mechanism of evolution—mutations + natural selection. Mutations produce gradual improvements, and natural selection means that organisms which have them are slightly more likely to leave offspring. So a later generation of organisms is slightly more complex, or higher up the slope of Mt Improbable. This process is repeated until the dizzy peaks are scaled by this ever-so-gradual process.[5]

2. Cooper, G. and Humber, P., Fraudulent report at AAAS and the 1986 Oxford University debate, www.samizdat.qc.ca/cosmos/origines/debate_gc.htm.
3. Downey, R., in *Eastsideweek*, 11 December 1996.
4. Johnson, P., If there is no God, what is the Oxford atheist scared of? *Spectator*, p. 19, 16 March 1996.
5. See my review, *J. Creation* 12(1):29–34, 1998; creation.com/dawkins.

In his largest book, *The Ancestor's Tale: A Pilgrimage to the Dawn of Evolution* (2004, 688 pages hardcover), Dawkins aimed to illustrate the history of life on Earth. This was a series of 40 tales, from the point of view of man's alleged evolutionary precursors,[6] and the name is a play on the Middle English classic *The Canterbury Tales* by Geoffrey Chaucer (c. 1343–1400).

This has made him probably the best known exponent of evolution in the world. Yet Ernst Mayr (1904–2005), one of the most influential evolutionists as far as biologists are concerned, says:

> "The funny thing is if in England, you ask a man in the street who the greatest living Darwinian is, he will say Richard Dawkins. And indeed, Dawkins has done a marvelous job of popularizing Darwinism. But Dawkins' basic theory of the gene being the object of evolution is totally non-Darwinian. I would not call him the greatest Darwinian."[7]

Apostle of Antitheism

Richard Dawkins not only regards Darwinism as compatible with atheism, but that atheism is a logical outcome of evolutionary belief. He has long promoted atheism both individually and as part of atheistic organizations. Dawkins is an Honorary Associate of the National Secular Society, a vice-president of the British Humanist Association (since 1996), a Distinguished Supporter of the Humanist Society of Scotland, a Humanist Laureate of the International Academy of Humanism, and a fellow of the Committee for Skeptical Inquiry. In 2003, he signed Humanism and Its Aspirations, published by the American Humanist Association.

In his 1991 essay "Viruses of the Mind", Dawkins singled out theistic religion as one of the most pernicious of these viruses. I.e. he regards theism as a kind of disease or pathology, and parents who teach it to their children are, in Dawkins' view, supposedly practising mental child abuse. But the sorts of criteria Dawkins applies have led critics to wonder whether Dawkins' own strident atheism itself could be a mental pathology—or 'atheopathy'.

After the 11 September 2001 terrorist attack, Dawkins argued:

> "Many of us saw religion as harmless nonsense. Beliefs might lack all supporting evidence but, we thought, if people needed a crutch for consolation, where's the harm? September 11th changed all that. Revealed faith is not harmless nonsense; it can be lethally dangerous nonsense.

6. See review by Weinberger, Lael, Long tails, tall tales, *J. Creation* **22**(1):37–40, 2008; creation.com/ancestors-tale.
7. Interview with Ernst Mayr, author of *What Evolution Is*, www.edge.org/3rd_culture/mayr/mayr_print.html, 2001.

Dangerous, because it gives people unshakeable confidence in their own righteousness. Dangerous, because it gives them false courage to kill themselves, which automatically removes normal barriers to killing others. Dangerous, because it teaches enmity to others labelled only by a difference of inherited tradition. And, dangerous, because we have all bought into a weird respect, which uniquely protects religion from normal criticism. Let's now stop being so damned respectful!"[8]

Dawkins somehow overlooked the record-breaking tens of millions killed by atheistic regimes last century. This was thoroughly documented by Rudolph Rummel (1932–), Professor Emeritus of Political Science at the University of Hawaii, who coined the term *democide* for murder by government.[9]

This antitheism continued with presenting a Channel 4 program in the UK, called *The Root of All Evil?* (2006). This title was Channel 4's choice, not Dawkins', but he argued that humanity would be better off without belief in God. The victims of the democides catalogued by Prof. Rummel might not agree. In this program, Dawkins interviewed a number of Christian leaders, and visited several holy sites and communities of major religions. However, some critics attacked the program for not having informed Christian responses. For example, Dawkins' fellow Oxford Don, Alister McGrath (1953–), Professor of Historical Theology (with a D.Phil. in molecular biophysics), claimed that after his responses Dawkins seemed uncomfortable, so was not surprised that his own contribution remained on the cutting room floor.[10]

Dawkins' defence of atheism produced his best-seller to date, *The God Delusion* (2006), with 1.5 million copies sold. Many high-profile atheists praised it, and naturally Christians criticized it. For example, Philip Bell, M.Sc. and former cancer researcher, published a detailed review,[11] and there are other books responding to it.[12] However, leading logician and Christian philosopher Alvin Plantinga (1932–), currently "John A. O'Brien Professor of Philosophy at the University of Notre Dame", was not impressed with Dawkins' excursions outside biology into philosophy, claiming that they could be called sophomoric were it not a grave insult to most sophomores.[13]

8.   Multiple contributors, Has the world changed? *The Guardian* (UK), 11 September 2001.
9.   Rummel, R.J., *Death by Government*, New Brunswick, N.J.: Transaction Publishers, 1994; www.hawaii.edu/powerkills/NOTE1.HTM.
10. McGrath, A., "Do stop behaving as if you are God, Professor Dawkins", *Mail Online*, 9 February 2007.
11. See Bell, P., Atheist with a Mission: Critique of *The God Delusion* by Richard Dawkins, *J. Creation* **21**(2):28–34, 2007; creation.com/delusion.
12. Slane, R., *The God Reality: A critique of Richard Dawkins' The God Delusion*, Day One, UK.
13. Plantinga, A., The Dawkins Confusion: Naturalism *ad absurdum*, *Christianity Today* (Books and Culture), March/April 2007; www.christianitytoday.com/bc.

Prof. McGrath himself responded to the book (co-authored with his wife).[14] This also revealed that Dawkins' support among atheists was not universal— famous evolutionary philosopher Michael Ruse writes in the blurb, "*The God Delusion* makes me embarrassed to be an atheist, and the McGraths show why." Ruse also said that the "new atheists" led by Dawkins are "a b****y disaster",[15] and said the following about the book:

"**Question:** What do you think of *The God Delusion* by Richard Dawkins? Your approach is a lot milder? (The book lays open on his bed in the hotel room in Amsterdam where Ruse is interviewed.)

"**Answer:** I am just as critical of this book as of the work of Intelligent Design authors like Michael Behe, despite the fact that I, as an agnostic, am closer to Dawkins, and am 99% in agreement with his conclusions. But this book is stupid, politically disastrous and bad academics. If someone spoke about biology and evolution as he does on theology, Dawkins would react without mercy.

"A good academic will inform himself in depth in a subject he is writing about. Dawkins did not. He is neither a philosopher nor a theologian. I am not a biologist myself, but at least I study the subject in depth before I write about it. And that arrogance and that pedantic attitude of his. ...

"Dawkins' book confirms my analysis of evolution as pseudo-religion. His secular humanism has quasi-religious characteristics."[16]

Another atheist, Terry Eagleton, Professor of Cultural Theory at the National University of Ireland, Galway, began his review of *The God Delusion* with these words:

"Imagine someone holding forth on biology whose only knowledge of the subject is the *Book of British Birds*, and you have a rough idea of what it feels like to read Richard Dawkins on theology."[17]

Eagleton continues:

"... does he imagine like a bumptious young barrister that you can defeat the opposition while being complacently ignorant of its toughest case? Dawkins, it appears, has sometimes been told by theologians that

14. McGrath, Alister and McGrath, Joanna Collicutt, *The Dawkins Delusion? Atheist fundamentalism and the denial of the divine*, SPCK, UK, 2007.
15. Kumar, J., http://talk.thinkingmatters.org.nz/, 19 August 2009
16. Ruse, Michael, interview with *De Volkskrant* (Netherlands), p. 7, 7 April 2007, (translated by Frans Gunnink).
17. Eagleton,T., Lunging, flailing, mispunching, *London Review of Books* **28**(20), 19 October, 2006, last accessed 25 January, 2007; www.lrb.co.uk.

he sets up straw men only to bowl them over, a charge he rebuts in this book; but if *The God Delusion* is anything to go by, they are absolutely right."[17]

Dawkins publicly debated his book with John Carson Lennox, Professor of Mathematics at Oxford. Lennox is also a Christian apologist and Intelligent Design supporter, and teacher of Science and Religion at Oxford, and the author of several books on the relations of science with religion and ethics. This debate did not cover evolution, but the wider Christianity vs atheism topics covered in *The God Delusion*.[18] Dawkins seemed quite red-faced and uncomfortable during the debate.

However, Dawkins refuses to debate best-selling author Dinesh D'Souza, author of *What's So Great about Christianity*[19] among others, even though D'Souza is a theistic evolutionist not a creationist.[20] Yet many of Dawkins' fellow 'new atheists' such as Christopher Hitchens and Daniel Dennett have been willing. In an open letter, D'Souza contrasted Dawkins' eagerness to entrap non-scientist Christians on his TV shows with a refusal to debate a strong opponent on level terms:

"To be honest, I find your behavior extremely bizarre. You go halfway around the world to chase down televangelists to outsmart them in an interview format that you control, but given several opportunities to engage the issues you profess to care about in a true spirit of open debate and inquiry, you duck and dodge and run away. ...

"If you are so confident that your position is right, and that belief in God is an obvious delusion, surely you should be willing to vindicate that position not only against Bible-toting pastors but also against a fellow scholar and informed critic like me!

"If not, you are nothing but a showman who takes on unprepared and unsuspecting opponents when you yourself control the editing, but when a strong opponent shows up you manufacture reasons to avoid him."[21]

Major defence of evolution

Now we come to Dawkins' current book, *The Greatest Show on Earth* (2009), deliberately published on the bicentennial of Darwin's birth. There is some

18. See *The God Delusion Debate* (DVD), available from CMI.
19. Regnery, Washington DC, 2007.
20. See review by Cosner, L., Mostly masterful defence of Christianity; pity it's slack on creation, *J. Creation* 22(2):32–35, 2008; creation.com/souza.
21. D'Souza, cited in: The rout of the New Atheists, http://voxday.blogspot.com, 21 July 2008.

irony right at the start of the preface (p. vii): many evolutionists have long touted Dawkins' books about evolution as its proof, yet Dawkins says:

> "*The Selfish Gene* and *Extended Phenotype* ... didn't discuss the evidence for evolution itself. ... My next three books ... *The Blind Watchmaker*, *River Out of Eden*[22] and ... *Climbing Mt Improbable* ... although they cleared away stumbling blocks, did not present the actual evidence that evolution was a fact. ... *The Ancestor's Tale* ... again assumed that evolution is true. ...
>
> "Looking back on these books, I realized that the evidence for evolution is nowhere explicitly set out, and that it seemed like a good gap to close."

In a brief review, Dr Henry Gee, senior editor of the leading science journal *Nature*, wrote:

> "Even some of Dawkins' admirers felt that *The God Delusion* was an embarrassment. *The Greatest Show on Earth* is 'not intended as an anti-religious book. I've done that, it's another T-shirt, this is not the place to wear it again,' [p. 6]. And so he moves on, with disarming lucidity."[23]

In this book, Dawkins is irate at what he calls 'history deniers', who deny evolution, and intends to show how wrong they are, as well as use the 'guilt by association' with 'Holocaust deniers'. He is especially distressed that polls show that at least 40% of Americans accept biblical creation, including the <10,000-year time scale, so his other name for 'history denier' is 'forty percenter'.

Why this book?

Although Dawkins has not worked in the science laboratory for decades, his books still have a widespread influence. They are a staple of atheists and humanists worldwide. An honest debate should address the strongest arguments for the opposing side, and Dawkins is an acknowledged champion of evolution and atheism. For example, here are some reviews (as they appeared on Dawkins' own site):

> "This is a magnificent book of wonderstanding: Richard Dawkins combines an artist's wonder at the virtuosity of nature with a scientist's understanding of how it comes to be."—**Matt Ridley, author of *Nature via Nurture.***

22. See review by Bohlin, R.G., *J. Creation* **10**(3):322–327, 1996.
23. *BBC Focus Magazine* 208:88, October 2009.

"'There is a grandeur in this view of life,' said Darwin, speaking of evolution. There is no one better qualified to convey this grandeur than his worthy successor, Richard Dawkins, who writes with passion, clarity, and wit. This may be his best book yet."—*V. S. Ramachandran*

"To call this book a defence of evolution utterly misses the point: *The Greatest Show on Earth* is a celebration of one of the best ideas humans have ever produced. It is hard not to marvel at Richard Dawkins's luminous telling of the story of evolution and the way that it has shaped our world. In reading Dawkins, one is left awed at the beauty of the theory and humbled by the power of science to understand some of the greatest mysteries of life."—**Neil Shubin, author of *Your Inner Fish***

"Up until now, Richard Dawkins has said everything interesting that there is to say about evolution—with one exception. In *The Greatest Show on Earth*, he fills this gap, brilliantly describing the multifarious and massive evidence for evolution—evidence that gives the lie to the notion that evolution is 'only a theory'. This important and timely book is a must-read for Darwin Year."—**Jerry Coyne, author of *Why Evolution is True***

"Whether or not you accept evolution, you will understand it after reading Dawkins's clear and fresh presentation of Evolution 101. His ability to explain science through choice analogies and metaphors (embryology as origami!) make accessible the newest research from paleontology to molecular biology, all the while capturing—and expressing—the excitement of the rapidly expanding field of evolutionary biology."—*Eugenie C. Scott, Executive Director, National Center for Science Education*

"Look out, creationists. There's a new sheriff in town, and he talks like an Oxford don … The author opens with guns a-blazing … (and) writes with terrific wit and considerable learning, but what is interesting here is his fire … Without the strictures of academia he relishes the opportunity to light into his opponents. Whether anyone will stand up to refute his notions remains to be seen, but for now Dawkins wins on points. A pleasure in the face of so much scientific ignorance—biology rendered accessible and relevant to the utmost degree."—*Kirkus Review*

Dawkins writes in a lucid style—he throws in much informative material from real science which keeps the reader interested, but this is mixed with many speculations, and not a few diversionary indulgences e.g. creationist-bashing.

His overall message is, however, anything but inspiring—we are robots programmed by DNA to replicate more copies of that DNA. His conclusion was expressed in *River Out of Eden:*

"The universe we observe has precisely the properties we should expect if there is, at bottom, no design, no purpose, no evil and no good, nothing but blind pitiless indifference." (*ROE*, p. 133)

In this, he was following Darwin himself, who said:

"According to all this, ones disgust at villain <ought to be> is nothing more than disgust at some one under foul disease, & pity accompanies both. Pity ought to banish disgust. P→P For wickedness is no more a man's fault than bodily disease!! (Animals do persecute the sick as if were their fault). If this doctrine were believed—pretty world we should be in!—But it could not be believed excepting by intellectual people—if I believed it—it would make not one difference in my life, for I feel more virtue more happiness— ...

"A man <reading> hearing bible by chance becomes good. This is effect of accident with his state of desire (neither by themselves sufficient) effect of birth & other accidents: may be congratulated, but deserves no credit. ..."[24]

And when Dawkins' fellow evolutionist, computer scientist Jaron Lanier, said:

"There's a large group of people who simply are uncomfortable with accepting evolution because it leads to what they perceive as a moral vacuum, in which their best impulses have no basis in nature."

Dawkins replied:

"All I can say is, That's just tough. We have to face up to the truth."[25]

Certainly we can agree to the last sentence. But the aim of this book is to show that evolution is *not* the truth, and there is something better than Dawkins' "blind pitiless indifference".

I have written a number of other books defending creation and rejecting evolution. But this book will presuppose no previous exposure to these. However, sometimes I will borrow from them, mainly to show that many of Dawkins' points had already been anticipated. I.e. while we try to address the strongest case for evolution, Dawkins has not always addressed the strongest creationist case. He frequently addresses arguments that no informed

---

24. Darwin, C., *Old and USELESS Notes about the moral sense & some metaphysical points written about the year 1837 & earlier*, p. 409, original punctuation; darwin-online.org.uk/.
25. 'Evolution: The dissent of Darwin', *Psychology Today* **30**(1):62, Jan–Feb 1997.

creationist makes, and attacks a number of 'soft targets' who don't even pretend to be scientists.

Dawkins is not alone among evolutionists in his extensive use of dubious tactics. These include such rampant strawman arguments as this book exposes in detail, and equivocation (bait-and-switch). It is this element of deception (perhaps accompanied by not a little self-deception, common in those who strongly reject their accountability to the Creator God[26]) that helps justify the word "hoax" in my book's title.

Of course, I believe the Bible (including Genesis) and the gospel of Christ to be the unalloyed truth. As such, those like Dawkins, who propagate belief in 'goo-to-you' evolution over millions of years, will indeed turn out to have engaged, no matter how unwittingly, in the "Greatest Hoax on Earth"—to the detriment of millions for eternity. This issue could scarcely be more important, which makes it doubly tragic when people are persuaded by "Greatest Show" without hearing the other side properly put.

Scientific evidence comes and goes, and some of the things in both Dawkins' book and mine will need scrapping or revision as time goes on. When one looks at the 'big picture', however, it seems clear that one can already reach the correct decision about ultimate reality with confidence. On that, at least, Richard Dawkins and I would be in agreement.

—∞—

---

26. Sometimes the evolutionary deception is *intentional*. E.g. evolutionist Bora Zivkovic argues that it's OK to deceive students as long as they end up believing in evolution—see documentation in creation.com/deceive, 24 September 2008.

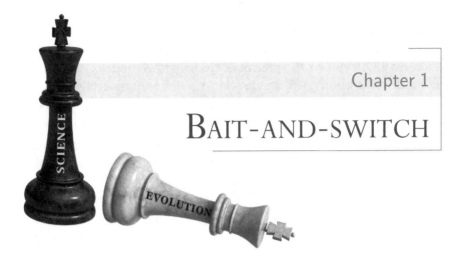

Chapter 1

BAIT-AND-SWITCH

In all discussions, it is important to define terms consistently and honestly. Socrates, in Plato's *Phaedo*, stated succinctly, "To use words wrongly and indefinitely is not merely an error in itself, it also creates evil in the soul." Many informal logical fallacies come from faulty or changing definitions.[1]

Evolution

The theory that Dawkins and other materialists are really promoting, and which creationists oppose, is the idea that particles turned into people over time, without any need for an intelligent designer. This "General Theory of Evolution" (GTE) was defined by the evolutionary biologist, Prof. G.A. Kerkut of Southampton University, as "the theory that all the living forms in the world have arisen from a single source which itself came from an inorganic form."[2]

However, one common logical fallacy is *equivocation* or 'bait-and-switch', that is, switching the meaning of a single word (evolution) part-way through an argument. Dawkins is unfortunately frequently guilty of this:

> "…when there *is* a systematic increase or decrease in the frequency with which we see a particular gene in a gene pool, that is precisely what we mean by evolution." (p. 33)

1. Sarfati, J., Loving God with all your mind: logic and creation, *J. Creation* **12**(2):142–151, 1998; creation.com/logic.
2. Kerkut, G.A., *Implications of Evolution*, Pergamon, Oxford, UK, p. 157, 1960. He continued: "the evidence which supports this is not sufficiently strong to allow us to consider it as anything more than a working hypothesis."

Similar definitions include evolution = "change in gene frequency with time" or "descent with modification". An example is the atheist Eugenie Scott, Executive Director of the pretentiously named National Center for Science Education, the leading US organization devoted entirely to pushing evolution.[3] She approvingly cited a teacher whose pupils said after her 'definition': "Of course species change with time! You mean that's evolution?!"[4]

However, if that were the issue, then I would be an evolutionist! In fact, I can't name anyone who doubts the occurrence of "systematic increase or decrease in the frequency with which we see a particular gene in a gene pool." Certainly much fewer than the 40 % that Dawkins is so concerned about.

This leads to another common fallacy, *knocking down a straw man*: refuting a caricature of the opponent's position. Since creation is defined as the opposite of evolution, if evolution is defined as per Dawkins, it leads to the caricature that creationists deny any sort of "systematic increase or decrease in the frequency with which we see a particular gene in a gene pool." Yet as will be seen, a large part of his book is concerned with showing that such change in gene frequency occurs, i.e. knocking down a straw man.

My chapter 2 defines the terms "species" and "kinds", showing that "kind" is much broader than "species". Biblical creationists realized this long before Darwin, and still do—rapid speciation is expected in the biblical model but is a surprise to many evolutionists.

Chapter 3 explains natural selection, and shows that it's not unique to evolution.

Chapter 4 deals with the worst equivocation in *Greatest Show:* examples of alleged evolution in action. These are invariably examples of change and natural selection, but have nothing to do with the GTE.

Only a theory?

This was the title of the first chapter of *Greatest Show*, showing his irritation with evolution-critics who claim "evolution is just a theory". On p. 185, Dawkins shows awareness of our "Don't Use" list,[5] yet he does not acknowledge that we (i.e. *Creation Ministries International*, or CMI) have also advised against "evolution is just a theory" in the same document. The section from that list reads:

"**Evolution is just a theory.**' What people usually *mean* when they say this is 'Evolution is not proven fact, so it should not be promoted

3. See Batten, D., and Sarfati, J., creation.com/how-religiously-neutral-are-the-anti-creationist-organisations.
4. Scott, E., Dealing with anti-evolutionism, *Reports of the National Center for Science Education* 17(4):24–28, 1997; quote on p. 26, with emphasis in original.
5. Arguments we think creationists should NOT use; creation.com/dontuse.

dogmatically.' Therefore people should say *that*. The problem with using the word "theory" in this case is that scientists usually use it to mean a well-substantiated explanation of data. This includes well-known ones such as Einstein's Theory of Relativity and Newton's Theory of Gravity, and lesser-known ones such as the Debye–Hückel Theory of electrolyte solutions and the Deryagin–Landau/Verwey–Overbeek (DLVO) theory of the stability of lyophobic sols, etc. It would be better to say that particles-to-people evolution is an unsubstantiated *hypothesis* or *conjecture*.

"All the same, the critic doth protest too much. *Webster's Dictionary* (1996) provides the #2 meaning as 'a proposed explanation whose status is still conjectural, in contrast to well-established propositions that are regarded as reporting matters of actual fact', and this usage is hardly unknown in the scientific literature. The dictionary further provides '6. contemplation or speculation. 7. guess or conjecture.' So the critic is simply wrong to say that it's a *mistake* to use theory to mean 'speculation', 'conjecture' or 'guess'; and that scientists *never* use theory this way in the literature. So the attack is really cheap point-scoring, but there is still no reason to give critics this opportunity."

Dawkins also acknowledges that the *Oxford Dictionary* likewise provides about the same meanings; Sense 1 is about the same as in our first paragraph, and Sense 2 is about the same as the #2 meaning. To avoid confusion, he proposes instead a neologism, 'theorum'. This is not the same as 'theorem', which is a mathematical theorem, which is logically deducible from axioms. Instead, Dawkins writes:

"A scientific theorem such as evolution or heliocentrism is a theory that conforms to the Oxford dictionary's 'Sense 1':

[It] had been confirmed or established by observation or experiment, and is propounded or accepted as accounting for the known facts; [it is] a statement of what are held to be the general laws, principles, or causes of something known or observed.

"A scientific theorum has not been—cannot be—proved in the way that a mathematical theorem can be proved. But common sense treats it as a fact in the same sense as the 'theory' that the Earth is round and not flat is a fact, and the theory that green plants obtain energy from the sun is a fact. All are scientific theorums: supported by massive quantities of evidence, accepted by all informed observers, undisputed facts in the ordinary sense of the word. As with all facts, if we are going to be pedantic, it is entirely possible that our measuring instruments, and the sense organs by which we read them, are the victims of a massive confidence trick. As Bertrand Russell said, 'We may all have come into existence five minutes ago, provided with ready-made memories, with holes in our socks and hair that needed cutting.' Given the evidence now available, for evolution to be anything other than a fact would require a similar confidence trick by the creator, something that few theists would wish to credit." (p. 15)

Whether the term 'theorum' will catch on is anyone's guess. However, as our Don't Use list stated, the other undoubted 'theorums' can be directly observed and tested, while evolution is a claim about the unobserved and unrepeatable past (see ch. 4 to refute claims that scientists have observed 'Evolution before our very eyes').

It is also disingenuous for an ardent antitheist like Dawkins to profess concern about a creator's alleged deception. However, biblical creationists respond that the real deception would be for a creator to use evolution then tell us in the Bible something diametrically opposed in every respect—the time frame,[6] the method,[7] the order of events,[8] and the origin of death and suffering.[9]

Furthermore, Bertrand Russell's 'created five minutes ago' scenario can't be disproven by empirical science, because even time measurement devices could have been created to read a false time period. This is one limit of the atheistic empiricism they both hold. But it *is* disprovable from the biblical axioms, since they teach a real history. In fact, there is no empirical way to prove the validity of empiricism itself; it is a 'faith' position.

The atheistic scientist must regard the orderliness of the universe as an *axiom*, a proposition accepted without proof, and which bears *no relation* to his other axiom of atheism. The biblical theist is in a better position because he can treat the orderliness of the universe as a *theorem, derived* from his axiom that the Bible's propositions are true, including that the universe was created by a God of order, not confusion. It is not surprising that the biblical axioms also gave rise to modern science, as shown in ch. 17.

Difficulties

In a friendly interview[10] about his book, Dawkins admitted that evolution has not solved every problem, and there are still "unsolved mysteries":

---

6. Grigg, R., How long were the days of Genesis 1? What did God intend us to understand from the words He used? *Creation* **19**(1):23–25 December 1996; creation.com/sixdays.
7. Mortenson, T., Genesis according to evolution: If evolution over millions of years was the way God created, He could easily have said so in simple words. *Creation* **26**(4):50–51, 2004; creation.com/gen-ev.
8. Manthei, D., Two world-views in conflict, *Creation* **20**(4):26–27 1998; creation.com/conflict. The Bible teaches that God created the earth before the sun, and whales and birds before land vertebrates, contrary to evolutionary order.
9. Sarfati, J., The Fall: a cosmic catastrophe: Hugh Ross's blunders on plant death in the Bible, *J. Creation* **19**(3):60–64, 2005; creation.com/plant_death.
10. Boyle, A., The not-so-angry evolutionist, http://cosmiclog.msnbc.msn.com, 14 October 2009.

"Dawkins cited four of his favourites ... during a talk at the University of Washington:

- **The origin of life:** It might surprise some of Dawkins' critics to hear that he offers no explanation for what kick-started life in the first place. 'That is a complete mystery,' he said. [See ch. 13 for why it's a major problem for his materialistic faith.]

- **The origin of sex:** Dawkins said scientists are also puzzling over 'what sex is all about'—in evolutionary theory, that is. After all, sexual reproduction isn't strictly necessary for the evolutionary process to do its thing. Some researchers surmise that sex helps weed out harmful mutations or provides more options for propagation. [This might go some way to explaining the persistence of sex, but not its *origin*.[11]]

- **The origin of consciousness:** Where does subjective consciousness come from? Dawkins sees this as the 'biggest puzzle' facing biology. Scientists have their ideas, and one of the latest ideas is that consciousness serves as the Wi-Fi network for an assortment of 'computers' inside your brain. [Come again? That explains where it comes from? See also ch. 9, p. 147.]

- **The rise of morality:** What drives us to do good, even for people we don't even know? The expectation of reciprocity provides a partial explanation, but 'it doesn't account for the extremely high degree of moral behavior that humans show,' Dawkins said. He surmises that altruism might have arisen as a 'mistaken misfiring' of neural circuits involved in calculating the mutual give and take among kin. [That might conceivably 'explain' an isolated example of altruism, but not its origin and widespread persistence (a person who sacrifices their life for someone else fails to pass on their gene for altruism, causing it to disappear). It also doesn't prove that it's objectively *right* to act altruistically. See also ch. 17, p. 314.]"

When confronted with difficulties, evolutionists often proclaim: "It's the scientists' job to solve problems." Fair enough. But the same evolutionists often find an alleged problem for creationists and demand an immediate answer or unconditional surrender. Yet the same allowance should be given to creationists: further research has often shown that an alleged problem is solved very well under a creation model, or that an alleged 'proof' of evolution is nothing of the kind.

—∞—

---

11. See also Sarfati, J., *Refuting Evolution 2*, ch. 11.

Chapter 2

SPECIES AND KINDS

THE Bible teaches creation of different kinds, which are broader than modern 'species'. There is much useful research on the created kinds, including hybridization studies. Biblical creationists have long taught variation and even speciation from these kinds. From the Ark account, they have long deduced that comparatively few Ark vertebrate kinds gave rise to a wide diversity of species.

However, by Darwin's day, the church had compromised with the long-age 'fixity of species' ideas of Lyell and others, which made an easy target. Modern science has shown how species have arisen at a surprisingly fast rate, much to the surprise of evolutionists. The various mechanisms of speciation are compatible with a properly understood biblical creation model, although they are often touted as 'evolutionary' mechanisms. But such mechanisms would not turn bacteria into biologists, as evolution requires.

Biblical creation model

Created kinds

Creationists, starting from the Bible, believe that God created different kinds of organisms, each of which reproduced "after their kind" (10 times in Gen. 1:11, 12, 21, 24, 25), where "kind" is the translation of the Hebrew word מִין (*mîn*). Each of these kinds was created with a vast amount of genetic information. There was enough variety in the information in the original creatures so their descendants could adapt to a wide variety of environments.

Kinds are not modern 'species'

But there has been an inadvertent equivocation stemming from the Latin translation of the Bible, the Vulgate (c. AD 400) by Jerome (Latin *Hieronymus*, 347–420)—he translated *mîn* with the Latin words *species* and *genus* (plural *genera*). For example, take Genesis 1:24–25; one popular English translation (NIV) reads:

> "And God said, 'Let the land produce living creatures according to their **kinds**: livestock, creatures that move along the ground, and wild animals, each according to its **kind**.' And it was so. God made the wild animals according to their **kinds**, the livestock according to their **kinds**, and all the creatures that move along the ground according to their **kinds**. And God saw that it was good."

Jerome translated it:

> *"dixit quoque Deus producat terra animam viventem in **genere** suo iumenta et reptilia et bestias terrae secundum **species** suas factumque est ita et fecit Deus bestias terrae iuxta **species** suas et iumenta et omne reptile terrae in **genere** suo et vidit Deus quod esset bonum"*

Linnaeus

The creationist founder of modern classification, Carl Linnaeus (1707–1778) of Sweden, wanted to name and classify these created kinds, taking inspiration from the biblical Adam in Genesis 2:19–20. Peter Harrison, Andreas Idreos Professor of Science and Religion and Director of the Ian Ramsey Centre at the University of Oxford, writes:

> "Swedish naturalist Carl von Linné (1707–1778) became known during his lifetime as a 'second Adam' because of his taxonomic endeavors. The significance of this epithet was that in Genesis Adam was reported to have named the beasts—an episode that was usually interpreted to mean that Adam possessed a scientific knowledge of nature and a perfect taxonomy. Linnaeus's soubriquet exemplifies the way in which the Genesis narratives of creation were used in the early modern period to give religious legitimacy to scientific activities and to taxonomy in particular. Allusions to Adam's work in the Garden of Eden thus became a way of investing the vocation of the naturalist with religious significance."[1]

1. Harrison, P., "Linnaeus as a second Adam? Taxonomy and the religious vocation", *Zygon* **44**(4):879–893, 19 November 2009; www3.interscience.wiley.com/journal/123188389/abstract.

It was not surprising that Linnaeus used the Latin terms in the Vulgate, given that his own surname was coined by his father from the Latin name of the giant linden tree in their family property (previously they had used patronymics, as in Iceland today[2]). In fact, his major work (or Latin *magnum opus*) was in Latin, as were most scientific works of his day: *Systema Naturae* (1735).[3] (Linnaeus took the surname von Linné after the Swedish king, Adolf Fredrik, granted him nobility in 1757, and after the privy council finally had confirmed this in 1761.)

However, the meanings of the *Linnaean* species and *biblical* species diverged over time, which led to the equivocation. The Bible talks of fixity of *kinds*, which in the Latin translation became fixity of *species*, but then an unwarranted switch took place to fixity of *Linnaean* species.

Fixity of species was taught by Darwin's mentor, Charles Lyell (see chapters 7 and 11), who rejected biblical history. Unfortunately, this provided an easy target for Darwin's most famous book, *On the Origin of Species by Means of Natural Selection, or the Preservation of Favoured Races in the Struggle for Life* (1859). Yet many people mistakenly think he disproved fixity of *biblical* kinds.

Biological species and created kinds

There is another term, *biological species*, which means a population of organisms that can interbreed to produce fertile offspring but that cannot so breed with other biological species. Each biblical kind would therefore have *originally* been a distinct biological species. But creationists point out that the biblical 'kind' is often larger than one of *today's* 'species'. Yet evolutionists often point to new biological species as if they have refuted the biblical model. Dawkins' own book devotes much of ch. 9 to proving that 'species' *change*, and that some new species have arisen.

The fixity of species charge can be refuted by considering further aspects of the biblical creation model. First, the Fall, which predicts deterioration from perfection, which I cover in chapters 14 and 15. Another important teaching is the global Flood.

---

2. E.g. take my chess friend Arinbjörn Guðmundsson, who once lost a memorable game to Bobby Fischer and now lives in Brisbane. His second name is not a surname, but is a patronymic after his father Guðmundur. In Iceland, any son would not have the last name Guðmundsson but Arinbjörnsson; and if a daughter would have the last name Arinbjörnsdóttir. Thus Icelandic families often have several last names, which confuses customs officers abroad.

3. Full title *Systema naturae per regna tria naturae, secundum classes, ordines, genera, species, cum characteribus, differentiis, synonymis, locis* or translated: "System of nature through the three kingdoms of nature, according to classes, orders, genera and species, with [generic] characters, [specific] differences, synonyms, places."

Noah's Flood

The Bible teaches in Genesis chapters 6 to 8 that the whole world was flooded, and that a male and female of every kind of land vertebrate (animals with biblical life in the Hebrew נֶפֶשׁ חַיָּה (*nephesh chayyāh*) sense) were saved on Noah's Ark. A few 'clean' animals were represented by seven individuals (Gen. 7:2). The Bible also teaches that this Ark landed on the mountains of Ararat.

Speciation after the Ark

Given this starting point, creationists conclude that these kinds multiplied and their descendants spread out over the earth. Bible believers have long realized the implications of this: that comparatively few land vertebrates gave rise to the large number of varieties/species we see today.

In 1668, Anglican Bishop John Wilkins (1614–1672), the founder of the metric system and the first secretary of the Royal Society (formed 350 years ago in 1660), argued that all the varieties of cattle today, including the American 'buffalo' or bison, would have arisen from two (or probably seven) cattle ancestors on the Ark:

> "There being much less difference betwixt these, than there is betwixt several Dogs: And it being known by experience what various changes are frequently occasioned in the same species, by several countries, diets, and other accidents."[4]

His contemporary, German Jesuit scholar Athanasius Kircher (1602–1680), renowned in his day as "master of a hundred arts",[5] had much the same idea in his meticulously illustrated book on Noah's Ark:[6]

> "Kircher expressed his belief that our modern species had developed by transmutation within definite series of forms."[5]

Kircher's insight has wrongly been equated with a brilliant pre-Darwinian idea of 'evolution', but this is really just the common bait-and-switch (see ch. 1). In reality, it shows that even early creationist scientists deduced from the Flood/Ark account in the Bible that species could change, i.e. fixity of species was false. Furthermore, that the species on the Ark had the potential to give rise to many varieties among their descendants.

4. Wilkins, J., *An Essay Towards a Real Character and a Philosophical Language*, Sa. Gallibrand and John Martin, London, p. 164, 1668.
5. Reilly, Conor, S.J., Father Athanasius Kircher, S.J.: Master of an Hundred Arts, *Studies: An Irish Quarterly Review* **44**(176):457–468, Winter 1955.
6. Kircher, A., *Arca Noë*, 1675.

Yet Dawkins in *Greatest Show* ch. 9 repeatedly quotes the following from Darwin's book *The Voyage of the Beagle* (1845).[7] Dawkins places what he calls the "key clause" in italics, and calls it "coming tantalizingly close to evolutionary ideas even before he had properly formulated his ideas" (p. 260):

"Seeing this gradation and diversity of structure in one small, intimately related group of birds, *one might really fancy that from an original paucity of birds in this archipelago, one species had been taken and modified for different ends.*"

Yet as shown, this would only have been news to proponents of the non-biblical fixity of species view, such as Darwin's deist (anti-Christian) mentor, Lyell. It clearly would not have been news to 17th-Century biblical creationist scientists Wilkins and Kircher, who taught the same thing!

Modern creationist biologists have found the Flood model very helpful in their studies of speciation. For example, Dr Arthur Jones obtained his Ph.D. in biology from the University of Birmingham in cichlid fish, which have huge diversity, with over 1,000 'species' (see p. 38–39 for more on them).

"My fish were supposedly strictly freshwater, but were found in the tropical fresh waters of three continents—from the Americas through Africa to Asia. I hypothesized that all, or at least most, fish kinds that survived the Flood must be able to survive both seawater and fresh, and much mixing of the two. After the post-Flood diversification within the kinds we should still find that, in marine kinds, there are some species that can tolerate much fresher water and, in freshwater kinds, some species that can tolerate much saltier water. With my cichlids I found that this was indeed the case. I was able to keep some species in pure seawater for more than two years with no harmful effects—they lived and reproduced normally. Literature searches again revealed that this was a common pattern throughout the fish classes."[8]

Contrasting the models

Once biblical creation is properly understood, it is possible to properly contrast it with the evolutionary model to see which one best deals with the data. The three diagrams below should help.

7.   The popular name for a book that had the formal title, *Journal of researches into the natural history and geology of the countries visited during the voyage of H.M.S. Beagle round the world, under the Command of Capt. Fitz Roy, R.N.* Quote from 2nd ed., p. 380, John Murray, London, 1845.
8.   Ashton, J., Ed., *In Six Days: Why 50 [Ph.D.] scientists choose to believe in creation,* Master Books, Green Forest, AZ, 2001; creation.com/jones.

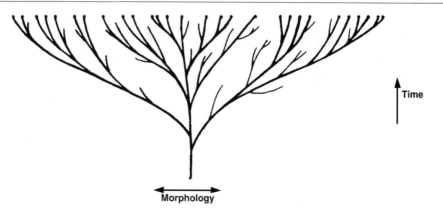

Figure 1: The evolutionary 'tree'—which postulates that all today's species are descended from the one common ancestor (which itself evolved from non-living chemicals). This is what evolution is really all about.

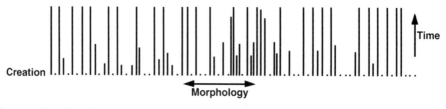

Figure 2: The alleged creationist 'lawn'—this represents the caricature of creationism presented by Dawkins—the Genesis 'kinds' did not change and were the same as today's species.

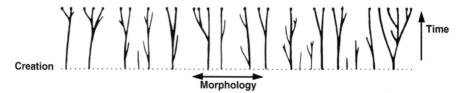

Figure 3: The true creationist 'orchard'—diversity has occurred with time within the original Genesis 'kinds' (creationists often call them *baramin*, from Hebrew *bara'* בָּרָא = create and *mîn* מִין = kind). Much of the evidence of variation presented by Dawkins refutes only the straw-man version of creationism in Fig. 2, but fits the true creationist 'orchard' model perfectly well.

What are the kinds?

Physicist Lawrence Lerner is typical of many anti-creationists, and mocks the idea of 'kind' by claiming:

> "In creationist literature, however, the breadth of a kind can vary from a species to a phylum, including everything in between."[9]

9. Lerner, L.S., *Good Science, Bad Science: Teaching Evolution in the States*, Thomas B. Fordham Foundation, 26 September 2000; see refutation, Sarfati, J., *Who's really pushing 'bad science'?* creation. com/lerner, 26 September 2000.

Hybridization criterion

One must wonder what creationist literature Lerner has actually studied. Based on the biblical criterion for kinds, creationists have extended the criterion used to assign 'biological species' to apply to the definition of kinds. That is, while members of the biological species can hybridize to produce fertile offspring, creationists deduce that as long as two modern creatures can hybridize with true fertilization, the two creatures are descended from the same kind.[10] This was first proposed in 1941 by Dr Frank Marsh, who explained:

"True fertilization is necessary because in hybridization the union of the gametes may result in an embryo which does not live beyond the gastrula stage; or the fetus may die at full period; or the hybrid may be a healthy individual in every way except that it is sterile; or the hybrid may be a completely normal, fertile individual. The requirement of *true* fertilization is met when the chromosome groups of *both parents* take part in formation of the early blastomeres of the embryo. This is a distinguishing requirement for a true hybrid because offspring may be produced where the germs cells of the male take no other part in the development of a new individual than to stimulate an artificial parthenogenesis whereby the egg will proceed with its development into an embryo."

The microbiologist Dr Siegfried Scherer of the University of Munich, Germany extended Marsh's criteria logically. He argued that, if two creatures can hybridize with the same third creature, they are all members of the same kind.[11] He also elaborated on Marsh's explanation of true fertilization:

"Two individuals belong to the same basic type if embryogenesis of a hybrid continues beyond the maternal phase, including subsequent co-ordinated expression of both maternal and paternal morphogenetic genes."[11]

The implication is one-way—hybridization can inform us that two creatures *are* the same kind. But it does *not* necessarily follow that if hybridization *cannot* occur then they are *not* members of the same kind (failure to hybridize could be due to degenerative mutations). After all, there are couples who can't have children, and we don't classify them as a different species, let alone a different kind.

---

10. Marsh, F.L., *Variation and Fixity in Nature*, Pacific Press, Mountain View, CA, USA, p. 37, 1976.
11. Scherer, S., Basic Types of Life, p. 197; ch. 8 of Dembski, Wm. A., *Mere Creation: Science, faith and intelligent design*, Downers Grove, IL, 1998.

Some atheistic skeptics have demanded that creationists should *list* every single 'kind'. Of course, to even begin to do so, it would be necessary to perform hybridization experiments on all sexually reproducing organisms, so this is unreasonable. No evolutionist has ever listed all biological species, anyway, as opposed to a list of organisms classified into arbitrary man-made groupings classified as species. And the skeptic's demand for a list of every single kind overlooks the fact that a *denotative definition* (i.e. exhaustive list) is not the only kind of definition. The hybridization criterion is a more reasonable *operational definition*, which could *in principle* enable researchers to list all the kinds.

Kind boundaries

The boundaries of the 'kind' do not always correspond to any given man-made classification such as 'species', genus or family. But this is not the fault of the biblical term 'kind'; it is actually due to inconsistencies in the man-made classification system. That is, several organisms classified as different 'species', and even different genera or higher groupings, can produce fertile offspring. This means that they are really the same *biological* species that has several varieties, hence a *polytypic* (many-type) species. A good example is Kekaimalu the wholphin, a fertile hybrid of two different so-called *genera*, the false killer whale and bottlenose dolphin.[12] There are more examples in reference 10.

Because of the inadequacies of manmade classification systems, creationists have devised a biblically-based system called *baraminology*, trying to find the boundaries of the created kinds.

A group of related organisms is called a *monobaramin*, but it may not be the complete created kind. Hybridization is *additive evidence*—it can enable us to *add* to the list of the members of a particular monobaramin—thus Marsh's and Scherer's "basic types" are really monobaramins.

Conversely, a group of organisms discontinuous with every other group is called an *apobaramin*.[13] Bats are an apobaramin; they are discontinuous from other creatures, but it is not clear how many created kinds are involved. Apobaramins can be determined by *subtractive evidence*, i.e. *removing* creatures from consideration as members of a kind. There are biblical criteria. For example, whales and birds do not share ancestry with land creatures

12. Batten, D., Ligers and wholphins? What next? *Creation* **22**(3):28–33, 2000; creation.com/liger.
13. Baraminology is a somewhat inelegant Hebrew-Greek hybrid; these other terms are Greek-Hebrew. Holobaramin comes from Greek ὅλος *hólos* whole; monobaramin from μόνος *mónos* one, only; apobaramin from ἀπό *apó* away from.

(Genesis 1:20–25), and mankind does not share ancestry with other animals (Genesis 1:26–27).

The whole created kind is called a *holobaramin*, which is thus an intersection of monobaramin and apobaramin. Further refinements are more difficult but creationist systematists work with features of discontinuity.[14,15]

Examples and mechanisms of speciation

Dawkins' chapter 9 includes "How species are born", and includes the importance of "islands", i.e. some means of isolation. Yet creationists have no problem with such speciation either. The important points follow:

Small populations

For one species to split into two, some differences must arise, e.g. losing different amounts of information such that they are no longer capable of interbreeding. This is most likely to happen in small, isolated populations. There is a bigger chance of a mutation being fixed in a small population simply by chance, and a greater chance of losing certain genes (genetic drift). In a larger population, it's harder to fix a mutation into the population, because of the cost of substitution—all the creatures lacking the gene must die off.[16] Also, it's harder to lose genes, because even if one individual doesn't pass on genes, there is a good chance that others will.

Allopatric speciation

Many varieties can arise rapidly from an initial population with large genetic variety. If this population splits into isolated small populations, each subgroup may carry a fraction of the total genetic information and/or different mutations. If these populations become subjected to different selective pressures, then they might become separate species. This is known as allopatric speciation, a term coined by Ernst Mayr.[17]

Biologists have identified several instances of rapid speciation, including guppies on Trinidad, lizards in the Bahamas, daisies on the islands of British Columbia, and house mice on Madeira.[18] Another good example is a new 'species' of mosquito that can't interbreed with the parent population, arising in the London Underground train system (the 'Tube') in only 100

14. ReMine, W.J., Discontinuity Systematics: A new method of biosystematics relevant to the creation model; in: Walsh, R.E. and Brooks, C.L., *Proc. Second Int. Conf. Creationism*, Creation Science Fellowship, Pittsburgh, PA, USA, pp. 207–213, 1990.
15. Wood, T., A baraminology tutorial with examples from the grasses (*Poaceae*), *J. Creation* **16**(1):15–25, 2002; creation.com/baramin.
16. ReMine, W.J., *The Biotic Message*, ch. 8, St. Paul Science, St. Paul, MN, USA, 1993.
17. From Greek ἄλλος *állos* (other) and πατρίς *patrís* (homeland).
18. Catchpoole, D. and Wieland, C., Speedy species surprise, *Creation* **23**(2):13–15, 2001; creation.com/speedy.

years. The rapid change has 'astonished' evolutionists, but *should* delight *informed* creationists.[19]

The following is an example of artificial 'allopatric' speciation, where the isolation was provided by the researcher:

"William R. Rice of the University of New Mexico and George W. Salt of the University of California at Davis demonstrated that if they sorted a group of fruit flies by their preference for certain environments and bred those flies separately over 35 generations, the resulting flies would refuse to breed with those from a very different environment."[20]

The mountainous environment of the Ark landing spot would provide natural isolation of different populations dispersing as they moved out to repopulate the earth.

Sympatric speciation

Not as well known is sympatric speciation, where reproductive isolation occurs without geographical isolation (Greek syn–/sym– with, same). But there are other factors that can cause division. For example, changes in song or colour might result in birds that no longer recognize a mate, so they no longer interbreed.

A major scientific conference on speciation held in Asilomar, California, in May 1996, showed that sympatric speciation is more widespread than Mayr thought.[21,22,23] For example, certain types of fruit-eating insects use the fruits of their host plant for courtship displays and mating. If one group decides to try a new type of fruit, then they will mate only with others which also choose the same plant. This results in reproductive isolation (speciation) even within the same geographical area.

As a further example, fish living in the same lake may become reproductively isolated because of genetically determined variation in food choices, and natural selection will favour the fittest size, and, thus, different mate choices. This could explain the hundreds of cichlid species in Lake Victoria. The following is a more recent description of the 300 species of cichlid fishes which have originated in only the last several thousand years:

19. See Wieland, C., Brisk Biters, *Creation* **21**(2):41, 1999.
20. 15 Answers to Creationist Nonsense, by John Rennie (Editor), *Scientific American* **287**(1):82–83. See refutation at creation.com/sciam and *Refuting Evolution 2*.
21. Gibbons, A., On the many origins of species, *Science* 273:1496–1499, 1996.
22. Morell, V., Starting species with third parties and sex wars, *Science* 273:1499–1502, 1996.
23. Wieland, C., Speciation Conference Brings Good News for Creationists, *J. Creation* **11**(2):135–136, 1997; creation.com/speciation-conference.

"Despite its young age, Lake Victoria has hundreds of endemic species and six endemic genera. The presumption is that all of the fishes evolved *in situ* within this very brief time."[24]

Dawkins is fond of the alleged rapid 'evolution' of these fish (pp. 266–7). But cichlid expert Arthur Jones (see p. 33) explains that this rapid diversification:

"was actually produced by the endless permutation of a relatively small number of character states: four colours, ten or so basic pigment patterns and so on. The same characters (or character patterns) appeared 'randomly' all over the cichlid distribution. The patterns of variation were 'modular' or 'mosaic'; evolutionary lines of descent were nowhere to be found. This kind of adaptive variation can occur quite rapidly (since it involves only what was already there) and some instances of cichlid 'radiation' (in geologically 'recent' lakes) were indeed dateable (by evolutionists) to within timespans of no more than a few thousand years."[8]

Genetic rearrangements

Biologists have identified several ways that a loss of genetic information through mutations (copying mistakes) can lead to new species. For example, the loss of a protein's ability to recognize 'imprinting' marks can result in the inability to mate successfully.[25,26] A chromosomal rearrangement can result in mutual infertility, as can 'jumping genes' (where the already existing gene moves around), [27,28] but this is reshuffling already existing information, not forming any new information. A polyploid organism, i.e. containing one or more extra sets of chromosomes, will often be unable to interbreed with the parent population. This is usually viable only in plants, not animals. However, polyploidy is the result of repetitious doubling of the same information, not generating new information (a brave student might try handing in two copies of the same assignment to see if he gets extra marks!).

Summary

- The Bible teaches the creation of separate created kinds. This inspired Linnaeus to try to classify them, and he was called a "second Adam" for his efforts.

24. Kaufman, L.S. *et al.*, Evolution in fast forward, *Endeavour* **21**(1):23, 1997.
25. Cohen, P., The great divide, *New Scientist* **160**(2164):16, 1998.
26. Jerlström, P., Genomic imprinting, *J. Creation* **13**(2):6–8, 1999.
27. Templeton, A.R., Mechanisms of speciation— a population genetic approach, *Annu. Rev.Ecol. Syst.* 12:23–48, 1981.
28. Jerlström, P., Jumping wallaby genes and post-Flood speciation, *J. Creation* **14**(1):9–10, 2000.

- Created kinds are broader than 'Linnaean species' and even broader than 'biological species'. Confusion arose because the Latin Vulgate Bible translated 'kind' as 'species', but it's illegitimate to transfer a modern meaning onto this word.

- The global Flood account in Genesis implies that comparatively few kinds of land vertebrates on board the Ark gave rise to a wide variety of land species. Creationist scientists long before Darwin realized this, although Dawkins treats it as a Darwinian insight that "one species had been taken and modified for different ends".

- The Flood account has provided useful insights into modern speciation research, such as cichlid adaptability to different salinities. The supposedly 'evolutionary' idea of allopatric speciation would work very well, especially as small populations dispersed after landing in the mountains of Ararat.

- By Darwin's day, much of the church had abandoned the historic Flood teaching, so adopted the old-earth fixity-of-species view promoted by Lyell. This made an easy target for Darwin, but his arguments did not refute the biblical view.

—∞—

Chapter 3

NATURAL SELECTION

MUCH of Dawkins' book is taken up by proving natural selection to be a fact, including citing many experiments. Yet creationists before Darwin already knew that, as do informed creationists today. So Dawkins is knocking down a straw man. Sexual selection is likewise a good explanation for some observations; ironically, it fails to explain the peacock tail, which is the very thing that Darwin invented the theory to solve.

Natural selection removes genes from a population, and can help it adapt to its environment. But the adaptations are not changes in the right *direction* to drive particles-to-people evolution. For instance, chloroquine-resistant malarial parasites show an 'edge' (boundary) to what mutation/selection can achieve: a mere two coordinated mutational changes, and even these are downhill. This is nowhere near enough to explain the machinery of life.

The Darwin/Dawkins theory requires a lot of small-effect mutations, but the smaller the effect of a mutation, the weaker the selection. Dawkins' computer models ignored this. More sophisticated computer programs show that realistic values of natural selection won't work.

Any substitution involves huge costs in the organisms selected against, and this limits how many substitutions can be achieved in a given time. Small bad mutations will not be eliminated by natural selection. So they would cause genetic breakdown of populations over time. The fact that humans have not broken down shows it is a strong argument against millions of years.

Natural selection works in only a very limited sense, cannot explain the origin of most biological functions, and cannot even stop genetic degeneration.

Natural selection occurs when a creature has some inheritable trait that gives it a better chance of passing on this trait to the next generation. Creatures without this trait are less likely to survive to reproduce, so they don't pass on their genes. Therefore this trait will become established in the population.

However, natural selection cannot create anything new; it only selects from what is available. Therefore, demonstrating that natural selection occurs does not prove that goo-to-you evolution occurs. Rather, it works by *removing* genes (of the unfit) from the population. Thus creationists long recognized natural selection as a *conservative* force, removing unfit organisms and thus hindering the effects of the Curse (but as will be shown below (p. 56 ff), not well enough). A creationist, the chemist/zoologist Edward Blyth (1810–1873), wrote thus about natural selection in 1835–7,[1] and as Stephen Jay Gould pointed out, "Natural selection ranked as a standard item in biological discourse" among the pre-Darwinian creationists.[2] William Paley's famous *Natural Theology* had also recognized the role of natural selection, although not by that name.[2]

According to Gould, Darwin's contribution was not natural selection *per se*, but *natural selection as a creative force*.[3] In this, he may have been anticipated by the Scottish fruit grower Patrick Matthew (in 1831) and the Scottish-American physician William Charles Wells (in 1813, published in 1818).[2]

Furthermore, Professor Paul Pearson of the University of Cardiff (Wales) discovered that James Hutton, better known as 'the father of modern (uniformitarian) geology' (see chapters 7 and 11), anticipated the concept of natural selection.[4] In 1794, Hutton wrote a little known work, *Elements of Agriculture*, and Pearson says, "Although he never used the term, Hutton clearly articulated the principle of evolution by natural selection."[5] Hutton argued that natural selection was creative in producing new traits, but he took it only as far as adapting species to new environments, not transforming them into other very different species.

Wells, Matthew and Darwin were all educated in Hutton's home town of Edinburgh, a place famous for its scientific clubs and societies, so they could all have been influenced by him. However, Pearson discounts the idea of Darwin stealing from Hutton:

1. Grigg, R., Darwin's illegitimate brainchild: If you thought Darwin's Origin was original, think again! *Creation* **26**(2):39–41, 2004; creation.com/brainchild.
2. Gould, S.J., *The Structure of Evolutionary Theory*, pp. 137–141, Harvard University Press, Cambridge, Massachusetts, 2002.
3. Historian Dr Noel Weeks has analyzed other influences on Darwin in Darwin and the search for an evolutionary mechanism, *J. Creation* **12**(3):305–311, 1998.
4. Pearson, P.N., In Retrospect, *Nature* **425**(6959):665, 2003.
5. Hutton's other unconformity, *Geological Society News (UK)*, 16 October 2003; www.geolsoc.org.uk/template.cfm?name=Hutton.

"There is no question of Darwin knowingly stealing Hutton's idea. But it is possible that an old half-forgotten concept from his student days later resurfaced, as he struggled to explain his many observations on species and varieties made voyaging around the world in *HMS Beagle*.

"Darwin rightly gets the credit for applying the principle to the transformation of species and assembling the evidence that convinced the scientific world."[5]

Dawkins likewise comments on:

"...the claim ... that other Victorian scientists, for example Patrick Matthew and Edward Blyth, had discovered natural selection before Darwin did, but I think the evidence shows that they didn't understand how important it is. Unlike Darwin and Wallace, they didn't see it as a general phenomenon with universal significance—with the power to drive the evolution of all living things in the direction of positive improvement." (p. 31).

Modern creationists also recognize natural selection as a way of producing many varieties from comparatively few created kinds. Therefore it is an important part of the Creation/Fall/Flood/Migration model, as will be shown.

Information—the real problem with evolution

The main scientific objection to evolution is *not* about whether changes occur through time, and neither is it about the *size* of the change (so use of the terms 'micro-' and 'macro-evolution' should be discouraged). It isn't even about whether natural selection happens. The key issue is the *type* of change required—to change microbes into men requires changes that *increase the genetic information content*. The three billion DNA 'letters' stored in each human cell nucleus convey a great deal more information (known as 'specified complexity') than the half a million DNA 'letters' of the simplest self-reproducing organism. The DNA sequences in a 'higher' organism, such as a human being or a horse, for instance, code for structures and functions unknown in the sort of 'primitive first cell' from which all other organisms are said to have evolved.

All (sexually reproducing) organisms contain their genetic information in *paired* form. Each offspring inherits half its genetic information from its mother, and half from its father. So there are two genes at a given position (*locus*, plural *loci*) coding for a particular characteristic. An organism can be heterozygous at a given locus, meaning it carries different forms (*alleles*) of this gene. For example, one allele can code for blue eyes, while the other one can code for brown eyes; or one can code for the **A** blood type and the other for the **B** type. Sometimes two alleles have a combined effect, while at other times only one allele (called *dominant*) has any effect on the organism, while the other does not (*recessive*).

With humans, the mother's and father's halves each have 25,000 genes, the information equivalent to a thousand 500-page books (3 billion base pairs or 'letters'). The ardent neo-Darwinist Francisco Ayala points out that humans today have an "average heterozygosity of 6.7 percent."[6] This means that for every thousand gene pairs coding for any trait, 67 of the pairs have different alleles, meaning 1,675 heterozygous loci overall. Thus any single human could produce a vast number of different possible sperm or egg cells—2^{1675} (or 10^{504}). The number of atoms in the whole known universe is 'only' 10^{80}, extremely tiny by comparison. So there is no problem for creationists explaining that the original created kinds could each give rise to many different varieties. In fact, the original created kinds would have had much more heterozygosity than their modern, more specialized descendants. No wonder Ayala pointed out that most of the variation in populations arises from reshuffling of previously existing genes, not from mutations. Many varieties can arise simply by two previously hidden recessive alleles coming together. However, Ayala believes the genetic information came ultimately from mutations, not creation. His belief is contrary to information theory; random changes act mainly to *degrade* information.

All the alleged proofs of 'evolution in action' to date do not show that functional new information is added to genes. Rather, they involve sorting and/or loss of information. To claim that mere change proves that such information-*increasing* change will occur is like saying that because a merchant can sell goods, he will sell them for a profit. The origin of information is an insurmountable problem for bacteria-to-biologists evolution.[7,8]

Information theory is a whole new branch of science that has effectively destroyed the last underpinnings of evolution—explained fully in the monumental work *In the Beginning was Information* by Dr Werner Gitt, recently-retired professor and Head of the Department of Information Technology at the German Federal Institute of Physics and Technology.[9] There is even a specialized branch called bio-informatics, the study of biological information.[10]

6. Ayala, F.J., The mechanisms of evolution, *Scientific American* **239**(3):48–61, September 1978, p. 55.
7. Wieland, C., Beetle Bloopers, *Creation* **19**(3):30, June–August 1997; creation.com/beetle.
8. Grigg, R., Information: A modern scientific design argument, *Creation* **22**(2):50–53, March–May 2000.
9. Gitt, W., 1997. *In the Beginning was Information*, CLV, Bielefeld, Germany.
10. See also Truman, R., The problem of information for the theory of evolution: Has Dawkins really solved it?, 1999 ; trueorigin.org/dawkinfo.asp.

Can beneficial mutations drive evolution?

Informed creationists do not deny that some copying mistakes (mutations) can be beneficial, by the normal definition that they help the organism. But in all known cases, they still add no new information.

There are many examples of obvious *losses* of information which are beneficial, such as wingless beetles that survive on windy islands because they can't fly, so won't be blown into the sea,[7] and animals in dark caves with shrivelled eyes that are less prone to damage, as explained in ch. 14, p. 250. On p. 69, some examples are given of information-losing mutations that confer antibiotic resistance on bacteria.

Still another example is a cattle breed called the *Belgian Blue*. This is very valuable to beef farmers because it has 20–30% more muscle than average cattle, and its meat is lower in fat and very tender. Normally, muscle growth is regulated by a number of proteins, such as *myostatin*. However, Belgian Blues have a mutation that *deactivates* the myostatin gene, so the muscles grow uncontrolled and become very large. This mutation has a cost, in reduced fertility.[11] A different mutation of the same gene is also responsible for the very muscular Piedmontese cattle. A similar mutation has caused human "superbabies". [12,13,14] In all these cases, a mutation causes information *loss,* even though it is 'beneficial'. Therefore, it is in the *opposite* direction required for particles-to-people evolution, which requires the generation of *new* information.

It's notable that Dawkins himself compares most examples of natural selection to a human sculptor removing clay, i.e. "chiselling" genes from the gene pool (p. 34).

How natural selection helps adaptation by removing genes[15]

We can show how this happens with many examples, both in practice and in principle. For example, suppose the original dog/wolf kind had the genetic information for a wide variety of fur lengths. Then most of the first animals probably had medium-length fur. In the simplified example illustrated at

11. Travis, J., Muscle-bound cattle reveal meaty mutation, *Science News* **152**(21):325, 22 November 1997.
12. Johnson, L., Doctors discover genetic mutation that makes toddler super strong, *Anchorage Daily News*, 23 June 2004, www.adn.com/.
13. Schuelke, M. *et al.*, Myostatin mutation associated with gross muscle hypertrophy in a child, *New England Journal of Medicine* 350(26):2682–2688, 24 June 2004, http://content.nejm.org/.
14. Sarfati, J., The superbaby mutation: Evolution of a new master race? *Creation* **27**(1):13, 2004; creation.com/superbaby.
15. Updated from Sarfati, J., *Refuting Evolution*, Creation Book Publishers, Australia, 1998/2008; creation.com/refuting. This explanation in a widely selling creationist book for over 10 years shows that Dawkins is knocking down straw men in his natural selection chapters.

the right,[16] a single gene pair is shown under each dog as coming in two possible forms. One form of the gene (L) carries instructions for long fur, the other (S) for short fur.

In row 1, we start with medium-furred animals (LS) interbreeding. Each of the offspring of these dogs can get one of either gene from each parent to make up their two genes.

In row 2, we see that the resultant offspring can have either short (SS), medium (LS) or long (LL) fur. Now imagine the climate cooling drastically (as in the post-Flood Ice Age). Only those with long fur survive to give rise to the next generation (line 3). So from then on, all the dogs will be a new, long-furred variety. Note that:

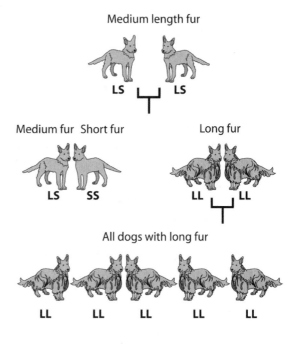

- They are now *adapted* to their environment.
- They are now more *specialized* than their ancestors on row 1.
- This has occurred through *natural selection.*
- There have been *no new genes* added.
- In fact, genes have been lost from the population—i.e. there has been *a loss of genetic information* (gene S for short hair), the opposite of what microbe-to-man evolution needs in order to be credible. Even worse, *all* the information carried by those dogs will be eliminated, since natural selection works on the whole organism. I.e. these dogs could have carried genes for the best sense of smell or fastest running ability, but these are also eliminated.
- Now the population is *less* able to adapt to future environmental changes—were the climate to become hot, there is no genetic information for short fur, so the dogs would probably overheat.

16. Based on Weston, P. and Wieland, C., Bears across the world, *Creation* **20**(4):31, September–November 1998; creation.com/adapt.

Wolves and poodles: a case study

This possibility (that creatures which are different species today are descended from an ancestral population that was less specialized, with more information/variability than its descendants) has been supported by experiment. In Berlin, a female wolf and (large!) male poodle were mated. The pups looked fairly similar to each other and nothing special, with genetic information from both parents. But the inbred 'grand-pups' were very different from each other: one was like its grandmother wolf in appearance and killer instincts, while the other looked clearly 'poodle' and still others were mixtures.[17]

This shows that:

• The poodle and wolf are the same kind, and even the same biological species.

• The first generation of pups had enough genetic variety to produce a wide variety of descendants.

• Therefore, it would have been possible in principle to have a single pair on the Ark with similar variation, to be subsequently sorted by natural selection into varieties, even separate species that are each more specialized than the parent population.

Note that one of the poodle's most famous traits, the long hair, is caused by an information-losing mutation—loss of ability to shed hair at the right length.

Dogs coming from wolves: evolution in history?

Creationists have often pointed out that Noah didn't need to take wolves, coyotes, dingoes, Chihuahuas, Great Danes, spaniels, dachshunds, etc. on the Ark, because it was sufficient to take a pair of wolf-like creatures with all the potential for diversifying into different varieties. And evolutionists now concede that domestic dogs came from wolves only a few thousand years ago, and are not really very different, although they, like Dawkins, insist on calling this 'evolution'.[18]

Dawkins provides interesting information on how wolves possibly diverged into dogs. Wolves will forage for food around humans, but will flee if humans approach closer than a certain distance, or won't approach closer than this. This minimum is called the 'flight distance'. Those wolves with smaller flight distances are of necessity 'tamer', and humans captured and bred from these, and progressively selected still tamer varieties (pp. 71–76).

17. Junker, R. and Scherer, S., *Evolution: Ein kritisches Lehrbuch*, Weyel Lehrmittelverlag, Gießen, Germany, 4th edition, p. 39, 1998.
18. Lange, K., Evolution of dogs: wolf to woof, *National Geographic*, p. 5, January 2001.

But how did distinctive dog characteristics arise? Apparently by *pleiotropy*: where one gene controls more than one characteristic, as Dawkins says:

"Presumably genes for floppy ears and piebald coats are pleiotropically linked to genes for tameness." (p.76)

This was shown by the fact that Russian geneticist Dmitri Konstantinovich Belyaev (Дмитрий Константинович Беляев, 1917–1985) produced many of the same changes while domesticating foxes; Dawkins shows pictures of Belyaev with some of his dog-like domesticated foxes (p. 75). This is nothing that informed creationists need dispute.

Many of the current varieties of domestic dog are due to further selective breeding or artificial selection. But this is mostly *elimination* of certain unwanted genes. E.g. to breed a Chihuahua-type tiny dog, breeders would exclude larger dogs, which entails excluding genes for largeness. It would be much the same *in principle* as in the diagram above.

Other examples involved mutations, which are downhill. Dawkins discusses the bulldog, and there is nothing objectionable about this either:

"...bulldogs get their Churchillian scowl from a genetic tendency towards slower growth of the nasal bones. This has knock-on effects on the relative growth of the surrounding bones, and indeed all the surrounding tissues. One of these knock-on effects is that the palate is pulled up into an awkward position, so the bulldog's teeth stick out and dribble. Bulldogs also have breathing difficulties, which are shared with Pekineses. Bulldogs even have difficulty being born because the head is disproportionately big. Most if not all the bulldogs you see today were born by caesarean section." (p. 36)

Indeed, purebreds have long been known to have many problems,[19] precisely because much information has been lost. Also, *inbreeding* allows mutational defects to be expressed. Normally, creatures carry lots of mutations, but since their information is in 'pairs', they possess the 'backup copy' of the 'good' gene which often masks the defect. But when two closely related dogs breed, they will tend to have the mutations in the *same* place. The offspring will have one chance in four of inheriting a pair of any given mutant gene, which will then be expressed as a defect. Since there are *many* mutations, there is a good chance that in *some* place, the offspring will inherit a pair of defective genes, and thus express a mutational disease.

19. Based on Weston, P. and Wieland, C., Bears across the world, *Creation* **20**(4):31, September–November 1998; creation.com/adapt.

Limits of natural selection

There are other chapters in *Greatest Show* allegedly demonstrating the fact of evolution. But as Dawkins himself says, natural selection (acting on random variation) is the only plausible *mechanism* of evolution. It is just double talk of many evolutionary propagandists to claim, "There is no dispute that evolution has occurred; the only dispute is how it occurred." The whole point of Darwin was to attempt to provide what no one disputes was lacking before: a supposedly plausible way for it to have occurred.

Dawkins shows some examples of what natural selection can achieve, but they must be extrapolated manyfold to explain the enormous complexity of life. So it's important to see how far natural selection can actually reach. First, an older example of Dawkins' …

Dawkins' Weaselling

Dawkins has previously touted computer programs that supposedly model natural selection, such as his Weasel program explained in *The Blind Watchmaker*. This program starts with a random sequence of 28 letters or spaces. It is then copied repeatedly, representing reproduction. Random copying errors are allowed, representing mutations. New sequences resulting from the errors that are closer to a target string are selected by the program ('natural selection') and then these are mutated again and ones resulting that are closer to the target are selected, and so on. This doesn't take many 'generations' to reach a target English sentence, in his case "Methinks it is like a weasel" from Shakespeare's *Hamlet*. But this analogy to evolution has a number of fatal flaws:

- The target sequence is known in advance, and the best match to this sequence is selected. But as Dawkins himself says, natural selection is a *blind* watchmaker.

- The genome was very small, the length of the sentence.

- The high reproductive rate in offspring is not realistic for land vertebrates.

- The mutation rate was much higher than for living organisms, which is $\sim 10^{-9}$ per nucleotide per generation. In reality, if living organisms behaved like Dawkins' simulation, error catastrophe would result, i.e. the genetic information would be destroyed by mutations so that all offspring are less fit than the parent/s so that selection cannot maintain the integrity of the genome. In reality, mutation rates must be inversely proportional to the size of the genome. So genomes as large as ours, or even as large as the simplest known living things, would need a very *low* mutation rate.

- The Weasel program has a very high chance of producing a 'beneficial' mutation, while in living organisms, beneficial mutations are only a tiny fraction of those which occur. And as discussed before, observed beneficial mutations are not the information-gaining type needed for evolution.

- Dawkins rightly says: "But most mutations are disadvantageous, if only because they are random and there are many more ways of getting worse than getting better. [Footnote in original to: This is especially true of mutations of large effect. Think of a delicate machine, like a radio or a computer. A large mutation is the equivalent of kicking it with a hobnailed boot, or cutting a wire at random and reconnecting it at a different place. It just might improve its performance, but it is not very likely. A small mutation, on the other hand, is equivalent to making a tiny adjustment to, say, one resistor, or to the tuning knob of a radio. The smaller the mutation, the more closely the probability of improvement approaches 50 per cent.] Natural selection promptly penalizes the bad mutations." (p. 352) But as will be shown below (p. 56), this is not true of bad 'near neutral' mutations, which is a huge problem for evolution and long ages.

- In his program, natural selection is perfect: a slightly closer match is the only one that is selected to reproduce for the next generation; it's as if anything else is a lethal genetic combination. But as Dawkins says, only small mutations have a realistic chance of being beneficial—however, he neglects to mention that the smaller the mutation, the smaller the selection coefficient.[20] So natural selection is less likely to select them.

- Slightly beneficial changes may not be the main factor for survival. For example, the fastest gazelle might by chance run into a waiting lioness while a slow one might escape. Another lioness might find a calf—and it wouldn't help the calf much if it happened to have good genes for adult speed. And it would seem that many extinct creatures were very 'fit', so some prominent evolutionary paleontologists refer to "survival of the lucky".[21] Indeed, computer simulations have shown that there is a 'selection threshold' of about 10^{-4}–10^{-3} below which a beneficial mutation will not be selected because random 'noise' swamps selective effects.[22]

---

20. If a mutation has a selection coefficient s = 0.001 or 0.1%, a supposedly typical value, then the number of surviving offspring is 0.1% greater for organisms with the mutant than without it.
21. A phrase coined by Kenneth Hsü, *The Great Dying,* Harcourt Brace Jovanovich, San Diego, 1986. David Raup also argued for elements of luck in *Extinction: Bad Genes or Bad Luck?* WW Norton, NY, 1991.
22. Sanford, J.C., Baumgardner, J.R. and Brewer, W.H., Selection threshold severely constrains capture of beneficial mutations, submitted for publication, 2010.

More advanced programs with realistic values for selection coefficients, genome size, reproductive and mutation rates show that Dawkins' mutation/ selection model would not work in real living creatures.[23,24,25]

Edge of Evolution

Biochemist Michael Behe (1952–) wrote *The Edge of Evolution (2007)*[26,27,28] *mainly about* the limits of what Dawkins would call Darwinian processes but which I simply call mutation and selection.

As Behe's Ph.D. research involved malaria, he applies his expertise to the malarial parasite (*Plasmodium falciparum*) and the mutations that have enabled humans to combat it, as well as the parasite's measures to counter human-made drugs.

One of the most effective anti-malarial drugs has been *chloroquine*, because the parasite took a while to develop resistance. Behe shows that chloroquine resistance likely involves *two* specific mutations occurring together in the one gene. I.e. one mutation is not enough to make a difference; there must be two for a great enough advantage that natural selection kicks in.

This explains why resistance to chloroquine took a long time to develop, whereas resistance to other anti-malarial drugs, which only need *one* mutation each, occurs within weeks. Behe works out the probability of this double mutation occurring in the same gene using other scientists' figures for the parasite's population.

If it took so much time for a double mutation to occur in an organism that has a huge population and short life cycle (and therefore a greater opportunity for all manner of mutations to occur), then how long would it take for a double mutation to occur in an organism like a human, with a relatively long lifespan and small population? Behe showed that it would never occur even with evolutionary time assumed. And this is just one double mutation in a gene. So, any adaptation that requires two or more specific mutations to work will

23. Ey, L., and Batten, D., Weasel, a flexible program for investigating deterministic computer 'demonstrations' of evolution, *J. Creation* **16**(2):84–88, 2002; creation.com/weasel.

24. Sanford, J.C., Baumgardner, J.R., Brewer, W.H., Gibson, P. and ReMine, W.R., Mendel's Accountant: A biologically realistic forward-time population genetics program, *Scalable Computing: Practice and Experience* **8**(2):147–165, June 2007; http://193.201.164.120/vols/vol08/no2/SCPE_8_2_02.pdf.

25. Sanford, J.C., Baumgardner, J.R., Brewer, W.H., Gibson, P. and ReMine, W.R., Using computer simulation to understand mutation accumulation dynamics and genetic load, in Y. Shi *et al.* (eds.), *Computational Science—ICCS 2007*, Part II, Lecture Notes in Computer Science 4488, Springer–Verlag, Berlin, Heidelberg, pages 386–392; www.springerlink.com/content/l636614g73322302.

26. Behe, M., *The Edge of Evolution: The search for the limits of Darwinism*, Free Press, NY, 2007.

27. This came in for severe criticism from the evolutionary gatekeepers, including Dawkins himself. See: Inferior Design, *New York Times*, 1 July 2007. For refutation, see Sarfati, J., Misotheist's misology: Dawkins attacks Behe but digs himself into logical potholes, creation.com/dawkbehe, 13 July 2007.

28. See also review of Ref. 27 by Batten, D., Clarity and confusion, *J. Creation* **22**(1):28–32, 2008; creation.com/edge-evolution.

never evolve in a human, yet such must have happened *numerous* times if humans arose through evolutionary processes.

Behe also points out that the chloroquine-resistant parasites do *worse* than the non-resistant ones where there is no chloroquine. This suggests that the double mutation is informationally downhill, as usual. It seems that the reason that the parasite is resistant to chloroquine is that concentration in the parasite's vacuole is reduced, and one mechanism is *impaired uptake*. According to one paper:

> "Chloroquine-resistant parasite isolates consistently have an import mechanism with a lower transport activity and a reduced affinity for chloroquine."[29]

This is the same *principle* that explains some antibiotic-resistant bacteria, where resistance is conferred by a mutation impairing a cell pump so the germ pumps in less of its would-be executioner.[30]

This leads to another of Behe's major points: *there is not so much an arms race as trench warfare or a* **scorched earth policy**. Many of the changes are *destroying machinery that the enemy could otherwise use*. E.g. defenders will destroy their own bridges to prevent an enemy crossing (or even better, right when the enemy is crossing), sabotage their own factories if the enemy is using them to churn out armaments, or burn their own crops so the enemy will run out of food.

Sickle cell anemia

This also explains some of the human defences to malaria, such as *sickle cell anemia*. Here, a mutation causes the hemoglobin to be more prone to clumping together. Although this is a favourite example of 'evolution', one of the world's leading authorities on sickle-cell anemia, Felix Konotey-Ahulu, explains:

> "These mis-shapen cells can block the smaller blood vessels, depriving tissues and organs of oxygen. However, sufferers have done very well *with proper treatment*, becoming doctors, lawyers etc."[31]

However, those with only *one* gene for sickle cell anemia only have half their hemoglobin molecules defective, so they won't clump on their own, so they don't suffer from those ill effects.

But the defect actually has an advantage.

29. Sanchez, C.P., Wünsch, S. and Lanzer, M., Identification of a Chloroquine Importer in *Plasmodium falciparum*: Differences in import kinetics are genetically linked with the chloroquine-resistant phenotype, *J. Biol. Chem.* **272**(5):2652–2658, 1997.
30. See Sarfati, J., Anthrax and antibiotics: Is evolution relevant? 2001–2005, creation.com/anthrax.
31. Exposing Evolution's Icon: World leader on sickle-cell anemia: "Nothing to do with evolution!" Jonathan Sarfati interviews Felix Konotey-Ahulu, *Creation* **29**(1):16–19, 2006.

The parasite feeds on the hemoglobin, which is very concentrated in our red blood cells. Behe points out that the sickle mutation makes the hemoglobin more prone to clumping together when the parasite enters the cell. This clumping distorts the shape, so the spleen detects the damaged cell and destroys it, along with the parasite. So those who carry only *one* gene will suffer no ill effects from anemia, and also enjoy protection from malaria.

However, Konotey-Ahulu cautions, "Demonstrating natural selection does not demonstrate that 'upward evolution' is a fact, yet many schoolchildren are taught this as a 'proof' of evolution." He pointed out that "the sickle-cell gene is still a defect, not an increase in complexity or an improvement in function which is being selected for". And he pointed out the unhappy downside, that "having more carriers of the sickle-cell genes results in more people suffering from this terrible disease."[31]

Clearly sickle cell hemoglobin is an example of scorched earth tactics: this useful oxygen carrier was sacrificed to destroy the invader.

Is natural selection as prevalent as claimed?

As stated, creationists have no problem with natural selection. But it doesn't explain everything that many evolutionists claim. Even protective colouration and mimicry for camouflage is not always so clear cut as it is in guppies, confirmed by Endler's careful experiments (see next chapter, p. 71). However, in the 1930s, ornithologist McAtee amassed much data on the contents of bird stomachs, and found that their prey were taken in accordance with availability, and the so-called protective adaptations made no difference:

> "In other words there is utilization of animals of practically every kind for food approximately in proportion to their numbers. This means that predation takes place much the same as if there were no such thing as protective adaptations. And this is only another way of saying that the phenomena classed by theorists as protective adaptations have little or no effectiveness. Natural Selection theories assume discrimination in the choice of prey. The principle of proportional predation so obvious from the data contained in this paper vitiates those theories for it denotes indiscrimination, the very antithesis of selection."[32,33,34]

32. McAtee, W.L., The Effectiveness in Nature of the So-Called Protective Adaptations in the Animal Kingdom, Chiefly as Illustrated by the Food Habits of Nearctic Birds, *Smithsonian Misc. Collection* **85**(7):1–201, 16 March, 1932.
33. A contemporary critic of McAtee, Ref. 33, faulted McAtee mainly for not offering an alternative to natural selection—to an evolutionist, this is the only game in town. Burt, W.H., *Condor* 34:196–198, July 1932, elibrary.unm.edu/sora/Condor/files/issues/v034n04/p0196-p0198.pdf.
34. McAtee, W.L., Protective resemblances in insects—experiment and theory, *Science* **79**(2051)361–363, 20 April 1934 | doi: 10.1126/science.79.2051.361.

These were presumably already highly evolved 'protective adaptations', yet they make little difference. *A fortiori,* the alleged incipient stages would make even less difference, so selection would be weaker still.

Breaking is easier than making

Behe provides a number of other examples showing how breaking something will help an organism in a battle with another. Yet this is no marvel of Darwinism. It is far simpler to break something than to make it, and there are many ways to break something while there are few ways to make it. Something as simple as sand can grind gears to a halt, and a wad of chewing gum can foul up other moving parts. Honey in the fuel tank can stop a car in its tracks. Some defensive mechanisms are like this: a sticky molecule that prevents a molecular machine from working.

Haldane's dilemma

Haldane's Dilemma[35] indicates that beneficial evolution is *too slow* to explain large-scale biological transformation in the *available time,* even given the claimed evolutionary timescale. It is named after J.B.S. Haldane (1892–1964), one of the world's former leading evolutionists (and quite a hero to Dawkins—*Greatest Show* chapter 8 especially).[36] He *wanted* evolution to work, but couldn't get around his dilemma, despite a half-hearted attempt.[37,38]

Take Dawkins' own bait-and-switch definition of evolution as change in gene frequency over time. For example, if a given Darwinian scenario claims an allele increased from one copy to a thousand copies in one generation, then a reproduction rate of one thousand is required. If the species has a smaller reproduction rate, then the Darwinian scenario is not plausible. In effect, the above logic is applied over and over again, to each generation in turn, and results in a speed limit to beneficial evolution.

A *cost of substitution* can be defined as the excess reproduction rate required specifically for substitutions under a given Darwinian scenario. In the above example, the cost of substitution is 999. There are also additional costs incurred by the scenario, and these costs all sum to the total reproduction rate required by the scenario.

---

35. Haldane, J.B.S.,. The Cost of Natural Selection, *J. Genetics* 55:511–24, 1957.
36. Dawkins doesn't mention that Haldane was chairman of the editorial board of the London edition of the Communist paper *Daily Worker*. As late as 1962, he described mass-murderer Stalin as "a very great man who did a very good job." Even Dawkins' fellow skeptic Martin Gardner was most unimpressed with such adulation: Notes of a Fringe-Watcher: The Sad Story of Professor Haldane, *Skeptical Inquirer* 6(3):244, Spring 1992.
37. Batten, D., Haldane's dilemma has not been solved, *J. Creation* 19(1):20–21, 2005.
38. ReMine, Cost theory and the cost of substitution—a clarification, *J. Creation* 19(1):113–125, 2005.

Take a population of 100,000. Imagine a scenario where a male and female each receive a new beneficial mutation, which substitutes into the population in one generation. In other words, the mutation goes from two to 100,000 copies in *one generation*. This would give the *maximum possible rate of evolution* and would require a reproduction rate of 50,000, with all members of the population not carrying the mutation dying out. Females would need to average at least 100,000 births. Even if evolution happened in this highly favourable but unrealistic manner continuously for 10 million years, only 500,000 mutations could be substituted. (With an effective generation time for an ape-human during that period of 20 years, the number of substituted mutations is 10 million divided by 20, which equals 500,000.)

Haldane's analysis assumed evolution occurs in a more realistic manner (yet he still included many unrealistic assumptions that greatly favour evolution). Under his analysis, the maximum speed sustainable over long-periods would be "one substitution per 300 generations."

Human and chimp DNA similarity?

Haldane's Dilemma can be applied to the alleged evolution of humans from the hypothetical common ancestor with apes, supposedly 10 million years ago. At one substitution every 300 generations, in this time frame, an ape-human-like lineage could substitute no more than about 1,700 beneficial mutations. Is this enough to explain the origin of all the unique human adaptations? Is it enough to explain the alleged tripling of brain size, upright posture, hand dexterity, speech, language, the distribution of hair, and the appreciation of music, to name a few (see ch. 9, p. 146 ff.)?

Compare that with the genetic changes we observe today, where *many alleles* are needed to explain the *relatively minor* modification in the beak of the Galápagos finch. By these comparisons, a mere 1,700 beneficial mutations is not sufficient to explain the origin of humans. All the theory and fundamental parameters for this problem come from evolutionary geneticists themselves, yet they obscured the problem from public view, and claimed the problem was solved when it wasn't. This is Haldane's Dilemma, a problem that has never been solved.

Furthermore, the human Y chromosome, owned by males, has been recently sequenced. The researchers noted the unexpected "extraordinary divergence" from the chimp Y chromosome, including "wholesale renovation".[39] Indeed, the researchers say:

---

39. Hughes, J.F. *et al.*, Chimpanzee and human Y chromosomes are remarkably divergent in structure and gene, *Nature*, advance online publication 13 January 2010 | doi:10.1038/nature08700content.

"Indeed, at 6 million years of separation, the difference in MSY gene content in chimpanzee and human is more comparable to the difference in autosomal gene content in chicken and human, at 310 million years of separation."

Substituting those changes would be a major problem for evolution.[40]

The woefully insufficient time to substitute the changes is a big problem for the evolution of man from an ape-like ancestor. Haldane's Dilemma applies most especially to species with low reproduction rates and large generation times. Even the evolutionary 'deep time' is not enough to make all the substitutions.

Human genome decay

As shown above (p. 50), Dawkins agrees that most mutations are harmful, and he rightly explains why this is: more ways to break something than make something. But he asserts, "Natural selection promptly penalizes the bad mutations" (p. 352). But is this so?

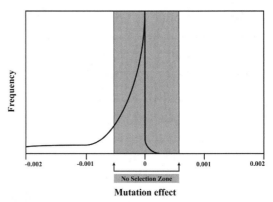

Plant geneticist Dr John Sanford, inventor of the gene gun, conclusively proves this is not so.[24,25,41,42] As stated

Figure 1. Most mutations have only a tiny effect and so are invisible to natural selection, accumulating in populations so as to destroy them over time; from Sanford, Ref. 42.

before, the smaller the mutation, the smaller the selective effects, something Dawkins consistently ignores. At a certain point (the 'selection threshold'), selection either for or against low-impact mutations breaks down completely, and all mutations below this point are unaffected by selection. Under realistic conditions, the large majority of mutations are so subtle that they are simply unaffected by selection.

Rather, most mutations are effectively *neutral*; i.e. unaffected by selection. Now *this* Dawkins acknowledges, although only for its purported usefulness

40. Hughes et al., Ref. 40: "We suggest that the extraordinary divergence of the chimpanzee and human MSYs was driven by four synergistic factors: the prominent role of the MSY in sperm production, 'genetic hitchhiking' effects in the absence of meiotic crossing over, frequent ectopic recombination within the MSY, and species differences in mating behaviour."
41. Sanford, J.C., *Genetic entropy and the mystery of the genome*, Ivan Press, 2005; see review of the book and the interview with the author in *Creation* **30**(4):45–47, 2008.
42. Sanford, J.C., *Genetic Entropy* (DVD), CMI, from presentation in Australia, 2009.

as a 'molecular clock' (p. 332). But the problem for evolution and long ages is that bad 'neutral' (really 'near neutral') mutations still greatly outnumber the good; i.e. very slightly harmful mutations will not be eliminated by natural selection.[43] So like tiny rust spots on a car, they accumulate through the gene pool. This contrasts with major damage that can be noticed and repaired, such as a flat tyre, smashed headlights, worn brakepads, or natural selection removing the very bad mutants. Eventually, as rust can eventually build up till it causes structural damage, the bad neutral mutations accumulate till the point of damage.

These mutations are accumulating much faster than previously thought— at least 100 nucleotide substitutions (single-letter 'typos') per person per generation, according to geneticist Kondrashov[44]—and the rate might be as high as 300.[45] And this doesn't include even larger changes such as deletions, insertions, duplications, translocations, inversions and micro-satellite mutations. Evolutionist Kondrashov himself asked, "Why aren't we dead 100 times over?"[46]

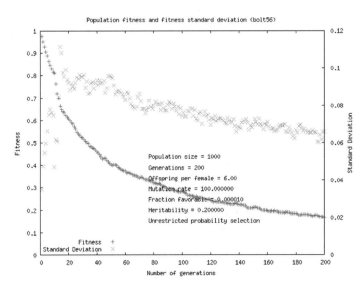

Figure 2. Young earth bottleneck–100 mutations; Simulation from Mendel's Accountant program, refs. 24 and 25; diagram from Ref. 43.

43. Gibson, P., Baumgardner, J.R., Brewer, W.H., Sanford, J.C., Selection threshold severely constrains elimination of deleterious mutations, submitted for publication, 2010. They found that the threshold is higher than expected, about 10^{-3}–10^{-4}.
44. Kondrashov, A.S., Direct estimation of human nucleotide mutation rates at 20 loci causing Mendelian diseases, *Human Mutation* 21:12–27, 2002.
45. Kondrashov, personal communication to Sanford, cited in *Genetic Entropy*, Ref. 42.
46. Kondrashov, A.S., Contamination of the genome by very slightly deleterious mutations: why have we not died 100 times over? *J. Theoret. Biol.* 175:583–594, 1995.

So according to this data, mutations are not the engine of evolution; rather, natural selection can't even stop mutations from gradually destroying populations.

Young age of the genome

A reasonable answer to Kondrashov's question is that the *human genome has not been around long enough to deteriorate to lethal levels.* Sanford and his colleagues working on supercomputer modelling on mutations plus selection have shown that our genome would already be fatally compromised if it had been around for many thousands

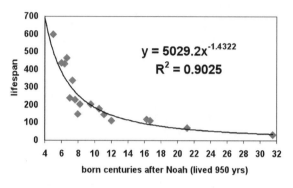

Figure 3. Declining lifespans of Noah's descendants; information from Genesis 11; diagram from ref. 43.

of generations. But the actual deterioration times match the shortening of the lifespans of the biblical patriarchs (Genesis 5,11), as shown by the graphs above. So the actual evidence, from realistic modelling of mutations and selection, is in favour of the biblical account, and a huge problem for evolutionary scenarios.

Summary

- Natural selection actually happens, and was accepted by creationists before Darwin, and by creationist scientists today.

- Natural selection works by 'chiselling' genes out of the gene pool; it generates no new information.

- It can help organisms adapt to the environment, but these specialized creatures have less information, so are less adaptable in the future.

- The vast majority of mutations that make a difference *remove* information, since breaking something is much easier (and more probable) than making. This even includes *beneficial* mutations such as wingless beetles on windswept islands and blind fish in caves, or "scorched earth" ones like sickle-cell anemia.

- Creationists have no problem with natural selection as such, but only oppose the reckless extrapolations that would make selection out to be omnipotent. So Dawkins' chapters on artificial selection, natural selection, dog breeds, etc. are merely proving something not disputed by creationist scientists, and are really just knocking down straw men.

- Some features alleged to have arisen by natural selection appear to have little selective advantage. And this is in their fully-formed stages; their alleged incipient stages would have had even less advantage and so they cannot be explained by natural selection.

- To substitute a new beneficial mutation in a population, creatures lacking this must be eliminated. This 'cost of selection' limits the amount of substitution.

- Natural selection can work quite well one mutation at a time, although not as well as Dawkins has claimed. But if a change requires two mutations to make a selectable difference, it will be hard; more than two would be too improbable.

- Most mutations are 'effectively neutral', i.e. of too small an effect to be affected by natural selection. Far more of these are slightly bad than slightly good. Humans accumulate 100–300 of these every generation, most of which natural selection can't eliminate. So the human race can't be very old, otherwise we would have suffered genetic meltdown and extinction.

—∞—

Chapter 4

EVOLUTION BEFORE
OUR VERY EYES?

DAWKINS caused much subsequent mirth when he said in an interview, "Evolution has been observed. It's just that it hasn't been observed while it's happening."[1] But in one chapter he attempts to show that evolution has been observed while it's happening. However, his chapter "Before our very eyes" should have been called "variation and natural selection before our very eyes". But the equivocation plays well in his game to paint creationists as ignorant of these.

Richard Lenski's decade-long experiment with bacteria shows indeed that they change through time, and due to natural selection; but the main changes have been downhill, i.e. losing function. Even with billions of bacteria and thousands of generations, they remain the same type of germ. No wonder that he moved for a time to computer simulations to try to prove evolution. Lenski recently found that one tribe of germs had acquired the ability to digest citrate under aerobic conditions. But even this was merely reactivating already existing machinery.

Likewise, sexual selection has been observed, e.g. John Endler's observations on guppies. Creationist biologists have no problem with that, despite the insinuations. However, people have been too eager to rush into sexual selection explanations, which just don't work for the peacock tail—the very feature for which Darwin concocted the idea, and he overlooked the thermoregulatory function of the huge toucan beak.

---

1. 'Battle over evolution', Bill Moyers interviews Richard Dawkins, *Now*, 3 December 2004, PBS network.

Antibiotic resistance is an old canard. But once again, natural selection—yes, evolution—no. I.e., often germs that are *already* resistant are selected for, but nothing new arises. Sometimes resistance arises through information-losing changes, which leave the germs less fit than the 'wild' types.

A long-tongued moth was supposedly a successful prediction of Darwin and Wallace, who reasoned that it must exist to pollinate an orchid with a long nectar channel. But this is equally a prediction of creation: that a long-channelled orchid would have a long-tongued moth designed to pollinate. Similarly, the way we deal with disease symptoms involves no practical difference whether we regard them as evolved or created for a function.

Lenski's bacteria: evolution in action?

If evolution were to be observed, single-celled organisms would be ideal since they reproduce so quickly. Hence Dawkins describes a decades-long experiment by Richard Lenski *et al.* This, Dawkins claims in a heading, was "Forty-five thousand generations of evolution in the lab". (p. 116) This is important to address, since this is an argument Dawkins spends many pages on, and he regards it as particularly powerful. First, he claims:

"Bacteria offer yet another priceless gift to the evolutionist. In some cases, you can freeze them for an indefinite length of time then bring them back again, whereupon they resume normal reproduction as if nothing had happened. This means that experimenters can lay down their own 'living fossil record', a snapshot of the exact point the evolutionary process had reached at any desired time. Imagine if we could bring Lucy, the magnificent pre-human fossil discovered by Don Johanson, back to life from a deep freeze and set her kind evolving anew! All this has been achieved with the bacterium *Escherichia coli,* in a spectacular long-term experiment by Richard Lenski and his colleagues at Michigan State University. ...

"*E. coli* is a common bacterium. ... There are about 100 billion billion of them around the world at any one time, of which a billion, by Lenski's calculation, are in your large intestine at this very moment. Most of them are harmless, or even beneficial, but nasty strains occasionally hit the headlines. Such periodic evolutionary innovation is not surprising if you do the sums, even though mutations are rare events. If we assume that the probability of a gene mutating during any one act of bacterial reproduction is as low as one in a billion, the numbers of bacteria are so colossal that just about every gene in the genome will have mutated somewhere in the world, every day. As Richard Lenski says, 'That's a lot of opportunity for evolution.' ...

"Lenski and his team have continued this daily routine for more than twenty years so far. This means about 7,000 'flask generations' and 45,000 bacterial generations—averaging between six and seven bacterial generations per day. To put that into perspective, if we were to go back 45,000 human generations, that would be about a million years, back to the time of *Homo erectus*, which is not very long ago. So whatever evolutionary change Lenski may have clocked up in the equivalent of a million years of bacterial generations, think how much more evolution might happen in, say, 100 millions of mammal evolution." (pp. 116–7, 119)

First, as shown in ch. 12, bacteria have been revived from cells allegedly millions of years old, by which time any DNA should have disintegrated. And they are often identical to living bacteria, despite supposedly billions of generations for modern ones to evolve.

Second, since as Dawkins says, this is comparable to the amount of time *H. sapiens* is said to have evolved from *H. erectus*, it would be interesting to see the *very best* that can be achieved by this experiment *under optimal conditions for evolution,* given the huge numbers and controlled experimental conditions.

Increasing body size

Dawkins lucidly describes the ingenious and careful experiments over the two decades. Lenski's team cultured different 'colour coded' populations of bacteria in fresh glucose-rich broth, which caused the population to increase massively. Then it levelled off as the glucose ran out and the bacteria starved. From this, a hundredth of the surviving germs were rescued and transferred to new glucose feeding grounds, and the process was repeated. Every 500 generations, samples were also frozen as 'fossils'.

Indeed, over the generations, the bacteria's fitness increased, i.e. they became better at exploiting scarce glucose. How precisely this occurred, Dawkins doesn't say, but one notable effect was increasing cell size in all the bacterial 'tribes', albeit at different rates. This suggests that large cell size helps in a glucose-poor environment. A graph of cell size vs. number of generations gives a nice curve called a *hyperbola*: that is, it increases rapidly over the first 2,000 generations, then the increase is much more gradual, almost levelling off. This curve is appropriate, given Dawkins' hyberbolic language about the significance:

"We have so far seen a beautiful demonstration of evolution in action: evolution before our very eyes, documented by comparing twelve independent lines, and also by comparing each line with 'living fossils', which literally instead of only metaphorically, come from the past." (p. 126)

This is the *best* that evolution can do? Increased cell size? And which almost levels off pretty quickly? No hint of evolution of multi-celled creatures? This need not even be an increase in information content; progressive degradation of a gene that initiates cell division at a certain size would result in a higher maximum size before they reproduce.

Dawkins also argued reasonably that there are a number of ways that a cell could grow larger. But then he tries a snow job:

"Lenski and a different set of colleagues investigated this phenomenon [bigger cells] by taking two of the [*E. coli*] tribes, called Ara+1 and Ara-1, which seemed, over 20,000 generations, to have followed the same evolutionary trajectory, and looking at their DNA. The astonishing result they found was that 59 genes had changed their level of expression in both tribes and all 59 had changes in the same direction. Were it not for natural selection, such independent parallelism, in all 59 genes independently, would completely beggar belief. The odds against it happening by chance are stupefyingly large. This is exactly the kind of thing creationists say cannot happen, because they think it is too improbable to have happened by chance. Yet it actually happened. And the explanation, of course, is that it did not happen by chance, but because gradual, step-by-step, cumulative natural selection favoured the same—literally the same—beneficial changes in both lines independently." (pp. 124–5)

Yet biochemist Michael Behe has also analyzed Lenski's experiment, and shows that the changes were not independent at all, but were ultimately due to changes in just *one* control gene:

"Another change was in a regulatory gene called *spoT* which *affected en masse how fifty-nine other genes worked,* either increasing or decreasing their activity. One likely explanation for the net good effect of this very blunt mutation is that it turned off the energetically costly genes that make the bacterial flagellum, saving the cell some energy."[2]

Indeed, since these germs have a rich glucose supply to feed on, there is no selection pressure to preserve other important functions, such as locomotion.

2.   Behe, M., *The Edge of Evolution: The search for the limits of Darwinism*, p. 142, Free Press, NY, 2007.

So we see deterioration, much like the blind cave creatures, as discussed in ch. 14. For example, none of the tribes could eat ribose any more, and some had even lost the ability to repair DNA. Such germs could not compete with 'wild' germs outside the pampered environment of the lab.

Apparently Lenski had given up on trying to observe genuine evolution in these real organisms, since he had calculated[3] that all possible simple mutations must have occurred several times over but without any addition of even one simple adaptive trait. So he switched to digital 'organisms' instead—his 'Avida' computer simulations, which he claims gave him the result he wanted in 15,000 generations.[4] Of course, this has little relevance to the real world of chemicals.[5] Chemicals obey the Second Law of Thermodynamics, and do not arrange themselves into self-sustaining metabolic pathways. Living cells have molecular machinery, whose assembly is directed by programmed instructions, to channel the chemistry in the right direction and amounts.

Yet a discovery in one of the lines revived Lenski's hopes and made him an overnight celebrity in the evolutionary community …

Citrate-eating bacteria?

There was "one dramatic exception" to the modest gradual changes: after 33,000 generations, one of the tribes, labelled Ara–3, had a sharp six-fold increase in 'cloudiness' because of the huge increase in the number of bacteria. This high maximum population was maintained in later generations; the graph shows a large step then a levelling off. Dawkins explains:

"… glucose was not the only nutrient in the broth. Another one was citrate (related to the substance that makes lemons sour[6]). The broth contained plenty of citrate, but *E. coli* normally can't use it, at least not when there is oxygen in the water. But if a mutant could 'discover' how to deal with citrate, a bonanza would open up to it. This is exactly what happened to Ara–3. This tribe, and this tribe alone, suddenly acquired the ability to eat citrate as well as glucose, rather than only glucose. The amount of food in each successive flask in the lineage therefore shot up. And so did the plateau at which the population in each successive flask daily stabilized." (pp. 127–8)

---

3. Holmes, Bob, Bacteria make major evolutionary shift in the lab, *NewScientist.com* news service, 9 June 2008.
4. Minnich, S., *Paradigm of Design: the Bacterial Flagellum DVD*, Focus on Origins series, 2003.
5. For a technical critique, see the two-part paper by Royal Truman, Evaluation of neo-Darwinian Theory using the Avida Platform, *PCID* 3.1.1, November 2004; http://www.iscid.org/papers/Truman_ComplexFeatures1_070104.pdf and http://www.iscid.org/papers/Truman_ComplexFeatures2_070104.pdf
6. True. Citric acid ($C_3H_5O(COOH)_3$) makes citrus fruits sour, hence the name; citrate ($C_3H_5O(COO)_3^{3-}$) is known as its *conjugate base*.

But then why was this mutation not seen in other tribes? Perhaps because the change required two (or three) mutations? Dawkins asserts, "the rarity of citrate metabolism suggests that we are looking for something more like the 'irreducible complexity' of creationist propaganda". Actually, two mutations would merely be Behe's 'edge of evolution', and no different in principle to the chloroquine resistance in malarial parasites, also requiring two mutations (see previous chapter, p. 51).

Dawkins tries to bolster his claim of new information arising by proposing:

"This might be a biochemical pathway in which the product of one chemical reaction feeds into a second chemical reaction, and *neither can make any inroads at all without the other.*" (pp. 128–9, emphasis in original)

Then he describes the painstaking experiments by Lenski's student Zachary Blount to show that indeed around generation 20,000, the germs had acquired the first mutation, priming them to be able to use the second. Once again, we have no problem with the *science*, just the *interpretation* of it. For example, even with huge numbers of bacteria and many thousands of generations, a new function requiring just two mutations was barely obtainable. Even three would probably have been out of reach.

But were the changes anything like (non-biochemist) Dawkins proposed? In reality, all living things use the Krebs cycle, otherwise known as the citric acid cycle, showing *that they already possess the ability to deal with citrate.* Normally, however, this is part of a wider cycle of metabolism of glucose. But *E. coli* can already use citrate directly under anaerobic conditions, a clue Dawkins inadvertently gave above (p. 65). This means the germs *already have* a whole suite of genes (operon) able to ferment citrate, including a citrate transporter gene that codes for a transporter protein embedded in the cell wall that takes citrate into the cell.[7] Indeed, Lenski himself noted:

"A more likely possibility, in our view, is that an existing transporter has been co-opted for citrate transport under oxic [high oxygen levels] conditions."

This operon is normally activated only under oxygen-free conditions. There is a good reason for this: such anaerobic respiration is less efficient than aerobic respiration, so there is good reason to have it switched off unless the oxygen required for aerobic respiration is lacking. But here, there is a

---

7. Pos, K.M., Dimroth, P. and Bott, M., The *Escherichia coli* Citrate Carrier CitT: a Member of a Novel Eubacterial Transporter Family Related to the 2-Oxoglutarate/Malate Translocator from Spinach Chloroplasts, *J. Bacteriol.* **180**(16):4160–4165, 1998; www.pubmedcentral.nih.gov/articlerender. fcgi?artid=107412.

loss of regulation allowing this anaerobic citrate respiration to work all the time, so it's informationally *downhill*. Biologist Don Batten suggests some possibilities as to how the change could have occurred via *information-losing* mutations, perfectly compatible with the biblical Creation/Fall model:

"So what happened? It is not yet clear from the published information, but a likely scenario is that mutations jammed the regulation of this operon so that the bacteria produce citrate transporter regardless of the oxidative state of the bacterium's environment (that is, it is permanently switched on). This can be likened to having a light that switches on when the sun goes down—a sensor detects the lack of light and turns the light on. A *fault* in the sensor could result in the light being on all the time. That is the sort of change we are talking about.

"Another possibility is that an existing transporter gene, such as the one that normally takes up tartrate,[8] which does not normally transport citrate, mutated such that it *lost specificity* and could then transport citrate into the cell.

"Such a loss of specificity is also an expected outcome of random mutations. A loss of specificity equals a *loss of information*, but evolution is supposed to account for the creation of new information; information that specifies the enzymes and cofactors in new biochemical pathways, how to make feathers and bone, nerves, or the components and assembly of complex motors such as ATP synthase, for example.

"However, mutations are good at destroying things, not creating them. Sometimes destroying things can be helpful (adaptive), but that does not account for the creation of the staggering amount of information in the DNA of all living things."[9]

Given the rarity, it seems likely that a loss of control of the transporter gene, leaving it permanently switched 'on', was just the priming mutation. Another change would turn on the citrate digesting machinery so it would work with oxygen present.

Antibiotic resistance

Dawkins finishes his section on bacterial 'evolution' with the old canard:

8. Blount, Z.D., Borland, C.Z. and Lenski, R.E., Historical contingency and the evolution of a key innovation in an experimental population of *Escherichia coli*, *PNAS* 105:7899–7906; published online on 4 June 2008, 10.1073/pnas.0803151105. This is Lenski's inaugural paper as a newly inducted member of the National Academy of Sciences, USA—yet another dyed-in-the-wool atheistic evolutionist in that august body (see: National Academy of Science is godless to the core—*Nature* survey; creation.com/godlessnas).
9. Batten, D., Bacteria "evolving in the lab"? "A poke in the eye for anti-evolutionists"? creation.com/citrate, 14 June 2008; partly based on Michael Behe's Amazon Blog, 6 June 2008; www.amazon.com/gp/blog/post/PLNK3U696N278Z93O.

"Many bacteria have evolved resistance to antibiotics in spectacularly short periods. After all, the first antibiotic, penicillin, was developed, heroically, by Florey and Chain as recently as the Second World War. New antibiotics have been coming out at frequent intervals since then, and bacteria have evolved resistance to every one of them." (p. 132)

Naturally Dawkins doesn't mention that Ernst Chain (1906–1979) was a devout Orthodox Jew (that is, he believed Genesis was real history, as Christian creationists do) and anti-Darwinian. His biography noted "Chain's dismissal of Darwin's theory of evolution", and his belief that "evolution was not really a part of science, since it was, for the most part, not amenable to experimentation—and he was, and is, by no means alone in this view". As an understanding of the development of life, Chain said, "a very feeble attempt it is, based on such flimsy assumptions, mainly of morphological-anatomical nature that it can hardly be called a theory." And speaking of certain evolutionary examples, he exclaimed, "I would rather believe in fairies than in such wild speculation."[10] This gives the lie to Dawkins' propaganda that evolution is necessary for the advancement of science; and the fight against human disease is the field of science most commonly held up as needing evolution.

And of course, Dawkins is using the old bait-and-switch yet again. A few years ago, I explained how antibiotic resistance can arise without any increase of information, i.e. the changes are irrelevant to germs-to-geniuses evolution:[11]

• Sometimes bacteria can pass on information to other bacteria, via loops of DNA called *plasmids*. Sometimes plasmids contain information for antibiotic resistance. But here too, the information *already existed*, so this is *not* evolution.

• Information-losing mutations can confer resistance. Such mutations are often harmful in an 'ordinary' environment without antibiotics. It is well documented that many 'superbugs' are really 'superwimps' for this reason. Also, some sorts of information-losing mutations evidently cause HIV resistance to antivirals, because the 'wild' types easily out-compete the resistant types when the drugs are removed. Despite that, this has been promoted as another 'proof' of evolution.

• So, how can an information *loss* confer resistance? Here are some *observed* mechanisms:

10. Clark R.W., *The Life of Ernst Chain: Penicillin and Beyond*, pp.146–148, Weidenfeld & Nicolson, London, 1985.

11. Sarfati, J., Anthrax and antibiotics: Is evolution relevant? creation.com/anthrax, 2001/2005. See also Anderson, K.L., Is bacterial resistance to antibiotics an appropriate example of evolutionary change? *CRSQ* **41**(4):318–326, March 2005.

o A *pump* in the cell wall takes in the antibiotic. A mutation *disabling* this pump will prevent the bacterium pumping in its own executioner. But in the wild, a bacterium with a disabled pump will be less fit than other bacteria because the pump also brings nutrients, etc., into the cell.

o A *control gene* regulates the production of an enzyme that destroys the antibiotic, e.g. penicillinase that destroys penicillin. (The information to make this complex enzyme was already in the gene pool prior to the discovery of penicillin. Despite the way an unwary reader might take Dawkins' earlier comment, penicillin—produced by a mould—pre-existed Chain and Florey.) A mutation *disabling* this gene destroys the regulation of the production, so far more enzyme is produced. Such a bacterium can cope with more antibiotic than others can, but in the wild, it would be less fit than normal because it's wasting valuable resources producing more enzyme than is needed.

o An *enzyme* is highly specialized to break down one specific type of chemical very well, and hardly affect other chemicals. A mutation could *reduce its specificity*, i.e. it no longer does its main job so well, and affects other chemicals to some extent too. Normally, a biological system with such a mutation would not function as well, and reduced specificity is reduced information *by definition*. But sometimes the other affected chemicals happen to be antibiotics, so this type of mutation confers resistance. Resistance to the antibiotic streptomycin can be caused by an information-losing mutation that degrades the surface of a bacterium's ribosome, where decoding of DNA information to proteins occurs. This *reduces* the binding ability of the drug to the ribosome, preventing it from ruining its operation.

• These principles should be enough to demonstrate that these latest claims about bacteria 'evolving' resistance are not a threat to biblical creation and do not give the claimed support to molecules-to-microbiologist evolution.

Dawkins also tells us about a pamphlet in his doctor's waiting room telling patients of the importance of finishing a course of antibiotics, even if the infection appears to have gone before then:

"Like any poison, antibiotics are likely to be dosage dependent [see ch. 16]. A sufficiently high dose will kill all the bacteria. A sufficiently low dose will kill none. An intermediate dose will kill some, not all. If there is genetic variation among bacteria, such that some are more susceptible to the antibiotic than others, an intermediate dose will be tailor-made to select in favour of genes for resistance. When the doctor tells you to take all your pills, it is to increase the chances of killing all the bacteria and avoid leaving behind resistant, or semi-resistant mutants. With hindsight we might say that if only we had all been better educated in Darwinian thinking, we would have woken up sooner to the dangers of resistant strains being selected." (pp. 132–3)

But in my article cited earlier,[11] I also pointed out that one doesn't need to accept goo-to-you evolution to realize the problems:

"Selection for resistant bacteria is a real danger when a patient fails to complete a prescribed course of antibiotics (60 days for Cipro)—i.e. stops taking the drug when the symptoms ease, which just means that *most* germs have been destroyed. The remnants require the final doses of antibiotic to finish them off, but if the treatment stops, they are free to multiply. This time the drug is far less effective, since the remnant population will tend to be the more resistant ones.

"This problem of selection of resistant varieties applies not only to the targeted germ, but all the other types affected by the same antibiotic. This is the main reason that the medical profession is concerned with people taking Cipro for a few days because of the anthrax scare. Indeed the over-use of Cipro could result in many germs that are resistant to this drug, so *the concern is very well founded*. Antibiotics as a preventative measure are warranted only where there's evidence that people were in a 'breathing zone' of the deadly airborne anthrax spores, not for the milder skin form of anthrax."[11]

Indeed, Dawkins should be happier with my explanation than the one in his doctor's surgery, because this irritated him with its anthropomorphic explanations "that bacteria are 'clever' and 'learn to cope' with antibiotics." (p. 132).[12]

Furthermore, I showed how Dawkins' historical revisionism about the need for Darwinism makes no sense even on the face of it:

"… many evolutionists crow about antibiotic resistance as an amazing 'prediction' of evolution. Even aside from the above points, this is revisionist history. Historically, antibiotic resistance at first took the medical profession by surprise—even as late as 1969, experts stated that

---

12. As this book was going to press, new research was published showing that antibiotics in low doses may stimulate "hypermutability", resulting in a "whole zoo of mutants", increasing the chance of these beneficial information-losing mutations. See Enserink, M., What Doesn't Kill Microbes, Makes Them Stronger, *ScienceNOW Daily News*, sciencenow.sciencemag.org, 11 February 2010.

'infectious diseases were a thing of the past'. I.e. antibiotic resistance was hardly a 'prediction' of evolution, but is really a phenomenon explained 'after the fact' by evolutionary language. But as shown, the biblical Creation/Fall model explains it better." [11]

Sexual selection

Dawkins appeals to interesting experiments to show the reality of sexual selection. I.e. some characteristics arose, not because they were fitter and thus favoured by natural selection, but preferred by the opposite sex in mate choice. This is potentially a strong effect, since only those creatures that find mates can pass on their genes to the next generation. Creationist biologists have no problem with sexual selection either, just, once again, with the bait-and-switch.

Guppies

Dawkins' colleague Dr John Endler studied many populations of guppies in mountain streams in Trinidad, Tobago and Venezuela (pp. 133–9). [13] Brightly coloured males seem to impress the females, who 'sexually selected' such colours. But they stand out to predators, who would 'naturally select' against this. As strong support for this, streams with strong predators contain drabber males, while streams with weak predators have more brightly coloured males with larger, gaudier spots.

Endler noticed that the 'drab' ones are camouflaged by spots as well, which blend in with the pebbles at the bottoms of their native streams. So he set up experiments in a number of ponds, half with fine gravel and half with coarse. He allowed guppies to breed freely. The number of spots shot up, presumably since only sexual selection was at work.

Then after six months, he left some ponds predator-free; in others, a fairly weak predator (given that no natural stream is really totally predator-free); and in the remaining, he introduced a strong predator, a pike cichlid. In the ponds with weak or no predation, the number of spots continued to rise, as sexual selection was still operating. But in the ponds with the strong predator, the number of spots dropped sharply. Evidently males with lots of spots were easily spotted and devoured, so despite the females' preferences, they had to be content with the survivors.

Also, Endler found that gravel size made a difference. Both strong and weak predators promoted larger spots in pools with coarse gravel, and smaller spots with finer gravel. This makes sense—the closer spot size matches gravel,

13. Endler, J.A., Natural and sexual selection on color patterns in poeciliid fishes, *Environmental Biology of Fishes* 9:173–190, 1983.

the more camouflaged the fish are. But in ponds with no predators, the reverse happened: fine gravel promoted larger spots and coarse gravel smaller. Again, this makes sense—the less camouflaged males stand out better to the females.

Evolution in action?

Dawkins relates a story Endler told about an encounter with a fellow domestic airline passenger. This passenger showed much interest in Endler's guppy research, and amiably asked what Endler himself calls "excellent questions … indicating that he was enthusiastically and intellectually following the argument." Yet when this passenger asked what theory underlined the experiments, Endler replied, "It's called Darwin's theory of evolution by natural selection." Then, by Endler's account, this passenger quit the conversation, which Endler calls, "really tragic". Dawkins calls this passenger "closed-minded" (p. 133).

But even if this account is unembellished, it doesn't prove what they claim. This passenger might have been justifiably annoyed at Endler's cheap bait-and-switch. Dawkins commits the same dishonest equivocation when he claims, "It is a spectacular example of evolution before our very eyes" (p. 139). It might have been better for the passenger to reply on the lines of, "Indeed, these are most ingenious experiments to support natural selection, a theory known to creationists before Darwin. But do guppies changing into guppies prove that fish evolved into fishermen? The changes don't show any new features, just different expressions of the same ones." Yet this type of change, *which doesn't add any new information*, is usually the best 'evidence' of evolution and alleged disproof of creation that evolutionists can come up with.

Furthermore, the Endler-passenger exchange shows that belief in particles-to-people evolution is not necessary to understand real science, *including experiments on natural and sexual selection.* And clearly belief in creation does not ruin fascination for such science. So Dawkins' scare-mongering about 'history deniers' destroying science education is shown—even by his own account—to be wide of the mark.

Peacock tail

No discussion on sexual selection would be complete without the peacock tail. Here is an even more blatantly cumbersome feature, surely a disadvantage to its wearer. Yet Darwin proposed that it evolved because females were impressed by gaudy tails. He did not explain precisely how the ingenious mathematical patterning of this tail came to be; i.e. no matter what females preferred, this would not generate the ingenious mathematical patterns and spectral colours.[14] Just like natural selection, it can select for *already-existing* characteristics, as Endler showed with guppies. But as an explanation for *new* features, sexual selection is as helpless as natural selection.[15]

Indeed, new research has damaged the sexual selection theory for peacock tails. It turns out that peahens aren't impressed with the peacock's display, and care more for the mating calls. The researchers summarize their seven-year study:

"We found no evidence that peahens expressed any preference for peacocks with more elaborate trains (i.e. trains having more ocelli, a more symmetrical arrangement or a greater length), similar to other studies of galliforms showing that females disregard male plumage. Combined with previous results, our findings indicate that the peacock's train (1) is not the universal target of female choice, (2) shows small variance among males across populations and (3) based on current physiological knowledge, does not appear to reliably reflect the male condition."[16]

A report on this research noted:

"The feather train on male peacocks is among the most striking and beautiful physical attributes in nature, but it fails to excite, much less interest, females, according to new research. The determination throws a wrench in the long-held belief that male peacock feathers evolved in response to female mate choice. It could also indicate that certain other elaborate features in galliformes, a group that includes turkeys, chickens, grouse, quails and pheasants, as well as peacocks, are not necessarily linked to fitness and mating success."[17]

It's not as if the researchers set out to contradict the theory—just the opposite in fact—they had planned to *confirm* it. So Charles Darwin's 'theory of sexual selection' *fails to explain the very thing Darwin concocted it for!* [18]

Toucan beak

Darwin also invoked sexual selection to explain the toucan's huge beak, about a third of its body length:

14. After Burgess, S., The beauty of the peacock tail and the problems with the theory of sexual selection, *J. Creation* **15**(2):94–102, 2001; creation.com/peacock. Stuart Burgess is Professor of Design and Nature and Head of Department, Mechanical Engineering, University of Bristol (UK), and a world expert on biomimetics. N.B. 'Professor' in the UK, and some British Commonwealth countries, is a title given only to the highest academic rank.
15. Bergman, J., Problems in sexual selection theory and neo-Darwinism, *J. Creation* **18**(1): 112–119, 2004.
16. Takahashi, M. *et al.*, Peahens do not prefer peacocks with more elaborate trains, *Anim. Behav.* 2007, doi:10.1016/j.anbehav.2007.10.004.
17. Viegas, J., Female Peacocks Not Impressed by Male Feathers, *Discovery News*, March 26, 2008; dsc. discovery.com/news/2008/03/26/peacock-feathers-females.html.
18. Catchpoole, D., Peacock tail tale failure, creation.com/tale, 2008.

"toucans may owe the enormous size of their beaks to sexual selection, for the sake of displaying the diversified and vivid stripes of colour with which these organs are ornamented."[19]

But now there is strong evidence that the beak is important for losing excess heat. It has 30% to 50% of the toucan's overall body surface area—although only about 5% of its weight—and is also supplied with a rich network of blood vessels close to its surface. And the amount of blood flow, hence heat loss, is closely regulated, even during sleep.[20]

So now that the beak's size is connected to its *function* (thermoregulation) rather than *hypothetical* sexual attractiveness, what explains its origins? The researchers still attributed the bill to evolution, but admitted, "the selective forces that led to the large bills of present-day toucans remain elusive".[20] That is, once again evolution provides no insights.

Successful evolutionary prediction: long proboscis?

Dawkins, like many evolutionary propagandists, talks about an allegedly successful prediction of evolution. Many plants are pollinated by insects, which means that they often have mutually compatible features. E.g. some flowers have tubes leading to the nectar, so insects need to have a long tongue (proboscis) to reach the nectar. On the way, they pick up pollen, ready to deposit on other flowers. Dawkins says:

"Both Darwin and his co-discoverer of natural selection, Wallace, called attention to an amazing orchid from Madagascar, *Angraecum sesquipedale* ... and both men made the same remarkable prediction, which was later triumphantly vindicated. This orchid has tubular nectaries that reach down to more than 11 inches by Darwin's own ruler. That's nearly 30 centimetres. A related species, *Angraecum longicalcar*, has nectar-bearing spurs that are even longer, up to 40 centimetres (more than 15 inches). Darwin, purely on the strength of *A. sesquipedale*'s existence in Madagascar, predicted in his orchid book of 1862 that there 'must be moths capable of extension to a length between ten and eleven inches.' Wallace, five years later (it isn't clear whether he had read Darwin's book) mentioned several moths whose prosboces were nearly long enough to meet the case. ...

"In 1903, after Darwin's death but well within Wallace's long lifetime, a hitherto unknown moth was discovered which turned out to fulfill

---

19. Darwin, C, *The Descent of Man: And Selection in relation to Sex*, John Murray, London, 1871, Volume II, 1st edition, 1871, p. 227; available online from darwin-online.org.uk/.
20. Tattersall, G. *et al.*, Heat exchange from the toucan bill reveals a controllable vascular thermal radiator, *Science* **325**(5939):468–470, 2009.

the Darwin/Wallace prediction, and was duly honoured with the sub-specific name *praedicta*. But even *Xanthopan morgani praedicta*, 'Darwin's hawk moth', is not sufficiently endowed to pollinate *A. longicalcar*, and the existence of this flower encourages us to suspect the existence of an even longer-tongued moth, with the same confidence as Wallace invoked the predicted discovery of Neptune. By the way, this little example gives the lie, yet again, to the allegation that evolutionary science cannot be predicted because it concerns past history. The Darwin/Wallace prediction was still a perfectly valid one, even though the praedicta moth must already have been in existence before they made it, They were predicting that, at some time in the future, somebody would discover a moth with a tongue long enough to reach the nectar in *A. sequipedale*." (pp. 49–50)

There is an important *logical* flaw in such arguments to consider before analyzing specifics.

Fallacy of verified prediction

While it is common to cite verified predictions as 'proof' of a scientific law, this commits a basic logical fallacy called *affirming the consequent*.[21,22] That can be seen if we analyze it ($\therefore$ = therefore):

1) Theory T predicts observation O;

2) O is observed;
   $\therefore$ T is true.

To see why this does not follow, consider:

1) If I had just eaten a whole pizza, I would feel very full;

2) I feel very full;
   $\therefore$ I have just eaten a whole pizza.

But I could feel very full for many different reasons, e.g. eating lots of another type of food. Similarly, there are potentially many possible theories that could predict a given observation.

On the other hand, the famous falsification criterion for a scientific theory devised by the Austrian-British philosopher of science Sir Karl Popper

---

21. Sarfati, J., *Loving God With All Your Mind: Logic and Creation*, *J. Creation* **12**(2):142–151, 1998; creation.com/logic.

22. Clark, G.H., *The Philosophy of Science and Belief in God*, The Trinity Foundation, Jefferson, MD, USA, 2nd ed, 1987.

(1902–1994)[23] is based on the valid form of argument known as *denying the consequent*:[21]

1) Theory T predicts O will not be observed;

2) O is observed;
∴ T is false.

However, some philosophers of science regard Popper as somewhat simplistic. The American historian of science Thomas Kuhn (1922–1996) pointed out that, in reality, in periods of 'normal science', scientists do not throw out the ruling paradigm readily, but tolerate a large number of 'anomalies'. It takes many anomalies to build up before there is a scientific revolution.[24]

The theory of the Hungarian-Jewish Imre Lakatos (1922–1974) has sometimes been regarded as a synthesis of Popper and Kuhn. He retained the falsification criterion in one sense, but also took into account that scientists in practice do not follow this strictly. But instead of Kuhn's sociological treatment, Lakatos put this in a logical perspective. He pointed out that core theories are not tested in isolation, but are 'protected' by auxiliary hypotheses. Denying the consequent only shows that one of the premises needs to be false, and it need not be the core theory. So the auxiliary hypotheses are modified instead.[25] In schematic form, the valid argument is as follows:

1) Theory T and auxiliary hypothesis A predict that O will not be observed;

2) O is observed;
∴ Either T or A is false.

For example, Newton's theory predicted certain motions of Uranus, provided there were no other massive objects interfering. When Uranus didn't move as predicted, either Newton's theory was falsified or there was another massive object perturbing the orbit—this turned out to be the planet Neptune, as Dawkins and Wallace alluded to.[26]

23. Popper, K., *The Logic of Scientific Discovery*, 1959; Routledge Classics 2002; translated from his *Logik der Forschung*, 1934.
24. Kuhn, T., *The Structure of Scientific Revolutions*, University of Chicago Press, Chicago, 1970.
25. Lakatos, I., Falsification and the methodology of scientific research programmes; in: Lakatos I. & Musgrave A., Eds., *Criticism and the Growth of Knowledge*; www.philosophy.ru/edu/ref/sci/lakatos.html.
26. For extensive discussion of the views of Popper and Lakatos, and other attempts to define science, see Bird, W.R., *The Origin of Species Revisited*, Philosophical Library, New York, Vol. II, chapters 9–10, 1991.

Alternative explanation

As shown above, the long proboscis may well be a successful prediction of Darwinian theory. But the logic shows that it is not a proof of it, because it might also be predicted by other theories. For example, it would also be a perfectly reasonable prediction of *design* theory. I.e., a creationist who finds an unusual feature would suppose that it was designed for a purpose, so a long nectar channel would be designed for pollination by a long-tongued creature, even if one had not been discovered.

Also, it could be a combination of design *and* natural selection, which, I must remind readers, is an important part of the biblical creation model. I.e. the basic orchid and moth kinds with nectar channels and proboscis were designed, and natural selection fine-tuned both for longer features.[27]

Darwinian medicine?

This sort of fallacy is quite common in evolutionary propaganda, and it recurs in the new area of 'Darwinian medicine'. The reasoning goes along the lines of, "We suppress coughs; had we thought in evolutionary terms, we would have realized that natural selection favoured the cough for a good reason, so it is probably adaptive. Thanks to Darwin, we have discovered that it's important for expelling gunk from the lungs." But a creationist medical doctor[28] could argue, "Things have been designed for a purpose, so it's highly likely that coughing is also useful for something. And indeed we find that it helps to expel gunk from the lungs."

The same goes for other disease symptoms. Should we suppress fever, when it's likely the result of natural selection for a temperature unfavourable to germs? Yet it's the same if it's a designed mechanism to cope with infection. Diarrhea should not be suppressed because it was adapted/designed to expel intestinal pathogens—pick one; the result *for all practical purposes* is the same.

The fallacy lies in equating adaptation to evolution, and presuming that a current advantage of a feature shows that it *evolved*, rather than was designed, for that purpose. There is no actual *evidence* that the feature arose by mutations + selection.

Summary

- Despite cautions about their overuse, creationists have no problem with natural or sexual selection as such. So Dawkins' chapters on artificial

27. For more on this combination of design and natural selection in orchids, see Grigg, R., The Love Trap, *Creation* 24(3):26–27, 2002; creation.com/orchid.
28. Such as Dr Carl Wieland, in Is evolution really necessary for medical advances? creation.com/ev-med, 28 October 2002.

selection, natural selection, sexual selection, dog breeds, etc. are merely proving something not disputed by creationists, and are really just knocking down straw men.

- Lenski's breeding of bacteria showed that even under the most favourable conditions for evolution, mutation + selection produces no change in the direction required for germs-to-geniuses evolution. Even his famous citrate-digesting bacteria merely show that already existing information was just turned permanently 'on', possibly by damaging genetic switches.

- Antibiotic resistance shows natural selection working, and sometimes deleterious mutations. But the resistant germs are usually less fit than the wild type except in the artificial environment of a patient taking antibiotics.

- Sexual selection has been observed, but again this gives no support to particles-to-people evolution. Also, sexual selection is demonstrably not the explanation of the peacock's tail, the very thing for which Darwin invented the theory.

- The long-tongued moth is claimed as a successful prediction of evolution— it had supposedly evolved for dealing with a long nectar channel. But using verified prediction as proof commits a logical fallacy. This would also be a successful prediction of creation: the moth was *designed* for the long-channelled flower, possibly with some natural selection accentuating the length as well.

- Proponents of 'Darwinian medicine' commit the same sort of fallacy: they argue that certain disease symptoms are adaptive, so should not be suppressed. Yet a creationist medical doctor could argue that these symptoms are designed reactions, so likewise should not be suppressed.

—∞—

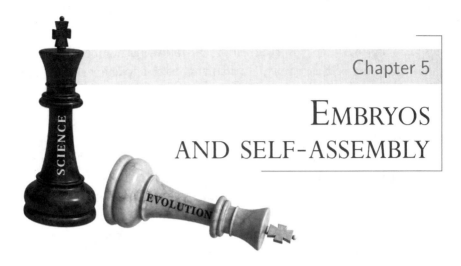

Chapter 5

EMBRYOS
AND SELF-ASSEMBLY

I N Greatest Show, ch. 8, Dawkins tries to show that embryonic development is all about simple local rules, which could supposedly enable natural selection to make small modifications so that different types of embryos could develop. However, as usual, Dawkins ignores a minimal complexity required, which includes the ability to form multicellular life in the first place. Also, while the individual local rules might be relatively simple, the organization on show involves that the sequence in which the rules are applied is anything but simple and is unlikely to have arisen without intelligent input.

Dawkins titled chapter 8 of *Greatest Show,* "You did it yourself in nine months." This comes from a riposte attributed to "irascible genius" J.B.S. Haldane (see also ch. 3, p. 54, and ch. 13, p. 229). After one of his public lectures, a woman expressed skepticism that it was possible to go from a single cell to a complicated human body, even in the alleged billions of years. Haldane responded: "But madam, you did it yourself. And it only took you nine months." (p. 211)

Various skeptics have tried this on us, and we have pointed out that the embryo has genetic instructions to build the body, which the hypothetical single-celled ancestor did not. Dawkins' chapter tries to address that charge, by showing that embryonic development follows a number of simple local rules including self-assembly. He also applies this to shapes of enzymes and viruses, and even the behaviours of flocks of birds.

Dawkins the theologian

Dawkins resorts to some amateurish theology:

> "And even if a divine intelligence did prove to be ultimately responsible for designing living complexity, it is definitely not true that he *fashions* living bodies in the way that clay modellers, for example, or carpenters, potters, tailors or car manufacturers go about their tasks. We may be 'wonderfully developed', but we are not 'wonderfully *made*'. When children sing, 'He made their glowing colours / He made their tiny wings', they are uttering a childishly obvious falsehood. Whatever else God does, he certainly doesn't *make* glowing colours and tiny wings. If he did anything at all, it would be to supervise the embryonic development of things, for example, by splicing together sequences of genes that direct a process of automated development. Wings are not made, they grow—progressively—from limb buds inside an egg.

> "God, to repeat this important point, which ought to be obvious, but isn't, never made a tiny wing in his eternal life. If he made anything (he didn't in my view, but let it pass, that's not what I'm about here), what he made was an embryological *recipe*, or something like a computer program for controlling the embryonic development of a tiny wing (plus lots of other things too). Of course, God might claim that it is just as clever, just as breathtaking a feat of skill, to design a recipe or a program for a wing, as to make a wing." (pp. 312–3)

Indeed, we have also pointed out that the Bible teaches that God's *creative* activity was *finished* on Day 6 of Creation Week—the Hebrew שָׁבַת *shābat*, translated 'rested' actually means 'ceased', not that God gets tired. His major activity now is *sustaining* this creation (Colossians 1:15 ff.) in a regular repeatable way that the founders of modern science equated with 'laws of nature' (see ch. 17). Yet Genesis 1 teaches that the chicken came before the egg, because God created it. The method of reproduction, involving a single cell and embryonic development, is ideal so that the genetic information from both parents is combined and a new unique individual is generated.

So Dawkins has committed the either-or fallacy, overlooking that God *both* made the ancestral adult form *and* the program to reproduce. We have also pointed out that overlooking the difference leads to error. For example, one Christian calendar had a picture of a panda with a biblical creation passage that implied that God directly created that *particular* panda. But this misleads. We wrote:

"The Bible clearly teaches that the heavens, the earth, and all they contain were made during the six days of Creation Week (Exodus 20:8–11). But was the panda in the photo made in Creation Week? Obviously not. The first of some ancestral kind were created at that time, with plan and purpose. The highly complex molecular machinery of which they were constructed, by the infinitely intelligent Designer, included the machinery by which they were to 'multiply and fill the earth'—i.e. reproduce— 'after their kinds'.

"The programmed instructions for this were written on the DNA within the first population of that kind. Today's panda was therefore not directly created in the same way as its first ancestors, though it is the eventual consequence of that original creative act. In fact, today's pandas would only contain a subset of the original information of their ancestral kind, marred further by accumulated genetic copying mistakes (mutations).

"Of course, God is still involved in everything that happens, including the 'natural laws' of reproduction. The God of Abraham is not some deistic notion of a watchmaker who started things off, then left them to their own devices. Scientific 'law' is merely a description of His normative action (cf. Colossians 1:17), miracles are His non-normative actions. But the point here is that without further explanation a misleading view of the world can result.

"Similarly, many small children are taught that 'God made me'. But unless this is more fully explained through the 'glasses' of a robust biblical worldview, the risk is that when the child later learns about the 'natural' laws and processes of reproduction, he comes to see these as the 'real' explanation in substitution for the idea of God as his Creator."[1]

The same calendar had another page with a picture of a spectacular canyon, with another creation passage. Yet as far as the Bible is concerned, any beauty it has is a merciful side effect of what was really the result of a worldwide water judgment on mankind's sin—the fast-moving channelized runoff from receding global floodwaters.[2] Similarly, the beautiful Fiordland National Park in New Zealand was likewise not a direct creation of God, but a

---

1. Wieland, C., The canyon and the panda (Editorial), *Creation* **23**(2):4, 2001; creation.com/canyon.
2. Austin, S., *Grand Canyon: Monument to Catastrophe,* Institute for Creation Research, USA, 1995.

delayed result of the same global judgment: the carving by immense glaciers during the Ice Age caused by the Flood.[3]

So indeed Dawkins was right, but for the wrong reasons, about the "childishly obvious falsehood". Once more, we see that the cure for a lot of the mistakes he complains about is not his antitheistic evolutionism, but proper biblical understanding. But then, at times it can seem as if Dawkins has never seen a straw man he doesn't like to knock down.

Recipe or blueprint?

Dawkins points out something we have also noted:[4] DNA is not really a blueprint but a *recipe* (pp. 213–215). That is, a literal blueprint from a house is a one-to-one map of the house's actual dimensions, so just as a house can be constructed by following the blueprint, the blueprint can be drawn from a complete house.

DNA is not like this: it is impossible to work out the DNA sequence from measurements of the organism, no matter how sophisticated. DNA is not even a one-dimensional representation of the three-dimensional structure. Conversely, "Nobody, reading the sequence of letters in the DNA of a fertilized egg, could predict the shape the animal is going to grow into." (p. 248) Similarly, measuring a cake doesn't enable us to reconstruct the recipe, or at least the exact words of the recipe. (p. 221)

Bottom-up programming: starling flock simulations

To try to explain embryonic development, Dawkins uses the analogy of computer programs for a flock of starlings, which "seems to behave as a single individual, wheeling and turning as one" (p. 218). They would not try to program the whole flock; rather, each 'robo-starling' would be programmed with:

"detailed rules on how to fly, and how to react to the presence of neighbouring starlings, depending on their distance and relative position. … These model rules would be informed by careful measurements of the real birds in action. Endow your cyber-bird with a certain tendency

---

3. There were not multiple ice ages, but advances and retreats of the single ice age. Obviously the climate would need to be colder. But global cooling by itself is not enough, because then there would be less evaporation, so less snow to form continental ice sheets. How is it possible to have both a cold climate and lots of evaporation? When 'all the fountains of the great deep' broke up, much hot water and lava would have poured directly into the oceans. This would have warmed the oceans, increasing evaporation. At the same time, much volcanic ash in the air after the Flood would have blocked out much sunlight, cooling the land. So the Flood would have produced the necessary combination of lots of evaporation from the warmed oceans and cool continental climate from the volcanic ash 'sunblock'. See Oard, M., *An Ice Age Caused by the Genesis Flood*, ICR, El Cajon, CA, USA, 1990, and Mammoth—riddle of the Ice Age, *Creation* **22**(2):10–15, 2000; creation.com/riddle.
4. E.g. Sarfati, J., DNA: marvellous messages or mostly mess? *Creation* **25**(2):26–31,2003; creation.com/message.

to vary its rules at random. Having written a complicated program to specify the behavioural rules of a single starling, now comes the definitive step I am emphasizing in this chapter. *Don't* try to program the behaviour of a whole flock, as an earlier generation of computer programmers might have done. Instead, clone the single computer starling you have programmed. Make a thousand copies of your robo-bird, maybe all the same as each other, or maybe with some slight variation among them in their rules. And now 'release' thousands of model starlings in your computer, so they are free to interact with each other, all obeying the same rules." (p.219)

Dawkins continues explaining that if the simulations are not quite right, the rules can be tweaked for the single robo-starling, which can then be cloned to replace the previous one. The process can be repeated until the simulation matches the real flock (pp. 219–220).[5]

It is hardly news that the real starlings are obeying local rules. However, a number of European researchers (including biologists, physicists and statisticians) in the Starling Project recently showed that the rules are much more complex than previously thought.[6,7] The previous explanation was that each bird simply keeps a set distance from its near neighbours. However, this is wrong. Instead, each starling seems to be continuously monitoring the positions of an average of six or seven of its neighbours, regardless of how far away they are. In other words, starlings have a pre-programmed, numeric, object-tracking ability, by 'computing' the *topological* distance (interactions) with other birds.

The researchers explain how this tracking method enables the flock to resist the attempts of predators to pick off stragglers because:

"By interacting within a fixed number of individuals the aggregation can be either dense or sparse, change shape, fluctuate and even split, yet maintain the same degree of cohesion."[6]

Embryonic development

The above explanation of starling flocks is not the first time that Dawkins makes very complex machinery seem much simpler than it really is. Then comes Dawkins' point:

5. The three *Lord of the Rings* films directed by New Zealander Peter Jackson did something similar with their computer-generated battle scenes: they programmed a dozen or so prototype 'soldiers' to react to soldiers and weapons close to them, and cloned them thousands of times.
6. Ballerini, M., *et al.*, Interaction ruling animal collective behavior depends on topological rather than metric distance: Evidence from a field study, *Proc. Natl Acad. Sci. USA* **105**(4):1232–1237, 2008.
7. After Bell, P., Bird behaviour beliefs overturned: A tale of the hummingbird and the starling, *Creation* **30**(3):9, 2008; creation.com/2bird.

"there is no choreographer and no leader. Order, organization, structure—these all *emerge* as by-products of rules which are obeyed *locally* and many times over, not globally. And that is how embryology works. It is all done by local rules, at various levels but especially at the level of the single cell. No choreographer. No conductor of the orchestra. No architect. In the field of development, or manufacture, the equivalent of this type of programming is called self-assembly.

"The body of a human, an eagle, a mole, a dolphin, a cheetah, a leopard frog, a swallow: these are so beautifully put together, it seems impossible to imagine that the genes that program their development don't function as a blueprint, a design, a master plan. But no: as with the computer starlings, it is all done by individual cells obeying local rules. The beautifully 'designed' body *emerges* as a consequence of rules being *locally* obeyed by individual cells, with no reference to anything that could be called an overall global plan. The cells of a developing embryo wheel and dance around each other like starlings in gigantic flocks. Unlike starlings, cells are physically attracted to each other in sheets and blocks: their 'flocks' are called 'tissues'." (p. 220)

Actually, again Dawkins hides some considerable complexity to bolster his claim of simple local rules explaining it all. Embryonic development applies only to multi-celled organisms. But the gap between single-celled and multi-celled organisms is another huge gap in evolution. Intermediates are not only non-existent in the fossil record (see chapters 7 and 8), but are an unsolved mystery in theory as well. There are completely different objectives in single-celled and multi-celled organisms. In the former, cells must simply multiply; in the latter, there must be controls *against* uncontrolled multiplication, usually called *cancer*. The cells from a single multi-cellular organism must also become different types of tissue, and their division is tightly controlled. There is an intricate mechanism called *serial differentiation*, which separates the self-renewing *stem cells* stage from the proliferative *transient amplifying cells* stage of cell division. The dilemma for evolutionists is: natural selection for such systems of control on cellular proliferation would require self-reproducing multi-cellular organisms, but they could not exist without those very systems already in place.[8]

---

8.   Doyle, S., Serial cell differentiation, *J. Creation* **22**(2):6–8, 2008; creation.com/serial. Also Multicellularity: what is required, *J. Creation* **23**(1):5–7, 2009; creation.com/multicellularity.

Stages

Dawkins explains how the early embryo develops, likening it to origami, the Japanese art of paper folding. The main difference is that the paper doesn't grow larger, while the developing embryo does, through cell multiplication. And as the area increases, the 'sheet' must buckle in some way (pp. 222–9). But first:

"The single fertilized cell divides to make two new cells. Then the two divide to make four. And so on, with the number of cells rapidly doubling and redoubling. At this stage, there is no growth, no inflation. The original volume of the cell is literally divided, as in slicing a cake, and we end up with a spherical ball of cells which is the same size as the original egg. It's not a solid ball but a hollow one, and it is called the blastula. The next stage, gastrulation ... typically involves a denting of the ... blastula, so that it becomes two-layered with an opening to the outside world. ... The outer layer of this 'gastrula' is called the ectoderm, the inner layer is the endoderm, and there are some cells thrown into the space between the ectoderm and the endoderm, which are called mesoderm. Each of these primordial layers is destined to make major parts of the body. For example, the outer skin and nervous system come from the ectoderm; the guts and other internal organs come from the endoderm; and the mesoderm furnishes muscle and bone.

"The next stage in the embryo's origami is called neurulation. ... In neurulation, as in gastrulation, invagination[9] is much in evidence. ... A section of the ectoderm invaginates (progressively backwards along the body like a zip fastener), rolls itself up into a tube, and is pinched off where the sides of the tube 'zip up' so that it ends up running the length of the body between the outer layer of the notochord. That tube is destined to become the spinal cord, the main nerve trunk of the body. The front end of it swells up and becomes the brain. And all the rest of the nerves are derived, by subsequent cell divisions, from this primordial tube." (pp. 226–8)

All this is perfectly reasonable. Yet although the steps are quite simple in principle, Dawkins commits a *fallacy of composition* here (as with: all atoms are microscopic, so an elephant composed of atoms is microscopic). It is the *sequence* of steps that makes the difference as to what forms at the end.

---

9.   Dawkins' note on p. 220: "Invaginate: 'fold inwards to form hollow', 'turn or double back within self' (*Shorter Oxford English Dictionary*)."

So chimp parents always produce chimp babies, not human ones. Similarly, computers follow lots of simple local rules, one might say—ultimately, they only deal with ones and zeroes. And they have simple rules in dealing with them, the *logic gates*, such as the AND gate, which produces a one in the output when *both* inputs are one; an OR gate where the output is one if *either* of the inputs is one; a NOT gate that inverts one to zero and vice versa, and such simple rules. Then the output of one gate becomes the input of another, and so on. But the computer and the program have predictable complex results because of the complex *organization* of these simple parts in space (hardware) and time (software). While the building block rules are relatively simple, that does not mean that the programs built on those rules are simple. The same is true of embryonic development and Dawkins omits this important distinction.

Nematode embryology

Dawkins explains how Sir John Sulston and his team have worked out the precise 'family tree' of every cell in the larva of the nematode worm *Caenorhabditis elegans*—all 558 of them (pp. 243–7). It takes only 10 cell doublings to reach this number. The main point is that at each doubling, the two daughter cells have identical DNA, but a different chemical environment. This means that different genes are turned on and off, and that changes the destiny of their descendant cells.

Dawkins again stresses:

"Let us hear the conclusion of the whole matter. There is no overall plan of development, no blueprint, no architect's plan, no architect. The development of the embryo, and ultimately of the adult, is achieved by local rules implemented by cells, interacting with other cells on a local basis. What goes on inside cells, similarly, is governed by local rules and in the cell membranes, interacting with other such molecules. Again, the rules are local, local, local." (p. 247)

Again, the local rules always cause the 558 cells of the *Caenorhabditis elegans* larva to land in the same place. If it were simply a matter of local rules, without some sort of *programming of the sequence*, then the same result each time would be highly unlikely. Also, while amount of DNA doesn't automatically correspond to the complexity of the organism, it is no accident that humans have many times more DNA 'instructions' than bacteria. A more complex organism requires a more complex program to oversee its development, Dawkins' 'local rules' notwithstanding.

Building the genetic recipe

Dawkins concludes:

"Haldane's interlocutor found it implausible that natural selection could put together in, say, a billion years, a genetic recipe for building her. I find it plausible although neither I nor anybody else can tell you the details of how it happened. The reason it is plausible is precisely that it is all done by local rules. In any one act of natural selection, the mutation it selected has had—in lots of cells and in lots of individuals in parallel—a very *simple* effect on the shape into which a protein chain spontaneously curls up into. This in turn, through catalytic action, speeds up, say, a particular chemical reaction in all the cells in which the gene is turned on. This changes, perhaps, the rate of growth in the primordium of the jaw. And this has consequential effects on the shape of the whole face, perhaps shortening the muzzle and giving a more human and less 'ape-like' profile. Now the natural selection pressures that favour or disfavour the gene can be as complicated as you like. … But the gene knows nothing of this. All it is doing, within different bodies and in successive generations, is rejigging a carefully sculpted dent in a protein molecule. The rest of the story follows automatically, in a branching cascade of local consequences, from which, eventually, a whole body emerges." (p. 249)

It's notable how Dawkins admits that the details of this supposed fact of evolution are unknown to him or anyone else. He also ignores the limitations of what natural selection can do (see ch. 4). And as will be seen next chapter, this is not even the way it *could* have worked. That's because evolution would predict that they come from homologuous genes and through homologous embryonic parts, yet often one or both of these is not true.

Summary

In response to a critic of the claim that a single cell could evolve into a human, J.B.S. Haldane responded that the critic did it herself in nine months. But the embryo was *programmed* to do that, whereas the alleged primordial single cell lacked such programming. Dawkins tries to minimize the difference by showing that embryonic development obeys simple local rules. Yet computer programs also use simple local rules; the difference is the *sequence*. Also, evolutionists have no explanations for the enormous changes needed to transform a single-celled organism into a multi-celled one, a pre-requisite for embryonic development in the first place.

Dawkins claims that a God, in whom he disbelieves anyway, never makes anything, and at best programs embryonic development. In reality, it's not either-or but both-and: God made adults in the beginning, but with the programming to reproduce via embryonic development. This enables a new unique individual which has genetic information from both parents. In general, God's creative acts finished at the end of Creation Week; His main activity now is *sustaining* His creation, including the programs of reproduction and embryonic development. Contrary to Dawkins, programs do not write themselves.

—∞—

Chapter 6

COMMON ANCESTRY OR COMMON DESIGN?

HOMOLOGY, or common features, has long been considered one of the strongest evidences for evolution. However, many supposed homologies turn out not to fit the evolutionary tree, so are explained away as 'homoplasies' or 'convergence'. Also, to fit evolutionary theory, homologous structures ought to be explained by homologous genes and developmental pathways, yet often this is not so. Common design is a better explanation, since this explains both homologies and homoplasies as the product of a single designer rather than many. It also encourages discovering physicochemical reasons for the similarities and differences.

Molecular homologies also fail to support evolution. The genetic code is not universal, despite Dawkins' claims. Also contrary to his assertions, comparison of different genes results in different proposed phylogenies.

Homology and analogy

In ch. 10 of *Greatest Show*, Dawkins explains what he thinks is the strongest argument for evolution: the common structures that are alleged to show descent from a common ancestor. This applies where the same underlying structure is modified to different uses. This is generally called 'homology'. A good example is the vertebrate limb pattern in Figure 1.

There is an underlying pattern of one upper limb bone connected to two, connected indirectly to the five digits, hence 'pentadactyl'. Yet they are put to different uses in human arm, bat wing, frog leg, and for that matter a

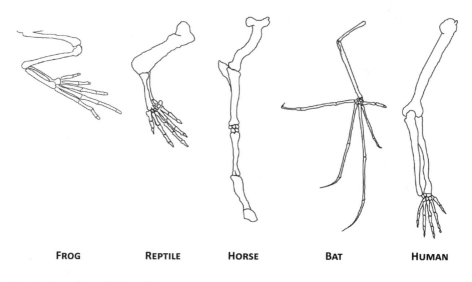

| FROG | REPTILE | HORSE | BAT | HUMAN |

Figure 1. 'Homologous' limbs of land vertebrates: they have different functions, but the same underlying structure.

Figure 2. Analogous wings of pterosaur, bat and bird. They all fly, but are structured differently.[1]

whale flipper. Dawkins argues that the land vertebrate skeleton as a whole shows homology, as does the crustacean exoskeleton.

The opposite is *analogous* structures,[1] where there is a similarity in use but a difference in the underlying structure. A good example is the wings of insects, pterosaurs, bats and birds—they all have the same function, to fly, but are structured very differently. A pterosaur wing relies on an extended 'little finger' to support a leathery wing (cf. Dawkins p. 288); a bat has a membrane supported by four elongated fingers, and the bird uses its 'arm' to support a feathered wing. Here, the evolutionary 'explanation' is 'convergence'.

Nowadays, evolutionists often *define* 'homologous' as 'descended from a common ancestor'. But this leads to circular reasoning if they then use homology as proof of common ancestors, since it becomes equivalent to: "these features,

---

1.   Romanes, J., *Darwin and after Darwin*, 1892, via *Wikipedia*.

descended from a common ancestor, prove that they descended from a common ancestor." Dawkins tries to overcome this with an independent test.

D'Arcy Thompson

On pp. 308–315 of *Greatest Show,* Dawkins admiringly cites a book that fascinated me in my university days, *On Growth and Form* (1917), by Scottish zoologist and mathematician Sir D'Arcy Wentworth Thompson (1860–1948). Dawkins says, "D'Arcy Thompson himself wasn't very interested in evolution" (p. 310), but this is an understatement. Even by itself, it shows once more how excellent science can be done without evolution, but D'Arcy Thompson went further. He thought that evolution by means of natural section was over-emphasized, and a more fruitful research program in biology would be to consider physical laws and mechanical constraints. He showed that many biological features make sense that way.

For example, D'Arcy Thompson showed that the shape of a medusa jellyfish resembles the shape of a water drop deforming as it slowly falls through oil. He also showed that the hollow bones of birds were reinforced in a similar way to the Warren's Truss.[2,3] A very well-known example was his demonstration that patterns of leaves on stems and the spiral patterns of sunflower seeds were related to the Fibonacci Sequence.[4]

But Thompson's most famous chapter, and the one Dawkins discusses, is chapter XVII, "The Comparison of Related Forms", where he showed that many differences in related animals could be described with relatively simple mathematical transformations. This was an admirable achievement, and Dawkins understandably wonders what Thompson would have achieved with a computer. Dawkins explains:

> "He would draw the animal on graph paper, and then he would distort the graph paper in a mathematically recognizable way and show that the form of the animal had turned into another, related animal. You could think of the original graph paper as a piece of rubber, on which you draw your first animal. Then the transformed graph paper would be equivalent to the same piece of rubber, stretched or pulled out of shape in some mathematically defined way." (pp. 308–10)

2. McIntosh, A., 100 years of airplanes—but these weren't the first flying machines! *Creation* **26**(1):44–48, 2003; creation.com/airplanes. Dr Andy McIntosh is Professor of Thermodynamics and Combustion Theory at the University of Leeds, and teaches advanced aerodynamics.
3. Vertebrate bones in general are analogous to girders in the building industry, but bones have a huge advantage over man-made girders, in that they are constantly rebuilding and redesigning themselves to cope with changing stress directions. Wieland, C., Bridges and bones, girders and groans, *Creation* **12**(2):20–24, 1990; creation.com/bones.
4. Wieland, C., and Grigg, R., Golden numbers, *Creation* **16**(4):26–29, 1994; creation.com/golden-numbers.

Homeomorphy

Although Thompson's own achievements were *despite* evolutionary theory, not because of it, Dawkins invokes his work to provide a more rigorous definition of homology:

"At the beginning of this chapter I introduced the idea of 'homology', using the arms of bats and humans as an example. Indulging an idiosyncratic use of language, I said that the skeletons were identical but the bones were different. D'Arcy Thompson's transformations furnish us with a way to make this idea more precise. In this formulation, two organs—for example, bat hand and human hand—are homologous if it is possible to draw one on a sheet of rubber and then distort the rubber to make the other one. Mathematicians have a word for this: 'homeomorphic'. ...

"The bat wing and human arm are homeomorphic: you can transform one into the other by distorting the rubber on which it is drawn. You cannot tranform a bat wing into an insect wing this way, because there are no corresponding parts. The widespread existence of homeomorphisms, which are not defined in terms of evolution, can be used as evidence for evolution. It is easy to see how evolution could go to work on any vertebrate arm and transform it into any other vertebrate arm, simply by changing the relative rates of growth in the embryo." (pp. 312–3)

But then it proved not so easy on computer programs to make such transformations, as Dawkins says:

"Therefore, it should have been very possible to start with, say, an *Australopithecus* skull drawn on the undistorted 'rubber', and breed your way through creatures with progressively shorter muzzles—progressively more human-like, in other words. In practice it proved very difficult to do anything like that, and I think the fact is, in itself, interesting." (p. 314)

I think so too, because it shows that they are not as similar as evolutionists would have us believe. As shown in ch. 9, australopithecines are a distinct basic type, further from both humans and apes than they are from each other. But Dawkins continues:

"I think one reason it was difficult is ... that D'Arcy Thompson's transformations change one *adult* form into another. ... that is not how genes in evolution work. Every individual animal has a developmental history. It starts as an embryo and grows, by disproportionate growth of different parts of the body, into an adult. Evolution is not a genetically controlled distortion of one adult form into another; it is a genetically controlled alteration in a developmental program." (p. 314).

So he says, but as will be shown (p. 94), this has major problems. Returning to Dawkins' evidence for evolution in homeomorphy, there are problems with that:

Homoplasy

Common structures that can't be explained by common ancestry are called *homoplasies*, and are frequently found in the alleged transitional series. Yet they are homeomorphic. But appeal to homoplasy is really explaining *away* evidence that doesn't fit evolution. Indeed such explaining away is ubiquitous. One paper admitted:

"Disagreements about the probable homologous or homoplastic nature of shared derived similarities between taxa lie at the core of most conflicting phylogenetic hypotheses."[5]

Homoplasies are said to be the result of 'convergence', i.e. evolution having 'converged' on a similar-looking outcome in each of the individual lines. However, this is far more *ad hoc* than using 'convergence' to explain the similarities between insect and bat wings, which are regarded as analogous, not homologous. But these are *not* homeomorphic, as Dawkins acknowledges, whereas homeoplasies *are*, which is why they were thought to be homologies.

Another evolutionary explanation is 'lateral gene transfer' [LGT], which creationist Walter ReMine predicted in 1997 would become increasingly common to explain away homoplasies.[6] Indeed, two evolutionists, microbiologist Carl Woese and physicist Nigel Goldenfeld, both at the University of Illinois at Urbana-Champaign, argue that LGT was the major mode of evolution while Darwinism (descent with modification from a common ancestor) played only a minor role (Woese was the one who defined the new domain Archaea and invented the RNA World hypothesis—see ch. 13, p. 234).[7]

It seems as though Dawkins himself would resort to this rather than abandon his evolutionary faith:

5 .   Luckett, W.P. and Hong, N., Phylogenetic relationships between the orders Artiodactyla and Cetacea, *J. Mammalian Evolution* **5**(2):130, 1998.
6 .   ReMine, W.J., *The Biotic Message: Evolution Versus Message Theory*, Saint Paul Science, Saint Paul, Minnesota, USA, 1993; see review: Batten, D., *J. Creation* **11**(3):292–298, 1997; creation.com/biotic.
7.   Buchanan, M., Horizontal and vertical: The evolution of evolution, *New Scientist* **205**(2744), 26 January 2010.

"Nevertheless, ... if [LGT] were as common in animals as it is in bacteria, it would make it harder to disprove the 'designer hypothesis'. What if chunks of bird genome could be ferried across, perhaps by bacterial or viral infection, and implanted in a bat's genome? Maybe a single species of bat might suddenly sprout feathers, the feather-coding DNA information having been borrowed in a genetic version of a computer's 'Copy and Paste'." (p. 303)

Ch. 8 provides a number of examples of homoplasies, e.g. the neck region of *Tiktaalik* is said to be homoplastic with that of *Mandageria*,[8] and the mesonychid teeth and skull were homoplastic with those of 'early' whales. Many of the alleged transitional series are replete with homoplasies.

Homoplasies are clear counter-examples to Dawkins' claim that homeomorphies are the result of inheritance from a common ancestor.

Non-homologous origin of 'homologies'

Dawkins argued that homologous structures are explained by alterations in the embryonic development program. If so, then the homologous structures in the adult organism should develop from homologous structures in the embryo. Jonathan Wells (1942–), who earned a second Ph.D. in Molecular and Cell Biology from UC Berkeley, specializing in embryology, pointed out that this was often not true. Wells is a supporter of intelligent design,[9,10] but he cites embryologist Sir Gavin de Beer (1899–1972), an ardent evolutionist, who wrote a book with the telling title *Homology, an Unsolved Problem* (1971).[11] Rather, as de Beer pointed out:

"The fact is that correspondence between homologous structures cannot be pressed back to similarity of position of the cells in the embryo, or of the parts of the egg out of which the structures are ultimately composed, or of developmental mechanisms by which they are formed."[12]

More recently, developmental biologist Pere Alberch pointed out that it is "the rule rather than the exception" that "homologous structures form from distinctly dissimilar initial states."[13]

8. Johanson, Z., Ahlberg, P., Ritchie, A. The braincase and palate of the tetrapodomorph sarcopterygian *Mandageria fairfaxi*: morphological variability near the fish-tetrapod transition, *Palaeontology* **46**:271–293, 2003.
9. Wells, J. *Icons of Evolution: Science or Myth? Why much of what we teach about evolution is wrong*, Regnery, Washington, 2000; see review by Truman, R., *J. Creation* **15**(2):17–24, 2001; creation.com/icons.
10. Wells, J., Homology in Biology: A problem for naturalistic science, *Origins and Design* **18**(2), Fall 1997; www.trueorigin.org/homology.asp.
11. de Beer, G., *Homology, an Unsolved Problem,* Oxford University Press, 1971.
12. de Beer, G., *Embryos and Ancestors,* p. 152, 3rd ed., Clarendon Press, Oxford, 1958.
13. Alberch, P., Problems with the Interpretation of Developmental Sequences, *Systematic Zoology* **34**(1):46-58, 1985.

Wells shows that even more recently:

"Evolutionary developmental biologist Rudolf Raff, who studies two species of sea urchin that develop by radically different pathways into almost identical adult forms, restated the problem in 1999: 'Homologous features in two related organisms should arise by similar developmental processes ... [but] features that we regard as homologous from morphological and phylogenetic criteria can arise in different ways in development.'"[14]

Wells also points out:

"The lack of correspondence between homology and developmental pathways is true not only in general, but also in the particular case of vertebrate limbs. The classic example of this problem are salamanders. In most vertebrate limbs, development of the digits proceeds from posterior to anterior—that is, in the tail-to-head direction. This accurately describes frogs, but their fellow amphibians, salamanders, do it differently. In salamanders, development of the digits proceeds in the opposite direction, from head to tail. The difference is so striking that some biologists have argued that the evolutionary history of salamanders must have been different from all other vertebrates, including frogs."[15]

Non-homologous genes

If homologies were due to mutation + selection, we would expect homologous structures to be controlled by homologous genes. Yet this is often not the case. As de Beer put it:

"Because homology implies community of descent from ... a common ancestor it might be thought that genetics would provide the key to the problem of homology. This is where the worst shock of all is encountered ... [because] characters controlled by identical genes are not necessarily homologous ... [and] homologous structures need not be controlled by identical genes."[11]

Wells cites the example of fruit flies, which need the *even-skipped* gene to form body segments, while locusts and wasps make segments perfectly well without it. Fruit flies also need the gene *sex-lethal* for sex differentiation, but other insects manage to produce males and females without it.[16]

---

14. Raff, 1999, cited in Wells Ref. 9, p. 72.
15. Wells, Ref. 9, p. 72.
16. Wells , Ref. 9, p. 73–74.

At other times, non-homologous structures arise from non-homologous genes. E.g. the gene *distal-less* is involved in development in creatures across different phyla, including sea urchin, spiny worm, velvet worm and mouse.[17]

These recent discoveries reinforce the "unresolved problem" of homology that led de Beer to ask:

> "What mechanism can it be that results in the production of homologous organs, the same 'patterns', in spite of their not being controlled by the same genes? I asked this question in 1938, and it has not been answered."[18]

Common designer

The homology argument has always been partly theological: "Why would a Creator make such similar features?" So it's acceptable to make theological arguments in reply.

First of all, why wouldn't a designer do that? Even human designers do that. For example, the original Porsche and Volkswagen 'Beetle' cars both have air-cooled, flat, horizontally-opposed, 4-cylinder engines in the rear, independent suspension, two doors, boot (trunk) in the front, and many other similarities ('homologies'). But this is explained very easily because they were both designed by Ferdinand Porsche (1875–1951).

Second, in reverse: what if everything were totally different; there were no similarities at all? Then it could look like they were made by more than one designer, resulting in polytheism. The observed uniformity is consistent with a particular subset of intelligent design: the biotic message theory, as proposed by Walter ReMine. That is, the evidence from nature points to a single designer (the homologies), but with a pattern which thwarts evolutionary explanations (the homoplasies). That is, unlike evolution, biotic message theory not only explains homologies but also homoplasies and convergences.[6]

Third, in most cultures around the world, such a pattern of commonality would bring honour to a Designer, and would also indicate the Designer's authority over and mastery of His designs.[19]

Uniformity of the universe

This uniformity is even more notable with subatomic particles, e.g. all electrons in the universe have exactly the same mass and charge, and exactly the opposite charge to all protons. This can't be explained by evolution, as the

---

17. Wells , Ref. 9, p. 74–75.
18. de Beer, Ref. 11, p. 16.
19. Holding, J.P., 'Not to Be Used Again': Homologous structures and the presumption of originality as a critical value, *J. Creation* **21**(1):13 –14, 2007; creation.com/original.

great Scottish physicist James Clerk Maxwell (1831–1879) pointed out with regard to molecules (since subatomic particles had not yet been discovered):

"No theory of evolution can be formed to account for the similarity of molecules, for evolution necessarily implies continuous change.... The exact equality of each molecule to all others of the same kind gives it ... the essential character of a manufactured article, and precludes the idea of its being eternal and self-existent."[20]

The universe as a whole also has a uniformity of temperature throughout, as shown by the cosmic microwave background (CMB) radiation, to within 1 part in 100,000. This is a problem for evolutionists, because for the temperature to be so even after the extreme unevenness of the alleged big bang, energy must have been transferred from hot parts to cold parts. The fastest this can occur naturally is at the speed of light, but even given the evolutionary age of the universe, light could only have traversed about a tenth of the distance needed to equilibrate the temperature. Incidentally, this is a light-travel time problem for believers in the big bang.[21]

Cosmologists call this the *horizon problem,* and they have invented a number of mathematical fudges like 'inflation' and claims that light travelled faster in the past to try to solve it. But the observations of uniformity in the entire cosmos are consistent with a single Creator of space and time Who holds the universe together (Colossians 1:17).

Scientific superiority of common designer explanation

It's one thing to say that evolution *could* have changed one form to another homeomorphic one, but quite another to demonstrate that it *did* so change it. As shown above, although one would expect that homologies arise from homologous genes via homologous embryonic development, this doesn't happen. And without a naturalistic *mechanism* to produce homologies via non-homogous genes and pathways, it fails to provide proof of Darwinism. Furthermore, as shown in the next two chapters, the fossil record doesn't demonstrate such transitions as a foreleg on a land reptile becoming a bird's wing. Indeed, there are problems in proposing a viable intermediate in many cases.

There are more fruitful explanations for homologies that dispense with evolution, and which have provided useful research insights. For example,

---

20. Maxwell, J.C., Discourse on Molecules, a paper presented to the British Association at Bradford in 1873. See also Lamont, A., James Clerk Maxwell (1831–1879), *Creation* **15**(3):45–47, 1993; creation.com/maxwell.
21. Lisle, J., Light travel-time: a problem for the big bang, *Creation* **25**(4):48–49, 2003; creation.com/lighttravel.

if a protein has an identical sequence of amino acids in many different types of creature, it is called 'highly conserved', e.g. osteocalcin, a vital protein involved in building vertebrate bones.[22] Evolutionists attribute this to natural selection weeding out deviations from this sequence which is constrained by physicochemical laws—in osteocalcin's case, the need to match up with the crystal lattice of hydroxyapatite in bone. Creationists attribute this to a Designer aware of exactly these constraints. This is not surprising, since in the biblical model, the 'laws' are our descriptions of the regular way the Creator upholds the universe (as explained in ch. 17). But *practical* research would be concerned with the fact that 'highly conserved' sequences point to some constraints to be discovered, regardless of how the conserved sequence arose. For example, D'Arcy Thompson would have omitted the 'middle man' of evolution, and just explained the physico-chemical laws involved.

Dr Larry Thaete, a medical research scientist at Northwestern University Feinberg School of Medicine, argues that explaining similar structures by common design has been more helpful:

"Scientific understanding is always dependent on the assumptions that are made at the outset, because that makes a difference on how observations are interpreted. Take for example the observation that cellular proteins are observed to be similar across certain types of creatures. If origins are assumed to be a matter of chance, then these protein similarities are interpreted as 'proof' that these creatures evolved from a common ancestor. Further, their similar structure is explained as being 'conserved' by natural selection. But if the existence of the biblical God is assumed, and that He designed life, the question may be 'What particular features of the organisms and their cellular processes required this particular design?' Creationists still make comparisons between similar life forms, but with the idea that these similarities result from a need for a similar design rather than common descent."[23]

Biochemist Bob Hosken, senior lecturer in food technology at the University of Newcastle, Australia, explains how the slight differences in the similar structures can often be explained by their physiological requirements better than their alleged evolutionary ancestry:

"I worked with a team to determine the amino acid sequences of myoglobin and hemoglobin from a range of Australian marsupials and monotremes, with the aim of determining the phylogenetic relationships of these unique animals. ...

22. Sarfati, J., Bone building: perfect protein, *J. Creation* **18**(1):11–12, 2004; creation.com/bone.
23. Saving the other patient: Lita Cosner chats with prenatal medical researcher Dr Larry Thaete, *Creation* **32**(1):47–49, 2010.

"While these findings were very interesting, the most exciting thing for me about this work was the opportunity it provided for relating the molecular architecture of each species of hemoglobin to the unique physiological requirements of the animal species studied.

"In other words, in a study of the relation between the structure and function of hemoglobin in various marsupial and monotreme species, I found it more meaningful to interpret hemoglobin structure in relation to the unique physiological demands of each species. A marsupial mouse has a greater rate of metabolism than a large kangaroo, so small marsupials need a hemoglobin with a structure designed to deliver oxygen to the tissues more efficiently than that required in large animals, and I found this to be actually the case. I also investigated the relation of hemoglobin structure and oxygen transport in the echidna and platypus, and again found the oxygen delivery system of the platypus was well suited to diving, while in the echidna it was suited to burrowing. The bill of the platypus has been found to be equipped with incredibly sensitive electroreceptors, capable of sensing muscular contraction of tiny prey, including dragonfly or mayfly larvae. This enables the platypus to find food in the murky waters in which it lives. These kinds of findings indicate to me that each animal is in some way uniquely designed to suit its particular environment, and I cannot help but attribute the complexity of the design to a Creator, rather than to random evolutionary forces."[24]

This underlines that evolution is a common 'gloss' in scientific papers, but it contributes nothing to our understanding of living things and in fact can stifle enquiry.

Molecular homologies

On pp. 315 ff. of *Greatest Show,* Dawkins discusses homologies at the molecular level—genes and proteins. First, he claims:

"Just as the vertebrate skeleton is invariant across all vertebrates while the individual bones differ, and just as the crustacean exoskeleton is invariant across all crustaceans while the individual 'tubes' vary, so the DNA code is invariant across all living creatures while the individual genes vary. This is a truly astounding fact, which shows more clearly than anything else that all living creatures are descended from a common ancestor." (p. 315)

---

24. Hosken, B., in Ashton, J., Ed., *In Six Days: Why 50 [Ph.D.] scientists choose to believe in Creation*, New Holland Publishers, Australia, 1999; creation.com/hosken.

But this is false—there are exceptions, some known since the 1970s. An example is *Paramecium*, where a few of the 64 (4^3 or 4x4x4) possible codons code for different amino acids. More examples are being found frequently. Also, some organisms code for one or two extra amino acids beyond the main 20 types.[25] But if one organism evolved into another with a different code, all the messages already encoded would be scrambled, just as written messages would be jumbled if computer keys were switched. This is a huge problem for the evolution of one code into another.

However, there *is* substantial consistency in the code, which is not surprising, since there is one Creator—one Mind behind it all. And the inconsistencies are sufficient to throw a spanner in evolutionists' attempts to explain the code. So much for Dawkins' clearest proof for evolution.

Furthermore, note how the observation of substantial consistency in the code does nothing to explain the *origin* of the code, and particularly an *optimized* code, which the DNA code is (see also ch. 13).[26]

Molecular evidence sometimes contradicts morphology

Dawkins argues:

"What Darwin didn't—couldn't—know is that the comparative evidence becomes even more convincing when we include molecular genetics, in addition to the anatomical comparisons that were available to him." (p. 315)

However, usually the evidence goes against anatomical expectations. For example, take the whales, where 'homologous' morphology suggested one set of ancestors, but molecular analysis suggested another. A 2001 press release stated:

"Until now paleontologists thought whales had evolved from mesonychians, an extinct group of land-dwelling carnivores, while molecular scientists studying DNA were convinced they descended from artiodactyls [even-toed hoofed animals, such as camels, cattle, pigs, deer, giraffes and hippopotamuses].

"'The paleontologists, and I am one of them, were wrong,' Gingerich said [Professor Philip Gingerich, of the University of Michigan in Ann Arbor]."[27]

---

25. Certain Archaea and eubacteria code for 21st or 22nd amino acids, selenocysteine and pyrrolysine—see Atkins, J.F. and Gesteland, R., The 22nd amino acid, *Science* **296**(5572):1409–10, 2002; commentary on technical papers on pp. 1459–62 and 1462–66.
26. Truman, R. and Borger, P., Genetic code optimisation: Part 1, *Journal of Creation* **21**(2):90–100, 2007; creation.com/images/pdfs/tj/j21_2/j21_2_90-100.pdf.
27. Fossil Finds Show Whales Related to Early Pigs, *Reuters*, 19 September 2001.

Another example is invertebrate compound eyes, which certainly *seem* a good candidate for homologous structure. But molecular evidence counts strongly against the idea that compound eyes all evolved from a common ancestor, and instead points to multiple independent origins. The researchers claimed:

"These results illustrate exactly why arthropod compound eye evolution has remained controversial, because one of two seemingly very unlikely evolutionary histories must be true. Either compound eyes with detailed similarities evolved multiple times in different arthropod groups or compound eyes have been lost in a seemingly inordinate number of arthropod lineages."[28]

Note here again the straitjacket of the evolutionary thinking: not for a moment is the very idea of evolution, that makes for such an unlikely scenario, questioned.

Overstating the case

In a friendly interview about his book, Dawkins summarizes what he explains in much more detail:

"You can actually plot a picture of the pattern of resemblances and differences between every animal and plant and every other animal and plant, and you find out that it fits on a beautiful, hierarchical, branching tree, which can only sensibly be interpreted as a family tree. When you do the same thing with a different gene, you get the same tree. Do the same thing with a third gene, and you get the same tree. It's overwhelmingly powerful evidence."[29]

However, this is a highly irresponsible, inaccurate claim. Almost always, comparisons with different genes support *mutually incompatible* evolutionary trees. For example, an evolutionary paper[30] shows that all

---

28. Oakley, T.H., and Cunningham, C.W., Molecular phylogenetic evidence for the independent evolutionary origin of an arthropod compound eye, *Proc. Nat. Acad. Sci. USA* **99**(3):1426–1430, 2002.
29. Boyle, A., The not-so-angry evolutionist, http://cosmiclog.msnbc.msn.com, 14 October 2009.
30. Huerta-Cepas, J. *et al.*, The human phylome, *Genome Biology* 8:R109, 13 June 2007 doi:10.1186/gb-2007-8-6-r109. The caption in their Figure 2, shown as our Figure 3, reads: The alternative phylogenetic relationships among the taxa involved in the three evolutionary hypotheses considered. (a) Placental mammals: primates, laurasatheria and rodents. (b) Ecdysozoa versus Coelomata hypothesis: relationships among arthropods, chordates and nematodes. And (c) the Unikont hypothesis: relationship among opisthokonts, amoebozoans and other eukaryotic groups. The numbers indicate the number of trees supporting each topology. For each alternative topology numbers on the top row refer to the total number of trees with a given topology, and what percentage of the total it represents; numbers in the middle row refer to those trees for which the posterior probabilities of the two partitions shown in the figure are 0.9 or higher. Numbers in the bottom row refer to the number and percentage of gene families supporting each topology.

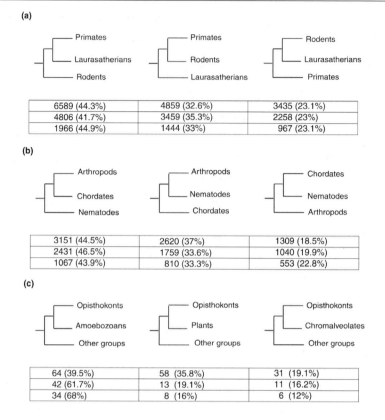

Figure 3: The alternative evolutionary relationships among three sets of three different taxa (groupings), showing that all these mutually incompatible trees have significant support, depending on which genes are chosen for comparison. From Ref. 30, Fig. 2.

possible phylogenies in the groups they studied were supported by significant numbers of genes (see Figure 3). Intelligent Design theorist Bill Dembski notes about this paper in relation to Dawkins' claim:

"The incongruence of gene and species trees is a standing obstacle, or research problem, in molecular phylogenetics.

"In the context of Dawkins's claim, this means that gene A supports grouping X, but gene B supports grouping Y, whereas gene C supports grouping Z, and so on. In short, one doesn't get the same species tree from any given gene. This problem of gene and species tree incongruence is so widely known in molecular systematics that it now arguably represents an entire field of study."[31]

31. Dembski, W., Shilling for Darwin—The wildly irresponsible evolutionist, www.uncommondescent.com, 15 October 2009.

Indeed, the paper notes:

"The finding that all three possible topologies, including the one widely considered as wrong in the literature, are supported by a significant number of trees illustrates the inherent difficulty of resolving the species phylogeny from gene phylogenies. We have found similar topological diversity in the three scenarios considered (see below) and also, to smaller degrees, in apparently undisputed evolutionary relationships (results not shown). Similar results showing variability in the relative positions of arthropods, nematodes and chordates have also been found in topological analyses of the phylogenies of 507 eukaryotic orthologous groups and of 100 protein families. These deviances from the species phylogeny might be the result of different processes, including convergent evolution or varying evolutionary rates."[30]

A molecular biologist commented on this paper:

"Just getting the best-supported topology is not enough, and even using all genes in a genome may not help you come to an unambiguous solution. This is because different genes produce different biases, and rigorous criteria for selecting the genes to be used to build a species tree are necessary to get less ambiguous results, as has been done in other work... *The important message from this part of the study is that, whatever the true tree may be, trees derived from single genes are more likely than not to point to a wrong topology.*"[32]

This means that the gene comparisons that result in different trees from the favoured one must be explained away. So much for Dawkins' claims about "overwhelmingly powerful evidence" for the "same tree" from different gene comparisons.

Summary

- Homology is where the same underlying structure is used for different functions; analogy means that the same functions are achieved with widely different underlying structures.

- Homology, when defined as structures inherited from a common ancestor, becomes circular when used as evidence for evolution. Dawkins resorts to another definition, homeomorphies—structures that can be transformed merely by changing the shape of the same underlying parts. Homeomorphies are used as evidence for evolution.

---

32 . Castresana, J., Topological variation in single-gene phylogenetic trees, *Genome Biology* **8**(6): 216, 13 June 2007. doi: 10.1186/gb-2007-8-6-216 (emphasis added).

- Yet some homeomorphies are homoplasies—the similarities don't fit the evolutionary story, so evolutionists explain this as 'convergence'.

- Dawkins explains homeomorphic structures by alterations in the embryonic development program of a common ancestor. If so, then the homologous structures in an adult organism should develop from homologous structures in the embryo, and they should be controlled by homologous genes. Yet often the homologous structures are controlled by non-homologous genes and have different embryonic pathways. The reverse also happens: that almost identical genes control structures that are not remotely homologous.

- A *single* common designer would explain all the similarities, including homoplasies; if living things had no similarities, then it would look like many creators instead of one. Also, common design would bring great honour to a Creator in most cultures that have ever existed.

- Common design theory leads to fruitful research as researchers try to find out the reasons for the slight differences, rather than try to explain it by evolution.

- Dawkins claims that the genetic code is universal and proof of common ancestry of all life. Yet it is demonstrably *not* universal—and evolving from one code to another would result in scrambled proteins, just as switching keys on a keyboard would result in scrambled messages.

- Contrary to Dawkins' claims, molecular homologies often conflict with morphological ones. In fact, molecular homologies can conflict with *other* molecular homologies.

- Dawkins' best evidence for evolution proves not to be good evidence at all.

—∞—

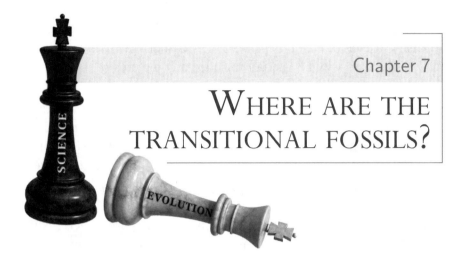

Chapter 7

WHERE ARE THE TRANSITIONAL FOSSILS?

MISSING intermediate forms have been a major problem for evolutionists ever since Darwin. Indeed, fossils in general are strong evidence not for eons of evolution but for rapid burial, especially soft-bodied creatures that Darwin claimed could not fossilize at all. Polystrate fossils are further evidence of rapid formation of many layers at once. One of the biggest problems of all is the 'Cambrian explosion', where a huge number of phyla appear, and no phyla since (according to evolutionary dating). Specific claims of transitional fossils are addressed in the next chapter.

The transitional fossils problem

Many evolutionists, starting with Darwin himself, have long admitted that the fossil record does not demonstrate evolution from one type of creature to another. He wrote:

> "But just in proportion as this process of extermination has acted on an enormous scale, so must the number of intermediate varieties, which have formerly existed, be truly enormous. Why then is not every geological formation and every stratum full of such intermediate links? Geology assuredly does not reveal any such finely-graduated organic chain; and this, perhaps, is the most obvious and serious objection which can be urged against the theory."[1]

---

1. Darwin, Charles, *Origin of Species*, pp. 264–5, 1st edition, John Murray, London, 1859; available online from darwin-online.org.uk/. I will quote from the first edition as this is the one Dawkins prefers, since he claims, "later editions, especially the sixth, pandered to more than public opinion". He calls his copy from the first print run of 1,250 "one of my most precious possessions, given me by my benefactor and friend Charles Simonyi." (p. 403)

Over a century later, Dr Colin Patterson, Senior Palaeontologist of the British Museum of Natural History, wrote a book, *Evolution* (1978). In reply to a query as to why he had not included any pictures of transitional forms, he wrote:

> "I fully agree with your comments about the lack of direct illustration of evolutionary transitions in my book. If I knew of any, fossil or living, I would certainly have included them. ... I will lay it on the line—there is not one such fossil for which one could make a watertight argument."[2,3]

In my own introductory geology class in 1983, the geology professor,[4] a paleontologist, said explicitly, "The fossil record does not support Darwinian evolution! Rather, it seems to support a series of divine creations." He went on to assure the large class in the lecture theatre, "I am not a divine creationist." He then explained *away* the problem, or it certainly seemed to my hearing to be special pleading, even though at the time I was not disposed towards creation.

Contrary to cliché, absence of evidence *is* evidence of absence; it's just not *proof* of it. So it is legitimate to argue that the widespread absence of fossils documenting major evolutionary changes counts as evidence against evolution.

Are fossils necessary for evolution?

But Dawkins says he is not at all worried. He claims:

> "Creationists fondly (very fondly) imagine that these gaps are an embarrassment for evolutionists. ... there is more than enough evidence for the fact of evolution in the comparative study of modern species (Chapter 10) and their geographical distribution (Chapter 9). We don't need fossils—the evidence for evolution is watertight without them; so it is paradoxical to use gaps in the fossil record as though they were evidence against evolution. We are, as I say, lucky to have fossils at all." (pp. 145–6)

Yet as shown above, Darwin agreed that it was legitimate to argue that the fossil record should be "full of such intermediate links" if his theory were right. Darwin likewise excused the lack of transitional fossils by arguing on similar lines for "the extreme imperfection of the fossil record."[1]

---

2. Patterson, C., letter to Luther D. Sunderland, 10 April, 1979, as published in *Darwin's Enigma*, Master Books, 4th ed. 1988, p. 89. Patterson later tried to backtrack somewhat from this clear statement, apparently alarmed that creationists would utilize this truth.

3. See also Bates, G., That quote!—about the missing transitional fossils: Embarrassed evolutionists try to 'muddy the waters', *Creation* 29(1):12–15, 2006; creation.com/pattquote.

4. Prof. Paul Vella, the eponym for Vella Flat, coastal flat to the south of Lake Cole in the NW part of Black Island, Ross Archipelago, Antarctica.

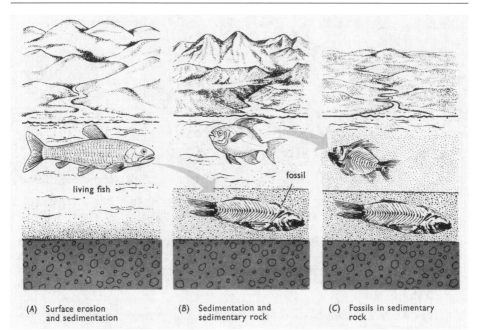

(A) Surface erosion and sedimentation

(B) Sedimentation and sedimentary rock

(C) Fossils in sedimentary rock

Figure 1: The above illustration featured as Figure 15a-b on p. 296 of the textbook *Biological Science: the web of life*, 2nd ed., *Australian Academy of Science*, 1973, with the caption:

"A sequence showing the physical changes (erosion, sedimentation and formation of a sedimentary rock) associated with fossilization in a stream bed. Silica, carbonates and other inorganic materials from ground water infiltrate the bones of the dead fish and slowly mineralize the bones to rock. Disturbances of the earth's crust may later cause the fossil-bearing rocks to become elevated, and erosion may later expose them."

Fossils: proof of rapid burial

It is true that fossilization requires specific conditions, and we would indeed be "lucky" to have any—if they were formed slowly and gradually as Darwin believed. We simply don't see fish fossilizing at the bottom of rivers and oceans. Nor are farms filling with fossils of sheep and cattle. Why not? Because most dead animals are scavenged and disintegrate quickly. In the ocean, a dead fish floats, contrary to the pervasive textbook model which shows it sinking (e.g. see diagram, above). And such a floating dead fish rots and is eaten by scavengers. Even if some parts reach the bottom, the scavengers such as crayfish take care of them. Scuba divers don't find the sea floor covered with dead fish being slowly fossilized. The same applies to land animals. Millions of buffaloes (bison) were killed in North America last century, but there are very few fossils. An ichthyosaur was fossilized at almost the end of the birth process (see picture on the next page), and it makes little sense to argue that it was lying on the ocean floor giving birth for millions of years while slowly being covered by sediment.

Figure 2: This incredible fossil of an *ichthyosaur*, buried while giving birth, is clear evidence of its having been buried quickly by water-borne sediments. Note that as an air-breathing creature, the baby had to be born tail-first; a head-first birth would make the breathing reflex start while it was stuck in the water. But like dolphins and whale babies today, they could come out of the birth canal completely before swimming to the surface to take the first breath. So the above baby had almost finished being born before it and its mother were rapidly entombed and fossilized. From *Staatliches Museum für Naturkunde*, Stuttgart.

Given Darwin's emphasis on slow and gradual processes, it's no wonder he said, "No organism wholly soft can be preserved."[5] Yet hundreds of fossil giant jellyfish, with many specimens measuring over 50 cm (20 in) across, were found in a Wisconsin sandstone quarry.[6,7] Such fossils certainly could not have formed gradually—how long do dead jellyfish normally retain their features (along with the ripple marks in the sand)?

These are also, incidentally, the biggest-ever fossil jellyfish found, yet they are in Cambrian ('dated' at 510 million years) strata—which doesn't support the 'big-evolved-from-little' idea.

To form a fossil, the best plan might be to dump a load of concrete on top of the creature! This way, it would be protected from scavengers, and be held in place rather than fall apart. Even if the soft tissues decompose, the minerals in the mud would slowly replace the bone, atom by atom, leaving a mineral cast of the original bone. Fossilization of soft-bodied creatures would be rarer still, because the mineralization must occur before they decompose. No wonder Darwin could not imagine such a thing. Yet the global Flood would provide huge amounts of sediments, exactly what's needed to bury many things quickly, so they can fossilize.[8]

5. Darwin, Ref. 1, p. 422.
6. Hagadorn, J.W., Dott, R.H. and Damrow, D., Stranded on a Late Cambrian shoreline: Medusae from central Wisconsin, *Geology* **30**(2):147–150, 2002.
7. Catchpoole, D., Hundreds of jellyfish fossils! *Creation* **25**(4):32–33, September 2003; creation.com/jellyfossils.
8. And all that is needed for the sediments to harden rapidly into rock is the presence of a cementing agent, e.g. from dissolved minerals, or even buried microbes—see Catchpoole, D., From sand to rock—quickly! creation.com/sand-to-rock, November 2009.

Is the record incomplete?

Michael Denton[9] points out that 97.7% of living orders of land vertebrates are represented as fossils, and 79.1% of living families of land vertebrates—87.8% if birds are excluded, as they are less likely to become fossilized.[10] For example, all 32 mammal orders appear abruptly and fully formed in the fossil record. The evolutionist paleontologist George Gaylord Simpson wrote in 1944:

> "The earliest and most primitive members of every order already have the basic ordinal characters, and in no case is an approximately continuous series from one order to another known. In most cases the break is so sharp and the gap so large that the origin of the order is speculative and much disputed."[11]

Missing geological time?

As evidence for the imperfection of the geological record, Darwin asserted that there are long periods between the geological formations:

> "But the imperfection in the geological record mainly results from another and more important cause than any of the foregoing; namely, from the several formations being separated from each other by wide intervals of time. When we see the formations tabulated in written works, or when we follow them in nature, it is difficult to avoid believing that they are closely consecutive. But we know, for instance, from Sir R. Murchison's great work on Russia, what wide gaps there are in that country between the superimposed formations; so it is in North America, and in many other parts of the world. The most skilful geologist, if his attention had been exclusively confined to these large territories, would never have suspected that during the periods which were blank and barren in his own country, great piles of sediment, charged with new and peculiar forms of life, had elsewhere been accumulated. And if in each separate territory, hardly any idea can be formed of the length of

---

9. Dawkins claims that Denton is "beloved of creationists who conveniently overlook the fact that, in his second book, *Nature's Destiny* [1998] he recanted his earlier anti-evolutionary stance [ref. 10, 1985], while remaining theistic." (p. 370, footnote). This is not the case; in neither book was Denton defending a theistic viewpoint, and the second book still rejects Darwinian evolution in favour of a planned process: "The entire process of biological evolution from the origin of life to the emergence of man was somehow directed from the beginning." Earlier, evolutionist and atheist Jim Lippard reported: "The truth is that Denton has neither retracted his entire book nor remained entirely unswayed by his critics (though the latter is closer to the truth than the former—he still believes that the neo-Darwinian theory of evolution is 'a theory in crisis')." How Not To Argue With Creationists, *Creation/Evolution* 11(2):9–21, Winter 1991–1992. Both Denton and Dawkins were interviewed for the DVD *From a Frog to a Prince*, stocked by CMI. Raw footage of Dawkins' interview can be viewed at "Was Dawkins Stumped? Frog to a Prince critics refuted again", creation.com/dawkinsstumped, 12 April 2008.
10. Denton, M., *Evolution, a Theory in Crisis*, ch. 7, Adler & Adler, Bethesda, Maryland, 1985.
11. Simpson, G.G., *Tempo and Mode in Evolution*, pp. 105–6, Columbia University Press, New York, 1944.

time which has elapsed between the consecutive formations, we may infer that this could nowhere be ascertained."[12]

Darwin points out that much sediment is found between the same layers at different locations, and uses this as evidence for the huge time gap. Yet the actual geological evidence, as I discuss below, shows that there could not have been much time between the layers. So this indicates that the sediment found elsewhere must have been deposited rapidly. This makes sense because of the fossils found in them.

Figure 3: Valley of the Colorado River viewed from Dead Horse Point in Utah. The arrows point to two gaps where about 10 and 20 million years is 'missing' ('Ma' in diagram = mega-annum = million years). The canyon is 600 m (2,000 ft) deep. From Ref. 14.

Figure 4: Knife-edge contact between Coconino Sandstone (top) and Hermit Shale (below), Grand Canyon, supposedly represents a time gap of about 6 million years, but shows no sign of such prolonged erosion. From Ref. 14.

Flat gaps

As Darwin says, observation of these adjacent layers would not lead to the conclusion of large time gaps between them. In fact, the boundaries between such layers, called *paraconformities*, are a problem for the millions of years that Dawkins accepts without question.[13,14]

Think how the surface of most landscapes, like the area around Grand Canyon, is jagged and uneven due to erosion (see Figure 3). Rainfall, streams and rivers keep cutting deeper gullies, canyons, and valleys. But often the layers through which the canyons are carved are flat and parallel. Darwin claims that these layers were deposited eons of time apart. But if the top of each layer had been exposed for millions of years, it should be as

12. Darwin, *Origin*, Ref 1, p. 289.
13. Roth, A.A., 'Flat gaps' in sedimentary rock layers challenge long geologic ages, *J. Creation* **23**(2):76–81, 2009.
14. 'Millions of years' is missing: interview with biologist and geologist Ariel Roth, *Creation* **31**(2): 46–49, 2009.

jagged as the surface. For instance, in the Grand Canyon, the Coconino sandstone overlies the Hermit shale and the surface between them is flat and smooth. Yet there is supposedly a 10 million year gap in time. Shale is a soft rock, and should have been eroded badly if it had been exposed to the weather for millions of years.

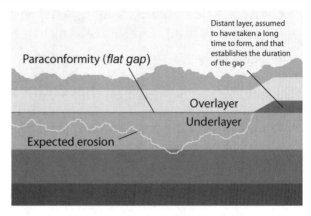

Figure 5: Above: diagram of rock layers showing a flat gap or paraconformity—this is the line in the middle of the diagram. To the right is a layer that was laid down before the overlayer—evolutionists assume that it took millions of years to deposit. From Ref. 14.

Furthermore, many paraconformities contain ephemeral[15] markings, i.e. features that should disintegrate quickly. For example, how long would one of your footprints last if exposed to the elements? So animal tracks, raindrop marks, and ripple marks, at the boundaries of paraconformities, show that the upper rock layer has been deposited immediately after the lower one, eliminating many millions of years of supposed 'gap' time.

So contrary to Darwin, the large amounts of sediment between the same layers is not evidence for vast time gaps. Rather, it is evidence for rapid deposition.

Polystrate fossils[16]

Further evidence against long time gaps comes from *polystrate[17]fossils*, i.e. those that cut through many layers. Derek Ager, Emeritus Professor of Geology, University College of Swansea, and an anti-creationist, describes some polystrate fossil tree trunks that he illustrated in his book:

"If one estimates the total thickness of the British Coal Measures as about 1,000 m, laid down in about 10 million years, then, assuming a

---

15. 'Ephemeral' comes from the Greek ἐφημέρος *ephēmeros*, literally 'lasting only a day', from ἡμέρα *hēmera*, day.
16. Walker, T., Polystrate fossils: evidence for a young earth, *Creation* **29**(3):54–55, 2007; creation.com/polystrate.
17. An ugly linguistic hybrid, from Greek πολύς *polys*, many; and Latin *stratum*, layer. A better term would be *multistrate*, but "polystrate" seems to have stuck, just like the other Latin-Greek hybrid *stratigraphy*, from Greek γραφή *graphē* (and the most famous hybrid word, *television*, from Greek τῆλε (*tēle*) meaning 'far' and the Latin *visio* from *videre* meaning 'to see').

constant rate of sedimentation, it would have taken 100,000 years to bury a tree 10 m high, which is ridiculous.

"Alternatively, if a 10 m tree were buried in 10 years, that would mean 1,000 km in a million years or 10,000 km in 10 million years (i.e. the duration of the coal measures). This is equally ridiculous and we cannot escape the conclusion that *sedimentation was at times very rapid indeed* and at other times there were long breaks in sedimentation, *though it looks both uniform and continuous*" [emphasis added].[18]

Like Dawkins' idol Darwin, Ager continues to believe in millions of years, *although it's not what it looks like.*

Rapid layer formation

While Darwin believed that the sedimentary layers formed very slowly over millions of years, evidence in both the field and laboratory shows that many finely laminated layers can form quickly. The experiments of the French sedimentologist Guy Berthault, sometimes working with non-creationists, have shown that fine layers do not need to be formed one at a time, one per year over many years. Rather, many thin layers can form all at once by a self-sorting mechanism during the settling of differently sized particles, as long as there is horizontal flow.[19]

In one of Berthault's experiments, finely layered sandstone and diatomite rocks were broken into their constituent particles, and allowed to settle from water flowing at various speeds. It was found that the same layer thicknesses were reproduced, regardless of flow rate. This suggests that the original rock was produced by a similar self-sorting mechanism, followed by cementing of the particles together—not over millions of years.[20] The prestigious journal *Nature* reported similar experiments by evolutionists a decade after Berthault's first experiments.[21]

Also, recent catastrophes show that violent events like the Flood described in Genesis could form many rock layers very quickly. The Mt St Helens eruption in Washington State produced 7.6 metres (25 feet) of finely layered sediment in a single afternoon![22] And a rapidly-pumped sand slurry was observed to deposit about a metre (3–4 feet) of fine layers on a beach over an area the

18. Ager, D.V., *The New Catastrophism*, p. 49, Cambridge University Press, 1993.
19. Julien, P., Lan, Y., and Berthault, G., Experiments on stratification of heterogeneous sand mixtures, *J. Creation* **8**(1):37–50, 1994.
20. Berthault, G., Experiments on lamination of sediments, *J. Creation* **3**:25–29, 1988; creation.com/sedexp.
21. Makse, H.A., *et al.*, Spontaneous stratification in granular mixtures, *Nature* **386**(6623):379–382, 27 March 1997. See also Snelling, A., Nature finally catches up, *J. Creation* **11**(2):125–6, 1997.
22. Austin, S., Mount St Helens and catastrophism, *Proc. First International conference on Creationism* 1:3–9, ed. R.E. Walsh, R.S. Crowell, Creation Science Fellowship, Pittsburgh, PA, USA, 1986.

size of a football field.[23] This all shows that as long as there is horizontal flow and differently sized particles, fine alternating layers can form. Conversely, a problem for long-age ideas is keeping each layer smooth and uncontaminated for at least many months before the next layer is deposited on top.

Rapid mud and clay deposition[24]

More recent flume experiments by different researchers show that even extremely fine clay and mud particles will deposit from flowing water.[25] Previously, it was claimed that only very still water would allow tiny particles to settle, and extremely slowly at that. Yet the experimenters used simple observation to show that this can't be right:

> "All you have to do is look around. After the creek on our university's campus floods, you can see ripples on the sidewalks once the waters have subsided. Closely examined, these ripples consist of mud. Sedimentary geologists have assumed up until now that only sand can form ripples and that mud particles are too small and settle too slowly to do the same thing."[26]

So they experimented, and found:

> "They accumulated at flow velocities that are much higher than what anyone would have expected."

A commentary on this research states:

> "The results call for critical reappraisal of all mudstones previously interpreted as having been continuously deposited under still waters. Such rocks are widely used to infer past climates, ocean conditions and orbital variations."[27]

They were also used to infer millions of years of time by those such as Charles Lyell who wanted to "free science from Moses" and overturn the Bible's history, the biblical timescale.

Cambrian Explosion

The Cambrian Explosion is a mystery for evolutionists. The term explosion refers to the fact that fossils of all the major groups (phyla) of animals appeared in what they call the Cambrian period ('dated' 542–488 Ma, named after

23. Batten, D., Sandy stripes: Do many layers mean many years? *Creation* **19**(1):39–40, 1996; creation.com/sandy.
24. Walker, T., Mud experiments overturn long-held geological beliefs: A call for a radical reappraisal of all previous interpretations of mudstone deposits, *J. Creation* **22**(2): 14–15, 2008; creation.com/mud.
25. Schieber, J., Southard, J. and Thaisen, K., Accretion of mudstone beds from migrating floccule ripples, *Science* **318**(5857):1760–1763, 2007 | doi: 10.1126/science.1147001.
26. As waters clear, scientists seek to end a muddy debate, Physorg.com, 13 December 2007.
27. Macquaker, J.H.S. and Bohacs, K.M., On the accumulation of mud, *Science* **318**(5857):1734–1735, 2007 (perspective on Ref. 23).

Cambria, the classical name for Wales)—**including the vertebrate (phylum Chordata)** *Haikouichthys*.[28] Furthermore, *no new phyla have appeared since,* i.e. *no new major body plans* (according to evolutionary dating).[29,30] Jeffrey Levinton, Professor of Ecology and Evolution at the State University of New York, calls this evolution's "deepest paradox".[31,32] In fact, compared to the 30+ animal phyla today, many estimate that as many as 100 existed in the Cambrian.

Dawkins tries to address the problem:

"The biggest gap, and the one the creationists like best of all, is the one that preceded the so-called Cambrian Explosion. A little more than half a billion years ago, in the Cambrian era [*sic*, it's the Cambrian Period of the Paleozoic Era according to uniformitarian geology], most of the great animal phyla—the main divisions within the animal world—'suddenly' appear in the fossil record. Suddenly, that is, in the sense that no fossils of these animal groups are known in rocks older than the Cambrian, not suddenly in the sense of instantaneously: the period we are talking about covers about 20 million years. Twenty million years feels short when it is half a billion years ago. But of course it represents exactly the same amount of time for evolution as 20 million years today! Anyway, it is still quite sudden, and, as I wrote in a previous book [*The Blind Watchmaker*, 1986], the Cambrian shows us a substantial number of major animal phyla 'already in an advanced state of evolution, the very first time they appear. It is as though they were just planted there, without any evolutionary history. Needless to say, this appearance of sudden planting has delighted creationists.'" (pp. 147–8)

Then he grumbles about "quote-mining", and that a Google search showed that the above paragraph has often been quoted without the next one:

---

28. Shu, D.G. *et al.*, Head and backbone of the Early Cambrian vertebrate *Haikouichthys*, *Nature* **421**(6922):526–529, 30 January 2003 | doi:10.1038/nature0126
29. Valentine, J.W., Why no new phyla after the Cambrian? Genome and ecospace hypotheses revisited, *Palaios* **10**(2):190–194, April 1995.
30. The sober *Encyclopædia Britannica* says: "At least 11 extant animal phyla (Annelida, Arthropoda, Brachiopoda, Chordata, Ctenophora, Echinodermata, Hemichordata, Mollusca, Onychophora [velvet worms], Porifera, and Priapulida), including most of those with a fossil record, first appear in Cambrian rocks. Most of these rapidly diversified as they seemingly adapted to numerous unfilled ecological niches. Another five phyla (Nemertea, Phoronida, Platyhelminthes, Pogonophora, and Sipuncula) may also trace their origin back to the Cambrian fossils, though questions still remain about them. The only extant animal phylum with a good fossil record that is not known from Cambrian rocks are the Bryozoa (moss animals), which first appear in rocks of Early Ordovician age." www.britannica.com
31. Levinton, J., The Big Bang of Animal Evolution, *Scientific American* 267:84–91, November 1992.
32. See also Wieland, C., Exploding evolution: Creatures found as fossils in 'Cambrian' rocks have no evolutionary ancestors. And no new basic body plans have appeared since, *Creation* **16**(2):38–39, 1994.

"Evolutionists of all stripes believe, however, that this really does represent a very large gap in the fossil record." (p. 148)

Yet how does leaving this sentence out show quoting out of context? Obviously an anti-evolutionist would not imply that Dawkins denies evolution—the whole point is that he is a *hostile witness*, who *must* believe that there is a major gap. Furthermore, some anti-evolutionists have indeed missed out that sentence—but quoted the *previous* sentences *which supply just the same context that Dawkins complains was missing*:

"Eldredge and Gould certainly would agree that some very important gaps really are due to imperfections in the fossil record. Very big gaps, too. For example the Cambrian strata of rocks, vintage about 600 million years, are the oldest ones in which we find most of the major invertebrate groups."

Punctuated equilibria

Niles Eldredge (1943–) and Stephen Jay Gould (1941–2002), staunch anti-creationists, are famous for 'punctuated equilibria', the idea that evolutionary history is mainly stasis (no significant change; hence 'equilibria') with episodes of relatively rapid speciation (hence 'punctuated'), mainly in small, isolated populations on the peripheries of the main population. This is what they said about the Cambrian Explosion:

"The fossil record had caused Darwin more grief than joy. Nothing distressed him more than the Cambrian explosion, the coincident appearance of almost all complex organic designs ..."[33]

"The Cambrian evolutionary explosion is still shrouded in mystery."[34]

Darwin's dilemma[35]

As Gould notes, Darwin himself recognized the problem of sudden appearance of major groups (but note that in his day, the 'Silurian' series defined by Sir Roderick Murchison (1792–1871) overlapped 'Cambrian' strata named by Adam Sedgwick (1785–1873), an old-earth creationist and one of Darwin's mentors who became a critic[36]):

"Consequently, if my theory be true, it is indisputable that before the lowest Silurian stratum was deposited, long periods elapsed, as long as, or probably far longer than, the whole interval from the Silurian age to

33. Gould, Stephen Jay, *The Panda's Thumb*, pp. 238–239, 1980.
34. Eldredge, N., *The Monkey Business*, p. 46, 1982.
35. The title of a new DVD documentary about the Cambrian Explosion and the problems for evolution, starring Stephen Meyer and Paul Nelson, Illustra Media, 2009.
36. Grigg, R., Darwin's Mentors, *Creation* **32**(1):50–52, 2010.

the present day; and that during these vast, yet quite unknown periods of time, the world swarmed with living creatures. To the question why we do not find records of these vast primordial periods, I can give no satisfactory answer.

"… the sudden manner in which whole groups of species appear in our European formations; the almost entire absence, as at present known, of fossiliferous formations beneath the Silurian strata, are all undoubtedly of the gravest nature."[37]

Dawkins says (p. 148) he addressed the Cambrian explosion in depth in his book *River Out of Eden*. In this, he takes issue with claims that Darwinian gradualism could not have resulted in such diversity in a short evolutionary time:

"The fallacy is glaring! Even creatures as radically different from one another as mollusks and crustaceans were originally just geographically separated populations of the same species. For a while, they could have interbred if they had met, but they did not. After millions of years of separate evolution, they acquired the characteristics which we, with the hindsight of modern zoologists, now recognize as those of mollusks and crustaceans respectively." (*ROE*, p. 11)

But is it a fallacy? That's the whole point! Under the Darwin/Dawkins model, there should have been a huge amount of diversification, first to form new species, then new genera, then new families, … then new phyla, such as Dawkins' molluscs and crustaceans. Or: *increasing diversity of the lower taxa (species) should precede the disparity of the higher taxa (phyla)*. Instead, there is wide disparity between the taxa and low species diversity, or *The disparity of the higher taxa (phyla) precedes the diversity of the lower taxa such as species* (see diagrams on the next page[38]).

The fossil record does not show any such pattern as Dawkins claims must have happened. It does not show a diversity of species becoming specialized over time into the different phyla. That's the whole point of the problem about the Cambrian; the phyla just appear 'out of nowhere'.

Two evolutionary palaeontologists recognize the problem:

"The required rapidity of the change implies either a few large steps or many and exceedingly rapid smaller ones. Large steps are tantamount to saltations and raise the problems of fitness barriers; small steps must be numerous and entail the problems discussed under microevolution.

---

37. Ref 1, pp. 307, 310.
38. www.veritas-ucsb.org

The periods of stasis raise the possibility that the lineage would enter the fossil record, and we reiterate that we can identify *none of the postulated intermediate forms*. Finally, the large numbers of species that must be generated so as to form a pool from which the successful lineage is selected are *nowhere to be found*. We conclude that the probability that species selection is a general solution to the origin of higher taxa is not great, and that neither of the contending theories of evolutionary change at the species level, phyletic gradualism or punctuated equilibrium, seem applicable to the origin of new body plans."[39] (my emphasis)

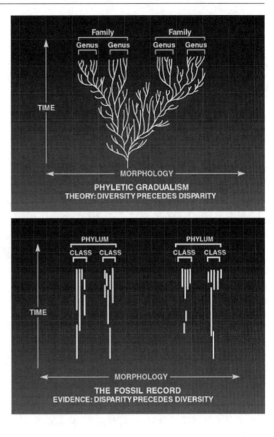

A geneticist pointed out that such rapid diversification would seem to require far more rapid change than known rates of genetic change would allow, and makes an unusual suggestion:

"It now appears that this Cambrian explosion, during which nearly all the extant animal phyla have emerged, was of an astonishingly short duration, lasting only 6–10 million years. Inasmuch as only a 1% DNA base sequence change is expected in 10 million years under the standard spontaneous mutation rate, I propose that all those diverse animals of the early Cambrian period, some 550 million years ago, were endowed with nearly identical genomes, with differential usage of the same set of genes accounting for the extreme diversities of body forms."[40]

39. Valentine, J., and Erwin, D. , Interpreting Great Developmental Experiments: The Fossil Record, p. 96 in: Raff, R.A. and E.C., Eds., *Development as an Evolutionary Process,* NY: Alan R. Liss, Inc., 1985.
40. Susumu Ohno, The notion of the Cambrian pananimalia genome, *Proc. Nati. Acad. Sci. USA*, 93:8475–8478, August 1996.

So the major changes to cause the diverse Cambrian body plans were *not* caused by a wide diversity of genes? Yet since the Cambrian, there *has* been wide diversity of genes without causing any more phyla? Yet changes are alleged to be the result of natural selection working on genes. How plastic evolution must be, if minor changes in genes can result in major changes in form, while major gene changes cause relatively minor form change.

Explosion into new niches?

Some have argued that somehow a lot of vacant new ecological niches drove this rapid diversification. But then, as Levinton points out, why did no new phyla appear after the 'Permian Extinction', 'dated' at 250 Ma?[31] This, according to evolutionary geology, was a far worse extinction even than the more famous 'Cretaceous extinction' that supposedly killed the dinosaurs 65 million years ago—57% of all families and 83% of all genera were killed off, including 96% of marine species. Yet no new phyla arose. Clearly vacant ecological niches are shown to be inadequate to explain the Cambrian diversity.

Flatworms: a counter-example?

Dawkins thinks he has a knock-down argument against the Cambrian explosion problem:

> "I have dealt with the Cambrian Explosion at length before. Here I'll add just one new point, illustrated by the flatworms, *Platyhelminthes*. This great phylum of worms includes the parasitic flukes and tapeworms, which are of great medical importance. My favorites, however, are the free-living turbellarian worms, of which there are more than 4,000 species: that's about as numerous as all the mammal species put together. They are common, both in water and on land, and presumably have been common for a very long time. You'd expect, therefore, to see a rich fossil history. Unfortunately, there is almost nothing. Apart from a handful of ambiguous trace fossils, not a single fossil flatworm has ever been found. The *Platyhelminthes*, to a worm, are 'already in an advanced state of evolution, the very first time they appear. It is as though they were just planted there, without any evolutionary history.'

> "But in this case, 'the very first time they appear' is not the Cambrian but today. Do you see what this means, or at least ought to mean for creationists? Creationists believe that flatworms were created in the same week as all other creatures. They have therefore had exactly the same time in which to fossilize as all other animals. During all the

centuries when all those bony or shelly animals were depositing their fossils by the millions, the flatworms must have been living happily alongside them, but without leaving the slightest trace of their presence in the rocks. What, then, is so special about gaps in the record of those animals that *do* fossilize, given that the past history of the flatworms is *one big gap*: even though the flatworms, by the creationists' own account, have been living for the same length of time? If the gap before the Cambrian Explosion is used as evidence that most animals suddenly sprang into existence in the Cambrian, exactly the same 'logic' should be used to prove that the flatworms sprang into existence yesterday.

"Yet this contradicts the creationist's belief that flatworms were created during the same creative week as everything else. You cannot have it both ways. This argument, at a stroke, completely and finally destroys the creationist case that the Precambrian gap in the fossil record can be taken as evidence against evolution." (pp. 148–9)

Dawkins is knocking down yet another straw-man: even though he refers to the "creative week" his argument confuses by implying that creationists believe that the creatures of the Cambrian explosion appeared in the Cambrian, i.e. as if we believe that there was such a period half a billion years ago. However, the fossil record is not a sequence of evolution over eons, but a sequence of burial by the year-long global Flood of Noah and its after-effects. But even such a flood would not be expected to fossilize too many small soft-bodied creatures—but it certainly explains the soft-bodied creatures that *are* fossilized, something Darwin said was impossible (see p. 108).

Creationists draw attention to the *evolutionist* belief in a Cambrian explosion as being inconsistent with their evolutionary belief; it is a contradiction. It is a form of the *reductio ad absurdum* argument. Surely Dawkins understands this.

Dawkins is also apparently wrong about there being no fossils of flatworms. Not only are there traces such as tracks (which he does allude to), but there is at least one report of a flatworm from rocks just below those classified as Cambrian.[41]

Dawkins does admit the lack of fossils leading to the creatures represented in 'Cambrian' rock, but then resorts to the old just-so story that the Precambrian animals were soft-bodied and therefore not preserved:

---

41.   Allison, C.W., Primitive fossil flatworm from Alaska: New evidence bearing on ancestry of the Metazoa, *Geology* 3(11):649–652, 1975.

"Why, on the evolutionary view, are there so few fossils before the Cambrian era? Well, presumably, whatever factors applied to the flatworms throughout geological time to this day, those same factors applied to the rest of the animal kingdom before the Cambrian. Probably, most animals before the Cambrian were soft-bodied like modern flatworms, probably rather small like modern turbellarians— just not good fossil material. Then something happened half a billion years ago to allow animals to fossilize freely—the arising of hard, mineralized skeletons, for example." (pp. 149–50)

Yet the absence of turbellarian fossils (as far as we know) is nothing like the absence of the huge number of fossil ancestors of the Cambrian creatures that are represented by abundant fossils. That there are no fossils of flatworms in the Cambrian when there are none in other rocks does not seem that significant. The problem of the Cambrian explosion relates to those *creatures that have abundant fossil evidence* for which there are no ancestors. It does not relate to those creatures that have no fossil evidence, for which there can be no 'Cambrian explosion'. Dawkins' flatworms are irrelevant to the argument.

Not just that, but the evidence is absent for other branches of the expected huge species diversification. And surely some of the intermediates leading up to the hard, mineralized animals would have intermediate partial skeletons that could have been fossilized?

This is all special pleading, Dr Dawkins, which is hardly science.

Ediacaran fauna

Indeed, research on Precambrian formations has discovered conditions so favourable for fossilization that many soft-bodied creatures have been found, contrary to Dawkins' claim. A good example is the wide variety of creatures discovered from the 'Ediacaran Period' ('dated' at 635–542 Ma, and named after the Ediacara Hills of South Australia). Even though many Ediacaran fossils included soft bodied organisms, none are ancestral to the Cambrian creatures.[31] Indeed, recent research has even identified an 'Avalon Explosion', whereby:

"A comprehensive quantitative analysis of these fossils indicates that the oldest Ediacara assemblage—the Avalon assemblage (575 to 565 Ma)—already encompassed the full range of Ediacara morphospace."[42]

---

42. Shen, B., Dong, L., Xiao, S. and Kowalewski, M., *The Avalon* explosion: evolution of Ediacara morphospace, *Science* 319:81–84, 2008.

So this hardly solves the problem for evolutionists—rather, they have *two* unrelated explosions of new creatures with no evidence of evolutionary ancestry.[43]

Summary

Abundant transitional forms should exist if evolution were true. So Dawkins in this chapter is clearly attempting to explain away their absence and soften up the reader for a fall-back excuse in his next chapter. There Dawkins deals with some specific examples of claimed transitional links ... Perhaps he knows that the claims are not that convincing, in the light of the overall pattern of the lack of transitional fossils that the evolutionist fossil expert Dr Colin Patterson pointed out so clearly.

Dawkins discusses the Cambrian explosion as if this was the only problem for the evolution myth. But this is just a part of a much larger overarching pattern of lack of transitional fossils; lack of evidence for common ancestry (aka evolution). For the Cambrian explosion, Dawkins offers the excuse that the ancestors of the creatures whose fossils are in the Cambrian might have been soft-bodied. But many of the Cambrian creatures were hard bodied so why don't we find their hard-bodied ancestors? Further, many of the Precambrian fossils were soft bodied, so why were not some soft bodied ancestors of the Cambrian explosion fossilized too?

The next chapter will address his claims of evolutionary transitions. This also shows that the links are missing even for very hard-skeletoned creatures, which makes Dawkins' excuse above even less tenable. The fossil record is very rich in 'end forms'; the only real 'evidence' for paucity is the lack of transitional forms—then this paucity is used as an excuse for the lack!

—∞—

43.   Doyle, S., creation.com/ediacaran-explosion, 5 March 2008.

Chapter 8

THE LINKS ARE STILL MISSING

D ESPITE claims by Dawkins and other evolutionists that "perfect missing links" have been discovered, the claims evaporate under careful analysis. This includes *Archaeopteryx* between reptiles and birds, *Tiktaalik* between fish and land creatures, *Pakicetus* and *Basilosaurus* between land mammals and whales. The earliest bats, pterosaurs, turtles/tortoises and distinctive types of dinosaurs and amphibians were already clearly recognizable representatives, not in-between forms.

As shown in the previous chapter, Dawkins has never been fond of the fossil record as evidence for evolution, and neither was Darwin. But he nevertheless tries to show that fossil intermediates are a bonus proof of evolution.

Archaeopteryx

Dawkins says:

"Another meaning [of 'missing link'] concerns the alleged paucity of so-called 'transitional forms' between major groups: between reptiles and birds, for example, or between fish and amphibians. 'Produce your intermediates!' Evolutionists often respond to this challenge from history-deniers by throwing them the bones of *Archaeopteryx*, the famous 'intermediate' between 'reptiles' and birds. This is a mistake, as I shall show. *Archaeopteryx* is not the answer to a challenge, because there is no challenge worth answering. To put up a single famous fossil like *Archaeopteryx* panders to a fallacy. In fact, for a large number of fossils, a good case can be made that every one of them is an intermediate between something and something else. The alleged challenge that seems to be answered by *Archaeopteryx* is based on an outdated conception, the one that used to be known as the Great Chain of Being ..." (p. 151)

This is rather weak: if everything is an intermediate, the word loses meaning. As shown in the previous chapter, Darwin knew very well that there were gaps between major groups. As for *Archaeopteryx*, there are a number of problems: its timing is wrong, and it did not have intermediate *features*; rather, it had many fully avian features:

• The dating, even by evolutionary methods, shows that the order is wrong. *Archaeopteryx* is allegedly 153 million years old, and even the beaked bird *Confuciusornis* is dated to 135 million years; but their alleged feathered dinosaur ancestors such as *Sinosauropteryx* and *Caudipteryx* are 'dated' to 125 million years old. Thus, by the evolutionists' own methods, *Archaeopteryx* and *Confuciusornis* are dated as being millions of years older than their alleged dinosaur ancestors. Evolutionary paleo-ornithologist Alan Feduccia, a well-known critic of the dino-to-bird dogma, often quips that you can't be older than your grandfather! Dino-bird believers respond that sometimes a grandfather can outlive his grandson. But while correct, it's hard to understand that an 'advanced' beaked bird like *Confuciusornis* could appear 10 million years before there is a trace of its 'feathered dino ancestors'. Also, one of the major 'evidences' of evolution is how the evolutionary order supposedly matches the fossil sequence. Therefore the gross mismatch with the dino-birds is a severe challenge to the evolutionary explanation.

• Perching foot.[1] This means that its wings would have needed to be sophisticated enough to produce the special wing turbulences (leading edge vortices) like those of modern birds, so that it could land.[2]

• Classical elliptical wings like modern woodland birds.[1]

• Fully-formed flying feathers (including asymmetric vanes and ventral, reinforcing furrows as in modern flying birds).[1]

• A large wishbone for attachment of strong muscles responsible for the downstroke of the wings.

1. Feduccia, A., Evidence from claw geometry indicating arboreal habits of *Archaeopteryx*, *Science* **259**(5096):790–793, 5 February, 1993.
2. Sarfati, J., Fancy flying from advanced aeronautics: The design of swifts and jet fighters, *Creation* **29**(1):37–39, 2006, creation.com/swift; after Videler, J.J., Stamhuis, E.J. and Povel, G.D.E., Leading-edge vortex lifts swifts, *Science* **306**(5703):1960–1962, 10 December 2004.

- *Archaeopteryx* possessed the unique avian lung design with air sacs[3] and one-directional airflow,[4] highly efficiently designed to flow in the opposite direction to the blood for maximum oxygen uptake.[5] This is totally different from the bellows-like lungs of a reptile,[6] even *Sinosauropteryx*.[7,8] One of the first intermediate forms would have a hole in the diaphragm, so natural selection would work against it.[9] The air sacs require a fixed thigh bone for support, yet dinosaurs had movable thighs, so could not have supported an avian lung system.[10] Paleo-ornithologist Alan Feduccia's major work on bird evolution doesn't even touch this problem.[11]

- A brain like a modern bird's, three times the size of that of a dinosaur of equivalent body size. The brain had large optic lobes to process the visual input needed for flying.[12]

- An inner ear with a cochlear length and semicircular canal proportions in the range of a modern flying bird's. This implies that *Archaeopteryx* could hear in a similar way, and also had the sense of balance required for coordinating flight.[12]

Note also, these obvious avian features are *totally incompatible* with the idea that *Archaeopteryx* was a forgery, a dinosaur fossil with fake feather imprints, as some have claimed. These features show that it was a true bird— neither a missing link nor a forgery.[13]

3. Christiansen, P. and Bonde, N., Axial and appendicular pneumaticity in *Archaeopteryx*, *Proc. Roy. Soc. London, Series B.* 267:2501–2505, 2000.
4. K. Schmidt-Nielsen, How birds breathe, *Scientific American* **225**(6):72–79, 1971.
5. Engineers make much use of this principle of *counter-current exchange* which is common in living organisms as well—see P.F. Scholander, The Wonderful Net, *Scientific American* 196:96–107, April 1957.
6. Denton, M., Evolution, a Theory in Crisis, pp. 199–213, Adler & Adler, Bethesda, MD, 1986; Blown away by design: Michael Denton and birds' lungs, *Creation* 21(4):14–15, 1999; creation.com/birdlung.
7. Ruben, J.A., *et al.*, Lung structure and ventilation in theropod dinosaurs and early birds, *Science* **278**(5341):1267–1270, 1997.
8. Evolutionist Ruben argues that *Sinosauropteryx's* "bellowslike lungs could not have evolved into the high-performance lungs of modern birds."— quoted in Ann Gibbons, Lung fossils suggest dinos breathed in cold blood, *Science* **278**(5341):1229–1230, 1997.
9. Ruben, Ref. 7, argues: "The earliest stages in the derivation of the avian abdominal airsac system from a diaphragmatic-ventilating ancestor would have necessitated selection for a diaphragmatic hernia [i.e. hole] in taxa transitional between theropods and birds. Such a debilitating condition would have immediately compromised the entire pulmonary ventilatory apparatus and seems unlikely to have been of any selective advantage."
10. Quick, D.E. and Ruben, J.A., Cardio-pulmonary anatomy in theropod dinosaurs: Implications from extant archosaurs, *J. Morphology*, **270**(10):1232–124620 May 2009. | doi:10.1002/jmor.10752. "The thin walled and voluminous abdominal air-sacs are supported laterally and caudally to prevent inward (paradoxical) collapse during generation of negative (inhalatory) pressure: the synsacrum, posteriorly directed, laterally open pubes and specialized femoral-thigh complex provide requisite support and largely prevent inhalatory collapse."
11. Feduccia, A., *The Origin and Evolution of Birds*, Yale University Press New Haven and London, 1996. However, this book shows that the usual dinosaur-to-bird dogma has many holes.
12. Alonso, P.D., *et al.,* The avian nature of the brain and inner ear of *Archaeopteryx*, *Nature* **430**(7000): 666–669, 5 August 2004; Witmer, L.M, Inside the oldest bird brain, a Perspective in the same issue, pp. 619–620.
13. Sarfati, J., *Birds: fliers from the beginning*, creation.com/not-hoax, 2000–2004.

Crocoducks and fronkeys

As is Dawkins' wont, he picks on soft targets, i.e. those who demand the showing of half-way stages between crocodiles and ducks, or frogs and monkeys (as if creationist biologists demand such things). True enough, evolutionists don't believe that such *modern* animals are descended from one another, but that they had a common ancestor which may not have looked much like either.

But the major creationist organisations have always pointed out that most types of creatures appear fully formed, without any ancestors. They are not demanding anything like a 'catobat'; rather, if flying creatures arose from non-flying creatures, where are the creatures which have incipient half-way *structures*, as opposed to *Archaeopteryx* which is at best a *mosaic*. No, creationists have long simply requested a sequence of creatures with certain characteristics consistently following a series, e.g., 100% leg/0% wing → 90% leg/10% wing → … 50% leg/50% wing … → 10% leg/90% wing → 0%leg/100% wing. Similarly, it is hardly unreasonable to demand evidence that distinctive types of dinosaur arose from other types, with creatures that have intermediate *structures*.

But the reality is different, as a recent study shows:

"In summary, rather than being simply a rapid accumulation of changes at or near the origin of Aves, bird flight appears to have been a stepwise series of punctuated evolutionary modifications."[14]

Note that punctuated steps is really evolspeak for gaps. Thus there are significant missing links in the chain.

Does one gap become two gaps?

Dawkins raises the old canard:

"Every time a fossil is found which is in between one species and another, you guys say, 'ah, now we've got two gaps there, where there previously was only one.'" (p. 198)

This is disingenuous. For example, consider a hypothetical world in which the only creatures known were fish and humans, then a fossil reptile was discovered. In a sense, this fills in a gap between fish and humans, but there are still huge gaps between the fish and reptile, and between reptile and human. It is no great argument to have two *very large* gaps instead of one *extremely large* gap.

---

14. Dececchi, T. A., and Larsson, H.C.E., Patristic evolutionary rates suggest a punctuated pattern in forelimb evolution before and after the origin of birds, *Paleobiology* **35**(1)1–12, 2009; p. 11.

When it comes to the famous *Archaeopteryx*, Dawkins' friend Jerry Coyne describes the situation before the mid-1990s rush of alleged feathered dinosaur claims, and does just what Dawkins complains about:

"After the discovery of *Archaeopteryx,* no other reptile-bird inter-mediates were found for many years, leaving a gaping hole between modern birds and their ancestors."[15]

Another example of filling in one gap and creating others comes from evolutionary cladistics, that tries to chart 'relatedness'.

"It might be expected that the addition of new fossil finds and reanalysis of older ones would improve the fit of age data to a fixed sample of cladograms, by the filling of gaps and by corrections of former taxonomic assignments. ... In other words, as a result of 26 years of work, new discoveries and reassignments had improved the fit in 20% of cases, but caused mismatches of clade and age data in a further 20% of cases. Sometimes a new fossil does not fill a gap, but creates additional gaps on other branches of a cladogram."[16]

This shows that it's hardly fair to attack creationists for something leading evolutionists practise as well.[17]

Bats and pterosaurs

For example, with the distinctive flying mammals and reptiles, bats and pterosaurs—the oldest known (by evolutionary 'dating' methods) fossil representatives are fully formed. Evolutionary paleontologist Paul Sereno admitted:

"For use in understanding the evolution of vertebrate flight, the early record of pterosaurs and bats is disappointing: Their most primitive representatives are fully transformed as capable fliers."[18]

In like manner, evolutionary paleontologist Robert Carroll said:

"The fossil record does not provide evidence for the transition towards either pterosaurs or bats: The earliest known members of these [bat] groups had already evolved an advanced flight apparatus."[19]

15. From Coyne, J., *Why Evolution is True,* p. 40, Penguin, NY, 2009; see refutation, Woodmorappe, J., Why evolution is not true, *J. Creation* **24**(1):24–29, 2010.
16. Benton, MJ., Testing the time axis of phylogenies, *Philosophical Transactions of the Royal Society of London* B349:8, 1995.
17. Woodmorappe, J., Does a 'transitional form' replace one gap with two gaps? *J. Creation* **14**(2):5–6, 2000; creation.com/onegap.
18. Sereno, Paul C., The evolution of dinosaurs, *Science* **284**(5423):2137–2147 (quote on p. 2143), 1999.
19. Carroll, R.L., *Patterns and Processes of Vertebrate Evolution,* p. 277, Cambridge University Press, NY, 1998.

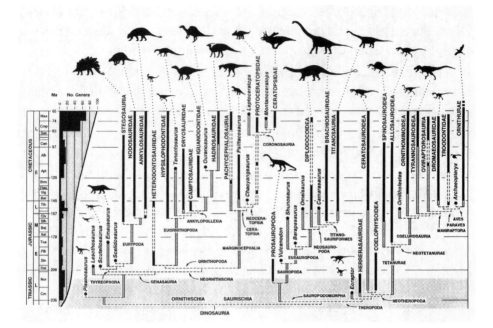

Figure 1: Fossil record of dinosaurs; Sereno, Paul C., The evolution of dinosaurs, *Science* 284: 2137–2147, 1999.

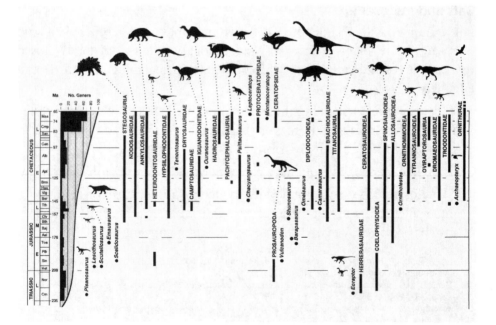

Figure 2: Fossil record of dinosaurs: modified from Figure 1 to show only the fossil evidence (by Don Batten).

With bats, the problem is even more acute, because they have sophisticated echolocating machinery: i.e. they have a sonar system where they locate objects from echos from squeaks they emit. Yet the 'earliest' bats were echolocators too, with no fossil evidence that such a system evolved. One evolutionist admitted:

"The oldest bat fossils, belonging to an extinct lineage, were unearthed from rocks about 54 million years old, but the creatures that they represent aren't dramatically different from living bats, says Mark S. Springer, an evolutionary biologist at the University of California, Riverside.

"Hallmark features of these creatures include the elongated fingers that support the wing membranes and the extensive coiling of bony structures in the inner ears, a sign that they were capable of detecting the high-frequency chirps used in echolocation." [20]

Another problem for Darwinists is that most echolocating bats use vocal cords to create their echoes, but some megabats use tongue clicks. Did they evolve separately, or did one type diverge?[21]

Dinosaurs

The dinosaurs were a famous extinct group of very distinctive creatures, which left an excellent fossil record. There are many more than a thousand fossils or part-fossils in the world's museums that provide evidence for the existence in the past of huge sauropods, carnivorous theropods, duck-billed dinosaurs, armoured ankylosaurs, horned dinos, etc. Figure 1, by the same Dr Sereno mentioned earlier under "Bats and pterosaurs", shows that the major groups of dinosaurs are recognizable from their fossils (dark lines).

However, there are no fossils showing the transitional forms or common ancestors; *none*.[22] In Figure 1, the dashed lines show the *conjectured* ancestors, in the absence of fossil evidence. The unfilled bars show the supposed fossil ranges extended beyond the fossil evidence to make the conjectured common ancestors feasible. To make it clear, Figure 2 shows *only* the fossil evidence, which makes it clearer that the distinctive types of dinosaurs have no fossil evidence for their supposed common ancestors.[23]

'The ancestors were soft-bodied, therefore didn't fossilize' is clearly an unacceptable excuse when it comes to dinosaurs. This shows up the shallowness of the Dawkins/Darwin excuse for the lack of Cambrian ancestors (previous chapter).

20. Perkins, S., Learning to listen: How some vertebrates evolved biological sonar, *Science News* **167**(20):314, 2005.
21. Bergman, J., Evidence for the evolution of bats [a critique], *Origins* (BCS) 47:10–15, February 2008.
22. Werner, C., *Evolution the Grand Experiment*, New Leaf Press, pp. 127–128, 2007.
23. See also Bergman, J., The evolution of dinosaurs: much conjecture, little evidence, *CRSQ* **46**(2):119–126, 2009.

Fish to tetrapods

Dawkins discusses the transition between sea creatures and land, which was an undoubted large gap spanning a long period of evolutionary time, and even had a name, "Romer's Gap", after the American paleontologist A.S. Romer (1894–1973):

> "'Romer's Gap' … stretches about 360 million years ago, at the end of the Devonian period, to about 340 million years ago, in the early part of the Carboniferous, the 'Coal Measures.' After Romer's Gap, we find unequivocal amphibians crawling through the swamps, a rich radiation of salamander like creatures … Before that, however, was Romer's Gap. And before his gap, Romer could see only fish, lobe-finned fish, living in water. Where were the intermediates, and what led them to venture out on to the land." (pp. 164–5)

Indeed, the evolution of land limbs and life on land in general requires many changes, and the fossil record has no evidence of such changes. Geologist Paul Garner writes:

> "[T]here are functional challenges to Darwinian interpretations. For instance, in fish the head, shoulder girdle, and circulatory systems constitute a single mechanical unit. The shoulder girdle is firmly connected to the vertebral column and is an anchor for the muscles involved in lateral undulation of the body, mouth opening, heart contractions, and timing of the blood circulation through the gills[24] However, in amphibians the head is not connected to the shoulder girdle, in order to allow effective terrestrial feeding and locomotion. Evolutionists must suppose that the head became incrementally detached from the shoulder girdle, in a step-wise fashion, with functional intermediates at every stage. However, a satisfactory account of how this might have happened has never been given." [25]

Yet some recent discoveries are alleged to have filled this gap.

Ichthyostega and *Acanthostega*

Dawkins discusses these two 'intermediates', although they have fully-formed pelvic girdles and limbs, unlike the *Eusthenopteron*, a lobe-finned fish. But

---

24. Gudo, M. and Homberger, D.G., Functional morphology of the coracoid bar of the Spiny Dogfish (*Squalas acanthias*): implications for the evolutionary history of the shoulder girdle of vertebrates, 43rd Annual Meeting of the Palaeontological Association, Manchester, 19–22 December 1999; www.palass.org/index. html, 4 April 2003. Click on 'Abstracts' then 'Manchester 1999'.
25. See the thorough analysis, Garner, P., The fossil record of 'early' tetrapods: evidence of a major evolutionary transition? *J. Creation* **17**(2):111–117, 2003; creation.com/tetrapod.

who was the predecessor of whom? It depends on which characteristic one looks at: e.g. *Ichthyostega's* skull seems more fish-like than *Acanthostega's*, but its shoulder and hips are more robust and land-animal–like.[26] *Ichthyostega* is allegedly the more amphibian-like, but *Acanthostega* possesses two 'amphibian' features that *Ichthyostega* does not.[27,28]

Indeed, even according to evolutionary 'dating', they are contemporaries (see Figure 3). Furthermore, *Panderichthys*, which Dawkins describes as "slightly more amphibian-like, and slightly less fish-like, than *Eusthenopteron*" (p. 168), is dated earlier. And even the limbed creatures predate the fully-fish *Coelacanth*.

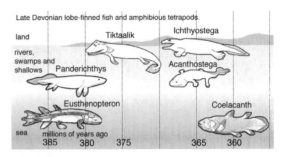

Figure 3: Fossil record of alleged fish-tetrapod transition, Wikipedia.

Dawkins also notes the unusual digit numbers: *Acanthostega* had eight, while *Ichthyostega* had seven (pp. 167–8). He tries to wave away this contradiction:

"It seems that the early tetrapods enjoyed more freedom to experiment than we have today. Presumably at some point the embryological processes fixed upon five, and a step was taken that was hard to reverse. Although, admittedly, it is not as hard as all that. There are individual cats, and indeed humans, who have six toes. The extra toes probably arose from a duplication error in embryology." (p. 167)

But still, evolutionists often appeal to the common pentadactyl 5-digit pattern as evidence for their common ancestry from a 5-digited creature. Yet the nearest creatures they have to a common ancestor *did not have five digits!*

Tiktaalik

Dawkins is delighted with the discovery of *Tiktaalik roseae*,[29,30,31] supposedly closing a gap between *Panderichthys* and *Acanthostega*:

26. *Ichthyostega*, www.devoniantimes.org/Order/re-ichthyostega.html, Devonian Times, accessed 11 April 2006.
27. Fang pair on parasymphysial plate, Anterior end of anterior coronoid; Ahlberg, P.E., Lukševičs, E. and Mark-Kurik,E., A near-tetrapod from the Baltic Middle Devonian, *Palaeontology* 43(3):533–548, 2000.
28. See also Lamb, A., *Livoniana*—have they (finally!) found a missing link? *J. Creation* 16(1):4–6, 2002; creation.com/livoniana.
29. Daeschler, E.B., Shubin, N.H. and Jenkins, F.A., Jr., A Devonian tetrapod-like fish and the evolution of the tetrapod body plan, *Nature* **440** (7085):757–763, 6 April 2006.
30. Shubin, N.H., Daeschler, E.B. and Jenkins, F.A., Jr, The pectoral fin of *Tiktaalik roseae* and the origin of the tetrapod limb, *Nature* **440**(7085):764–771, 6 April 2006.
31. See also Sarfati, J., *Tiktaalik*—a fishy 'missing link', *J. Creation* 21(1): 53–57, 2007; creation.com/tiktaalik.

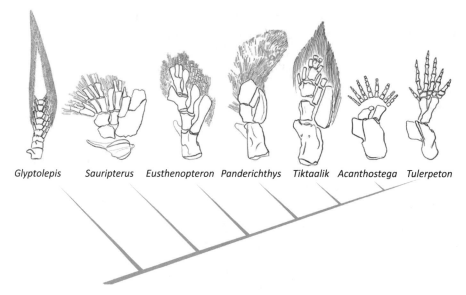

Glyptolepis   Sauripterus   Eusthenopteron   Panderichthys   Tiktaalik   Acanthostega   Tulerpeton

Figure 4: Cladogram of the pectoral fins on the tetrapod stem.

"*Tiktaalik* is the perfect missing link—perfect, because it almost exactly splits the difference between fish and amphibian, and perfect because it is missing no longer." (p. 169)

Dawkins is following the infectious enthusiasm of evolutionary palaeontologists who claimed that this is "a link between fishes and land vertebrates that might in time become as much of an evolutionary icon as the proto-bird *Archaeopteryx*."[32]

But how intermediate is it really? One of those enthusiastic palaeontologists cited above, Jennifer Clack (University of Cambridge, UK), admitted:

"There remains a large morphological gap between them and digits as seen in, for example, *Acanthostega*: if the digits evolved from these distal bones, the process must have involved considerable developmental repatterning. …

"Of course, there are still major gaps in the fossil record. In particular we have almost no information about the step between *Tiktaalik* and the earliest tetrapods, when the anatomy underwent the most drastic changes, or about what happened in the following Early Carboniferous period, after the end of the Devonian, when tetrapods became fully terrestrial."[32]

32. Ahlberg, P.E. and Clack, J.A., Palaeontology: A firm step from water to land, *Nature* **440**(7085):747–749, 6 April 2006.

Indeed, *Tiktaalik's* fins that are supposed to have become legs were not connected to the main skeleton, so could not have supported its weight on land. The discoverers claim that they could have helped to prop up the body as the fish moved along the sea bottom,[31] but evolutionists had similar high hopes for the coelacanth fin. However, a living coelacanth (*Latimeria chalumnae*) was discovered in 1938. Later, it was found that the fins were not used for walking but for deft maneuvring when swimming.

Thus all the claims about *Tiktaalik* are mere smokescreens, exaggerating mere tinkering around the edges while huge gaps remain unbridged by evolution. And it is hardly unreasonable for creationists to point out that there are still two large gaps rather than one huge gap (see p. 126).

The series of corresponding limbs (Figure 4, left) does not appear to show a clear progression. Even from looking at it, it is not obvious that the *Panderichthys* limb belongs in between the adjacent ones in the series. It has fewer small bones. And a later study indeed argued that *Panderichthys'* fin may be *closer* to tetrapods in morphology than *Tiktaalik.*[33,34]

The *Tiktaalik* discoverers themselves appear to recognize that there are some anomalies:

"In some features, *Tiktaalik* is similar to rhizodontids such as *Sauripterus*. These similarities, which are probably homoplastic, include the shape and number of radial articulations on the ulnare, the presence of extensive and branched endochondral radials, and the retention of unjointed lepidotrichia."[30]

As explained in ch. 6, 'homoplastic' essentially means a common feature that can't be explained by inheritance from a common ancestor. But appealing to homoplasy is really *explaining away* evidence that doesn't fit the paradigm, and indeed such explaining away is ubiquitous. Two evolutionists admit:

"Disagreements about the probable homologous or homoplastic nature of shared derived similarities between taxa lie at the core of most conflicting phylogenetic hypotheses."[35]

In fact, when more characteristics than just one are analyzed, homoplasies become even more necessary to explain away anomalies. Another

33. Boisvert, C.A., Mark-Kurik, E. and Ahlberg, P.E., The pectoral fin of *Panderichthys* and the origin of digits, *Nature* 456:636–638, 2008, doi:10.1038/nature07339.
34. Doyle, S., *Panderichthys*—a fish with fingers? creation.com/panderichthys, 9 December 2008.
35. Luckett, W.P. and Hong, N., Phylogenetic relationships between the orders Artiodactyla and Cetacea, *J. Mammalian Evolution* 5(2):130, 1998.

example is that the neck region of *Tiktaalik* is said to be homoplastic with that of *Mandageria*.[36]

In reality, *Tiktaalik* appears to be another *mosaic* or *chimera*, like *Archaeopteryx*. It has some fish-like aspects, some unique features such as the hyomandibula,[37] and some tetrapod-like features. Under an evolutionary scenario, this would mean that they are all at different stages of evolution. However, natural selection can only work on organisms as a *whole*, not on parts; therefore a new trait cannot be selected for outside of the context of the whole organism. Moreover, mosaic evolution does not identify an evolutionary lineage; evolutionists have only identified traits that seem to change in complex, independent and contradictory ways in an evolutionary framework.[38]

But a designer could create different creatures with different *modules*, that fit no consistent evolutionary pattern. This is contrary to Dawkins' claim that there is "no borrowing" across different types of creatures unless there is a common ancestor which had the common feature (p. 297).

Polish footprints undermine story[39]

Tracks of footprints found on the surface of large limestone slabs from Zachelmie Quarry in the Holy Cross Mountains of Poland have turned the palaeontological world upside down.[40,41,42] This is because they are evidence of a 2-metre-long four-limbed walking creature 'dated' at 397 million years old. This predates all the alleged fish-to-tetrapod transitional forms, including the now-famous *Tiktaalik,* and the more fish-like *Panderichthys*, and is 12 million years older than the undoubted fish *Eusthenopteron*.

Other evolutionists were equally shocked, including the *Tiktaalik* enthusiasts of Ref. 32:

- "They force a radical reassessment of the timing, ecology and environmental setting of the fish-tetrapod transition, as well as the completeness of the body fossil record."[40]

36. Johanson, Z., Ahlberg, P., Ritchie, A. The braincase and palate of the tetrapodomorph sarcopterygian Mandageria fairfaxi: morphological variability near the fish-tetrapod transition, *Palaeontology* 46:271–293, 2003.
37. The hyomandibula is a pair of deep bones or cartilage in the hyoid (neck) region in most fishes, which usually helps suspend the jaws.
38. Doyle, S., *Tiktaalik*—sticking its head out of water? creation.com/tiktaalik2, 12 December 2008.
39. Walker, T., Tetrapods from Poland trample the *Tiktaalik* school of evolution, *J. Creation* 24(1):55–59, 2010; creation.com/tetrapod-footprints.
40. Niedzwiedzki, G., Szrek, P., Narkiewicz, K., Narkiewicz, M and Ahlberg, P., Tetrapod trackways from the early Middle Devonian period of Poland, *Nature* 463(7227):43–48, 2010.
41. Editor's Summary, Four feet in the past: trackways pre-date earliest body fossils, *Nature* 463(7227), 2010; nature.com/nature.
42. Bryne, J., Four-legged creature's footprints force evolution rethink, www.livescience.com, 6 January 2010.

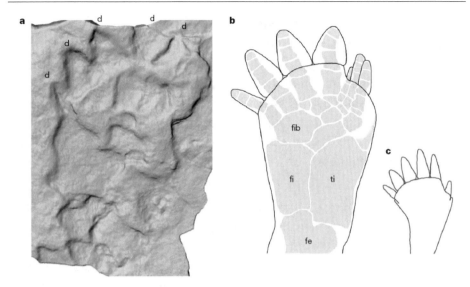

Figure 5: Laser scan of surface showing detail of individual print and diagram relating it to an animal's foot (from Ref. 29).

- "[It] will cause a significant reappraisal of our understanding of tetrapod origins."[41]
- "We thought we'd pinned down the origin of limbed tetrapods. We have to rethink the whole thing."[43]
- "These results force us to reconsider our whole picture of the transition from fish to land animals."[44]
- "[They] could lead to significant shifts in our knowledge of the timing and ecological setting of early tetrapod evolution."[45]
- "That's surprising, but this is what the fossil evidence tells us."[46]

Furthermore, the tracks look five-toed, although the paper reconstructs them as six- or seven-toed (Figure 5). If the prints rather than the reconstructions reflect reality, it would show 5-digited tetrapods long predating their alleged ancestors that had more digits, i.e. were 'less evolved'.

This all goes to show that grand claims and story-telling pass as evolutionary 'science' and just one small fossil discovery can undo years of 'rock-solid' evidence for evolution.

43. Clack, J., cited in: Curry, M., Ancient four-legged beasts leave their mark, *ScienceNOW Daily News,* sciencenow.sciencemag.org, 6 January 2010.
44. Paleontologist Per Ahlberg of Uppsala University, Sweden; in: Fossil Footprints Give Land Vertebrates a Much Longer History, *ScienceDaily* sciencedaily.com/, 8 January 2010.
45. Roach, J., Oldest land-walker tracks found—pushes back evolution, *National Geographic News,* nationalgeographic.com, 6 January 2010.
46. Paleontologist Philippe Janvier from the National Museum of Natural History, Paris, France; in: Amos, J., Fossil tracks record 'oldest land-walkers', *BBC News,* news.bbc.co.uk, 6 January 2010.

Whale evolution?

Dawkins claims that just as land creatures began in the sea, some later land creatures returned (pp. 170–171), including whales and dugongs. For a long time Darwin and his followers didn't even have remotely plausible fossil evidence, but they had faith. E.g. evolutionary whale experts like the late E.J. Slijper admitted in 1962: "We do not possess a single fossil of the transitional forms between the aforementioned land animals [i.e. carnivores and ungulates] and the whales."[47]

The first thing to ask is, *which* land creatures? Dawkins says:

"Whales have long been an enigma, but recently our knowledge of whale evolution has become rather rich. Molecular genetic evidence … shows that the closest living cousins of whales are hippos, then pigs, then ruminants. Even more surprisingly, the molecular evidence shows that hippos are more closely related to whales than they are to the cloven-hooved animals (such as pigs and ruminants) which look much more like them. This is another example of the mismatch that can sometimes arise between closeness of cousinship and degree of physical resemblance. … Hippos stayed, at least partly, on land, and so resemble their more distant land-dwelling cousins, the ruminants, while their closer cousins, the whales, took off into the sea and changed so drastically that their affinities with hippos escaped all biologists except molecular geneticists." (p. 170)

This indeed seems to be the current favoured evolutionary explanation. But Dawkins fails to mention that it wasn't long ago that palaeontologists thought that whales were descended from mesonychids, an order of extinct carnivorous mammals quite unlike hippos. This was the explanation in *Teaching about Evolution and the Nature of Science* (1998), the teachers' guidebook from the National Academy of Sciences (USA).[48] Yet now, the supposedly overwhelming evidence of mesonychid ancestry, presented dogmatically as a fact, has to be explained away. That is, the supposedly homologous features of mesonychids and whales, mainly teeth and skull anatomy, once attributed to common ancestry, have to now be explained away as homoplastic/convergent, i.e. having nothing to do with common ancestry.[49]

---

47. Slijper, E.J., *Dolphins and Whales,* University of Michigan Press, 1962, p. 17.
48. See my book *Refuting Evolution* (1998, 2008), ch. 5, for refutation of their material on whale evolution; creation.com/rech5.
49. See Woodmorappe, J., Walking whales, nested hierarchies, and chimeras: do they exist? *J. Creation* **16**(1):111–119, 2002; creation.com/walkingwhales.

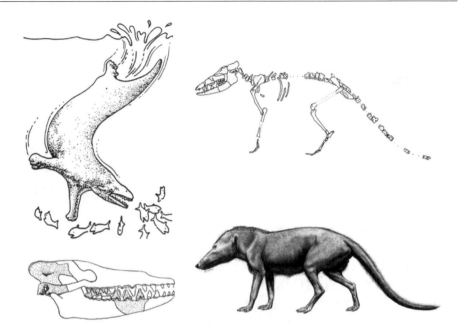

Figure 6:

Top left: Gingerich's first reconstruction of *Pakicetus*;[50,51] **bottom left:** what he had actually found;[50,51] **top right:** more complete skeleton;[52] **bottom right:** more reasonable reconstruction.[53]

Fossil record

Dawkins also reproduces a diagram of supposed whale ancestry, saying:

"Note the careful way this picture is drawn. It is tempting—and older books used to do this—to draw sequences of fossils with arrows from older to younger ones. But nobody can say, for example, that *Ambulocetus* was descended from *Pakicetus*. Or *Basilosaurus* was descended from *Rodhocetus*. Instead, the diagram follows the more cautious policy of suggesting that, for example, whales are descended from a contemporary cousin of *Ambulocetus* which was probably rather like *Ambulocetus* (and might even have been *Ambulocetus*). The fossils shown are representatives of the stages of whale evolution. The gradual disappearance of the hind limbs, the transformation of the front limbs from walking legs to swimming fins, the flattening of the tail into flukes, are among the changes that emerged in an elegant cascade." (pp. 171–2)

Of course, the diagram looks nice when all these creatures are drawn to about the same size, with no mention that, for example, *Basilosaurus* was 10 times longer than *Ambulocetus*. Some of the other claims are not what they seem either.

Pakicetus

For example, *Pakicetus* ('whale from Pakistan') was first drawn as an aquatic creature,[50] based on a few skull bones and teeth.[51] Its discoverer, Philip Gingerich, triumphantly proclaimed:

"In time and in its morphology, *Pakicetus* is perfectly intermediate, a missing link between earlier land mammals and later, full-fledged whales."[50]

Since Gingerich, like Dawkins, is a committed materialist, evolution is the only game in town. So he must *interpret* fossils in an evolutionary framework. Therefore it's not surprising that a few scraps of bone are wishfully thought to be a 'missing link'.

However, when the rest of its skeleton was found, it was realized to be a fast-running land creature[52] (then drawn by the same artist as the diagram in Dawkins' book[53])—see Figure 6, above. This is hardly the only example of evolutionists misleading the public, exaggerating the evidence from a few scraps of bones. The moral of the story, as one evolutionist put it, is: "Fossils are fickle. Bones will sing any song you want to hear."[54]

Basilosaurus

Basilosaurus is Greek for 'king lizard', though it was actually a serpent-like sea mammal about 21 m (70 feet) long, with a 1.5 m (5 foot) long skull. However, *Basilosaurus* was fully aquatic, so hardly transitional between land mammals and whales. Also, Barbara Stahl, a vertebrate paleontologist and evolutionist, points out:

"The serpentine form of the body and the peculiar shape of the cheek teeth make it plain that these archaeocetes [like *Basilosaurus*] *could not possibly have been the ancestor of modern whales.*"[55]

Both modern branches of whales, the toothed whales (Odontoceti) and baleen whales (Mysticeti), appear abruptly in the fossil record. And Stahl points out that the skull structure in both types

"shows a strange modification *not present, even in a rudimentary way*, in *Basilosaurus* and its relatives: in conjunction with the backward migration of the nostrils on the dorsal surface of the head, the nasal

50. Gingerich, P.D., *J. Geol. Educ.* 31:140–144, 1983.
51. Gingerich, P.D. *et al., Science* **220**(4595):403–6, 22 April 1983.
52. Thewissen, J.G.M., *et al.*, Skeletons of terrestrial cetaceans and the relationship of whales to artiodactyls, *Nature* 413:277–281, 20 September 2001
53. *Pakicetus* ... eight years on. Illustration: Carl Buell www.neoucom.edu/Depts/Anat/Pakicetid.html.
54. Shreeve, J., Argument over a woman, *Discover* **11**(8):58, 1990 (in reference to human evolution, but nevertheless apt).
55. Stahl, B.J., *Vertebrate History: Problems in Evolution*, p. 489, Dover, 1985; emphasis added.

bones have been reduced and carried upwards and the premaxillary and maxillary elements have expanded to the rear to cover the original braincase roof."[55]

Basilosaurus did have small hind limbs (certainly too small for walking), and some have claimed they were vestigial. But they were probably used for clasping during copulation, according even to other evolutionists. For example, Philip Gingerich said, "It seems to me that they could only have been some kind of sexual and reproductive clasper."[56]

Tortoises and turtles

These are quite distinctive reptiles, grouped together as chelonians. As Dawkins says (p. 174), British usage reserves 'tortoise' for land-dwellers and 'turtle' for sea-dweller, and they also have 'terrapin' for those living in fresh or brackish water; to Americans they are all 'turtles'.[57] Australians generally follow British usage; New Zealanders even more so. Dawkins says:

"I now want to turn to another group of animals that returned from the land to the water: a particularly intriguing example because some of them later reversed the process and returned to the land a second time. Sea turtles are, in one important respect, less fully given back to water than whales or dugongs, for they still lay their eggs on beaches. Like all vertebrate returners to the water, turtles haven't given up on breathing air, but in this department, some of them go one better than whales. These turtles extract additional oxygen from the water through a pair of chambers at their rear end that are richly endowed with blood vessels." (p. 173)

For a long time, even evolutionists admitted that chelonian origin was an enigma.[58] For example, "Intermediates between turtles and cotylosaurs, the primitive reptiles from which [evolutionists believe] turtles probably sprang, are entirely lacking."[59] This was even more vexing, because Darwin's

---

56. As quoted in *The Press Enterprise*, 1 July, 1990, p. A–15.
57. Dawkins cites G.B. Shaw's quip, "England and America are divided by a common language." As an Australian/New Zealander happily married to an American, I can relate to that.
58. See Bergman, J. and Frair, W., Evidence for turtle evolution, *J. Creation* **21**(3):24–26, 2007; creation.com/turtle.
59. 'Reptiles', *Encyclopædia Britannica* 26:704–705, 15th Ed., 1992.

usual excuse of an incomplete fossil record fails, because "turtles leave more and better fossil remains than do other vertebrates."[59]

Shell origins

The turtle/tortoise armour comprises the convex *carapace* on top and the flat bottom part, the *plastron*. So how did such shelled creatures evolve from non-shelled creatures? One hypothesis is that the turtle carapace gradually evolved from "elements of the primitive reptilian integument."[60] Chelonian expert Olivier Rieppel argued that a big "problem for an evolutionary biologist is to explain these transformations in the context of a gradualistic process."[61] Rieppel argues that turtles could not evolve by a gradual process, as favoured by Darwin and Dawkins, and concluded that they may be an example of 'hopeful monsters',[61] the result of a sudden macro change.[62]

Santanachelys

In 1998, the 20-cm–long *Santanachelys gaffneyi* was described as the "oldest known sea turtle", and 'dated' to 110 Ma. But this was a fully formed turtle, and even had a fully developed system for excreting salt, without which a marine reptile would quickly dehydrate. This is shown by skull cavities which would have held large salt-excreting glands around the eyes.[63]

Proganochelys

Until 2008, the oldest known chelonian was *Proganochelys quenstedti*, 'dated' to 210 Ma, about 1 metre long, and what British commonwealth English would call a 'tortoise' (*Greatest Show* p. 178). According to evolutionists, it "literally[64] pops into the fossil record as a completely formed turtle,"[65] as it had a skeleton, "characteristic of turtles—carapace, plastron, scapular girdle inside the rib cage (unique among vertebrates)."[66] Yet it didn't answer how chelonians evolved from non-chelonians:

> "With *Proganochelys,* our trail into the past runs cold. We do not know from whence it came. We may be not be much closer to knowing today than we were more than a century ago, in the 1880s, when *Proganochelys*

60. Burke, A.C., Development of the turtle carapace: implications for the evolution of a novel bauplan, *Journal of Morphology* **199**(3):363–378, 1989; p. 363.
61. Rieppel, O., Turtles as hopeful monsters, *BioEssays* 23:987–991, 2001; p. 990.
62. A term coined by geneticist and non-Darwinian evolutionist Richard Goldschmidt, *The Material Basis of Evolution*, pp. 205–206, New Haven, CT: Yale University Press, 1940.
63. Ren Hirayama, 'Oldest known sea turtle', *Nature* **392**(6678):705–708, 16 April 1998 | doi:10.1038/33669. Comment by Henry Gee, p. 651, same issue.
64. A non-literal use of the word 'literally'!
65. Spotila, J.R., *Sea Turtles A Complete Guide to Their Biology, Behavior, and Conservation,* The Johns Hopkins University Press, Baltimore, MD, p. 57, 2004.
66. Garcia-Porta, J. and Casanovaso-Vilar, I., The origin and first evolutionary stages of turtles: new perspectives, *Reptilia (The European Herpetology Magazine)* 19:47–51, 2001; p. 48.

was first discovered ... the possible choices for the original turtle span almost the entire range of reptiles, living and extinct."[67]

Odontochelys

In 2008, a mainly Chinese team plus Rieppel discovered an even 'older' chelonian, this time a turtle, about 30 cm long. They named it *Odontochelys semitestacea* ('toothed turtle with a half-shell').[68] The paper admits the sad (for evolutionists) state of affairs in chelonian origins before their own fossil was discovered:

> "The origin of the turtle body plan remains one of the great mysteries of reptile evolution. The anatomy of turtles is highly derived, which renders it difficult to establish the relationships of turtles with other groups of reptiles. The oldest known turtle, *Proganochelys* from the Late Triassic period of Germany, has a fully formed shell and offers no clue as to its origin."[68]

But this new creature is supposed to solve problems. Dawkins says:

> "The most instantly noticeable feature of the chelonians is their shell. How did it evolve, and what did it look like? Where are the missing links? What (a creationist zealot might ask) is the use of half a shell? Well, amazingly a new fossil has just been described which eloquently answers these questions. ... unlike a modern turtle or tortoise, it had teeth, and it did indeed have half a shell. It also had a much longer tail than a modern turtle or tortoise. All three of those features mark it out as prime 'missing link material'. The belly was covered by a shell, the so-called plastron, in pretty much the same way as that of a modern sea turtle. But it almost completely lacked the ... carapace. Its back was presumably soft, like a lizard's, although there were some hard, bony bits along the middle above the backbone, as in a crocodile, and the ribs were flattened, as though 'trying' to form the evolutionary beginnings of the carapace." (pp. 174–5)

First of all, why are "teeth" primitive? Some modern creatures have them, and some extinct ones do not. And a loss of teeth means loss of information, so it sheds no light on the *origin* of these elaborate structures.[69]

67. Orenstein, R., *Turtles, Tortoises & Terrapins: Survivors in Armor*, Firefly Books, Buffalo, NY, p. 26, 2001.
68. Li, Ch., Wu, X.-Ch., Rieppel, O., Wang, L.-T. and Zhao, L.-J., An ancestral turtle from the Late Triassic of southwestern China, *Nature* 456:497–501, 27 November 2008 | doi:10.1038/nature07533.
69. E.g. recent discoveries about so-called 'defects' in teeth show they suppress the growth of cracks, making enamel very tough though composed of a brittle mineral. Herzl Chai *et al.*, Remarkable resilience of teeth, *PNAS* **106**(18):7289–7293, 13 April 2009 | doi: 10.1073/pnas.0902466106; Sarfati., J., Tooth enamel: sophisticated materials science: Teeth are hard to crack due to 'defects' and other fine structure, *Creation* **32**(3), 2010; creation.com/enamel, 14 May 2009.

Same with tails. And the "half shell" is hardly a half-*evolved* shell; rather, it is a *completely formed* bottom part without a top part. A partly-formed top or bottom shell would likely provide little protection and would hinder escape from a predator.[70]

Second, as Dawkins acknowledges, there was a perspective in *Nature* by two Canadian biologists on this paper.[71] Rather than solving problems, they say:

"The evolutionary relationships and ecology of turtles through time, and the developmental and evolutionary origins of the shell are major controversies in studies of vertebrate evolution."

They dispute the interpretation that *Odontochelys* is a primitive form on the way to evolving a shell on both top and bottom. Rather, they argue that it had *lost* part of its upper shell, so it was really a *loss* of information. As I've pointed out before, a loss can be advantageous sometimes; this could save weight, and a sea turtle swimming near the surface is in more danger of attacks from below than from above, so is in less need of armour on top (Dawkins says much the same, p. 176). The *Nature* Perspective argues:

"Although this evolutionary scenario is plausible, we are particularly excited by an alternative interpretation and its evolutionary consequences. We interpret the condition seen in *Odontochelys* differently—that a carapace was present, but some of its dermal components were not ossified. The carapace forms during embryonic development when the dorsal ribs grow laterally into a structure called the carapacial ridge, a thickened ectodermal layer unique to turtles. The presence of long, expanded ribs, a component of the carapace of all turtles, indicates that the controlling developmental tissue responsible for the formation of the turtle carapace was already present in *Odontochelys*. The expanded lateral bridge that connects the plastron to the carapace in other turtles is also present, implying that the plastron was connected to the laterally expanded carapace. Thus, an alternative interpretation is that the apparent reduction of the carapace in *Odontochelys* resulted from lack of ossification of some of its dermal components, but that a carapace was indeed present.

"This interpretation of *Odontochelys* leads us to the possibility that its shell morphology is not primitive, but is instead a specialized

---

70. Martin, R., The Phantom Bridge Exposed: The Latest Turtle Attack, *Creation Res. Soc. Quart.* **33**(1):17, 1996.
71. Reisz, R.J. and Head, J.J., Paleontology: Turtle origins out to sea, *Nature* 456:450–451, 27 November 2008 | doi:10.1038/456450a.

adaptation. Reduction of dermal components of the shell in aquatic turtles is common: soft-shelled turtles have a greatly reduced bony shell and have lost the dermal peripheral elements of the carapace. Sea turtles and snapping turtles have greatly reduced ossification of the dermal components of the carapace, a condition similar to that seen in *Odontochelys*."[71]

Thus *Odontochelys* doesn't seem to solve the problems of chelonian *origins*. Dawkins says:

"But *Odontochelys* throws speculation back into the melting pot. We now have three possibilities, all equally intriguing.

1. *Proganochelys* and *Palaeochersis* might be survivors of the land-dwelling animals that had earlier sent some representatives to the sea, including the ancestors of *Odontochelys*. This hypothesis would suggest that the shell evolved on land early, and *Odontochelys* lost the carapace in the water, retaining the ventral plastron.

2. The shell might have evolved in water, as the Chinese authors suggest, with the plastron over the belly evolving first, and the carapace over the back evolving later. In this case, what do we make of *Proganochelys* and *Palaeochersis*, who lived on land after *Odontochelys* lived, with its half shell, in water? *Proganochelys* and *Palaeochersis* might have evolved the shell independently. But there is another possibility.

3. *Proganochelys* and *Palaeochersis* might represent an earlier return from the water to the land. Isn't that a startlingly exciting thought?" (p. 179)

However, this shows that evolution has become so flexible that it's compatible with two opposite stories. It suggests that evolution itself is unfalsifiable in Dawkins' mind.

Summary

- For evolution to be remotely plausible, there should be lots of fossils exhibiting transitional structures. The best evolutionists normally come up with are curious mosaics like *Archaeopteryx* and *Tiktaalik*, which had a mixture of fully-developed features, not in-between ones.

- *Archaeopteryx* had fully formed bird wings and perching claws. Evolutionists also lack an explanation for their unique lung design.

- The 'earliest' pterosaurs and bats were fully-formed fliers. Furthermore, the 'earliest' bats had fully-developed echolocation.

- The distinctive dinosaur groups lack fossil ancestors; sometimes this is obscured in books by shaded or dotted lines indicating *postulated* ancestors in the absence of fossils.

- The fish-to-tetrapod transition still has many large gaps even with the discovery of *Tiktaalik*. The alleged transitional sequence is out of 'date' order, and is even inconsistent in structural order. The recent Polish footprint discovery put undoubted tetrapods before their claimed fishy 'ancestors'. Also, the common five-digit pattern in tetrapods is adduced as evidence for a common ancestor, but the touted ancestors did not have five digits.

- The whale-from-land-mammal transition leaves major gaps unfilled. There has been conflict about *which* land mammals are ancestral, from mesonychid to artiodactyl: this means that evidence dogmatically adduced as common ancestry with mesonychids must now be explained away as homoplasy. *Pakicetus* was first drawn as a sea creature, based on no bones below the neck, and claimed to be a "perfect intermediate". A more complete skeleton was found, showing that it was a fast-running land mammal. The enormously long *Basilosaurus* had features showing that it could not be ancestral to modern whales.

- Tortoises and turtles have a superb fossil record because of their tough shells, but their ancestors remain an enigma. The earliest representatives had fully-formed shells, leading some evolutionists to conclude that turtles were "hopeful monsters". Even the recently discovered *Odontochelys semitestacea* is hardly convincing; some evolutionary experts believe that it *lost* the carapace, which leaves unexplained where the fully-shelled turtles came from.

- In conclusion, the creatures with the best fossil record have no transitional forms, etc. It is where the fossil record is sparse that evolutionists try to claim examples of transitional fossils. But all it takes is one little discovery and it all unravels. The fossil record overall contradicts evolutionary expectations—that's why Dawkins wants to downplay its significance.

—∞—

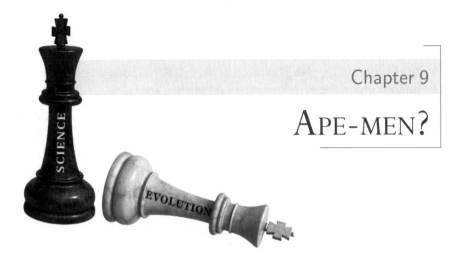

Chapter 9

APE-MEN?

DARWIN'S book *The Descent of Man* proposed that humans evolved from apes. But Alfred Wallace thought that human special abilities were beyond the reach of natural selection, and needed a "Higher Power". Language of even young children would baffle chimps. Children can also put themselves into the perspective of another person, something no chimp can do.

Dawkins argues that similarities and various intermediate fossils support Darwin's totally materialistic view. Dawkins describes his 'debate' with a non-scientist, telling her to "go to a museum" and see all the missing links. Yet there are ways of drawing reconstructions of creatures based on dead bones to make them *appear* transitional. Other alleged ape-human links are based on fragmentary evidence, such as *Ardipithecus ramidus kadabba*.

Detailed analysis of a number of various ape-man candidates shows that they are either fully ape-like or fully human, not transitional or even mosaic. Australopithecines were not ancestral to modern man, and Lucy was a knuckle-walker. *Homo habilis* is a 'taxonomic wastebin'. *Homo erectus* was a variety of *Homo sapiens*, with overlapping cranial capacity and morphology, and even seafaring ability.

Dawkins admits familiarity with CMI's "Don't Use" list when it comes to Java Man (*H. erectus*), but this doesn't stop him knocking down other straw men in the same list.

In his ch. 7: "Missing persons? Missing no longer", Dawkins says:

"Darwin's treatment of human evolution in his most famous work, *On the Origin of Species*, is limited to twelve portentous words: 'Light will be thrown on the origin of man and his history.' ...

"Darwin deliberately deferred his treatment of human evolution to another book, *The Descent of Man*. Perhaps it is not surprising that the two volumes of that later work devote more space to the topic of its subtitle, *Selection in Relation to Sex* (investigated largely in birds), than to human evolution. Not surprising because, at the time of Darwin's writing, there were no fossils at all linking us to our closest relatives among the apes. Darwin had only living apes to look at, and he used them well, arguing correctly (and almost alone) that our closest living relatives were all African (gorillas and chimpanzees—bonobos were not recognized as separate from chimpanzees in those days, but they are African too), and therefore predicting that if ancestral fossils were to be found, Africa was the place to search. Darwin regretted the paucity of fossils, but he maintained a bullish attitude to it. Citing Lyell, his mentor and the great geologist of the time, he pointed out that 'in all the vertebrate class the discovery of fossil remains has been an extremely slow and fortuitous process ... .'" (pp. 183–4)

This inadvertently shows that evolution was accepted for reasons other than fossil evidence. And as shown in the two previous chapters, the fossil record is very rich; it merely lacks the transitional forms predicted by evolution. It's also notable that Darwin's book on human evolution didn't deal much with the title. Then Dawkins goes through a few of the fossils found since then, claiming to show the evolution of man from ape-like ancestors.

Human distinctives

Dawkins doesn't try to explain the origin of such distinctive features of humans that go beyond the physical. In fact, he doesn't even explain much about the physical distinctives such as much greater brain capacity, upright posture and opposable thumbs.

Human v chimp minds

Dawkins shows a baby chimp skull, which is supposed to be more similar to a human baby's than the corresponding adult skulls. But the real difference is the minds. The hugely publicized PBS-Nova 7-part series *Evolution* (2001)[1]— which featured Dawkins among many other prominent evolutionists—tried to explain away the problem.

---

1. See refutation at creation.com/pbs, 2001.

Episode 6 turns to psychologist Andrew Whiten of the University of St Andrews in Scotland, who tested how young children learned. (Incidentally, on the lintel above the entryway to the school, was the Latin *In principio erat Verbum*, the Vulgate translation of John 1:1, 'In the beginning was the Word'.) He tested children with small models of people, where one 'person' puts an object in one place, goes away, then another 'person' takes this object and hides it somewhere else. Then the first 'person' returns, whereupon the child is asked where he or she would look for the object. A 3-year-old suggests the new hiding place, while a 5-year-old correctly realizes that the first 'person' would have no way of knowing that the object had been moved, and would look in the place he left it. (Sometimes this is called the 'Sally-Anne' test, where the 'Sally' doll hides something in the presence of 'Anne'.) Whiten concluded that by the age of three:

"A child cannot ascribe actions to others. But by the age of five, the child's brain has developed the capacity for stepping into someone else's mind."

The program contrasts this with chimpanzees, which are incapable of this at any age, "No chimp has passed the test of attribution of false belief."

Consciousness

How come we are self-aware? Dawkins himself admitted that evolutionists don't have an answer (see ch. 1, p. 27). Richard Gregory, evolutionist and professor of neuropsychology and director of the brain and perception laboratory at the University of Bristol in England, explained the dilemma:

"If the brain was developed by Natural Selection, we might well suppose that consciousness has survival value. But for this it must, surely, have causal effects. But what effects could awareness, or consciousness, have?

"Why, then, do we need consciousness? What does consciousness have that the neural signals (and physical brain activity) do not have? Here there is something of a paradox, for if the awareness of consciousness does not have any effect—if consciousness is not a causal agent—then it seems useless, and so should not have developed by evolutionary pressure. If, on the other hand, it is useful, it must be a causal agent: but then physiological description in terms of neural activity cannot be complete. Worse, we are on this alternative stuck with mentalistic explanations, which seem outside science."[2]

2.   Gregory, R.L. "Consciousness", in: Duncan, R. Anmd Weston-Smith, M. (eds.), The Encyclopaedia of Ignorance, pp. 276–7, Pergamon), 1977.

Language

There are about 6,300 languages in the world today. They all have certain constraints, and obey strict rules, called syntax. This enables us to hierarchically organize information, which is something chimps cannot do, even with the best training in signing.

In particular, non-human primates are incapable of using 'recursion', the process by which concepts are contained within concepts. For example, "He saw that the chimp could not understand him"; "the chimp could not understand him" is the concept within "he saw". Even a child could easily understand this sentence, but it would confuse any ape.[3] A 2006 study on communication in macaque monkeys admits:

> "…these regions [of the brain that in humans are involved in language] are clearly not performing linguistic computations in the macaque".

> It does, though, go on to speculate about possible "prelinguistic functions" that those areas of the brain might serve.[4]

Language doesn't have to be spoken. Deaf people actually process sign language with the same areas of the brain that hearing people use to process spoken language, including Broca's area and Wernicke's area. This is shown by deaf patients who have damage to either area—they have an equivalent type of aphasia (language impairment) in sign language to what a hearing person suffers in spoken language.[5]

Furthermore, to underscore the difference between children and chimps, in Nicaragua, a group of about 500 deaf children developed their own unique sign language. Judy Kegl, a behavioural neuroscientist at Rutgers, describes this as "the first documented case of the birth of a language."[6] An article reports:

> "It displays characteristic rules of grammar such as noun and verb agreement, subject-verb-object sentence construction, and a distinct number of hand-shape and movement building blocks. But in contrast to ASL [American Sign Language], which has been handed down for generations, this new language has sprung from nowhere. 'There is

3. Cosner, L., Monkeying around with the origins of language, creation.com/monkeying, 22 August 2006.
4. Gil-da-Costa, R. *et al.*, Species-specific calls activate homologs of Broca's and Wernicke's areas in the macaque, *Nature Neuroscience* 9:1064–1070, 2006.
5. Hickok, G., Bellugi, U. and Klima, E.S., Sign language in the brain, *Scientific American* **284**(6):42–49, 2001.
6. Radetsky, P., Silence, Signs, and Wonder: What is it about our brains that gives us the capacity for language? Neuroscientist Ursula Bellugi is looking for the answer in a language that evolved in the absence of sound, *Discover*, August 1994; http://discovermagazine.com/1994/aug/silencesignsandw409.

nothing that they could have used as a model,' says Kegl. 'It's clear evidence of an innate language capacity.'"[6]

Evolution of language?

Since true language skills are unique to humans, evolutionists must try to explain their origins. PBS-Nova *Evolution* series interviewed Dawkins himself about the origin of language; it's interesting that the only topic that the *Evolution* series interviewed Dawkins about was language, although his field is biology, not linguistics. True to form, Dawkins resorted to just-so story telling, about how language conferred a selective advantage, so its possessors left more offspring.

However, it's one thing to claim that languages evolved, but it's another to provide a *mechanism*. Evolutionists usually claim that languages evolved from animal grunts. Some even claim that the continuing change of languages is just like biological evolution. However, actual observations of language present a very different picture.

First, ancient languages were actually extremely complex with many different inflections. There is no hint of any build-up from simpler languages. For example, in the Indo-European family, Sanskrit, Classical Greek and Latin had many different noun inflections for different case, gender and number, while verbs were inflected for tense, voice, number and person. Modern descendants of these languages have greatly reduced the number of inflections, i.e. the trend is from complex to simpler, the opposite of evolution. English has almost completely lost inflections, retaining just a few like the possessive "–'s".

English has also lost 65–85% of the Old English vocabulary, and many Classical Latin words have also been lost from its descendants, the Romance languages (Spanish, French, Italian, etc.).

Second, most of the changes were not random, but the result of *intelligence*. For example: forming compound words by joining simple words and derivations, by adding prefixes and suffixes, by modification of meaning, and by borrowing words from other languages including calques (a borrowed compound word where each component is translated and then joined).

There are also unconscious, but definitely non-random, changes such as systematic sound shifts, for example those described by Grimm's Law (which relates many Germanic words to Latin and Greek words).[7,8]

---

7. Steel, A., The development of languages is nothing like biological evolution, *J. Creation* **14**(2), 2000; creation.com/language_development.
8. May, K., Talking Point, *Creation* **23**(2):42–45, March–May 2001; creation.com/talking-point.

Brain: over-designed?

Another problem for evolution is that our brain seems far more complex than would be needed simply for survival. This was a problem for none other than Darwin's co-discoverer Alfred Wallace, who believed that man's higher capacities such as the human spirit, the mind, and the faculties of speech, art, music, mathematics, humour and morality were beyond the reach of natural and sexual selection:[9]

"Natural Selection could only have endowed the savage with a brain a little superior to that of an ape, whereas he actually possesses one but very little inferior to that of the average members of our learned societies."[10]

When Darwin read this, he scribbled "No" in the margin with lots of exclamation marks and triple underlining.

In the same article Wallace added:

"… we must therefore admit the possibility, that in the development of the human race, a Higher Intelligence has guided the same laws [of variation, multiplication, and survival] for nobler ends."[10]

Darwin wrote a letter to Wallace, even before Wallace's paper was published, evidently knowing something of its content: "I hope you have not murdered too completely your own and my child."[11] Afterwards, he wrote to Wallace that he differed grievously from him.[12] Note that Wallace's 'Higher Intelligence' was not the God of the Bible.

Some of this 'over-design' is evident in 'idiot savants', as portrayed by Dustin Hoffman in the film *Rain Man*. These people are normally regarded as mentally handicapped, yet they can display extraordinary abilities in one field such as mathematics, chess, music, or memory. Natural selection would hardly favour such abilities, given that 'normal' folk reproduce just fine without them. Instead, natural selection would be more likely to eliminate mentally handicapped individuals rather than favour these extraordinary but specialist abilities.[13]

However, the main point is that 'idiot savants' demonstrate the extraordinary capacity of the human brain for all manner of incredible mental feats; feats far beyond those needed to be fit to survive.

9. Grigg, R., Alfred Russel Wallace—'co-inventor' of Darwinism, *Creation* 27(4):33–35, 2005; creation.com/wallace

10. Wallace, A., Essay S146: 1869, titled 'Sir Charles Lyell on Geological Climates and the Origin of Species'. Source: www.wku.edu/~smithch/wallace/S146.htm, 18 January 2005.

11. Letter from Darwin to Wallace, March 1869.

12. Letter from Darwin to Wallace, 14 April 1869.

13. Wieland, C., The brain—brainier than believed before, creation.com/brainier, 31 March 2009.

Another good example is the phenomenon of cortical plasticity or neuroplasticity, i.e. 're-wiring' the brain. As shown above, deaf people can put the 'hearing' areas of the brain to other uses. Similarly, when blind people read Braille, the visual areas of the brain are active.[14] But why would natural selection favour such a capacity? Rather, it would eliminate deaf and blind individuals in the first place. Even taking into account caring fellow humans, it would not explain enough, since the group as a whole does not need such a 'backup capacity' to survive, even to thrive.[13]

The above shows a little of how distinct humans are, and how many unique human abilities are beyond the reach of natural selection. But Dawkins concentrates on the physical features and the alleged ape-men.

"Just go and look in a museum"

This is a prime example of the way Dawkins goes for what he thinks are soft targets instead of answering informed opponents of evolution. On pp. 198–202, he presents a transcript of his interview with Wendy Wright, President of Concerned Women for America, who never claimed to be a scientist. Another example was Andy Schlafly (p. 131), editor of *Conservapedia*, who likewise is not a scientist and doesn't pretend to be. The book shows a much more extensive transcript with Miss Wright than what was shown in his Channel 4 documentary *The Genius of Charles Darwin*. It includes the lack of transitional forms:

Wendy: Show it to me, show me the, show me the bones, show me the carcass, show me the evidence of the in-between stages from one species to another.

Richard: Every time a fossil is found which is in between one species and another, you guys say, 'ah, now we've got two gaps there, where there previously was only one.' I mean, every fossil you find is intermediate between something and something else."

Here we have this old saw again. Our response is either: so one super-huge gap is now two huge gaps, leaving the origin of the distinctive features still unexplained. Or: the alleged intermediate is just a variety within the kind, and explains nothing about how the kind evolved. For more, see previous chapter.

Then their debate turns to human origins:

---

14. See also Brain rewires itself in deaf, blind people–U.S. study, www.udel.edu/billf/caudillart.html, 30 November 1998; and this commentary by University of Delaware student in cognitive science, Krista Caudill who is deaf-blind herself, www.udel.edu/billf/caudill.html.

Wendy [laughs]: If that were the case, the Smithsonian Natural History Museum would be filled with these examples but it isn't.

Richard: It is, it is … in the case of humans, since Darwin's time there's now an enormous amount of evidence about intermediates in human fossils and you've got various species of *Australopithecus* for example, and … then you've got *Homo habilis* — these are intermediates between *Australopithecus* which was an older species and *Homo sapiens* which is a younger species. I mean, why don't you see those as intermediates?

Wendy: …if evolution has had the actual evidence then it would be displayed in museums not just in illustrations.

Richard: I just told you about *Australopithecus, Homo habilis, Homo erectus, Homo sapiens*—archaic *Homo sapiens* and then modern *Homo sapiens*—that's a beautiful series of intermediates.

Wendy: You're still lacking the material evidence so ...

Richard: The material evidence is there. Go to the museum and look at it … "I don't have them here, obviously, but you can go to any museum and you can see *Australopithecus,* you can see *Homo habilis,* you can see *Homo erectus,* you can see archaic *Homo sapiens* and modern *Homo sapiens*. A beautiful series of intermediates. Why do you keep saying, 'Present me with the evidence' when I've done so? Go to the museum and look.

Wendy: And I have. I have gone to the museums and there are so many of us who are still not convinced. …

Richard: Have you seen *Homo erectus?* Have you seen *Homo habilis?* Have you seen *Australopithecus?* I've asked you that question.

Wendy: What I've seen is that in the museums and in the textbooks whenever they claim to show the evolutionary differences from one species to another, it relies on illustrations and drawings … not on any material evidence.

Richard: Well you might have to go to the Nairobi Museum to see the original fossils but you can see casts of fossils—exact copies of the fossils in any major museum you care to look at.

But as Miss Wright says, she has been to the museums, as have I. The point is, there is *evidence*, and there are *stories* about the evidence. For comparison, see my written critique of an attempt to link dinosaurs to birds in the Australian National Museum.[15] When it comes to humans, there are also ways to make an evolutionary story.

Fragmentary evidence: case study, *Ardipithecus ramidus kadabba*

Another problem is that claims of intermediate fossils, both 'ape-men' and other creatures, are often based on fragmentary fossil remains, while the museum puts them all together and arranges them in a supposed evolutionary scheme.

For example, *Time* magazine reported on a specimen called *Ardipithecus ramidus kadabba*[16], 'dated' between 5.6 and 5.8 million years old.[17] *Time* claimed that this new specimen was already walking upright, at (what they claim was) the dawn of human evolution:

"But unlike a chimp or any of the other modern apes that amble along on four limbs, *kadabba* almost certainly walked upright much of the time. The inch-long toe bone makes that clear."[17]

Dawkins claims on much the same lines:

"There are a few, albeit rather fragmentary traces. *Ardipithecus*, which lived 4–5 million years ago, is known mainly from teeth, but enough cranial and foot bones have been found to suggest, at least to most anatomists who have attended to it, that it walked upright." (p. 204)

But how clear is this really? *Time* reports the opinion of the discoverer of 'Lucy', Donald Johanson:

"Beyond that, he's dubious about categorizing the 5.2 million-year-old toe bone with the rest of the fossils: not only is it separated in time by several hundred thousand years, but it was also found some 10 miles away from the rest."[17]

Note that this toe was the major 'evidence' for uprightness, yet, at being found ten miles away, it boggles the mind how it could be regarded as part of the same specimen![18] As one researcher put it regarding the fossils and human evolution, "Fossils are fickle. Bones will sing any song you want to hear."[19] When the various fossils are analyzed in depth, they turn out not to be transitional or even mosaic.

15. Skeptics/Australian Museum 'Feathered Dinosaur' display: Knockdown argument against creation? creation.com/dinodisplay, 26 November 2002.
16. The name comes from the local Afar language: *ardi* = ground or floor; *ramid* = root; *kadabba* = basal family ancestor.
17. Lemonick, M.D. and Dorfman, A., One Giant Step for Mankind, *Time* magazine cover story, 23 July 2001.
18. E.g. see Sarfati, J., *Time's* alleged 'ape-man' trips up (again) *J. Creation* **15**(3):7–9, 2001; creation.com/kadabba.
19. Shreeve, J., Argument over a woman, *Discover* **11**(8):58, 1990.

Some of the other fossils Dawkins mentions are based on even flimsier evidence, such as *Orrorin tugenensis* or the 'Millennium Man' (p. 204), based on 13 fossil fragments comprising broken femurs, jaw bones and teeth. Another very 'old' ape-man, *Sahelanthropus tchadensis* or 'Toumaï' (p. 204), might have been a gorilla,[20] and is rejected as a human ancestor by leading evolutionists.[21]

Dawkins says about these last two:

"Other palaeoanthropologists are sceptical of the claims of bipedality that have been made on behalf of *Orrorin* and *Sahelanthropus* by their discoverers. And as a cynic might note, for each such problematic fossil some of the doubters include the discoverers of the others!" (p. 204)

I might note that *all* the doubters are right—humans didn't evolve from *any* of these, because they did not evolve, full stop.

Evolutionary illustrations

Even when the fossil remains are not so fragmentary, there is still much flexibility in illustrating what the living creature might have looked like. For example, leading medical illustrator and creationist Ron Ervin, who has featured on TV shows in Virginia, explains some of the ways that drawings based on bones can be made to look more transitional than they are. He drew for medical textbooks, but the same would apply to museum illustrations:

"I was told to make the illustrations either more or less human or modern—whatever the subject was. I was pleased as an artist to have the freedom to create a drawing no one could question, because they didn't know for sure themselves what the creature looked like. But I was uncomfortable as a Christian to be told that they wanted more 'ape-like' or more 'human-like' qualities."[22]

With fossils, we have *bones*—not hair and skin, let alone their colour; lips or nose. Ervin said that with any illustration of 'normal' anatomy, he can turn it, twist it, and picture it in any position while keeping it anatomically correct. But what about fossils of alleged ape-men? Ervin says:

"With this *Australopithecus* I was told to re-create something that was a big 'maybe', and then make it look believable."[22]

---

20. Chalmers, J., Seven million-year-old skull 'just a female gorilla', *The Sun-Herald* (Sydney), 14 July 2002, www.smh.com.au, 23 August 2004.
21. Wolpoff, M., *et al.*, *Sahelanthropus* or *'Sahelpithecus'*? *Nature* **419**(6907):581–582, 2002.
22. Doolan, R., and Wieland, C., Filling in the blanks: Interview with illustrator Ronald J. Ervin, *Creation* **17**(2):16–18, 1995; creation.com/ervin.

But he originally drew this *Australopithecus* as too human-like for the book's authors. So he was asked to alter his picture to conform to what the evolutionist authors of the biology textbook wanted:

> "I was told to make her more ape-like, or more 'transitional' in appearance. I had been given a cast of a skull, and I was shown some drawings other artists had done of 'Lucy', and was asked to improve on these—to make her look more transitional. I had to make some things up, while keeping the anatomical bones intact, like the temple bone and other features which are standard."

> "I added more body hair, and did another sketch. 'No', they said, 'she's got to have more this and more that.' I just kept adding and subtracting until I got what they wanted."[22]

Ron Ervin's illustration of an australopithecine (like the famous 'Lucy' fossil).He was asked to alter his picture to conform with the evolutionary transitional creature which a biology textbook's authors wanted.

Humans are distinct from australopithecines[23]

Another problem is that visitors to a museum might not pick up anything more than superficial similarities. But when there is enough fossil evidence to analyze carefully, the story doesn't fit Dawkins' neat picture.

There have been a number of fossils classified as *Homo*, and their features are tabulated in Table 9.1 overleaf. If these creatures had been the evolutionary transitional series that Dawkins claims, gradually progressing from australopithecines to modern *Homo sapiens*, this table should show many intermediate features (I). However, these features are either like modern humans (H) or like australopiths (A). In fact, it's even worse for the evolutionist—these creatures do not even qualify as a *mosaic* of australopithecine and *Homo sapiens* attributes. The different creatures do not increase in the number of human traits in this line towards modern man. Rather, the six constellations of traits are either almost always all-human or all-australopithecine.

---

23. Neurologist and biophysicist Dr Peter Line has written a detailed two-part article, in *J. Creation* **19**(1), 2005: Fossil evidence for alleged apemen—Part 1: the genus Homo, pp. 22–32, creation.com/apemen1; Part 2: non-Homo hominids, pp. 33–42, creation.com/apemen2.

Thus the data show that humans are distinct from ape-like creatures such as the australopithecines, as shown by the analysis of a number of characteristics.[24] This indicates that *Homo ergaster, H. erectus, H. neanderthalensis* as well as *H. heidelbergensis*, were most likely 'racial' variants of modern man. Conversely, many specimens classified as *H. habilis* and another specimen called *H. rudolfensis* were just types of australopithecines.[25]

For some years now, many evolutionist specialists have agreed that *H. habilis* ("Handy Man"), one of Dawkins' favourites in his above dialogue, was probably always a phantom taxon with fossils belonging to both *H. erectus/ergaster* and *Australopithecus* thrown together into this 'taxonomic wastebin'. This expression was used in an interview with Dr Fred Spoor, a Dutch-born paleoanthropologist in the UK, and joint editor of the *Journal of Human Evolution*.[26]

The assignments by the evolutionists Wood and Collard (see Table 9.1 below) match those of the slightly earlier ones by creationist paleoanthropologist Dr Sigrid Hartwig-Scherer, research fellow at the Institute for Anthropology and Human Genetics, Ludwig-Maximilian University, Munich. She concluded

Table 9.1: Summary of the results of analyses of characteristics of fossil *Homo* species [After Table 7 in Wood and Collard[24]]. 1) body size, 2) body shape, 3) locomotion, 4) jaws and teeth, 5) development and 6) brain size. H = like modern humans, A = australopith-like, I = intermediate ? = data unavailable.

Species name	1	2	3	4	5	6
H. rudolfensis	?	?	?	A	A	A
H. habilis	A	A	A	A	A	A
H. ergaster	H	H	H	H	H	A
H. erectus	H	?	H	H	?	I
H. heidelbergensis	H	?	H	H	?	A
H. neanderthalensis	H	H	H	H	H	H

that *H. erectus/ergaster*, Neandertals and *H. sapiens* were members of the same basic type (created kind—see ch. 7), Homininae. But she assigned to another basic type, Australopithecinae, the fossils called *Australopithecus afarensis, A. anamensis, A. africanus, A. robustus, A. aethiopithecus, A. boisei* and possibly *Ardipithecus ramidus*.[27]

24. Wood, B. and Collard, M., The human genus, *Science* **284**(5411):65–71, 1999.
25. Woodmorappe, J., The non-transitions in 'human evolution'—on evolutionists' terms, *J. Creation* **13**(2):10–13, 1999; creation.com/non-transitions.
26. Interview on *The Image of God* DVD, Keziah Productions.
27. Hartwig-Scherer, S., Apes or ancestors? ch. 9 of Dembski, Wm. A., *Mere Creation: Science, faith and intelligent design*, Downers Grove, IL, 1998.

Australopithecus africanus and A. afarensis (Lucy)

The above also matches anatomist Charles Oxnard's[28] earlier multivariate analysis of different bones of australopithecines, an objective analysis from which he concluded that it did not walk upright in the human manner and that the australopithecine fossils:

> "clearly differ more from both humans and African apes, than do these two living groups from each other. The australopithecines are unique."[29]

Since creationists have long cited Oxnard, it shows that Dawkins is wrong to say, "If creationist apologists are right, *Australopithecus* is 'just an ape'." Rather, although the name means "Southern Ape" (p. 204), that is not what Oxnard said; he made it clear that *Australopithecus* was not transitional between apes and humans. More recently, Oxnard made the following comments about the australopithecines:

> "It is now recognized widely that the australopithecines are not structurally closely similar to humans, that they must have been living at least in part in arboreal [tree] environments, and that many of the later specimens were contemporaneous [living at the same time] or almost so with the earlier members of the genus *Homo*."[30]

Further, Oxnard showed that the big toe of the famous 'Lucy' (*Australopithecus afarensis*) stuck out as in chimpanzees. Also, Dr Fred Spoor, Professor of Evolutionary Anatomy at University College London, UK, and joint editor of the *Journal of Human Evolution*, performed CAT scans of australopithecine inner ear canals, the organs of posture and balance. This showed that they did not walk habitually upright.[31]

This is all contrary to Dawkins' claim that Lucy "walked upright on her hind legs, as we do ... on two feet which were pretty much like ours although its brain was the size of a chimpanzee's" (pp. 188–9). Indeed, evidence now suggests that Lucy had wrist-locking abilities "classic for knuckle walkers", which is hardly consistent with Dawkins' claim that Lucy walked upright like we do.[32,33]

28. Formerly Professor of Anatomy and Biological Sciences at the University of Southern California, now Professor of Human Anatomy and Human Biology, University of Western Australia.
29. Oxnard, C.E., in *Fossils, Sex and Teeth—New Perspectives on Human Evolution,* University of Washington Press, Seattle and London, p. 227, 1987. Oxnard had previously concluded much the same thing in an earlier paper, The place of the australopithecines in human evolution: grounds for doubt? *Nature* 258:389–395, 4 December 1975 | doi:10.1038/258389a0.
30. Oxnard, C.E., *The Order of Man,* Yale University Press, New Haven, 1984.
31. Spoor, F, Wood, B., and Zonneveld, F., Implications of early hominid morphology for evolution of human bipedal locomotion, *Nature* **369**(6482):645–648, 1994.
32. Stokstad, E., Hominid ancestors may have knuckle walked, *Science* **287**(5461):2131, 2000, citing the first author of Richmond, B.G. and Strait, D.S., Evidence that humans evolved from a knuckle-walking ancestor, *Nature* **404**(6776):382, 2000.
33. See also Oard, M., Did Lucy walk upright, *J. Creation* **15**(2):9–10, 2001; creation.com/lucy.

Museum illustrations now discarded

Another problem for Dawkins' browbeating is that many exhibits of "human evolution" once shown are no longer regarded as human ancestors. It's not just the obvious ones such as Nebraska Man (based on a single tooth of a pig) and Piltdown Man (hoax). Some far more respectable examples have now been demoted and removed.

My colleague Dr Carl Wieland remembers when he was about nine years old being strongly influenced by *National Geographic's* touting *Zinjanthropus boisei* ('Nutcracker Man') as a human ancestor, which is completely discounted today. More recently, when I was in high school, *Ramapithecus* was taught as a human ancestor, but now it's thought to be a variety of orangutan.

This applies to many other alleged missing links. Evolutionist Derek Ager admits:

> "It must be significant that nearly all the evolutionary stories I learned as a student, from Trueman's *Ostrea/Gryphaea* to Carruthers' *Zaphrentis delanouei*, have now been 'debunked'. Similarly, my own experience of more than twenty years looking for evolutionary lineages among the Mesozoic Brachiopoda has proved them equally elusive."[34]

Museums once featured *Australopithecus africanus* as an ancestor to humans—*A. africanus* includes "Mrs Ples" (now thought to be a small "Mr Ples") and the Taung child (Dawkins pp. 189–193). Donald Johanson, the discoverer of 'Lucy', places *Australopithecus africanus* in a side-branch not leading to man[35] and many museums have now demoted this once certain human ancestor to a non-ancestor.

As we saw above, Charles Oxnard is one of several experts who do not believe that *any* of the australopithecines were on the human line, contrary to what Dawkins told Wendy Wright. However, museums will not remove all the australopithecines, like they should; this is because their displays of 'human evolution' will collapse without them.

Two rival evolutionary views

There are two major evolutionary views of the origin of modern man. As Dawkins says, they follow Darwin's advice that we should look for our ancestors in Africa. One major theory is called the 'Out of Africa' or single-origin model, or even the 'Noah's Ark model'. This states that modern humans came out of Africa and replaced less evolved hominids that had emerged from

---

34. Ager, D.V., The nature of the fossil record, *Proceedings of the Geologists' Association*, **87**(2):131–160, 1976.
35. Johanson D.C. and White T. D., A Systematic Assessment of Early African Hominids, *Science* 203:321-330, 1979.

Africa much earlier. But there is another evolutionary idea, called the 'multi-regional' or 'regional-continuity' model, or even the 'Noah's Sons' model. This proposes that the hominids that allegedly emerged from Africa 2 million years ago evolved into modern humans separately in many parts of the world.

This is one of the most vitriolic debates among paleoanthropologists—the acrimony between the proponents of these rival theories is due, according to the anthropologist Peter Underhill, of Stanford University, to: "Egos, egos, egos. Scientists are human." I think that *both* sides are right—in their criticisms of each other—because humans did not evolve at all![36]

Dr Hartwig-Scherer has proposed a single-origin model that fits in with a human basic type, and is consistent with human migration patterns after the Babel dispersion described in Genesis 11:

"Three migration waves may have occurred originating from the Afro-Arabian shield. During the first migration, a population with unknown morphology spread into different directions and developed the typical *ergaster* morphology in Africa and *erectus* traits in Southeast Asia. A second migration wave produced the Neanderthal morphology in the comparatively isolated Europe. Finally, a third migration wave filled the world with modern *Homo sapiens*. The mosaic features, a combination of Pleistocene forms, may be considered the consequence of either hybridization between members of the different migration waves or the expression of hidden traits in the (polyvalent?) ancestral gene pool or a mixture of both."[37]

Homo erectus

Dawkins notes that the first 'missing links' were found in Asia rather than Africa, contrary to what Darwin predicted (pp. 184–5). One of the famous ones was 'Java Man', which Dutch anthropologist Eugène Dubois (1858–1940) discovered in 1891 in Trinil, in what is now Indonesia. This is now called *Homo erectus,* but named by its discover as *Pithecanthropus erectus.* This name meant 'erect ape-man', showing that Dubois thought he had found the missing link between apes and humans.

Dawkins informs us about the egos involved in these discoveries, and things have hardly been different since:

"Fiercely protective about, not to say protective of, his fossil, Dubois believed that only Java Man was the true missing link. To emphasise

---

36. For an explanation of both the out of Africa and regional-continuity ideas and a biblical alternative, see Wieland, C., No bones about Eve, *Creation* **13**(4):20–23, September–November 1991; creation.com/eve2; and Hartwig-Scherer, Ref. 27.
37. Hartwig-Scherer, Ref. 27, pp. 229–230.

the distinction from the various Peking Man fossils, he described them as far closer to modern man, and his own Java Man of Trinil as an intermediate between man and ape [citing Dubois:].

'*Pithecanthropus* [Java Man] was not a man, but a gigantic genus allied to the gibbons, however superior to the gibbons on account of its exceedingly large brain volume and distinguished at the same time by its faculty of assuming an erect attitude and gait. It had the double cephalisation [ratio of brain size to body size] of the anthropoid apes in general and half that of a man. ...

'It was the surprising volume of the brain—which is very much too large for an anthropoid ape, and which is small compared with the average, though not smaller than the smallest human brain—that led to the almost general view that the "Ape Man" of Trinil, Java, was really a primitive man. Morphologically, however, the calvaria [skullcap] closely resembles that of anthropoid apes, especially the gibbon.'"

However, *Homo erectus* was just a variety of real human. This was shown by the morphological analysis of various traits, which are all human except supposedly for the 'intermediate' brain size (see Table on p. 156). But even in this trait, their cranial vault size overlapped with that of modern people,[38] as even Dubois admitted above.

Contrary to Dubois' claim, It was shown to have a "strikingly modern feature",[39] a strongly bent or "flexed" cranial base. The paleoanthropologist Dan Lieberman of Harvard University said:

"This is an important find because it is the first *H. erectus* find with a reasonably complete cranial base, and it looks modern."[39]

Of course, Lieberman would see *H. erectus* as a human ancestor, but this evidence is consistent with *H. erectus* being just a variant of the human created kind.

And as recently as 2001, Wolpoff *et al.* showed that the features of various human skulls indicated that there must have been interbreeding among 'modern-looking' *Homo sapiens* and Neanderthals and even *Homo erectus*.[40]

The cultural abilities of *H. erectus* are also strong evidence of their humanity. They even had evidence of seafaring skills! This was shown by butchered elephant bones on a small Indonesian island, too small and

38. Woodmorappe, J., How different is the cranial vault thickness of *Homo erectus* from modern man? *J. Creation* **14**(1):10–13, 2000; creation.com/cranium.
39. Gibbons, A., Java skull offers new view of *Homo erectus*, *Science* **299**(5611):1293, 28 February 2003.
40. Wolpoff, M., *et al.*, Modern human ancestry at the peripheries: A test of the replacement theory, *Science* **291**(5502):293–297, 12 Jan 2001; comment by Pennisi, E., p. 231, Skull study targets Africa-only origins.

resource-poor to sustain a settlement, with tools and dating that identify *'Homo erectus'* as the only candidate (in evolutionists' minds) for the butcher, but the island had to be reached by boat over quite a stretch of deep water.[41,42,43] Thus there must have been migration of *H. erectus* from island to island, across straits ranging in size from several kilometres to a few tens of kilometres, and quite deep water. The islands involved included Lombok, Bali, Sumbawa, and Flores.[44] Clearly, *H. erectus* must have crossed the straits that separate the islands, and this implies at least some seafaring ability. And according to conventional dates, this happened some 800,000 years ago. The original researchers wrote:

> "Furthermore, they [our findings] indicate that, somewhere between 800,000 and 900,000 years ago, *Homo erectus* in this region had acquired the capacity to make water crossings."[44]

The seafaring skills of *H. erectus* were also highlighted by the noted 'multi-regional' advocate Wolpoff as support for his views. Interestingly, the ardent 'out of Africa' advocate Chris Stringer said that these seafaring skills would be evidence that *H. erectus* "was more human, just like us." Indeed.

Arguments creationists should not use

Dawkins makes a curious detour after quoting Dubois above:

> "It can't have improved Dubois' temper that others took him to be saying that *Pithecanthropus* was just a giant gibbon, not intermediate between them and humans at all, and he was at pains to reassert his earlier stand: 'I still believe, now more firmly than ever, that the *Pithecanthropus* of Trinil is the real "missing link".'

> "Creationists from time to time used as a political weapon the allegation that Dubois backed off from his claim that *Pithecanthropus* was an intermediate ape-man. The creationist organization Answers in Genesis has, however, added it to their list of discredited arguments which they now say should not be used. It is to their credit that they maintain such a list at all." (p. 185)

It's nice that Dawkins gives credit for maintaining such a list, although it should be given to *Creation Ministries International*,[45] since I was the

41. Morwood, P.B. *et al.*, Fission-track ages of stone tools and fossils on the east Indonesian island of Flores, *Nature* **392**(6672):173–176, 12 March 1998.
42. *New Scientist* **157**(2125):6, 14 March 1998; based on Morwood *et al.*, Ref. 41.
43. See also *Creation* **21**(1):9, 1998.
44. Bednarik, R.G., Hobman, B. and Rogers, P., Nale Tasih 2: journey of a Middle Palaeolithic raft, *Int.J.Nautical Archaeology* **28**(1)25–33, 1999.
45. Arguments we think creationists should NOT use; creation.com/dontuse.

anonymous author of most of it (before our Australian ministry, and three others bearing the same name, rebranded in 2006).[46] The list says:

> **"'Dubois renounced Java man as a "missing link" and claimed it was just a giant gibbon.'** Evolutionary anthropology textbooks claimed this, and creationists followed suit. However, this actually misunderstood Dubois, as Stephen Jay Gould has shown. It's true that Dubois claimed that Java man (which he called *Pithecanthropus erectus*) had the proportions of a gibbon. But Dubois had an eccentric view of evolution (universally discounted today) that demanded a precise correlation between brain size and body weight. Dubois' claim about Java man actually *contradicted* the reconstructed evidence of its likely body mass. But it was necessary for Dubois' idiosyncratic proposal that the alleged transitional sequence leading to man fit into a mathematical series. So Dubois' gibbon claim was designed to *reinforce* its 'missing link' status."

And the 'Don't Use' list referred to an article from 1991, showing that it's hardly news. However, we wonder how much of the article Dawkins has read, since it also says:

> "Many of these arguments have never been promoted by CMI, and some have not been promoted by any major creationist organization (so they were not directed at anyone in particular), but are instead straw men set up by anti-creationists.

> "It is notable that some skeptics criticise creationists when they retract doubtful arguments, but these are also the same people who accuse creationists of being unwilling to change their minds!"

The first paragraph in particular describes Dawkins, since his book contains many of the straw men specifically addressed in this list, such as (quoting whole sections):

> **"'If we evolved from apes, why are there still apes today?'** [cf. Dawkins p. 155] In response to this statement, some evolutionists point out that they don't believe that we descended from apes, but that apes and humans share a common ancestor. However, the evolutionary paleontologist G.G. Simpson had no time for this 'pussyfooting', as he called it. He said, 'In fact, that earlier ancestor would certainly be called an ape or monkey in popular speech by anyone who saw it. Since the terms ape and monkey are defined by popular usage, man's ancestors

---

46. As shown in the accompanying DVD in Ref. 45, and the relatively condensed version, Sarfati, J., Moving forward: Arguments we think creationists shouldn't use, *Creation* **24**(2):20–24, 2002.

were apes or monkeys (or successively both). It is pusillanimous if not dishonest for an informed investigator to say otherwise.'"

However, the main point against this statement is that many evolutionists believe that a small group of creatures split off from the main group and became reproductively isolated from the main large population, and that most change happened in the small group which can lead to *allopatric speciation* (a geographically isolated population forming a new species—see p. 37). So there's nothing in evolutionary theory that requires the main group to become extinct.

It's important to note that allopatric speciation is not the sole property of evolutionists—creationists believe that most human variation occurred after small groups became isolated (but not speciated) at Babel, while Adam and Eve probably had mid-brown skin colour. The quoted erroneous statement is analogous to saying, 'If all people groups came from Adam and Eve, then why are mid-brown people still alive today?'

So what's the difference between the creationist explanation of people *groups* ('races') and the evolutionist explanation of people *origins*? Answer: the former involves separation of already-existing information and loss of information through mutations; the latter requires the generation of tens of millions of 'letters' of *new* information.

'There are no transitional forms.' [Dawkins ch. 6] Since there are *candidates*, even though they are highly dubious, it's better to avoid possible comebacks by saying instead: 'While Darwin predicted that the fossil record would show numerous transitional fossils, even 140 years later, all we have are a handful of disputable examples.'"

But then, if Dawkins removed those straw men, his book would be only a fraction of its size and hardly convincing, even for his fans who want to be convinced.

Summary

- Human non-physical attributes are well beyond those of chimps. Even Alfred Russel Wallace thought that natural selection could not explain many human special abilities such as art, music, mathematics, humour and morality.
- Young children can use real language, including recursion (concepts within concepts), beyond the capacity of the smartest chimp. Deaf children have even invented their own language, whereas it is difficult to even teach a chimp very rudimentary sign language.

- Even a 5-year-old child can put himself in another person's mind, something no chimp can do.

- The human brain is capable of considerable 're-wiring' after injury or physical disability. But natural selection would have eliminated such a badly injured individual in nature before their recovery.

- Dawkins' chapter on "Missing persons" shows his proclivities for attacking soft targets and knocking down straw men. He browbeats the president of Concerned Women for America to go and look at the missing links in the museum, but she already had, and is aware of the limitations of museum presentations.

- Some of the ape-man candidates are based on very fragmentary remains, such as *Ardipithecus* and *Orrorin*.

- Artists are told to make their drawings look 'more transitional'; there is plenty of leeway since skin, hair, lips and noses are not fossilized.

- The more plausible candidates have either almost all human traits, or almost all australopithecine traits. They lack intermediate traits, and don't even show mosaic traits.

- Australopithecines are more different from both humans and apes than they are from each other, so are a distinct type of creature. Some evolutionists reject them as human ancestors. Lucy was a knuckle walker which did not walk like humans at all.

- Many highly promoted human ancestors are now believed—by evolutionists—to be on a side branch (not human ancestors). This includes *Zinjanthropus boisei* and *Australopithecus africanus*.

- *Homo erectus,* including Java Man, was just a post-Babel variety of *Homo sapiens*, and had seafaring ability, for example.

- Dubois did not renounce Java Man as a missing link. Dawkins gives credit to the CMI-authored list of "Arguments that creationists should not use" that advises against this argument. But this doesn't stop him knocking down a number of other straw men that the list shows are not arguments that creationist scientists use.

—∞—

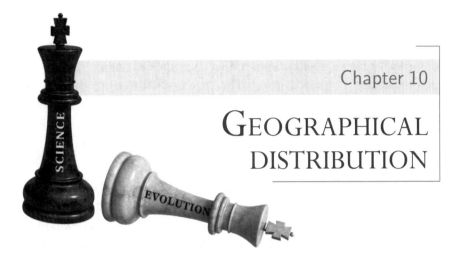

GEOGRAPHICAL DISTRIBUTION

Dawkins' ch. 9 is "Ark of the Continents", and first discusses speciation via isolation, then argues that the geographical distribution (biogeography) of plants and animals supports evolution. Darwin invoked the distribution of living organisms across the world as evidence of evolution. In reality, this distribution was only a problem for the unbiblical view that species were created unchanging and in their current location. It is compatible with the biblical model of dispersion after the Flood.

Also, Darwin presupposed a *fixed* distribution of continents. But Dawkins regards geographical distribution as strong evidence for evolution on a *moving* continents model. Yet there are anomalies here too, such as similar species separated across oceans, but supposedly evolving long after the continents split.

Dawkins' favoured slow-and-gradual model of plate tectonics has a number of problems, such as insufficient energy, and the presence of still-cool deep slabs of subducted crust. But these 'problems' are mostly solved by a catastrophic plate tectonics model, which is also a possible explanation for many aspects of the biblical Flood.

Darwin *vs* a faulty creation model

To understand Darwin's reasoning properly, it is necessary to be aware of what he was reacting to. The main rival view at the time was Fixity of Species, but as already mentioned, this did not come from the Bible but from ancient Greek philosophy. In particular, Darwin took issue with one of his own mentors, Charles Lyell. To explain the limited geographical distribution of various species, Lyell proposed that each species had a 'centre of creation' in a habitat best designed for it. The species would sometimes go extinct as the habitat changed over the vast eons he advocated, so he proposed different creative episodes over time.[1] Lyell specifically rejected pre-Darwinian ideas of evolution, such as those of Jean Baptiste Lamarck (1744–1829); but both of them referred to it by the more logical term *transmutation of species*.

However, Darwin showed that the Galápagos Islands contained the same types of animals that inhabited Ecuador, but with clear differences between the island varieties and mainland ones. This was hard to explain even under an expanded creation radius. So Darwin discredited this unbiblical model, and eventually won over Lyell.

Biblical model unaffected

The biblical model is very different from Darwin's straw-man target. The Bible teaches that a global flood wiped out all land vertebrates outside Noah's Ark; such would have totally rearranged the earth's surface. As shown in ch. 7, there is good geological evidence for this in the fossils and sedimentary layers.

This drastic geographical rearrangement means that there's no way that anything could have been created in its present location. Also, all modern land vertebrates would be descendants of those which disembarked from the Ark in the mountains of Ararat—over generations, they migrated to their present locations. It should therefore be no surprise to biblical creationists that animals on the Galápagos Islands would be similar to those in northwestern South America—they migrated to the islands *via* this continent.

How did animals get to remote islands?

Dawkins knocks down a quasi-Lyellian straw-man model of creation to mock the biblical account, in a number of examples.

Australian marsupials

Dawkins says:

"… an even more famous example is the Australian mammal fauna. In Australia, there are, or were until recent extinctions possibly caused by the arrival of the aboriginal people, the ecological equivalents of wolves, cats, rabbits, moles, shrews, lions, flying squirrels and many others.

1. Bowler, P.J., *Evolution: The History of an Idea*, University of California Press, 2003. Prof. Peter Bowler was featured in the documentary *The Voyage that Shook the World* (2009).

Yet they are marsupials, quite different from the wolves, cats, rabbits, moles, shrews, lions and flying squirrels with which we are familiar in the rest of the world, the so-called placental mammals. The Australian equivalents are all descended from just a few, or even one, ancestral marsupial species, 'taken or modified for different ends' [quoting Darwin]. This beautiful marsupial fauna has produced creatures for which it is harder to find a counterpart outside Australia. The many species of kangaroo mostly fill antelope-like niches (or monkey or lemur-like niches in the case of the tree kangaroos) but get around by hopping rather than galloping. They range from the large red kangaroo (and some even larger extinct ones, including a fearsome, bounding carnivore) to the small wallabies and tree kangaroos. There were other giant, rhinoceros-sized marsupials, Diprotodonts, related to modern wombats but 3 yards long, 6 feet tall at the shoulder, and weighing 2 tons." (p. 268)

How flexible evolutionary theory must be: the Australian niches are so similar to those elsewhere that mutation + selection produced such amazingly similar features in unrelated mammal classes. But then they produced such dramatic differences in kangaroo locomotion (compared to quadruped placental grazers). See also ch. 6.

There is a lot of assertion above, such as the wide variety of marsupials evolving from one or a few. However, biblical creationists would have no problem with all varieties of kangaroos being one created kind, as opposed to the fixity-of-species straw-man idea.

Dawkins continues, in a more overt straw-man argument:

"It is almost too ridiculous to mention, but I'm afraid I have to because of the 40 per cent of the American population, who ... accept the Bible literally:[2] think what the geographical distribution of animals should look like if they'd all dispersed from Noah's Ark. Shouldn't there be some sort of law of decreasing species diversity as we move away from an epicentre—perhaps Mount Ararat? I don't need to tell you that that is not what we see." (p. 268)

Why should we expect this? Yes, certainly if we were looking a short time after the beginning of the dispersion, but not necessarily thousands

---

2.   I don't know anyone who does: rather, informed creationists accept the Bible in a *textualist/originalist* way, using the grammatical and historical context to work out *what the Bible meant to its original audience.* So we interpret parts of the Bible in a historical narrative genre as history, the poetic parts as poetry, figurative language as figurative.

of years later. Competition pressures may force some kinds of animals to migrate away from the epicentre, so over time diversity near the epicentre would decrease.

Also, Dawkins' own book points out that speciation occurs most commonly with geographical isolation. A mountainous region would be ideal to isolate small populations from each other as they diverged, producing new species. Dawkins' questions about presumed creationist expectations presupposes the fixity of species.

We can see the fallacy of Dawkins' claims in more recent times. Early settlers released a very small number of rabbits in a small area of Australia. Wild rabbits are now found at the very opposite corner of (in fact, nearly all over) this vast continent. There is not the slightest trace of "a law of decreasing species diversity as we move away from an epicentre".

How did animals get to Australia?[3]
Then Dawkins asks:

> "Why would all those marsupials—ranging from tiny pouched mice through koalas and bilbys to giant kangaroos and Diprotodonts—why would all those marsupials but no placentals at all, have migrated en masse to Australia? What route did they take? And why did not a single member of their straggling caravan pause along the way, and perhaps settle—in India, perhaps, or China, or some haven along the Great Silk Road?" (pp. 268–9)

The ancestors of present-day kangaroos possibly did spread out across the world. In the process, they may have left "straggler" populations in several parts of the world, but most of these populations subsequently became extinct. Perhaps those marsupials only survived in Australia because they migrated there ahead of the placental mammals, and were then isolated from the placentals and so protected from competition and predation.

Just because an animal was not fossilized, doesn't mean it didn't once live in a region. There is ample historical evidence that lions once lived in the Middle East, from both biblical and other records, but none live there today and there are no fossil lions from the area. Furthermore, millions of bison that once roamed the United States of America have left virtually no fossils. So why should it be a surprise that small populations, presumably under migration pressure from competitors and/or predators, and thus living in any one area for a few generations at most, should leave no fossils?

3. For a more detailed answer, see Batten, D., (contributing editor), Catchpoole, D., Sarfati, J., and Wieland, C., Chapter 17: How did the animals get to Australia?, *Creation Answers Book*, Creation Book Publishers, 2008; creation.com/cab.

Another explanation is that humans selectively moved them. They may have chosen marsupials because they are mostly nocturnal and can retain dormant young in their pouches.[4]

Transport by humans may explain the Falklands Island Wolf (*Dusicyon australis*), which perplexed Darwin himself. How did it manage to cross 500 km from Argentina to the archipelago, which has no other native mammals, even rodents? Unfortunately, the last one was shot in 1876. Recent research has not really solved the problem:

> "Because the islands were never connected to the mainland, the Falklands wolf must have crossed the sea from South America by clinging to logs or an ice floe, the researchers conclude."[5]

These researchers ruled out human involvement, because their (fallacious) dating of the genetic split of the wolves from their closest relatives on the mainland (the maned wolf *Chrysocyon brachyurus*) predates any possible human involvement. Yet as shown in ch. 11, these dating methods have many flaws. And apart from 'dating', there is nothing against human involvement with bringing distinctive fauna to Australia.

However, if evolutionists can propose that wolves drifted across 500 km of sea to the Falklands, I don't see why it is such a problem for marsupials to cross the lesser water barrier between south-east Asia and Australia (remembering that this would have been at a minimum at the peak of the post-Flood Ice Age).

Problems for evolutionary view

The currently popular evolutionary view has problems explaining the distribution of marsupials, for example. They are not mainly in Australia 'because they evolved there'. Evolutionists have to concede that 'earlier' (by their own timeline) marsupials once lived *exclusively* in Europe, Asia and North America (in profusion in the latter), but now are largely absent (except for opossums in the Americas). Two evolutionists admit:

> "Living marsupials are restricted to Australia and South America … In contrast, metatherian [marsupial] fossils from the Late Cretaceous are exclusively from Eurasia and North America … This geographical switch remains unexplained."[6]

Actually, it's even more of a problem: living marsupials can also be found in Papua New Guinea (north of Australia) and westwards from there

4. Woodmorappe, J., Causes for the Biogeographic Distribution of Land Vertebrates After the Flood. *Proc. Second ICC,* Pittsburg, pp. 361–367, 1990.
5. Morell, V., Whence the Falklands Wolf? *ScienceNOW Daily News*, 2 November 2009.
6. Cifelli, R.L., and Davis, B.M., Marsupial origins, *Science* 302:1899–1900, 2003.

into Indonesia—even on the major Indonesian island of Sulawesi.[7] And the Australian possum now also lives in New Zealand due to human help, where it is seen as a major pest. And it is much more similar to the rare Chilean opossum *Dromiciops* (or *Monito del Monte,* Spanish for "little mountain monkey") than *Dromiciops* is similar to other South American marsupials.[8,9,10]

Similarly, monotremes, or egg-laying mammals (platypus and spiny anteater) were once thought to be unique to Australia. But the discovery in 1991 of a fossil platypus tooth in South America was a shock to the scientific community.[11]

As for placentals, it turns out that they were in Australia from an early stage rather than recent arrivals (according to evolutionary 'dating'), shown by a fossil allegedly 120 million years old. So now some evolutionists suggest that placentals might have evolved first in the southern hemisphere, migrated north, and then disappeared 'down under'.[12] So what's wrong with most marsupials dying out elsewhere?

Lemurs in Madagascar

Dawkins writes, in a glaring example of knocking down the fixity-of-species straw man, as well as a straw-man form of the biblical post-Flood dispersion model:

"An ancestral lemur, again very possibly just a single species, found itself in Madagascar. Now there are thirty-seven species of lemur (plus some extinct ones). They range in size from the pygmy mouse lemur, smaller than a hamster, to a giant lemur, larger than a gorilla and resembling a bear, which went extinct quite recently. And they are all, every last one of them, in Madagascar. There are no lemurs anywhere else in the world, and there are no monkeys in Madagascar. How on Earth do the 40 per cent history-deniers think this state of affairs came about? Did all thirty-seven or more species of lemur troop in body down Noah's gangplank and hightail it (literally in the case of the ringtail) for

7. Weston, P. and Wieland, C., The Sulawesi Bear Cuscus, *Creation* **24**(3):28–30, 2002).
8. Allaby, M., Dromiciopsia, in A Dictionary of Zoology, Oxford University Press, 1999; encyclopedia.com.
9. This is a member of a 'clade' (Microbiotheria) earlier thought to have become extinct more than ten million years ago. Lobos, G. *et al.*, Presence of *Dromiciops gliroides* (Microbiotheria: Microbiotheriidae) in the deciduous forests of central Chile, *Mammalian Biology—Zeitschrift für Saugetierkunde* **70**(6):376–380, 2005.
10. Catchpoole, D., The 'Lazarus effect': rodent 'resurrection'! *Creation* **29**(2):52–55, 2007; creation.com/lazarus.
11. Platypus tooth bites hard into long-held beliefs, *Creation* **14**(1):13, 1992; based on *New Scientist*, 24 August 1991.
12. Flannery, T., Forum: A Hostile Land—Could One Tiny Fossil Overthrow Australia's Orthodoxy? *New Scientist* **157**(2116):47, 10 January 1998.

Madagascar, leaving not a single straggler by the wayside, anywhere throughout the length and breadth of Africa?" (p. 269)

Of course, the biblical model would suggest just what Dawkins suggests we deny, but this is nothing new. That is, a single ancestral lemur population, descended from a single lemur pair on the Ark, arrived in Madagascar and diversified into all the new vacant niches.

And most likely there were stragglers in other parts of Africa, but no traces are left of them, simply because they were not rapidly buried.

Meanwhile Dawkins ignores the very stark difficulties that Madagascar's lemurs present to evolutionists. In addition to the lack of fossil transitional forms[13] and other "awkward" fossil evidence,[14,15] the whole area of lemur taxonomy, and particularly how the very distinctive aye-aye might relate (in an evolutionary sense) to 'other' lemurs, has been described as "notoriously problematic".[16] And evolutionists themselves have the problem of explaining how lemurs crossed the huge stretch of deep ocean to Madagascar, as, to be consistent with their evolutionary time-frame, they have to assume that the island was in its present place before these creatures arrived.

Hence their suggestion that "the only possible means of access to Madagascar was by 'rafting': floating across the Mozambique Channel from Africa on matted tangles of vegetation."[17]

Of course, if creationists had said that these mammals hitched a ride across hundreds of kilometres of open sea on huge floating islands, it would have been ridiculed as special pleading. In relation to discussion of how animals dispersed after Noah's Flood, the reality of such transport possibilities is a valuable concession by evolutionists—of which Dawkins appears to be unaware (or perhaps would rather ignore?).

Marine iguanas in the Galápagos
Dawkins discusses these creatures that fascinated but also disgusted Darwin:[18]

13. Sarfati, J., Micro-primates ... a transitional form or just heel-bone hype? creation.com/microprimates, 22 March 2000.
14. Trivedi, B., Do Pakistan fossils alter path of lemur evolution?, *National Geographic Today*, news. nationalgeographic.com/news/2001/10/1022_TVlemur.html, 22 October 2001.
15. Out of Asia?, *Creation* **28**(3):11, 2006; creation.com/asia.
16. Horvath, J. *et al.*, Development and application of a phylogenomic toolkit: Resolving the evolutionary history of Madagascar's lemurs, *Genome Research* 18:489–499, 2008.
17. Tattersall, I., Madagascar's lemurs, *Scientific American*, January 1993, pp. 90–97; Hitchhiking lemurs, *Creation* **15**(4):11, 1993.
18. Hennigan, T., Darwin's 'imps of darkness': the marine iguanas of the Galápagos, *Creation* **31**(2): 28–30, 2009.

"Since marine iguanas are so good at swimming, it might be supposed that they, rather than the land iguanas, made the long crossing from the mainland and subsequently speciated, in the archipelago, to give rise to the land iguana. This is almost certainly not the case, however. The Galápagos land iguana is not greatly different from iguanas still living on the mainland, while the marine iguanas are unique to the Galápagos archipelago. No lizard with the same marine habits has ever been found elsewhere in the world. We are nowadays confident that it was the land iguana that originally arrived from South America, perhaps carted on driftwood like the modern ones from Guadeloupe that were blown to Anguilla.[19] On Galápagos, they subsequently speciated to give rise to the marine iguana.

"And it was almost certainly the geographical isolation permitted by the spaced-out pattern of the islands that made possible the initial separation between the ancestral land iguanas and the newly speciating marine iguanas. Presumably some land iguanas were accidentally rafted across to a hitherto iguana-free island, and there adopted a marine habit, free from contamination by genes from the land iguanas on the original island. Much later, they spread out to other islands, eventually returning to the island from which their land ancestors had originally hailed. By now they could no longer interbreed with them, and their genetically inherited marine habits were safe from contamination by land iguana genes." (pp. 261–2)

We can agree that the marine iguana came from land iguanas, much like Dawkins says. But he is just wrong that they can no longer interbreed: the marine iguana (genus *Amblyrhynchus*) and female land iguana (genus *Conolophus*) can form viable hybrids—even though they belong not only to different species but different genera.[20,21] Naturally Dawkins didn't expect this, because of his millions-of-years dogma, but it makes sense if the marine iguana diverged only in the last few thousand years.

Plate tectonics

Evolution does not explain the geographical distribution as well as Darwin thought. But he was restricted to a fixed continent model. Yet some very

---

19. See Surfing lizards wipe out objections, *Creation* **21**(2):7–9, 1999. This shows that animals could have migrated to quite distant islands on flotsam after the Flood.
20. Rassmann, K. *et al.*, Tracing the Evolution of the Galápagos Iguanas, in: *Iguanas: Biology and Conservation,* pp. 71–83, University of California Press, 2004.
21. There is good footage of the hybrid in the documentary *The Voyage that Shook the World* (2009), and interviews with evolutionists who were surprised that a hybrid was possible.

similar species are separated on different continents across thousands of miles of ocean. These are called *disjunct distributions,* and the phenomenon is called *range fragmentation.*

Modern evolutionists such as Dawkins claim that plate tectonics explains these, and that this evidence provides strong support for long ages. That is, the earth once contained one land mass, which broke up. The large fragments separated to form today's continents. Supposedly they always moved as slowly as today, carried on giant convection currents of semi-molten rock below the crust (*Greatest Show*, pp. 273–83). And these fragments carried separate groups from the same ancestral population, explaining their similarity.

There are many problems with the slow-and-gradual model, but many would be solved if the movement was much quicker at one time—catastrophic plate tectonics, discussed below (p. 177); i.e. instead of 'continental *drift*' it was once a 'continental *sprint*'. However, first it's worth discussing some problems with geographic distribution with the model of gradual continental drift over millions of years.

Biogeographical anomalies[22]

For continental drift to explain the disjunct populations, obviously the ancestral group must have arisen before the split. Yet even according to evolutionary dating, many of them arose in the different locations long after the land was separated.[23,24] For example, species of cactus, which supposedly evolved in South America 30 million years ago, are also found in Africa, yet these continents are said to have separated 70 million years before. The same applies to rodents and a number of other creatures, also found on both continents, yet are meant to have emerged long after the separation.[25]

Furthermore, continental drift doesn't explain disjunct species that are often found on continents that never bordered one another. For example, many plants and insects display range fragmentation across the Pacific Ocean.[26,27]

22. Thanks to Dominic Statham, *Evolution: Good Science? Exposing the Ideological Nature of Darwin's Theory,* ch. 6, Day One, UK, 2009; Biogeography, *J. Creation* **24**(1)72–77, 2010.
23. George, W. and Lavocat, R., The Africa–South America Connection, p. 159, Clarendon Press, Oxford, 1993.
24. Davis, C.C. *et al.,* High-Latitude Tertiary Migrations of an Exclusively Tropical Clade: Evidence from Malpighiaceae, *International Journal of Plant Sciences* **165**(4):S107–S121, 2004; people.fas.harvard.edu/~ccdavis/pdfs/Davis_et_al_IJPS_2004.pdf.
25. George and Lavocat, Ref. 23, ch. 9.
26. Thorne, R., Major Disjunctions in the Geographic Ranges of Seed Plants, *Quarterly Review of Biology* **47**(4): 365–411, 1972.
27. Buffalo Museum of Science (New York), Panbiogeography: Pacific Basin Tracks, sciencebuff.org/pacific_basin_tracks.php.

There are many other examples where the similarities of disjunct species don't match the pattern expected by evolution and slow continental drift. For example, animals in central and southern Africa are closer to those of southern Asia than those of northern Africa.[28] Plants in Madagascar are remarkably similar to the flora of Indonesia rather than mainland Africa, as Dawkins might expect according to his lemur example (p. 170, above).[29] Crowberries (*Empetrum*) are found only in the more northern latitudes of the northern hemisphere and in the very southern regions of the southern hemisphere.

About 150 seed plant genera are common to eastern Asia and eastern North America but are not found in the intervening western North America.[30] Many of these are even of the same species, showing that they must have diverged recently, not millions of years ago. Significantly, some of the plants (and animals) found in eastern Asia and eastern North America are identical at the species level, indicating that the disjunctions occurred very recently (that is, within the last few thousand years). Indeed, many of our crop plants can be traced back to the 'Fertile Crescent'—the plain of Shinar—consistent with the biblical account of human dispersion from Babel, bringing along their plants (and domestic cats[31]).[32]

Another example is the cactus, a specialized desert-adapted plant. One genus, *Rhipsalis*, is native to Africa, Madagascar, and Sri Lanka.[33] So did they predate the breakup of the southern supercontinent Gondwana, or were its seeds secondarily introduced by ocean-crossing birds?

So what can be done about disjunct species? When it comes to those shared by Africa and South America, evolutionists have proposed that they had either crossed the south Atlantic, or had migrated indirectly across the northern supercontinent Laurasia.[34] Indeed, to 'explain' whether faunas are shared or not between Africa and South America, evolutionists resort to *ad hoc* openings and closings of the Laurasian route,[35] which shows how plastic evolutionary theory can be.

28. Beck , W. *et al., Life. An Introduction to Biology*, 3rd ed., p. 1324, HarperCollins, NY, 1991.
29. Schatz, G., Malagasy/Indo-Australo-Malesian Phytogeographic connections, in Lourenço, W.R. (ed.), *Biogeography of Madagascar*, Editions ORSTOM, Paris, 1996; mobot.org.
30. Hong Qian, Floristic Relationships between Eastern Asia and North America: Test of Gray's Hypothesis, *American Naturalist* **160**(3):317–332, 2002.
31. Driscoll, C.A., and 12 others, The Near Eastern origin of cat domestication, *Science* **317**(5837):519–523, 2007.
32. Catchpoole, D., creation.com/cats-from-shinar-not-egypt, 16 October 2007.
33. Nyffeler, R., Phylogenetic relationship in the Cactus Family (Cactaceae) based on evidence from TrnK/MATK and TrnL-TrnF sequences, *American J. Botany* **89**(2)312–326, 2002.
34. Davis, C.C. *et al.*, Laurasian migration explains Gondwanan disjunctions, *PNAS (USA)* **99**(10)6833–6837, 2002.
35. Davis *et al.*, Ref. 34, p. 6837.

The fossil record also presents problems for evolutionary explanations of biogeography. For example, there are many similar plant fossils in western North America and eastern Asia, yet the evolutionary timescale 'dates' them to a time when Alaska and Russia still had thousands of miles of ocean between them.[36]

So much for Dawkins and his fellow atheopath Jerry Coyne claiming,

"The biogeographic evidence for evolution is now so powerful that I have never seen a creationist book, article, or lecture that has tried to refute it. Creationists simply pretend that the evidence doesn't exist." (*Greatest Show*, p. 263[37])

What is plate tectonics?[38]

Most geologists believe that the earth once contained one land mass, which broke up. The large fragments separated to form today's continents. In fact, it was a creationist, Antonio Snider-Pellegrini (1802–1885), who first proposed in 1858 that a land mass broke up catastrophically during the Genesis Flood and separated into our continents.[39] He gained this idea from Genesis 1:9–10 which suggests one land mass before the Flood.

But in the uniformitarian climate of his day, he was ignored. Then Alfred Wegener (1880–1930) proposed a slower form of separation, based on the fit of continents like a jigsaw, and some similarities in rock formations and fossils. But he had no mechanism.

This was later supported by a zebra-striped pattern of magnetic reversals parallel to mid-ocean floor rifts, in the volcanic rock formed along the rifts. This was interpreted as seafloor spreading very slowly, and magnetic field reversals, supposedly every few hundred thousand years, being recorded in the solidifying rock.

Most geologists explain these observations by the theory of plate tectonics. That is: the earth's crust comprises a mosaic of rigid plates, each moving relative to adjacent plates. These 'float' on the *asthenosphere*, a portion of the upper mantle that is mechanically weak and easy to deform plastically (from Greek ἀσθενὴς *asthenēs* = weak). Deformation occurs at the edges of the plates by three types of horizontal motion:

36. Smiley, C., Pre-Tertiary Phytogeography and Continental Drift: Some Apparent Discrepancies, in Gray, J. and Boucot, A., (eds.), Historical Biogeography, Plate Tectonics and the Changing Environment, pp. 311–319, Oregon State University Press, 1976.

37. From Coyne, J., *Why Evolution is True*, Penguin, NY, 2009; see refutation, Woodmorappe, J., Why evolution is not true, *J. Creation* **24**(1):24–29, 2010.

38. See also Batten *et al.*, Ref. 3, ch.11.

39. Snider, A., *Le Création et ses Mystères Devoilés*, Franck and Dentu, Paris 1858.

1. Extension occurs as the sea floor pulls apart at rifts, or splits; molten lava pours in and forms new oceanic crust, mainly basalt.

2. Transform faulting occurs where one plate slips horizontally past another (e.g., the San Andreas Fault of California).

3. Compression deformation occurs when one plate subducts beneath another.

Problems with slow and gradual continental drift

However, there are problems with the slow-and-gradual view (uniformitarian plate tectonics (UPT)), which are solved if the plates moved apart much more quickly in the past, as Snider-Pellegrini originally suggested. Catastrophic Plate Tectonics (CPT), explained next section, proposes a continent speed of metres per second, which is billions of times that of uniformitarian plate tectonics (1–2 cm/year), and this better explains the following:

- The zebra-stripe pattern of *surface* magnetism is real, but this polarity also changes vertically as well—*every* drill core sample of sea floor rock that penetrates the basement basalt shows magnetic mottling—something Dawkins fails to mention (p. 281). This is consistent with *rapid* formation of the basalt, combined with rapid field reversals, predicted by the Humphreys model of the earth's magnetic field (see ch. 12, p. 208).

- CPT explains other high pressure (HP) minerals, such as those in the metamorphic blueschist rocks as well as ultra high pressure (UHP) mineral phases such as coesite and diamond found in ancient (i.e., Flood related) subduction zone environments. The best explanation is that crustal rock was carried down in these subduction zones, to depths of 20–30 km in the case of HP rocks and up to 150–200 km in the case of UHP minerals, metamorphosed at the increased pressures. Then, they were rapidly returned to the surface because of the buoyancy of crustal rock before they had a chance to heat up much. This scenario is plausible in the framework of CPT but inconsistent with UPT.

- Under UPT, plates are moving too slowly to penetrate past the upper layers of the mantle; rather, they should blend in long before they reach the lower mantle. Yet studies show that the subducted plates have penetrated much further, and are still relatively cool.[40,41,42] This is consistent with the subduction being fast enough to penetrate the mantle, and recently enough so they haven't had time to heat up.

40. Grand, S.P., Mantle shear structure beneath the Americas and surrounding oceans, *Journal of Geophysical Research* 99:11591–11621, 1994.
41. Vidale, J.E., A snapshot of whole mantle flow, *Nature* 370:16–17, 1994.
42. Vogel, S., *Anti-matters, Earth: The Science of Our Planet*, pp. 43–49, August 1995.

- Significant simultaneous uplift of all of today's high mountains occurred during Pliocene-Pleistocene times (using uniformitarian designations). The non-volcanic mountain ranges are produced by thickening of the crust at plate collision boundaries, mainly by subduction, and this crust then rises due to *isostasy*.[43] In standard UPT, most of the crustal thickening was produced by tectonic processes (by uniformitarian reckoning) before the uplift took place. This implies an implausibly long isostatic response time, while in CPT, the time is only tens to hundreds of years, which makes far better mechanical sense. Also, the dramatically higher plate speeds of CPT would be much more likely to generate such thickened zones in the first place.

Catastrophic Plate Tectonics (CPT)[44]

Dr John Baumgardner, working at the Los Alamos National Laboratories (New Mexico), used supercomputers to model processes in the earth's mantle to show that tectonic plate movement could have occurred very rapidly, and spontaneously.[45] He was acknowledged as having developed the world's best 3-D supercomputer model of plate tectonics.[46]

Baumgardner's model begins with a pre-Flood super-continent. While uniformitarian models assume that the ocean plates have always had the temperature profile they display today, Baumgardner started with some additional cold rock in regions just offshore surrounding the super-continent. Since this rock was colder, it was denser than the mantle below. At the start of the Flood year, this began to sink.

But how can it sink more rapidly than ocean plate subducts today? The answer lies in laboratory experiments that show that the silicate minerals that make up the mantle can weaken dramatically, *by factors of a billion or more*,

43. Isostasy means tectonic plates 'float' on the weaker underlying asthenospheric rock at an elevation depending on their thickness and density. Compare this to icebergs: they always float in the sea so that the same *proportion* is above the surface (about 10%, hence the expression, 'the tip of the iceberg'). So if the iceberg grows perhaps by snow adding ice to its top surface, then although its bottom would sink deeper into the water, the buoyancy forces would adjust its height such that about 10% of its mass still lies above the water. Similarly, isostasy describes how buoyant forces make thicker sections of the crust both deeper and taller.
44. Not all creationists agree with CPT; see Forum on catastrophic plate tectonics, *J. Creation* 16(1):57, 2002; creation.com/cpt_forum. I think it is still the most promising theory, explaining the data supporting uniformitarian plate tectonics, and solving a number of its problems. It also provides a mechanism for observed quick field reversals (above), and a source for the hydrothermal solutions that likely carved massive caves (Silvestru, E., Caves for all seasons, *Creation* 25(3):44–49, 2003). But CPT is not a direct teaching of Scripture, and multiple models are a good thing in science, especially when it comes to trying to understand what happened in the unobservable past.
45. Baumgardner, J.R., Catastrophic Plate Tectonics: the physics behind the genesis flood, *Fifth International Conference on Creationism*, Creation Science Fellowship, Pittsburgh, Pennsylvania, August, 2003; globalflood.org/
46. Beard, J,. How a supercontinent went to pieces, *New Scientist* 137:19, 16 January 1993.

at mantle temperatures and stresses. If a cold blob of rock is sufficiently large, it can enter a regime in which the stresses in the envelope surrounding it become large enough to weaken the rock in that envelope, which allows the blob to sink faster, resulting in the stresses becoming a bit larger still, and causing the rock inside the surrounding envelope to weaken even more. Moreover, as the blob sinks ever faster, the volume of the envelope of weakened rock grows ever larger. Rather quickly the sinking velocity of the blob of dense rock can reach values of several km/hour, on the order of a billion times faster than is happening today. This is called *runaway subduction*.

The sinking ocean floor would drag the rest of the ocean floor along, in conveyor belt fashion, and would displace mantle material, starting large-scale movement throughout the entire mantle. However, as the ocean floor sank and rapidly subducted adjacent to the pre-Flood super-continent's margins, elsewhere the earth's crust would be under such tensional stress that it would be torn apart (rifted), breaking up both the pre-Flood super-continent and the ocean floor.

Thus, ocean plates separated along some 60,000 km where seafloor spreading was occurring. Within these spreading zones hot mantle material was rising to the surface to fill the gap caused by the rapidly separating plates. Being at the ocean bottom, this hot mantle material vapourized copious amounts of ocean water, producing a linear chain of superheated steam jets along the whole length of the spreading ridge system. This is consistent with the biblical description of the 'fountains of the great deep' (Genesis 7:11; 8:2).

This steam would disperse, condensing in the atmosphere to fall as intense global rain ("and the flood-gates of heaven were opened" Genesis 7:11). This could account for the rain persisting for 40 days and 40 nights (Genesis 7:12).

Baumgardner's CPT global flood model for Earth history is able to explain more geological data than the conventional plate tectonics model with its many millions of years. For example, rapid subduction of the pre-Flood ocean floor into the mantle results in new ocean floor that is dramatically hotter, especially in its upper 60 miles, not just at spreading ridges, but everywhere. Being hotter, the new ocean floor is of lower density and therefore rises 3,000 to 6,000 feet higher than before, causing a dramatic rise in global sea level.

This higher sea level floods the continental surfaces and makes possible the deposition of large areas of sedimentary deposits on top of the normally high-standing continents. The Grand Canyon provides a spectacular window into the amazing layer-cake character of these sediment deposits that in many cases continue uninterrupted for more than 1,000 km. Uniformitarian ('slow and gradual') plate tectonics simply cannot account for such thick continental sediment sequences of such vast horizontal extent.

Moreover, the rapid subduction of the cooler pre-Flood ocean floor into the mantle would have resulted in increased circulation of viscous fluid (note: plastic, not molten) rock within the mantle. This mantle-flow (i.e., 'stirring' within the mantle) suddenly altered the temperatures at the core-mantle boundary, as the mantle near the core would now be significantly cooler than the adjacent core, and thus convection and heat loss from the core would be greatly accelerated. The model suggests that under these conditions of accelerated convection in the core, rapid geomagnetic reversals would have occurred. These in turn would be expressed on the earth's surface and recorded in the so-called magnetic stripes. However, these would be erratic and locally patchy, laterally and at depth, just as the data indicate.

This model provides a mechanism that explains how the plates could move relatively quickly (in a matter of a few months) over the mantle and subduct. And it predicts that little or no movement would be measurable between plates today, because the movement would have come almost to a standstill when the entire pre-Flood ocean floor was subducted. From this we would also expect some of the trenches adjacent to continental regions today to be filled with largely undisturbed post-Flood sediments. We do observe sediments consistent with this scenario.

Aspects of Baumgardner's mantle modelling have been independently duplicated and thus verified by others. Furthermore, Baumgardner's modelling predicts that because this thermal runaway subduction of slabs of cold ocean floor occurred relatively recently, during the Flood (about 4,500 or so years ago), then those slabs would not have had sufficient time since to be fully assimilated into the surrounding mantle. So, evidence of the slabs above the mantle-core boundary (to which they sank) should still be found today. Indeed, evidence for such unassimilated relatively cold slabs has been found in seismic studies.

Plate collisions would have pushed up mountains, while cooling of the new ocean floor would have increased its density, causing it to sink and thus deepen the new ocean basins to receive the retreating Flood waters. It may be significant, therefore, that the "mountains of Ararat" (Genesis 8:4), the resting place of the Ark after the 150th day of the Flood, are in a tectonically active region at what is believed to be the junction of three crustal plates.

Dawkins is vaguely aware of the existence of rapid plate tectonics theory. But he thinks he can dismiss this with one or two one-liners, such as "It is an arresting image: South America and Africa speeding away from each other faster than a man can swim, for forty days continuously" (p. 283). But what matters is not Dawkins' paucity of imagination when dealing with views he does not like, but the *evidence* that plates really did move much faster in the past.

Summary

- Darwin's target was a faulty long-age creation model, with fixity of species and centres of creation: i.e. species were created in their present form and location. But island species are similar though not identical to those of the nearby mainland. Darwin explained this better as migration followed by variation.

- However, the biblical creation model involves the Flood, followed by dispersion from the landing site of the Ark in the mountains of Ararat. So this would predict that animals migrated to islands from continents, followed by variation. But Dawkins is still knocking down the same straw man as Darwin. For example, biblical creationists would actually agree with Dawkins that an ancestral lemur migrated from Africa to Madagascar, although more recently than evolutionists believe.

- Darwin thought that the geographical distribution supported evolution under a fixed continent view; Dawkins claims that a moving continent view supports evolution. How plastic evolutionary theory must be to cope with such diametrically opposed versions of Earth history!

- The distribution of marsupials in Australia is supposed to be a problem for creationists and explainable by evolution. Yet the Chilean opossum is closer to the Australian marsupials than to other South American ones. And fossil marsupials, from an 'earlier' evolutionary age, are found just where modern ones are not, leading evolutionists to admit, "This geographical switch remains unexplained."

- Marine and land iguanas on the Galápagos Islands can still hybridize, contrary to Dawkins' assertion based on his faith in long ages of evolution.

- If separated similar species are explained by continental drift, then the ancestral group must have arisen before the continents split. Yet according to evolutionary 'dating', many of them arose in the different locations long *after* they were separated.

- Some widely separated species are *not* in locations that were once joined.

- The slow and gradual model of plate tectonics that Dawkins advocates has a number of serious problems. Catastrophic plate tectonics explains the horizontal and vertical magnetic patterns on seafloor rock, ultra-high-pressure minerals, significant simultaneous uplift of all of today's high mountains, and slabs of crust that penetrated deep into the mantle but are still relatively cool.

- Contrary to Dawkins' confident assertions, his evolutionary approach has nothing to offer over the *biblical* creation model, which also explains the anomalies.

—∞—

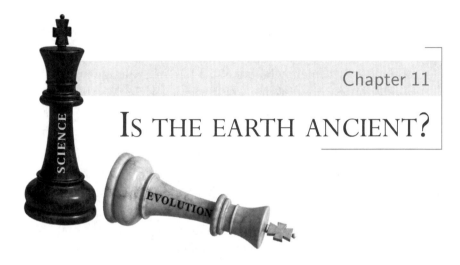

Chapter 11

IS THE EARTH ANCIENT?

D ARWIN'S ideas of gradual change in biology over eons were an extension of Lyell's ideas of gradual change in geology over eons. Without long ages evolution is not possible. So for Dawkins it is also imperative to demonstrate long ages.

All radioisotope 'dating' methods first need to postulate a history, and that involves at least three assumptions. A reliable eyewitness, however, trumps such assumptions.

Dawkins explains radiometric dating, but seems unaware of the weakness of its assumptions. There is evidence that half lives were vastly accelerated at some time in the past. Moreover, radioactive 'clocks' are not always 'zeroed', as shown by wrong dates on rocks of known age. Also, the presence of C-14 in 'billion-year-old' diamonds shows that they can't be more than about 100,000 years old; i.e., here is actual radiometric evidence *against* long ages. It is common for radiometric dates to be ignored or explained away when they disagree with accepted 'ages'.

Finally, tree-ring dating and other methods that assume 'annual' phenomena are not always annual after all, compromising their ability to provide absolute dates.

Chapter 4 of *Greatest Show* is called "Science and slow time". Dawkins begins by railing against opponents, and includes some 'elephant hurling'[1]:

"If the history deniers who doubt the fact of evolution are ignorant of biology, those who think the world began less than ten thousand years ago are worse than ignorant, they are deluded to the point of perversity. They are denying not only the facts of biology but those about physics, geology, cosmology, history and chemistry as well." (p. 86)

Anti-creationists like Dawkins realize quite keenly how essential the concept of an ancient earth is to their entire framework. In fact, old-earth geology provided the crucial underpinnings for Darwin's theory, which explains Dawkins' vehement defence of long ages. It turns out that long ages are not nearly so soundly based as his vehement attack on long-age skeptics would suggest.

Darwin and Lyell

One of the greatest influences on Darwin, for example, was a book he took on the *Beagle* voyage, *Principles of Geology,* by Charles Lyell (1797–1875). In this book Lyell pushed the idea of slow and gradual geological processes occurring over millions of years, and denied the global Noachian Flood. This idea was termed 'uniformitarianism' by the great historian and philosopher of science, William Whewell (1794–1866), who also invented the term 'catastrophism', the old-earth theory dominant just prior to Lyell.

Lyell's book convinced Darwin, who was actually more of a geologist than a biologist at the time. Much later, Darwin linked slow and gradual *geological* processes with slow and gradual *biological* processes. For example, Lyell claimed that mountains were the products of thousands of small rises. So Darwin argued that if small changes over ages can produce mountains, so small changes accumulating over ages in animals can produce new structures.

Even some modern evolutionists acknowledge that Lyell was biased and unscientific, driven by antibiblical philosophical assumptions, whereas the 'catastrophists' of his day (who believed in huge catastrophes although not necessarily in a young earth) were more empirically based followers of the scientific method (though most of them did not believe that the global Flood was responsible for most of the sedimentary rock layers and did also

---

1. This occurs when the critic throws summary arguments about complex issues to give the impression of weighty evidence, but with an unstated presumption that a large complex of underlying ideas is true, and failing to consider opposing data, usually because they have uncritically accepted the arguments from their own side. But we should challenge elephant-hurlers to offer *specifics* and challenge the *underlying assumptions*.

believe in an earth much older than the Bible teaches). Stephen Jay Gould (1941–2002), himself a leading evolutionist, wrote:

"Charles Lyell was a lawyer by profession, and his book is one of the most brilliant briefs ever published by an advocate ... In fact, the catastrophists were much more empirically minded than Lyell. The geologic record does seem to record catastrophes; rocks are fractured and contorted; whole faunas are wiped out. To circumvent this literal appearance, Lyell imposed his imagination upon the evidence. The geologic record, he argued, is extremely imperfect and we must interpolate into it what we can reasonably infer but cannot see. The catastrophists were the hard-nosed empiricists of their day, not the blinded theological apologists." [2]

One infamous example of Lyell's bias was his decision to ignore eyewitness accounts of the rate of erosion of Niagara Falls, and publish a different figure to suit his purpose.[3]

In chapter 7, we saw how Darwin explained away gaps in the fossil record by appealing to deep time, and how the geological evidence points towards rapid processes. In this chapter, we answer Dawkins' main 'proofs' of long ages.

Determining the age of something

In Q&A sessions after my creation talks, I am sometimes asked about the age of things. I show this picture of a measuring cylinder: it contains 300 ml of liquid, and it is currently dripping in at 50 ml per hour. So how long did it take to fill up to its current level?

Someone usually answers, "Six hours."

I reply that the answer showed impeccable *mathematics*, dividing the amount of water in the cylinder (300 ml) by the rate (50 ml per hour). But then I say that the answer was *wrong*. It actually took far less time. How so?

The answer *assumed* that it had started from zero, whereas it really started from 100 ml.

2.   Gould, S.J., *Natural History* p. 16, February 1975.
3.   Pierce, L., Niagara Falls and the Bible, *Creation* **22**(4):8–13, September–November 2000; creation.com/niagara.

The answer also *assumed* that the current rate has been constant; in reality, during my chemistry lab days, I would turn a tap on full to quickly reach almost the desired level, then turn down the flow to drip slowly to reach the right level accurately without overflowing. What they see now is only the dripping, without knowing the much faster flow in the past.

They also presupposed that the only source of water was the tap. But I had a 'helpful' student top up a lot of the water, unbeknown to them. They also didn't see the small leak at the back ... I.e. they assumed that the system was *closed*—nothing else came in or out.

But an eyewitness (like me) would be able to know whether those three assumptions were true.

The same principle applies to the age of the earth. It makes more sense to trust an eyewitness who was there at the beginning: the Creator Himself, who has revealed the age in His Book, the Bible.[4] And there were other eyewitnesses too, including Noah and his descendants who meticulously recorded the years elapsed since the global Flood.

But Dawkins ignores this eyewitness information,[5] and relies on dating methods that resort instead to speculative and dubious assumptions. Actually, *given the same sorts of assumptions he accepts for the minority of the old-earth chronometers,* he ignores far more chronometers that point to an age far too young for evolution.[6] This will be the subject of the next chapter.

Radiometric dating

Atomic theory

Dawkins presents a junior high-school level explanation of atomic theory, and sneers, "which I think everyone accepts, even creationists" (p. 91). But why wouldn't creationists accept it, when creationists were instrumental in *discovering* it, as with most other branches of modern science (see also ch. 17)?

---

4. See also this clever illustration of how eyewitnesses should trump assumptions: Wiebe, G., *The Parable of the Candle* creation.com/candle.
5. On pp. 14–15 of *Greatest Show*, Dawkins tries to undermine the reliability of eyewitnesses by citing an experiment by Prof. Daniel J. Simons at the University of Illinois. He showed a film of a ring of young people tossing a basketball to each other, and asks the audience to count the number of passes. Then he asked, "how many saw the gorilla?", which most didn't, including Dawkins. Allowing the audience to see the film again, ignoring basketball passes, and being forewarned, they saw the gorilla, much to their amazement. Yet all this shows is that people can be distracted and overlook something; the number of passes counted is likely to be accurate. It does not show that circumstantial evidence about the past should overcome a *reliable* eye witness.
6. Batten, D., *101 evidences for a young age of the earth and the universe*, creation.com/age-of-the-earth, 4 June 2009.

For example, Robert Boyle (1627–1691), the founder of modern chemistry, first overturned the Greek idea of four elements (the belief that everything was composed of earth, air, fire and water) and replaced it with the modern idea of an element—namely that an element is a substance that cannot be separated into simpler components by chemical methods. He also discovered that gas volume is inversely proportional to pressure, now called Boyle's Law. This helped him develop atomic theory, explaining that gases are compressible because there is much space between atoms, which are more closely packed in liquids and solids. His book *The Christian Virtuoso* explained how his scientific research was fulfilling God's dominion mandate (Genesis 1:28).[7] In his will, he endowed a series of academic lectures to prove the truth of the Christian religion against infidels—the *Boyle Lectures*.

Dawkins then explains how atoms comprise the massive nucleus consisting of protons and neutrons, orbited by much less massive electrons. Elements are defined by the number of protons, while some atoms of the same element have different neutron numbers—*isotopes*. Dawkins also explains how some isotopes have unstable atomic nuclei, so they decay into other isotopes, and then outlines a simplified explanation of radiometric dating methods.

Problems ignored

Dawkins is pulling a typical swifty here, as do all those who promote the reliability of radioactive dating. They often spend much time discussing the technical details of radioactive decay, half-lives, mass-spectroscopes, etc., some in much more detail than Dawkins. But they don't discuss the basic flaw in the methods: they don't really measure age at all, because no-one was present to measure the radioactive elements when the rock formed and no-one monitored the way those elements changed over its entire geological history.

It would be like the judges of a 100 m dash bragging about their state-of-the-art electronic timers, and explaining the crystal structure of the quartz crystal that regulates the electrical oscillation—but not admitting that no one actually saw the start of the race.[8]

So, the fatal problem with all radioactive dates is that they are all based on assumptions about the *past*. As will be shown, these methods rely critically on quantities measured only *in the present*. Moreover, there are many examples where a specific geological history is assumed *after the event*. They call it 'interpreting the results' (see p. 194).

---

7. Doolan, R., The man who turned chemistry into a science, Robert Boyle (1627–1691), *Creation* **12**(1):22–23, 1989; creation.com/boyle.
8. Walker, T. The fatal flaw with radioactive dating methods, *Creation* **32**(1):20–21, 2010; creation.com/fatalflaw.

Half-life

Dawkins correctly states:

"Every unstable or radioactive isotope decays at its own characteristic rate which is precisely known. Moreover, some of these rates are vastly slower than others. In all cases, the decay is exponential. Exponential means that if you start with, say, 100 grams of a radioactive isotope, it is not that a fixed amount, say 10 grams, turns into another element in a given time. Rather, a fixed *proportion* of whatever is left turns into the second element. The favoured measure of decay rate is the half-life. The half-life of a radioactive element is the same, no matter how many atoms have already decayed—that is what exponential decay means. You will appreciate that, with such successive halvings, we can never really know when there is none left." (p. 95)

Then he explains in principle how the age is calculated from the ratio of the radioactive element to the second (daughter) isotope,[9] "assuming that there was no [first element] to begin with ... i.e., it is necessary that our clock has the facility to be zeroed". But this is patently incorrect for almost all dating systems, such as the uranium-lead or the rubidium-strontium system. Only under very special circumstances does a scientist assume that there was zero daughter isotope to begin with. Rather, a number of methods and models have been developed to help make ostensibly plausible assumptions for the value of the initial quantity. The assumption of zero daughter initially is commonly made for the potassium-argon method, for example, because the daughter isotope, argon, is a gas which is assumed to escape. Even here, this assumption will be tested later (p. 192), but first, back to his claim that the rate is constant.

Has the rate been constant?

Yet for this method to work, the rates cannot have changed. Indeed, radioactive decay is not significantly influenced by such factors as temperature and pressure. However, we have tested decay rates for only about 100 years, so we can't be sure they were constant over the alleged billions of years. Indeed, beta (β) decay rate was sped up a *billion times* when atoms were stripped of their electrons.[10]

9. The time t since radioactive decay commenced can be given by $N/N0 = e^{-\lambda t}$, where N is the number of atoms measured in the present; $N0$ is the initial number; λ, the decay constant, which is related to the half-life $t_{1/2}$ by $\lambda = ln2/t_{1/2}$.
10. Bosch, F. *et al.*, Observation of bound-state β-decay of fully ionized ^{187}Re, *Physical Review Letters* 77(26)5190–5193, 1996; Woodmorappe, J., Billion-fold acceleration of radioactivity demonstrated in laboratory, *J. Creation* 15(2):4–6, 2001.

Later, Dawkins excoriates 'history deniers' for 'special pleading':

"Why on Earth should the known laws of physics change, just like that, and so conveniently? The history deniers would have to fiddle the half-lives of all the isotopes so that they all end up agreeing that the Earth began 6,000 years ago." (pp. 106–7)

However, according to "the known laws of physics", *tiny* changes in the nuclear potential energy well would have a *huge* effect on decay rate.[11] But Dawkins' question is in any case irrelevant if there is actual *evidence* that the decay has accelerated. Many scientists have discovered the *existence* of a phenomenon long before anyone could *explain* how it occurred. The philosopher of science Larry Laudan points out:

"For centuries scientists have recognized a difference between establishing the existence of a phenomenon and explaining that phenomenon in a law-like way. Our ultimate goal, no doubt, is to do both. …

"Galileo and Newton took themselves to have established the existence of gravitational phenomena, long before anyone was able to give a causal or explanatory account of gravitation. Darwin took himself to have established the existence of natural selection almost a half-century before geneticists were able to lay out the laws of heredity on which natural selection depended."[12]

Similarly, there are several lines of evidence suggesting that there has been a phenomenon—accelerated nuclear decay in the past—even though there is much uncertainty about what the mechanism was that caused this phenomenon.

- ^{14}C data showing the earth itself is only thousands of years old, so the billions of years of decay at present rates of the long half-life isotopes must have occurred at much higher rates to fit within this short time span.

- Huge numbers of ^{238}U and ^{210}Po, ^{214}Po, and ^{218}Po radiohalos in the same biotite flakes in granite plutons. The extremely short half-lives of polonium show that they must have formed in a few days at most, in rapidly hardening rock. Yet the uranium halos, with many rings, must have been formed *during the same short time*, although there is at least 100 million years worth of nuclear decay *if current rates were assumed*. This is consistent with an

11. Chaffin, E., Accelerated decay: Theoretical models, in: ed. Ivey, R.L., Jr., *Fifth International Conference on Creationism*, pp. 3–15, Creation Science Fellowship, Pittsburgh, Pennsylvania, August, 2003; www.icr.org/research/icc03/pdf/RATE_ICC_Chaffin.pdf.
12. Laudan, L., "Science at the Bar—Causes for Concern", in Ruse, M., editor, *But Is it Science?* pp. 351–355, Prometheus Books, Buffalo, NY, 1988. Laudan, himself an anti-creationist, was criticizing Judge Overton's reasoning that creation was 'unscientific', but the points apply equally here.

episode of *rapid decay* during the Flood, which also quickly produced the huge quantities of polonium that replenished the sites for Po-haloes.[13]

- The presence of helium atoms still within the rock where they were apparently formed by nuclear α-decay. The diffusion rate of helium through minerals would suggest that it would have escaped if the rocks were really billions of years old.
- High correlation of heat flow at the earth's surface with concentration of radioactive isotopes. This is consistent with a pulse of accelerated decay during the Flood year to produce heat that hasn't had time to dissipate. This explains a correlation that had been a mystery to geophysicists.[14]

Despite Dawkins' straw man (p. 187), none of the scientists who observed these accelerated decay rates has claimed that "they all end up agreeing that the Earth began 6,000 years ago". Rather, they show that the observed ratios of radioactive and daughter elements are not due to decay at constant rate. Thus the 'clock' rate is not constant—which means it is not a clock at all!

Carbon-14: evidence for a young earth

Dawkins explains how a certain form of carbon can be used for dating:

> "Carbon has three naturally occurring isotopes. Carbon-12 is the common one, with the same number of neutrons as protons: 6. There's also carbon-13, which is too short-lived to bother with, and carbon-14 which is rare but not too rare to be useful for dating relatively young samples, as we shall see." (p. 94)

Yet here, Dawkins makes a crass blunder: carbon-13 is **not** "too short-lived" but **stable!** If a creationist had made that blunder, Dawkins, true to form, would be using it as evidence of scientific incompetence—indeed, on p. 154 he mocks a couple of creationists (not associated with CMI) for some blunders.

But Dawkins rightly points out:

> "However, we can say that after a sufficient time has elapsed—say ten half lives—the number of atoms is so small that, for all practical purposes, it has all gone. For example, the half-life of carbon-14 is between 5,000 and 6,000 years. For specimens older than about 50,000–60,000 years, carbon dating is useless." (p. 95)

13. Snelling, A.A., Radiohalos in granites: evidence for accelerated nuclear decay, in: Vardiman, L., Snelling, A.A. and Chaffin, E.F. (Eds), *Radioisotopes and the Age of the Earth: Results of a Young-Earth Creationist Research Initiative*, Institute for Creation Research, California, and Creation Research Society, Missouri, pp. 101–207, 2005.
14. Baumgardner, J., Distribution of radioactive isotopes in the earth, ch. 3, Vardiman *et al.*, Vardiman, L., Snelling, A.A. and Chaffin, E.F., *Radioisotopes and the Age of the Earth*, El Cajon, California: Institute for Creation Research, and St. Joseph, Missouri: Creation Research Society, 2000.

Indeed, after 10 half lives, less than a thousandth would be left. So Dawkins' figures are reasonable. And there should be no doubt that none should be detectable after a million years—even in a lump of carbon-14 (^{14}C) as massive as the earth.[15] So if samples were really over a million years old, there should be no radiocarbon left. But is this what we find? Today, there are very sensitive detectors[16] that can detect only a ten-thousandth of the current tiny ratio of ^{14}C to C.

'Billion-year-old' diamonds and coal contain carbon-14[17]

Diamond is the hardest substance on Earth, so its interior should be very resistant to contamination. So any ^{14}C present must have been there from its formation. Diamond requires very high pressure to form—pressure found naturally on Earth only deep below the surface. They are alleged to have formed at a depth of 100–200 km, 1–3 billion years ago. The ones we find must have been transported supersonically[18] to the surface, in extremely violent eruptions through volcanic pipes.

Geophysicist and plate tectonics expert Dr John Baumgardner, part of the RATE research group (Radioisotopes and the Age of the Earth),[19] investigated ^{14}C in a number of diamond samples he sent to a radiocarbon lab for analysis.[20] There should be no ^{14}C at all if they really were over a billion years old, yet in *every* case the measured ^{14}C level exceeded the lab's background detection limit. Thus they had a radiocarbon 'age' far less than a million years! Baumgardner repeated this with six more alluvial (deposited from flowing water) diamonds from Namibia, and these had even more radiocarbon. The presence of radiocarbon in these diamonds where there should be none is thus sparkling evidence for a 'young' world.

Baumgardner has also shown that significant levels of C-14 exist in coal and fossilized wood, 'dated' by their locations in the geological record at *tens to hundreds of millions of years.*[20] This reality is also documented by scores of papers in the secular peer-reviewed radiocarbon literature.

15. The earth's mass is 6×10^{27} g; equivalent to 4.3×10^{26} moles of ^{14}C. Each mole contains Avogadro's number ($N_A = 6.022\times10^{23}$) of atoms. It takes only 167 halvings to get down to a single atom ($\log_2(4.3\times10^{26}$ mol x 6.022×10^{23} mol$^{-1}) = \log_{10}(2.58\times10^{50}) / \log_{10}2$), and 167 half-lives is well under a million years.
16. AMS (accelerator mass spectrometry) counts the atoms themselves, and can detect one ^{14}C in more than 1016 atoms, or measure a ^{14}C/C ratio of $<10^{-16}$ or 0.01% of the modern ratio (0.01 p_{MC}, percent modern carbon).
17. After Sarfati, J., Diamonds: a creationist's best friend: Radiocarbon in diamonds: enemy of billions of years, *Creation* **28**(4):26–27, 2006; creation.com/diamonds; based on the research in Baumgardner, Ref. 20. These also refute objections such as contamination, which is even less plausible with such a hard mineral as diamond.
18. Otherwise the diamond would anneal into graphite, so-called pencil 'lead'.
19. Vardiman, L., Snelling, A. and Chaffin, E., *Radioisotopes and the Age of the Earth*, Vol. II, ch. 8, Institute for Creation Research, El Cajon, CA, 2005.
20. Baumgardner, J., ^{14}C evidence for a recent global flood and a young earth; in Ref. 19, ch. 8.

Once again, in contradiction to Dawkins' straw man (p. 189) that creationists "would have to fiddle the half-lives of all the isotopes so that they all end up agreeing that the Earth began 6,000 years ago", the ^{14}C 'dates' for the diamonds of 55,700 years were still much older than the biblical timescale. However, we are not claiming that this 'date' is that actual age; rather, if the earth were just a million years old, let alone 4.6 billion years old, there should be no ^{14}C at all! Such calculations are normally only applied to samples that were once living and not to inorganic crystals such as diamond. And also not to once-living samples that are assumed to be 'millions of years' old. And even the 'date' obtained for relatively recent organic samples also rests on several assumptions, e.g. that the $^{14}C/C$ ratio has been constant. But the Flood would have disturbed the $^{14}C/C$ ratio in the atmosphere by releasing copious amounts of CO_2 into the atmosphere from volcanoes, as well as burying huge numbers of carbon-containing living creatures, and some of them likely formed today's coal, oil, natural gas and some of today's fossil-containing limestone. Studies of the ancient biosphere indicate that there was several hundred times as much carbon in the past, so the $^{14}C/C$ ratio would have been several hundred times smaller. This would explain the observed small amounts of ^{14}C found in 'old' samples that were likely buried in the Flood, thus giving rise to calculated 'ages' in the tens of thousands of years despite having been buried only some 4,300 years ago.

Are the clocks really zeroed?

Dawkins discusses potassium-argon dating, since potassium-40 decays into the inert gas argon-40 with a half-life of 1.26 billion years. As a gas, it is assumed that all argon-40 will escape from the liquid magma before the rock solidifies:

> "Imagine you start with some quantity of potassium-40 in an enclosed space with no argon-40. After a few hundred million years have elapsed, a scientist comes upon the same enclosed space and measures the relative proportions of potassium-40 and argon-40.[21] From this proportion—regardless of the absolute quantities involved—knowing the half-life of potassium-40's decay and assuming there was no argon to begin with, one can estimate the time that has elapsed since the process started—since the clock was 'zeroed', in other words. ...

> "When a crystal [in igneous rock] is newly formed, there is potassium-40 but no argon. The clock is 'zeroed' in the sense that there are no argon

---

21. Actually, only 11% of potassium-40 decays into argon-40, by electron capture. The remainder beta decays into calcium-40.

atoms in the crystal. As the millions of years go by, the potassium-40 slowly decays, and one by one, atoms of argon-40 replace potassium-40 atoms in the crystal. The accumulating quantity of argon-40 is a measure of time that has elapsed since the rock was formed." (pp. 96–7)

Excess argon problem

But, without eyewitnesses, how could anyone know for sure that there was no argon in the rock when it formed? There are many examples where the dating methods give 'dates' that are wrong for rocks of *known* historical age, where there *were* eyewitnesses. One example is rock from a new dacite lava dome at Mount St Helens volcano. Although we know the rock was formed in 1986, the rock was 'dated' by the potassium-argon (K-Ar) method as 0.35 ± 0.05 million years old. And dates on mineral concentrates from the rock samples gave 'dates' as old as 2.8 Ma.[22] Another example is K-Ar 'dating' of five andesite lava flows from Mt Ngauruhoe in New Zealand. The 'dates' ranged from <0.27 to 3.5 million years—but one lava flow occurred in 1949, three in 1954, and one in 1975!

It's widely accepted, by both creationist and evolutionist, that 'excess' argon from the magma (molten rock) was retained in the rock when it solidified. The retained argon is symbolized $^{40}Ar^*$, as opposed to radiogenic argon produced by the potassium in the rock, ^{40}Ar, but there is no way of telling these apart. So how is excess argon determined? By calculating it from the assumed age of the rock! The secular scientific literature also lists many examples of $^{40}Ar^*$ causing 'dates' of millions of years in rocks of known historical age. This excess appears to have come from the upper mantle, below the earth's crust. This is consistent with a young world—the argon has had too little time to escape.[23]

If excess^{40}Ar can cause exaggerated dates for rocks of *known* age, then why should it not have exaggerated the ages of rocks of *unknown* age?

22. Austin, S.A., Excess argon within mineral concentrates from the new dacite lava dome at Mount St. Helens volcano, *J. Creation* **10**(3):335–343, 1996, creation.com/lavadome; Swenson, K., Radio-dating in rubble, *Creation* **23**(3)23–25, 2001, creation.com/rubble, a simpler account which refutes many of Dr Austin's critics.
23. Snelling, A.A., The cause of anomalous potassium-argon 'ages' for recent andesite flows at Mt Ngauruhoe, New Zealand, and the implications for potassium-argon 'dating'; in: Walsh, R.E. Ed., *Proceedings of the Fourth International Conference on Creationism,* Creation Science Fellowship, Pittsburgh, pp. 503–525, 1998. This paper documents many examples: six were reported by Krummenacher, D., Isotopic Composition of Argon in Modern Surface Rocks, *Earth and Planetary Science Letters* 8:109–117, 1970; five were reported by Dalrymple, G.B., $^{40}Ar/^{36}Ar$ analysis of historic lava flows, *Earth and Planetary Science Letters* 6:47–55, 1969. Also, a large excess was reported in Fisher, D.E., Excess rare gases in a subaerial basalt from Nigeria, *Nature* 232:60–61, 1970.

Radiometric dates are *not* regarded as absolute

For all the talk about 'absolute' dating methods, they are not regarded as such in practice. When samples are submitted to radiodating labs, the forms usually have an entry for 'estimated age'. But why should this be, if the method were absolute? One expert admitted:

> "If a C14 date supports our theories, we put it in the main text. If it does not entirely contradict them, we put it in a footnote. And if it is completely 'out of date', we just drop it."[24]

And if the dates are rejected, the difference can be explained away—the technical term is 'interpreted'. A glaring example concerns the 'KBS tuff'. This is a layer of volcanic ash in East Africa, famous because of nearby fossils of our alleged ape-man ancestor.[25]

First, the potassium-argon method gave a 'date' of 230 Ma. But this disagreed with the accepted 'age' of the fossils, especially pigs (as well as elephant, ape and tools), so they rejected the date. Their excuse, or interpretation, was contamination with excess argon.[26] But their only 'evidence' for excess argon was that this supposedly absolute date disagreed with the fossil dates! It shows that exaggerated potassium-argon ages can be readily explained away—so Dawkins has no grounds for complaint *when the exact same explanation is used to counter ages that contradict the biblical record.*

The same researchers used new samples of feldspar and pumice from the tuff, and supposedly 'reliably dated' the tuff at 2.61 million years, which was compatible with the fossil 'dates'. Naturally, this 'date' was 'confirmed' by two other dating methods (paleomagnetism and fission tracks), and was widely accepted.

That is, until famous paleo-anthropologist Richard Leakey (1944–) found a skull, which he called KNM-ER 1470, *below* the KBS tuff, so it must be older. But this skull was too modern to have evolved as long ago as that date. So new researchers redated the KBS tuff using selected pumice and feldspar samples to 1.82 Ma.[27] This was compatible with the assumed evolutionary

---

24. Quoted by Säve-Söderberg., T. and Olsson, I.U., (Institute of Egyptology and Institute of Physics respectively, University of Uppsala, Sweden), "C14 dating and Egyptian chronology"; in Olsson, I.U., (ed.), *Radiocarbon Variations and Absolute Chronology, the 12th Nobel Symposium*, p. 35, John Wiley & Sons, Inc., New York, 1970.
25. Lubenow, M.L., The pigs took it all, *Creation* 17(3):36–38, 1995; creation.com/pigstook; Walker, T., How dating methods work, *Creation* 30(3):28–29, 2008.
26. Fitch, F.J. and Miller, J.A., Radioisotopic age determinations of Lake Rudolf artifact site, *Nature* 226(5242):226–228, 1970.
27. Curtis, G.H. *et al.*, Age of KBS Tuff in Koobi Fora Formation, East Rudolf, Kenya, *Nature* 258:395–398, 4 December 1975.

history of that skull. Then other scientists redid the paleomagnetic and fission-track dating and confirmed the lower date. And this date has been accepted since about 1980.

Absence of short-lived radionuclides (SLRNs)

Dawkins repeats another common old-earth argument:

"… it is worth pausing to consider another piece of evidence in favour of an old Earth, a planet whose age is measured in billions of years.

"Among all the elements that occur on Earth are 150 stable isotopes and 158 unstable ones, making 308 in all. Of the 158 unstable ones, 121 are either extinct or exist only because they are constantly being replenished, like carbon-14 … Now, if we consider the 37 that have not gone extinct, we notice something significant. Every single one of them has a half-life greater than 700 million years. And if we look at the 121 that have gone extinct, every single one of them has a half-life of less than 200 million years. Don't be misled, by the way. Remember we are talking *half-life* here, not life! Think of the fate of an isotope with a half-life of 100 million years. Isotopes whose half-life is less than a tenth or so of the age of the Earth are, for practical purposes, extinct, and don't exist except under special circumstances. With exceptions that are there for a special reason that we understand, the only isotopes that we find on earth are those that have a half-life long enough to have survived on a very old planet." (pp. 102–3)

However, this commits the fallacy of *arguing from silence,* from the *absence* of certain nuclides. Contrast that with the young-earth argument on p. 190 based on the *presence* of C-14.

Dawkins' argument against the biblical age of the earth presupposes that these short-lived isotopes would have been created in the first place (the word "extinct" begs this question)! However, there are good reasons on a biblical model for questioning this. The main one would be that short-lived isotopes, by definition, emit radiation more often. Also, the shorter the half-life, the higher the energy of decay in general, and definitely so with alpha decay. This is an even greater problem when most of these isotopes form very soluble compounds, so they could be leached into dangerous hot spots.

Indeed, many of these isotopes comprise the most troublesome *radioactive waste*, because of the need for long-term disposal. For example, the by-products of nuclear fission products, technetium-99 (half-life 220,000 years) and iodine-129 (half-life 15.7 million years), as well as some higher elements in spent fuel rods such as neptunium-237 (half-life two million years) and plutonium-239 (half-life 24,000 years). So to satisfy Dawkins, should God have created lots of, in effect, dangerous radioactive waste?

Another perhaps more likely answer involves accelerated nuclear decay rates (p. 188). In this case, God created these SLRN isotopes, but the same acceleration that accounts for some 90% of all uranium decay that has ever occurred also caused all the SLRN isotopes to disappear during Creation Week before life was formed.

Furthermore, in practice, if such a SLRN *were* discovered, it would be taken as evidence not for a young Earth, but as evidence that something is replenishing it. For example, in the Anarkardo basin formation, the ^{129}I (half-life = 15.7 Ma) present is *assumed* to have been produced by fission because the rock is said to be over 300 Ma old.[28]

Annual changes?

Dawkins spends a few pages (pp. 88–91) on certain cyclic processes that could be used as dating methods. But the problem is that so-called annual changes are often nothing of the kind.

Tree rings

It's commonly argued that the number of tree rings can give the number of years a tree lived. It is assumed that the dark thin ring is produced during the slow-growth season of winter, and the wider rings are produced during warmer times when the tree grows more quickly. So the idea is that one can count the rings to find how many years the tree was growing. Using this method the oldest *living* trees, the Bristlecone Pines (*Pinus longaeva*) of the White Mountains of Eastern California, were dated in 1957 at 4,723 years old.

Yet even in the common timber tree *Pinus radiata* (Monterey Pine), up to five rings per year can be produced and the extra rings are often indistinguishable, even under the microscope. Tree physiologist Dr Don Batten argues that:

"evidence of false rings in *any* woody tree species would cast doubt on claims that any particular species has *never* in the past produced false rings. Evidence from *within the same genus* surely counts much more strongly against such a notion."[29]

Although the oldest living tree has over 4,700 rings, most trees have only several hundred. Therefore, in order to construct tree-ring chronologies

---

28. Woodmorappe, J., *The Mythology of Modern Dating Methods, p. 26,* Institute for Creation Research, El Cajon, California, 1999.

29. Batten, D., *Tree ring dating (dendrochronology),* creation.com/tree-ring-dating-dendrochronology.

that are older than the biblical age of the earth, chronologists resort to linking many dead trees from peat bogs together into a long line—a process that depends on many unprovable assumptions. Dawkins discusses these methods, starting with correlations among rings of different trees, if they shared the same climate. That is, they would share a pattern of particularly wide rings in bumper growing seasons and narrow rings for bad years. Then he states:

"To use the overlap principle in dendrochronology, you take the reference fingerprint patterns whose date is known from modern times. Then you identify a fingerprint from the old rings of modern trees and seek the same fingerprint from the younger rings of long-dead trees. Then you look at the fingerprints from the older rings of those same long-dead trees and look for the same pattern in the younger rings of still older trees. And so on. You can daisychain your way back, theoretically for millions of years using petrified forests, although in practice dendrochronology is only used on archaeological timescales over some thousands of years. ... Unfortunately we don't have an unbroken chain, and dendrochronology in practice takes us back only about 11,500 years." (pp. 89–90)

This sounds reasonable, but it's not so simple, as these 'fingerprints' are not unique, as Batten explains:

"The biggest problem with the process is that ring patterns are not unique. There are many points in a given sequence where a sequence from a new piece of wood matches well (note that even two trees growing next to each other will not have *identical* growth ring patterns). Yamaguchi[30] recognized that ring pattern matches are not unique. The best match (using statistical tests) is often rejected in favour of a less exact match because the best match is deemed to be 'incorrect' (particularly if it is too far away from the carbon-14 'age'). So the carbon 'date' is used to constrain just which match is acceptable. Consequently, the calibration is a circular process and the tree ring chronology extension is also a circular process that is dependent on assumptions about the carbon dating system.[31]

"The extended tree ring chronologies are far from absolute, in spite of the popular hype. To illustrate this we only have to consider the publication and subsequent withdrawal of two European tree-ring

30. Yamaguchi, D.K., Interpretation of cross-correlation between tree-ring series, *Tree Ring Bulletin* 46:47–54, 1986.
31. Newgrosh, B., Living with radiocarbon dates: a response to Mike Baillie. *Journal of the Ancient Chronology Forum* 5:59–67, 1992.

chronologies. According to David Rohl,[32] the Sweet Track chronology from Southwest England was 're-measured' when it did not agree with the published dendrochronology from Northern Ireland (Belfast). Also, the construction of a detailed sequence from southern Germany was abandoned in deference to the Belfast chronology, even though the authors of the German study had been confident of its accuracy until the Belfast one was published. It is clear that dendrochronology is not a clear-cut, objective dating method despite the extravagant claims of some of its advocates."[29]

Varves

Dawkins claims, continuing his overstatement:

"Tree rings are not quite the only system that promises total accuracy to the nearest year. Varves are layers of sediment laid down in glacial lakes. Like tree rings, they vary seasonally and from year to year, so theoretically the same principle can be used, with the same degree of accuracy." (p. 90)

Each varve consists of two distinct layers of sediment, a lower layer of light coloured silty or sandy material and an upper layer of darker silt or clay. Annual changes are *assumed* to cause the light layers to be deposited in summer and the dark layers in winter.

You may have the impression that researchers obtain a long sample of sediment, and count the thousands and thousands of layers it contains. However, it is not like that. In Sweden each section of sediment is relatively short, and usually has less than 200 varves.[33] This is not surprising because lakes, especially pro-glacial lakes (those in front of the glaciers), tend to be relatively short lived. They either fill up with sediment or the water cuts the outlet and drains the lake.

De Geer developed his long chronology, which extended over 13,000 years, by collecting samples from different areas of Sweden and matching the layers. However, this process is very subjective, and even if the pattern of layers is similar you cannot be sure that the widely separated sediments were really deposited at the same time.

Although De Geer was able to measure and count the layers in one particular section accurately, the fact remains that he did not directly observe the layers

---

32. Rohl, D., *A Test of Time,* Arrow Books, London, Appendix C, 1996.
33. Oard, M.O., Varves—the first 'absolute' chronology, Part 1, *Creation Research Society Quarterly* **29**(2):72–80, 1992.

forming in the lakes, or the relationship of the sedimentary layers between one site and the next. So, the claim that short sequences can be matched to form one reliable long sequence is an assumption. So too is the idea that one varve couplet formed each year.

Furthermore, as explained in chapter 7 (pp. 112), recent laboratory sedimentation experiments show that multiple layers can form with sideways flow of differently-sized particles. The layers would build sideways beneath the moving water, like sand dunes in a desert wind, and many layers would form at the same time, all growing sideways in the direction of the water flow.

Summary

- Darwin imbibed theories of very slow changes in geology over eons; it was a small step to slow changes in biology over eons.

- Long ages are necessary, not sufficient, for evolution.

- Dating methods always rely on assumptions about initial conditions, constancy of rate, and a closed system—they need an assumed history.

- There is strong evidence that radioactive decay rates underwent a dramatic acceleration at one or more times in the past.

- Argon is present in rocks known to be young, showing that the assumption of zero argon in rocks of unknown age is an unreliable assumption. If potassium-argon dates fail on rocks of known age, why trust them on rocks of *unknown* age, when they contradict the reliable eyewitness dates of the Bible?

- Carbon-14 has a short decay half-life, so should not be present in samples over a few hundreds of thousands of years. But it occurs in essentially every fossil that still contains carbon, including those that are in strata dated by other methods at tens to hundreds of millions of years. And it occurs in diamonds allegedly billions of years old.

- Radiometric dates are not a primary dating method but are *interpreted*, by changing assumptions after the event, to match expectations from other methods. Then we are reminded of the fallibility of the assumptions.

- So-called 'annual' changes in tree rings and varves are not annual. Pine trees can form five growth rings in a year, and layered rock forms automatically when deposited from moving water.

—∞—

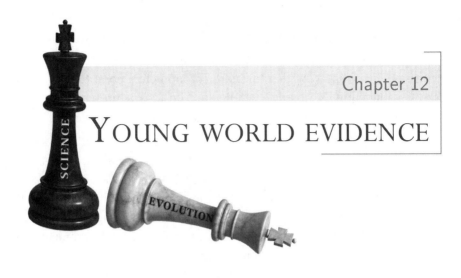

Chapter 12

YOUNG WORLD EVIDENCE

Even under evolutionists'/long-agers' own uniformitarian assumptions, there are many 'age' indicators that point to an age far less than billions of years. This would be fatal for the long-age view that Dawkins defends precisely because long ages are essential for evolution. This chapter presents further evidence, based on recent research, that the age of the earth is much too short for evolution.

Determining the age of something

As shown in the previous chapter, 'age' isn't really measured; rather, certain processes and amounts of materials are measured, and age is inferred via certain assumptions. Dawkins' main evidences for billions of years were shown to be wanting, and one of them, C-14 dating, is shown to be strong evidence for a much younger age. And as shown in chapter 7, the fossils themselves are evidence for a rapid burial. Furthermore, when fossils span multiple layers (polystrate), they show that all these layers were deposited in a short time scale. We also show in chapter 3 that the observable deterioration of the human genome indicates that humans can't have been around for millions of years, or else we would have suffered mutational meltdown.

Overcoming the opponent with his own weapons

Creationists have published a number of articles about scientific evidence for a young world, showing that far more chronometers point to a young age,[1,2] and this chapter will provide a detailed and up-to-date presentation of several of them, those not covered elsewhere in this book.

The point of these articles is to overcome the opponent's belief system (cf. 2 Corinthians 10:4–5) by turning its own axioms against it. This is a form of argument well-known to logicians called the *reductio ad absurdum*, i.e. showing that a premise is false by demonstrating that it implies an absurd conclusion. It is a technique that Christians can use to great effect, and Jesus Himself used this and many other types of logical arguments.[3] Many statements by anti-Christians might appear reasonable on the surface, but when each of these statements is turned on itself, it refutes itself, e.g.:[4]

- "There is no truth"—this would mean that **this** sentence itself is not true.

- "We can never know anything for certain"—so how could we know **that** for certain?

- "A statement is only meaningful if it is either a necessary truth of logic or can be tested empirically" (the once-popular *verification criterion for meaning* of the "Logical Positivists")—this statement itself is neither a necessary truth of logic nor can it be tested empirically, so it is meaningless by its own criteria.

- "There are no moral absolutes, so we ought to be tolerant of other people's morals"—but "ought" implies a moral absolute that toleration is good.

    Evolutionists rely on a principle sometimes called *uniformitarianism*: 'the present is the key to the past'. This is precisely the characteristic of the 'scoffers' prophesied in 2 Peter 3:4 "all things continue as *they were* from the beginning of the creation". Peter reveals the huge flaw of the uniformitarian scoffers: they are 'willingly ignorant' of special creation by God and a cataclysmic globe-covering (and fossil-forming) Flood.

---

1. An excellent summary is Batten, D., 101 evidences for a young age of the earth and the universe, creation.com/age-of-the-earth, 4 June 2009.
2. For detailed explanations of a number of them, see also my earlier book *Refuting Compromise*, ch. 11, Creation Book Publishers, 2004. This chapter will concentrate on evidence discovered since then.
3. E.g. Jesus' response to the Pharisees in Matthew 12:27, "And if I drive out demons by Beelzebub, by whom do your people drive them out? So then, they will be your judges." He was showing that if His opponents were right in their own assumptions, it would rebound against themselves. See further discussion in Sarfati, J., Loving God With All Your Mind: Logic and Creation, *J. Creation* **12**(2)142–151, 1998; creation.com/logic.
4. See also Koukl, G., Arguments that Commit Suicide, Stand to Reason, www.str.org/free/solid_ground/SG0107.htm, July/August, 2001.

The evidence in this chapter shows that the evolutionists' *own axiom of uniformitarianism* leads to conclusions contrary to their billions-of-years beliefs. If they wish to deny the conclusion of these articles, they must abandon their own axiom to do so. This is the whole point.

Four main points

1. Atheists have no ultimate basis for believing in the general uniformity of nature that makes science possible. It is impossible to prove that the universe is orderly, because all possible proofs presuppose the very order they are trying to prove. Conversely, Christians have a basis in the Creator God of the Bible—since "Jesus Christ is the same yesterday and today and forever" (Hebrews 13:8).[5] See also final chapter.

2. Atheists certainly have no logical basis for believing in a rigid uniformity (i.e. not just uniformity of physical law but uniformity of geological process rates[6]) in the past, which doesn't even have the merit of being amenable to observation or repeatable tests.

3. Since atheists generally have this belief, it is legitimate for Christians to show that it leads to conclusions that refute their long-age beliefs.

4. Christians should not try to reinterpret the Bible to fit in with essentially anti-theistic theories.

Some evidence for a young world

As already pointed out, we are not trying to prove the biblical age with science. Arguments of the sort presented below, whether offered in support of an 'old' or 'young' earth, are always subject to revision in the light of new data or different assumptions. Rather, we are showing that, even granting the long-agers' premises about uniformitarianism, the *science* is overwhelmingly in favour of an age far younger than billions of years.

Dinosaur blood cells and vessels, hemoglobin, and proteins

A number of dinosaur bones have been discovered with red blood cells including hemoglobin, and blood vessels which are still elastic. Proteins like collagen and osteocalcin have also been found. Proven decay rates rule out their survival for many millions of years. But the long-age paradigm reigns,

---

5. Although their faith in uniformity is not unreasonable in light of repeated everyday experience, philosophically this is an unsound basis. Leading 20th-Century logician Bertrand Russell referred to a turkey facing Thanksgiving who could argue that since every day so far had passed without getting its head chopped off, it was safe in presuming that this would never happen.

6. This was the definition of uniformitarianism I was taught in Geol 101 in 1983. But many geologists now merely believe in uniformity of natural laws, allowing for past catastrophes but not Noah's Flood. This is the New Catastrophism, the title of a book by Derek Ager (1993), who also called it "episodicity".

and now evolutionists either deny the findings or postulate unknown means of preservation.

Dino blood cells

In the mid 1990s, Mary Schweitzer, a student of the famous paleontologist 'Dinosaur' Jack Horner, was studying thin sections of *T. rex* bones under the microscope at Montana State University. Then, as she describes it:

> "The lab filled with murmurs of amazement, for I had focused on something inside the vessels that none of us had ever noticed before: tiny round objects, translucent red with a dark center. Then a colleague took one look at them and shouted, 'You've got red blood cells. You've got red blood cells!'"[7]

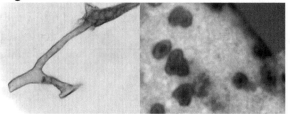

Left: The flexible branching structures in *T. rex* bone were justifiably identified as 'blood vessels'. **Right:** These microscopic structures were able to be squeezed out of some of the blood vessels, and do 'look like cells' as the researchers said. Photo M. H. Schweitzer.

Dino hemoglobin

Schweitzer then demonstrated that hemoglobin, the oxygen-carrying protein that gives red blood cells their colour, had also survived surprisingly well.[8] It gave the right spectroscopic signatures with multiple techniques, and also induced rats to produce antibodies that reacted with hemoglobin from modern creatures.[9]

Dino blood vessels

Then in 2005, Schweitzer announced a further sensational discovery in a different *T. rex* bone. After the mineral matrix was dissolved using the chelating agent EDTA, some soft tissue remained. This included what looked like transparent branching blood vessels that were still elastic, containing microscopic structures that looked like red blood cells. They even had nuclei, like those of modern reptiles—but unlike mammals, where the cells start off nucleated then lose their nuclei to become biconcave discs.[10]

7.   Schweitzer, M. and Staedter, T., The real Jurassic Park, *Earth*, pp. 55–57, June 1997.
8.   Schweitzer, M.H. et al., Heme compounds in dinosaur trabecular bone, *PNAS* 94:6291–6296, June 1997; www.pnas.org/cgi/reprint/94/12/6291.pdf.
9.   Wieland, C., Sensational dinosaur blood report! *Creation* **19**(4):42–43, 1997; creation.com/dino_blood, based on research by Schweitzer & Staedter, Ref 7.
10. Sid Perkins, Old Softy: Tyrannosaurus fossil yields flexible tissue, *Science News* **167**(13):195, 26 March 2005.

Dino proteins

Two years later, Schweitzer found the protein collagen in a *T. rex* bone,[11,12] and followed it with the discovery of collagen in hadrosaur bone,[13] dated as 'older' than the *T. rex* (80 Ma compared to 65 Ma). Yet analysis of collagen stability shows that it would last only 2.7 Ma at freezing point under the most favourable preservation conditions. At 10°C, the limit was 180,000 years, and 15,000 years at 20°C;[14,15] dinosaurs were supposed to live in a warm climate.

Furthermore, other researchers discovered bones of an *Iguanodon*, allegedly twice as old ('dated' to 120 Ma), which contained enough of the protein osteocalcin to produce an immune reaction.[16,17] Yet even at freezing point, this protein should not last this long—only 110 Ma.[14,15] Given the much warmer climates during the alleged Age of Dinosaurs, even this figure is implausible; given that osteocalcin would last 7.5 Ma at 10°C and 580,000 years at 20°C, the maximum lifetimes indicated by these two protein discoveries are even shorter: 15,000 and 580,000 years, respectively.

And other researchers found "cell-like structures comparable to those of living vertebrates" in a well-preserved hadrosaur fossil. Further analysis of the hadrosaur skin and a claw found amino acids (constituents of proteins) "suggesting that the cell-like structures were indeed cells".[18]

Power of the paradigm

Schweitzer's reaction was a perfect illustration of how one's bias determines the interpretation of the evidence:

> "It was exactly like looking at a slice of modern bone. But of course, I couldn't believe it. I said to the lab technician: 'The bones are, after all, 65 million years old. How could blood cells survive that long?'"[19]

Here is more sensible reasoning:

11. Schweitzer, M.H., et al., Analyses of soft tissue from Tyrannosaurus rex suggest the presence of protein, *Science* **316**(5822):277–280, 2007.
12. Doyle, S., Squishosaur scepticism squashed, creation.com/collagen, 20 April 2007.
13. Schweitzer, M.H. *et al.*, Biomolecular characterization and protein sequences of the Campanian hadrosaur *B. canadensis, Science* **324**(5927):626–631, 1 May 2009 | doi: 10.1126/science.1165069,
14. Nielsen-Marsh, C., Biomolecules in fossil remains: Multidisciplinary approach to endurance, *The Biochemist* **24**(3):12–14, June 2002; www.biochemist.org/bio/02403/0012/024030012.pdf.
15. Doyle, S., The Real Jurassic Park, *Creation* **30**(3):12–15, 2008; creation.com/real-jurassic-park.
16. Embery G. et al., Identification of proteinaceous material in the bone of the dinosaur *Iguanodon, Connect Tissue Res.* 44 Suppl 1:41–6, 2003; The abstract says: "an early eluting fraction was immunoreactive with an antibody against osteocalcin."
17. Muyzer G. *et al., Preservation of bone protein osteocalcin in dinosaurs. Geology* 20:871–874, 1992.
18. Hecht, J., Dinosaur "cells" shed light on life 66 million years ago, *New Scientist* **203**(2715):8, 4 July 2009.
19. Schweitzer, M.H., Montana State University Museum of the Rockies; cited on p. 160 of Morell, V., Dino DNA: The hunt and the hype, *Science* **261**(5118):160–162, 9 July 1993.

"This looks like modern bone; I have seen blood cells and detected hemoglobin, and real chemistry shows they can't survive for 65 million years. I don't see millions of years in my lab. So maybe *that* is the wrong premise."

Then after she found elastic blood vessels and other soft tissue, a report quoted her as follows:

"'It was totally shocking,' Schweitzer says. 'I didn't believe it until we'd done it 17 times.'"[20]

This repeated testing shows that she is a careful scientist, but would she have been so careful if the blood vessels were not so "shocking"—to the long-age paradigm?

After discovering collagen, she admitted that it wasn't predicted, but said:

"The presence of original molecular components is not predicted for fossils older than a million years, and the discovery of collagen in this well-preserved dinosaur supports the use of actualistic conditions to formulate molecular degradation rates and models, rather than relying on theoretical or experimental extrapolations derived from conditions that do not occur in nature."[11]

So, rather than falsifying her long-age beliefs, she postulated unknown 'conditions' that have allowed these structures to survive for millions of years—and these conditions must have *persisted* for millions of years.

Other scientists claimed that the blood vessels were really bacterial biofilms, and the blood cells were iron-rich spheres called framboids.[21] Yet this ignores the wide range of evidence Schweitzer adduced, and she has answered this claim in detail.[22,23]

Young age evidence would be explained away

More bias comes from the discoverers of preserved hadrosaur cells.[18] *New Scientist* reports them as follows:

"Manning says the presence of amino acids, rather than whole proteins, is a good sign. After 66 million years, proteins in soft tissue should have broken down into amino acids, so finding large proteins would likely be a sign of contamination. The high concentrations of amino acids in the fossil, compared with only traces found in the surrounding sediment, support the idea that they came from the fossil."[18]

20. Schweitzer, cited in *Science* 307:1852, 25 March 2005.
21. Kaye, T.G. et al., Dinosaurian Soft Tissues Interpreted as Bacterial Biofilms, *PLoS ONE* 3(7): e2808, 2008 | doi:10.1371/journal.pone.0002808.
22. Researchers Debate: Is It Preserved Dinosaur Tissue, or Bacterial Slime? blogs.discovermagazine.com, 30 July 2008.
23. Wieland, C., Doubting doubts about the Squishosaur, creation.com/squishosaur-doubts, 2 August 2008.

So if intact proteins had been found in the hadrosaur fossil, the researchers would have *denied the result*, instead dismissing it as 'contamination'.[24] Yet Schweitzer has already discovered such proteins. But it shows again the grip of the millions-of-years dogma.

And evolutionary paleontologist Hans Larsson has advocated ^{14}C testing of dino bones. I *agree*—any detectable [14]C *should* be regarded as further evidence against millions of years, as with diamonds (previous chapter). But Larsson would use it as evidence that the bones were contaminated by modern microbes! Once again, eons of time are sacrosanct—immune from evidence. Of course, bacteria would not explain collagen or osteocalcin, which are normal proteins in bone. And they can't explain ^{14}C in diamonds.

DNA, tissue and microbe survival after millions of years

The above is the best known of biological materials that have survived. But it is far from the only case:

- **Magnolia leaf DNA.** This was extracted from a magnolia leaf fossil reported to be 17–20 million years old.[25,26] The problem for evolutionists is that DNA degrades very quickly, even faster than proteins, hence if the fossils really were millions of years old, no DNA could be extracted.[27]

- **Bugs on ice.** Bacteria frozen in Antarctica 'dated' to 8 million years old have been revived in the lab.[28,29]

- **Amber bacteria.** Some have claimed to have 'resurrected' dormant bacteria found in amber supposedly 120 million years old.[30,31]

- **Salty microbes.** A paper in *Nature* in 2000 claimed to have revived bacteria found in salt crystals from 600 m (2,000 ft) below the surface in a mine in Mexico 'dated' to 250 million years.[32,33]

24. Catchpoole, D., Dino protein denial, *Creation* **32**(2):18, 2010; creation.com/dino-protein-denial.
25. Golenberg, E.M., et al., Chloroplast DNA sequence from a Miocene Magnolia species, *Nature* 344:656–658, 12 April 1990; commentary by Karl J. Niklas, K.J., Turning over an old leaf, same issue, p. 587.
26. Wieland, C., 'Oldest' DNA—an exciting find! *Creation* **13**(2):22–23, 1991; creation.com/oldestdna.
27. As Benjamin Kear, a long-age evolutionist and Research Fellow in Genetics at La Trobe University (Victoria, Australia) said: "The problem is when we're talking about ancient DNA, you're generally only talking a few tens of thousands of years at absolute maximum. DNA degrades very, very quickly … ." *The Science Show*, ABC Radio National, first broadcast 5 December 2009, www.abc.net.au.
28. Bidle, K.D. et al., Fossil genes and microbes in the oldest ice on Earth, *Proceedings of the National Academy of Sciences* **104**(33):13455–13460, 2007.
29. Catchpoole, D., 'Sleeping Beauty' bacteria, *Creation* **28**(1):23, 2005; creation.com/sleeping. See also Catchpoole, D., More 'Sleeping Beauty' bacteria, creation.com/moresleep.
30. Greenblatt, C.L. *et al.*, Diversity of microorganisms isolated from amber, *Microbial Ecology* 38:58–68, 1999.
31. Catchpoole, D., Amber needed water (and lots of it), *Creation* **31**(2):20–22, 2009.
32. Vreeland, R.H., Rosenzweig, W.D., Powers, D.W., Isolation of a 250 million-year-old halotolerant bacterium from a primary salt crystal, *Nature* **407**(6806):897–900, 2000.
33. Salty saga, *Creation* **23**(4):15, 2001; creation.com/saltysaga.

- **Shiny shells with ligaments.** Mud springs on the edge of the 'market town' of Wootton Bassett, near Swindon, Wiltshire, England, are 'pumping up' fossils that are supposed to be 165 million years old.[34] One evolutionary palaeontologist explained: "There are the shells of bivalves which still have their original organic ligaments and yet they are millions of years old."[35] Many also have "shimmering mother-of-pearl shells".

- **Muscle tissue from fossil salamander.** This allegedly 18 million-year-old fossil has muscle tissue preserved "organically" in three dimensions, with many fine microscopic details.[36] This included circulatory vessels "infilled with blood". The researchers commented that the tissue showed "very little degradation since it was originally fossilised... making it the highest quality soft tissue preservation ever documented in the fossil record."[37,38]

- **Fossil ink and ink sac.** A fossilized ink sac from a squid 'dated' at 150 million years old provided ink that was used to draw a picture of the squid and write its Latin name. An evolutionary geologist admitted, "The structure is similar to ink from a modern squid so we can write with it. They can be dissected as if they are living animals, you can see the muscle fibres and cells."[39,40]

Earth's magnetic field decay[41]

The earth's magnetic field has been decaying so fast that it couldn't be more than about 10,000 years old. Rapid reversals during the Flood year, and fluctuations shortly after, just caused the field energy to drop even faster. Creationist physicist Dr Russell Humphreys' model for planetary magnetic fields has made successful predictions where the evolutionary dynamo failed.

Cause of the earth's magnetic field

Materials like iron are composed of tiny magnetic domains, each of which behaves like a tiny magnet. The domains themselves are composed of even

34. Snelling, A. A., '165 million year' surprise, *Creation* **19**(2):14–17, March–May 1997; creation.com/ligaments165ma.
35. Nuttall, N., Mud springs a surprise after 165 million years, *The Times,* London, p. 7, 2 May 1996.
36. McNamara, M. et al., Organic preservation of fossil musculature with ultracellular detail, *Proceedings of the Royal Society B,* published online before print 14 October 2009 | doi: 10.1098/rspb.2009.1378.
37. 'Ancient muscle tissue extracted from 18 million year old fossil', www.physorg.com, 5 November 2009.
38. Wieland, C., Best ever find of soft tissue (muscle and blood) in a fossil, creation.com/muscle-and-blood-in-fossil, 11 November 2009.
39. Dr Phil Wilby of the British Geological Survey, cited in, Ink found in Jurassic-era squid, BBC News, news.bbc.co.uk/2/hi/uk_news/england/wiltshire/8208838.stm, 19 August 2009.
40. Wieland, C., Fossil squid ink that still writes! creation.com/fossil-squid-ink, 15 September 2009; *Creation* **32**(1):9, 2010.
41. Sarfati, J., The earth's magnetic field: evidence that the earth is young, *Creation* **20**(2):15–19, March–May 1998; creation.com/magfield. See also *Refuting Compromise,* ch. 11, 2004, for refutation of other evolutionary arguments, such as multipoles.

tinier atoms, which are themselves microscopic magnets, and are lined up within the domain. But most pieces of iron are not magnets, because normally the domains cancel each other out. However in magnets, such as a compass needle, more of the domains are lined up in a certain direction, and so the material has an overall magnetic field.

Earth's core is mainly iron and nickel, so could its magnetic field be generated the same way as a compass needle's? No—above a temperature called the Curie point, the magnetic domains are disrupted. The earth's core, at its coolest region, is about 3,400–4,700°C,[42] much hotter than the Curie points of iron (750°C)[43] and indeed, of all known substances.

But in 1820, Danish physicist H.C. Ørsted (1777–1851) discovered that a sustained electric current produces a magnetic field. Without this, there could be no electric motors, vital to modern technological society. So could an electric current be responsible for the earth's magnetic field? Electric motors have a power source, but electric currents normally decay almost instantly once the power source is switched off (except in superconductors).[44] So how could there be an electric current inside the earth, without a source?

The answer is the 1831 discovery by the great creationist physicist Michael Faraday that a changing magnetic field induces an electric voltage, the basis of electrical generators.[45] Imagine the earth soon after creation with a large electrical current in its core. This would produce a strong magnetic field. Without a power source, this current would decay. Thus, the magnetic field would decay, too. As decay is change, it would induce a current—lower than, but in the same direction as, the original one.[46] So we have a decaying current producing a decaying field, which generates a decaying current ... . If the magnetic field is strong enough, the current would take a while to die out—which can be observed when some appliances are switched off. The decay rate can be accurately calculated, and is *exponential*.[47] (The electrical

---

42. The Earth: Its Properties, Composition and Structure, *Encyclopædia Britannica* 17:600, 15th ed., 1992.

43. Curie point, *Encyclopædia Britannica* 3:800 (15th ed.), 1992, named after Pièrre Curie (1859–1906), who later won a Nobel Prize with his wife Marie for their work on radioactivity.

44. This is due to electrical resistance—the electrons collide with atoms and are soon moving randomly, rather than in a current. In superconductors, there is zero resistance, so currents can persist indefinitely. But superconductivity is a low temperature phenomenon and has never been observed at temperatures anywhere near those of Earth's extremely hot core.

45. See Lamont, A., *21 Great Scientists who Believed the Bible*, Creation Science Foundation, Australia, pp. 88–97, 1995.

46. This is the result of Lenz's Law (after H.F.E. Lenz 1804–1864), which states that the direction of an induced current is that which opposes the cause producing it. In this case, the cause is the decaying current, so the induced current is in the direction to retard decay.

47. For a simple electric circuit at time t with initial current I, resistance R and inductance L, the current is given by $i = I\exp(t/\tau)$, where τ is the time constant L/R—the time for the current to decay to $1/e$ (~37%) of its initial value. For a sphere of radius a, conductivity σ and permeability μ, $\tau = 4\pi\sigma\mu a^2$.

energy doesn't disappear—it is turned into heat, a process discovered by the creationist physicist James Joule in 1840.[48])

Consequence of decaying current

In the 1970s, the late creationist physics professor Dr Thomas Barnes noted that measurements since 1835 have shown that the main part[49] of the earth's magnetic field is decaying at 5% per century[50] (also, archaeological measurements show that the field was 40% stronger in AD 1000 than today[51]). Barnes, the author of a well-regarded electro-magnetism textbook,[52] proposed that the earth's magnetic field was caused by a *freely decaying electric current* in the earth's metallic core. That is entirely consistent with observations on the rate of decay and experiments on likely core materials.[53] Barnes calculated that the current could not have been decaying for more than 10,000 years, or else its starting strength would have been large enough to melt the earth. So the earth must be younger than that.

The decaying current model is obviously incompatible with the billions of years needed by evolutionists. So their preferred model is a *self-sustaining dynamo* (electric generator). The earth's rotation and convection is supposed to circulate the molten iron/nickel of the outer core. Positive and negative charges in this liquid metal are supposed to circulate unevenly, which would produce an electric current, generating the magnetic field. Scientists have not produced a workable *analytic* model, despite 40–50 years of research, and there are many problems.[54]

Humphreys model out-guns evolutionary model on planetary magnetic fields

Physicist Russell Humphreys refined Barnes' model, proposing that God first created the earth out of water.[55] He based this on several Scriptures, for

---

48. Lamont, ref. 45, pp. 132–141.
49. More technically, the 'main part' is the 'dipole' (two poles, north and south) part of the field, comprising over 90% of the field observed. The strength of the source of the dipole part, called the 'dipole moment' is what is decaying at 5% per century.
50. McDonald, K.L. and Gunst, R.H., *An analysis of the earth's magnetic field from 1835 to 1965*, ESSA Technical Report, IER 46-IES 1, U.S. Government Printing Office, Washington, 1967.
51. Merrill, R.T. and McElhinney, M.W., *The Earth's Magnetic Field*, Academic Press, London, pp. 101–106, 1983.
52. Barnes, T.G., *Foundations of Electricity and Magnetism*, 3rd ed., El Paso, Texas, 1977.
53. Stacey, F.D., Electrical resistivity of the earth's core, *Earth and Planetary Science Letters* 3:204–206, 1967.
54. Measurements of electrical currents in the sea floor pose difficulties for the most popular class of dynamo models—Lanzerotti, L.J. *et al.*, Measurements of the large-scale direct-current earth potential and possible implications for the geomagnetic dynamo, *Science* 229:47–49, 5 July 1986. Also, the measured rate of field decay is sufficient to generate the current needed to produce today's field strength, meaning that there is no evidence for a self-sustaining dynamo operating today, if one ever did.
55. Humphreys, D.R., The creation of planetary magnetic fields, *CRSQ* 21(3):140–149, 1984.

example 2 Peter 3:5 which concludes: "the earth was formed out of water and by water." After this, God would have transformed much of the water into other substances like rock minerals. Now water contains hydrogen atoms, and the nucleus of a hydrogen atom is a tiny magnet.[56] Normally these magnets cancel out so water as a whole is almost non-magnetic. Humphreys proposed that God created the water with many of the nuclear magnets aligned. In the model, immediately after creation, they formed a more random arrangement, which caused the earth's magnetic field to decay. This generated current in the core, which would then decay according to Barnes' model, apart from many reversals in the Flood year as Humphreys' model states.

Dr Humphreys also calculated the fields of other planets (and the sun) based on this model. The important factors are the mass of the planet, the size of the core and how well it conducts electricity, plus the assumption that their original material was water. His model explains features which are puzzles to dynamo theorists. For example, evolutionists refer to "the enigma of lunar magnetism"[57] — the moon once had a strong magnetic field although it rotates only once a month. Also, it never had a molten core according to evolutionary models, which is essential for a dynamo.

Also, Mercury has a far stronger magnetic field than dynamo theory expects from a planet rotating 59 times slower than Earth. One evolutionist admitted, "Magnetism is almost as much of a puzzle now as it was when William Gilbert (1544–1603) wrote his classic text *Concerning Magnetism, Magnetic Bodies, and the Great Magnet, Earth* in 1600!"[58] The 2008 *Messenger* spacecraft flyby showed that Mercury's magnetic field was a few per cent lower than that measured by the *Mariner* spacecraft in 1975,[59] as Humphreys predicted in 1984.[55]

That year, Dr Humphreys had also made some predictions of the field strengths of Uranus and Neptune, the two giant ice planets past Saturn. His predictions were about 100,000 times the evolutionary dynamo predictions. The two rival models were inadvertently put to the test when the *Voyager 2* spacecraft flew past these planets in 1986 and 1989. The fields for Uranus

56. This is the proton, with a magnetic moment of 2.79285 nuclear magnetons or 1.4106 x 10^{-26} J/T. The deuteron, the nucleus of the rare 'heavy hydrogen' isotope, has a magnetic moment less than a third of this. Source: Laby, G.W.C. and T.H., *Tables of physical and chemical constants*, cited in P.W. Atkins, *Physical Chemistry*, 2nd Ed., p. 645, Oxford University Press, 1982.
57. Hood, L.L., The enigma of lunar magnetism, *Eos* **62**(16):161–163.
58. Taylor, S.R., *Destiny or Chance: our solar system and its place in the cosmos*, pp. 163–164, Cambridge University Press, Cambridge, 1998.
59. Humphreys, D.R., creation.com/mercurys-magnetic-field-is-young, 26 August 2008.

and Neptune[60] were just as Humphreys had predicted.[61] Yet many anti-creationists call creation 'unscientific' because it supposedly makes no predictions! Humphreys' model also explains why the moons of Jupiter which have cores have magnetic fields, while Callisto, which lacks a core, also lacks a field.[62]

Magnetic field reversals

The major criticism of Barnes' young-earth argument is evidence that the magnetic field has *reversed* several times—i.e. compasses would point south instead of north. When grains of the common magnetic mineral *magnetite* in volcanic lava or ash flows cool below its *Curie point* (see p. 209) of 570°C (1,060°F), the magnetic domains partly align themselves in the direction of the earth's magnetic field *at that time*. Once the rock is fully cooled, the magnetite's alignment is fixed. Thus, we have a permanent record of the earth's field through time.

Although evolutionists have no good explanations for the reversals, they maintain that the straightforward decay assumed by Barnes is invalid. Also, their model requires at least thousands of years for a reversal. And with their dating assumptions, they believe that the reversals occur at intervals of millions of years, and point to an old Earth.

Humphreys model predicts rapid reversals

The physicist Dr Russell Humphreys believed that Dr Barnes had the right idea, and he also accepted that the reversals were real. He modified Barnes' model to account for special effects of a liquid conductor, like the molten metal of the earth's outer core. If the liquid flowed upwards (due to convection—hot fluids rise, cold fluids sink), this could sometimes make the field reverse quickly.[63] Geophysicist John Baumgardner proposes that subducting tectonic plates were greatly involved in the Genesis Flood

60. The Voyager measurements were 3.0 and 1.5 x 10²⁴ J/T for Uranus and Neptune respectively. Ness, N.F. et al., Magnetic fields at Uranus, *Science* 233:85–89, 1986; A.J. Dessler, 'Does Uranus have a magnetic field?', *Nature* 319:174–175, 1986; R.A. Kerr, 'The Neptune system in Voyager's afterglow, *Science* 245:1450–51.

61. Dr Humphreys had predicted field strengths of the order of 10²⁴ J/T — see D.R. Humphreys, Good news from Neptune: the Voyager 2 measurements, *CRSQ* **27**(1):15–17, 1990. The fields of Uranus and Neptune are hugely off-centred (0.3 and 0.4 of the planets' radii) and at a large angle from the planets' spin axis (60° and 50°). A big puzzle for dynamo theorists, but explainable by a catastrophe which seems to have affected the whole solar system—see W. Spencer, Revelations in the solar system, *Creation* **19**(3):26–29, 1997; creation.com/solarsystem.

62. See 'Magnetic moon findings support creationist's theory', Focus, *Creation* **19**(4):8, 1997.

63. Humphreys, R., Reversals of the earth's magnetic field during the Genesis Flood, *Proc. First International Conference on Creationism*, Creation Science Fellowship, Pittsburgh 2:113–126, 1986. The moving conductive liquid would carry magnetic flux lines with them, and this would generate new currents, producing new flux in the opposite direction. See also his interview in *Creation* **15**(3):20–23, 1993.

(see also ch. 10). Humphreys proposes that these plates would sharply cool the outer parts of the core, driving the convection.[64] This means that most of the reversals occurred in the Flood year, every week or two. And after the Flood, there would have been large fluctuations due to residual motion. This is supported by the fact that archaeological measurements on materials from about 1000 BC and AD 1000 show that the surface geomagnetic field *intensity* (**B**) slowly increased to a maximum at about the time of Christ, and then declined slowly, becoming approximately exponential about AD 1000 (see graph below). But the reversals and fluctuations could not halt the loss of *energy* (E). This would decay even faster and has decayed monotonically throughout the whole period. Note that the field energy is the volume integral of B^2, which is why the *intensity* could fluctuate up and down during and after the Flood, while the total field *energy* always decreased.

The Humphreys model also explains why the sun reverses its magnetic field every 11 years. The sun is a gigantic ball of hot, energetically moving, electrically conducting gas. Dynamo theorists have trouble explaining how the sun would not only reverse its field but also regenerate it and maintain its intensity over billions of years. But there is no problem if the sun is only thousands of years old.

Dr Humphreys also proposed a test for his model: magnetic reversals should be found in rocks known to have cooled in days or weeks. For example, he predicted that in a thin lava 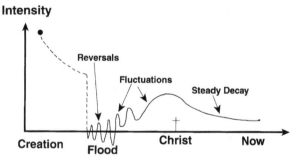 flow, the outside would cool first, and record Earth's magnetic field in one direction; the inside would cool a short time later, and record the field in another direction.

Three years after this prediction appeared in print, leading researchers Robert Coe and Michel Prévot found a thin lava layer that must have cooled within 15 days, and had 90° of reversal recorded continuously in it.[65] And it

---

64. Humphreys, R., Discussion of Baumgardner, J., 'Numerical simulation of the large-scale tectonic changes accompanying the Flood', *Proc. First International Conference on Creationism*, Creation Science Fellowship, Pittsburgh 2:29, 1986.
65. Coe, R.S. and Prévot, M., Evidence suggesting extremely rapid field variation during a geomagnetic reversal, *Earth and Planetary Science* **92**(3/4):292–298, April 1989. See also the reports by Ph.D. geologist Andrew Snelling, *Creation* **13**(3):46–50, **13**(4):44–48, 1991.

was no fluke—eight years later, they reported an even faster reversal.[66] This was staggering news to them and the rest of the evolutionary community, but strong corroboration for Humphreys' model.

Helium in zircons

Evolutionists assume that helium comes from alpha-decay of certain radioactive elements in the rocks. Helium atoms are very small and chemically unreactive so can quickly diffuse from rocks. Yet so much helium is still in some rocks that it couldn't have had time to escape—certainly not billions of years. This is also strong evidence that nuclear decay rates were much faster at some time in the past.

On Earth, helium is produced mainly by radioactive *alpha* (α)-decay. The great New Zealand physicist Ernest Rutherford (1871–1937) discovered that α-particles were really the nuclei of helium atoms. Radioactive elements in rocks—such as uranium, radium and thorium—produce helium this way. Yet helium is such a small, slippery molecule that it can slip through crystal lattices and eventually escape into the air, and the hotter the faster.

In some rocks, radioactive elements are often found in tiny crystals of zirconium silicate ($ZrSiO_4$), called *zircons*. Thus, they continuously produce helium, which should be escaping. But even the deep, hot zircons (197°C or 387°F) contained far too much helium—that is, if it had had billions of years to escape. But if there had really been only thousands of years for this helium to escape, then we shouldn't be surprised that there is so much left.[67]

Helium could not have been escaping for long

A RATE (Radioisotopes and the Age of the Earth) project confirmed this further.[68,69] This discovered:

• There must have been 1.5 billion years worth of decay—at current decay rates.

• Large amounts, up to 58%, of the helium are still there, while there is little in the surrounding material.

66. Coe, R.S., Prévot, M. and Camps, P., New evidence for extraordinarily rapid change of the geomagnetic field during a reversal, *Nature* **374**(6564):687–692, 1995; see also Snelling, A., The 'principle of least astonishment', *J. Creation* **9**(2):138–139, 1995; creation.com.magrev2.
67. Gentry, R.V., Glish, G.L. and McBay, E.H., Differential helium retention in zircons: implications for nuclear waste containment, *Geophysical Research Letters* **9**(10):1129–30, October 1982. See also Gentry's book: *Creation's Tiny Mystery*, Earth Science Associates, Knoxville TN, 3rd ed. 1992, pp. 169–170, 263–264.
68. Humphreys, R., Nuclear decay: evidence for a young world, *Impact* 352, October 2002; www.icr.org/pubs/imp/imp-352.htm.
69. Humphreys, D.R., Austin, S.A., Baumgardner, J.R. and Snelling, A.A., Helium diffusion rates support accelerated nuclear decay; in: ed. Ivey, R.L., Jr., *Fifth International Conference on Creationism*, pp. 175–196, Creation Science Fellowship, Pittsburgh, Pennsylvania, August, 2003; www.icr.org/research/icc03/pdf/Helium_ICC_7-22-03.pdf.

- Yet helium diffuses so rapidly out of zircon that it should have all but disappeared after about 100,000 years.

- The rate of helium leakage dates 'billion-year-old' zircons at 5,680 ± 2,000 years.

Therefore, the decay that produced the helium must have occurred within that timeframe. But then how could so much helium have been produced and accumulated in so little time? The best answer seems to be an episode of accelerated nuclear decay, during Creation Week or the Flood year, or more likely both.[70]

Of course, if nuclear decay had been accelerated in the past, that falsifies one key assumption of radiometric dating, i.e. that the decay rate has been constant. This is far from the only evidence for accelerated nuclear decay, as shown in the previous chapter.

Salt in the sea[71]

Salt is pouring into the sea much faster than it is escaping. The sea is not nearly salty enough for this to have been happening for billions of years. Even granting generous assumptions to evolutionists, the seas could not be more than 62 million years old—far younger than the billions of years believed by evolutionists. Again, this indicates a *maximum* age, not the *actual* age.

The ocean is essential for life on Earth, and also helps make the climate fairly moderate. However, although the ocean contains 1,370 million cubic kilometres (334 million cubic miles) of water, humans can't survive by drinking from it—it is too salty.

To a chemist, 'salt' refers to a wide range of chemicals where a metal is combined with a non-metal. Ordinary common salt is a compound formed when the metal sodium combines with the non-metal chlorine—sodium chloride. This contains electrically charged atoms, called ions, which attract each other, resulting in a fairly hard crystal. When salt dissolves, these ions separate. Sodium and chloride ions are the main ions in seawater, but not the only ones. The salty seas benefit man, because the ocean provides many useful minerals for our industries.

How old is the sea?

Many processes (see below) bring salts into the sea, while these salts don't leave the sea easily. So the saltiness is increasing steadily. We can work out how

---

70. See also Humphreys, R., Critics of helium evidence for a young world now silent, *J. Creation* **24**(1):14–16, 2010.
71. Sarfati, J., Salty seas: evidence for a young earth, *Creation* **21**(1):16–17, December 1998–February 1999; creation.com/salty.

much salt is in the sea, as well as the rates at which salts go into and out of the sea. Then, assuming how these rates varied in the past and how much salt was in the sea originally, we can calculate a maximum age for the sea.

In fact, this method was first proposed by Sir Isaac Newton's colleague Sir Edmond Halley (1656–1742), of comet fame.[72] More recently, the geologist, physicist and pioneer of radiation therapy, John Joly (1857–1933), estimated on this basis that the oceans were 80–90 million years old at the most.[73] But this was far too young for evolutionists, who believe that life evolved in the ocean billions of years ago.

More recently still, the geologist Dr Steve Austin and physicist Dr Russell Humphreys analyzed figures from secular geoscience sources for the quantity of sodium ion (Na^+) in the ocean, and its input and output rates.[74] The slower the input and faster the output, the older the calculated age of the ocean would be.

Every kilogram of seawater contains about 10.8 grams of dissolved Na^+. This means that there is a total of 1.47×10^{16} (14,700 million million) tonnes of Na^+ in the ocean.

Sodium input

Water on the land weathers minerals, especially clays and feldspars, and leaches the sodium out of them. This sodium is carried into the ocean by rivers. Some salt is supplied by water through the ground directly to the sea— called submarine groundwater discharge (SGWD). Such water often has a high mineral concentration. Ocean floor sediments release much sodium, as do hot springs on the ocean floor (hydrothermal vents). Volcanic dust also contributes some sodium.

Austin and Humphreys calculated that about 457 million tonnes of sodium now enter the sea every year. The minimum possible amount in the past, even if the most generous assumptions about inflow rates are granted to evolutionists, is 356 million tonnes/year.

Actually, a more recent study shows that salt is entering the oceans even faster than Austin and Humphreys thought, which means that the maximum

72. Halley, E., A short account of the cause of the saltness [sic] of the ocean, and of the several lakes that emit no rivers; with a proposal, by help thereof, to discover the age of the world, *Philosophical Transactions of the Royal Society of London* **29**:296–300, 1715; cited in Ref. 74.

73. Joly, J., An estimate of the geological age of the earth, *Scientific Transactions of the Royal Dublin Society, New Series,* **7**(3), 1899; reprinted in Annual Report of the Smithsonian Institution, 30 June 1899, pp. 247–288; cited in Ref. 74.

74. Austin, S.A. and Humphreys, D.R., The sea's missing salt: a dilemma for evolutionists, *Proc. Second International Conference on Creationism* **2**:17–33, 1990. This paper should be consulted for more detail than is possible here.

possible age of the ocean is even lower than they calculated.[75] Previously, the amount of submarine groundwater discharge was thought to be a small fraction (0.01–10%) of the water from surface runoff, mainly rivers. But this new study, measuring the radioactivity of radium in coastal water, shows that the groundwater discharge is as much as 40% of the river flow.[76]

Sodium output

People who live near the sea often have problems with rust in cars. This is due to salt spray—small droplets of seawater which escape from the ocean; the water evaporates, leaving behind tiny salt crystals. This is a major process that removes sodium from the sea. Another major process is called ion exchange—clays can absorb sodium ions and exchange them for calcium ions, which are released into the ocean. Some sodium is lost from the ocean when water is trapped in pores in sediments on the ocean floor. Certain minerals with large cavities in their crystal structure, called zeolites, can absorb sodium from the ocean.

However, the rate of sodium output is far less than the input. Austin and Humphreys calculated that about 122 million tonnes of sodium leave the sea every year today. The maximum possible amount, even if the most generous assumptions about sodium loss rate are granted to evolutionists, is 206 million tonnes/year.

Estimating the age of the ocean

Even with these generous assumptions, Austin and Humphreys calculated that the ocean must be *less* than 62 million years old. It's important to stress that this is *not* the *actual* age, but a *maximum* age. That is, this evidence is consistent with any age up to 62 million years, including the biblical age of about 6,000 years.

The Austin and Humphreys calculation assumes the lowest plausible input rates and fastest plausible output rates, sustained throughout geologic time. Another assumption favourable to long-agers is that there was no dissolved salt to start with. If we assume more realistic conditions in the past, the calculated maximum age is much less.

For one thing, God probably created the oceans with some saltiness, so that saltwater fish could live comfortably in it. Noah's Flood would have dissolved large amounts of sodium from rocks and sediment. This would

75. Moore, W.S, Large groundwater inputs to coastal waters revealed by 226Ra enrichments, *Nature* **380**(6575):612–614, 18 April 1996; perspective by Church, T.M., An underground route for the water cycle, same issue, pp. 579–580.
76. Church, Ref. 75, p. 580, comments: "The conclusion that large quantities of SGWD are entering the coastal ocean has the potential to radically alter our understanding of oceanic chemical mass balance."

have found its way into the oceans when the floodwaters retreated. Finally, the larger-than-expected submarine groundwater discharge would further reduce the maximum age.

Comets[77]

Comets lose so much mass every time they pass near the sun in their orbit that they should have evaporated after a few tens of thousands of years. To hold onto long ages, evolutionists have proposed *ad hoc* sources to replenish the comet supply. But observations of the region of the proposed Kuiper Belt fail to confirm its existence as a cometary source. And there is a total absence of observational evidence for the Oort Cloud, among other scientific difficulties for both notions.

What are comets?

Comets are "dirty snowballs" (or "dirty icebergs"[78,79]) that revolve around the sun in highly elliptical orbits. They are usually a few kilometres across, but Halley's is about 10 km and Hale-Bopp, seen in 1997, is about 40 km and one of the largest comets known. They contain dust and 'ice', which is not just frozen water but also frozen ammonia, methane and carbon dioxide. A recently discovered 'backwardly orbiting' comet is a problem for the 'nebular hypothesis' that tries to explain how the solar system formed naturalistically, a hypothesis that Dawkins no doubt accepts.[80]

How comets shine—problem for long-agers

When comets pass close to the sun, some of the ice evaporates, forming a coma about 10,000–100,000 km wide. Also, the solar wind (charged particles radiating from the sun) pushes a tail of ions (electrically charged atoms) directly away from the sun. And finally, solar radiation pushes away dust particles to generate a *second* tail that curves backwards along the comet's orbital path, gently away from the sun. The coma and tails have a very low density—even the best vacuums produced in laboratories are denser. The earth passed through a tail of Halley's Comet in 1910, and it was hardly noticeable. But these tails reflect the sun's light very strongly, which can

77. Sarfati, J., Comets: Portents of doom or indicators of youth? *Creation* 25(3):36–40 June–August 2003; creation.com.comets.

78. Frank Whipple's model, e.g., Whipple, F.L., Background of modern comet theory, *Nature* 263:15, 2 September 1976. He expressed it more formally as a 'dirty ice comet nucleus'.

79. Kuiper, G., Present status of the icy conglomerate model; in: *Ices in the Solar System*, J. Klinger, D. Benest, A. Dollfus and R. Smoluchowski (Eds.), D. Reidel Publishing, Dordrecht, Holland, pp. 343–366, 1984.

80. Sarfati, J., and Catchpoole, D., "Backwards" comet perplexes scientists, *Creation* 31(4):38–39, 2009; creation.com/backwards-comet.

make comets spectacular when they are close to both the sun and the earth. Their appearance like a hairy star is responsible for the term 'comet', from the Greek κομητη *comētē* (long-haired).

This loss of material means that the comet is gradually being destroyed every time it comes close to the sun. In fact, many comets have been observed to become much dimmer in later passes. Even Halley's Comet was brighter in the past. However, the pathetic appearance in its last visit in 1986 was more due to unfortunate viewing conditions. I.e. when it was at its brightest, at perihelion,[81] the earth was on the other side of the sun, which therefore blocked it from view. And even when it emerged from behind the sun, it was far from the earth.

Comets are also in danger of being captured by planets, like Comet Shoemaker-Levy crashing into Jupiter in 1994, or of being ejected from the solar system. A direct hit on Earth is unlikely, but could be disastrous because of the comet's huge kinetic (motion) energy.

Some evolutionists believe comets have caused mass extinctions. The mysterious aerial explosion in Tunguska, Siberia, in 1908, which flattened over 2,100 km² (800 sq. miles) of forest, has been attributed to a comet. However, no people were killed because the area was unpopulated.

The problem for evolutionists is that, given the observed rate of loss and maximum periods, comets could not have been orbiting the sun for billions of years since the solar system allegedly formed.[82,83]

Two groups of comets

Comets are divided into two groups: short-period (<200 years) comets, such as Halley's (76 years); and long-period (>200 years) comets. But the comets from the two groups seem essentially the same in size and composition. Short-period ones normally orbit in the same direction as the planets (prograde) and in almost the same plane (the ecliptic). However, one exception is Halley's Comet, which has retrograde motion and a highly inclined orbit. Long-period comets can orbit in almost any plane and in both directions. Some astronomers suggest that it was once a long-period comet, and strong gravity from a planet dramatically shrank its orbit, and thus the period. So long-period and Halley-type comets are grouped together and called 'nearly isotropic comets' (NICs).

---

81. Closest point to the sun, from Greek περὶ perí around; and ἥλιος hēlios sun.
82. Wieland, C., Halley's Comet: Beacon of Creation, *Creation* **8**(2):6–10, March 1986; creation.com/halley.
83. The most thorough article is Faulkner, D., Comets and the age of the solar system, *J. Creation* **11**(3):264–273, 1997; creation.com/comet.

The longest period that could be envisaged for a stable orbit would be about 4 million years if the maximum possible aphelion[84] were 50,000 AU.[85] This is a conservative estimate, because this is 20% of the distance to the nearest star, so there's a fair chance other stars could release the comet from the sun's grip.[86]

However, even with this long orbit, this would still have been time to make 1,200 trips around the sun if the solar system were 4.6 billion years old. But the comet would have been extinguished long before. The problem is even more acute with short-period comets.

Empty evolutionist explanations

Evolutionists need to invent a secondary hypothesis to preserve long ages. Their only solution is to propose hypothetical sources to replenish the supply of comets:

Short period: Kuiper Belt and Scattered Disc

Dutch astronomer Gerald Kuiper (1905–1973) proposed in 1951 that a doughnut-shaped reservoir of comets would be located at about 30–50 AU (beyond Neptune's orbit). But to work, there would need to be billions of comets in this belt. However, only about a thousand bodies (Kuiper Belt Objects, KBOs) have been discovered, and these are hardly comets, because they are far too large. They are over 100 km in diameter, so are at least ten times wider than comets, which means over a thousand times more massive. Indeed, the KBOs Orcus and Quaoar are over 1,000 km in diameter.

Furthermore, the more recent observations indicate that the Kuiper Belt is too stable to be a comet reservoir, so the origin of short-period comets is now considered to be the "Scattered Disc".[87] This is even further out, and the bodies (Scattered Disc Objects, SDOs) have highly elliptical orbits from 30–35 AU at perihelion to over 100 AU at aphelion. However, much the same problems apply: too few objects, and too large. For example, the SDO Eris with a diameter of 2,400 km, is even larger than Pluto, while another SDO called Sedna is larger than Quaoar.

---

84. Furthest point from the sun, from Greek ἀπό *apó* away from, which becomes ἀπ- *ap-* or ἀφ- *aph-* before an unaspirated or aspirated vowel, respectively.
85. AU = Astronomical Unit, the mean distance of the earth from the sun, 150 million km.
86. This comes from Kepler's 3rd Law of Planetary motion, $a^3 = p^2$, where a is the semi-major axis in AU, and p is the period in years.
87. Levison H.F. and Donnes, L., "Comet Populations and Cometary Dynamics". in McFadden, L.A.A. *et al.*, *Encyclopedia of the Solar System* (2nd ed.), Amsterdam; Boston: Academic Press, pp. 575–588, 2007.

Long period: Oort Cloud

Dutch astronomer Jan Hendrik Oort (1900–1992) proposed in 1950 that a spherical cloud of comets extending as far as three light-years from the sun could supply the long-period comets. Passing stars, gas clouds and galactic tides are supposed to be able to knock comets from the Oort Cloud into orbits that enter the inner solar system. But there is no *observational* support for such a cloud.[88]

Furthermore, collisions would have destroyed most comets. This would leave a combined mass of comets of only about one Earth, or at most 3.5 Earths with some doubtful assumptions,[89,90] instead of the 40 hoped for.

Also, if there really were an Oort Cloud, there should be about 100 times more comets than are actually observed. So evolutionary astronomers postulate an 'arbitrary fading function',[91] or that they are broken before we see them.[92] It seems desperate to propose an unobserved (and with present technology, unobservable even if it existed) source to keep comets supplied for the alleged billions of years, then make excuses for why this hypothetical source doesn't feed in comets nearly as fast as it should.

Summary

This chapter was not trying to 'prove' the Bible's timescale with science. Rather, it showed that, even granting uniformitarian assumptions, there are many physical processes that point to a 'young age'. Therefore, this turns the evolutionists' arguments against them. The following are the main arguments for a young earth discussed in this chapter and others:

- Many tissues and biomolecules remain in fossils allegedly millions of years old, although real chemistry shows that they could not have survived anywhere near that long. This includes collagen, blood cells and vessels from dinosaur bones; muscle tissue, shell ligaments, DNA and living bacteria.

- Zircons often contain abundant helium, produced by much radioactive decay. Yet such small atoms should long ago have diffused out of the crystals. This indicates that it was produced recently (about 6,000 years ago) by accelerated radioactive decay.

88. Sagan, C. and Druyan, A., *Comets*, Michael Joseph, London, p. 175, 1985.
89. Stern, S.A. and Weissman, P.R., Rapid collisional evolution of comets during the formation of the Oort Cloud, *Nature* **409**(6820):589–591, 2001.
90. Faulkner, D., More problems for the 'Oort comet cloud', *J. Creation* **15**(2):11, 2001; creation.com/oort.
91. Bailey, M.E., Where have all the comets gone? *Science* **296**(5576):2251–2253, 21 June 2002 (perspective on Levison, Ref. 92).
92. Levison, H.F. et al., The mass disruption of Oort Cloud comets, *Science* **296**(5576):2212–2215, 21 June 2002.

222 ~ THE GREATEST HOAX ON EARTH?

- Coal and diamond often contain carbon-14, but this decays so quickly that it would be undetectable in much less than a million years (see previous chapter).

- The earth's magnetic field is decaying exponentially, as a giant resistance/inductive circuit. This decay has been accompanied by rapid field reversals, recorded in thin, quickly-hardening lava flows.

- Salt is entering the sea quicker than it's leaving it; measured rates of inflow and outflow, and the current concentration place an upper limit of 62 million years. This is much less than the billions of years required for evolution.

- Comets lose so much mass every time they pass the sun (that's why we see their tails) that they would have evaporated after a few hundred passes. This means they could not have been orbiting for millions of years. Proposed hypothetical replenishing sources, such as the Kuiper Belt and Oort Cloud, have numerous problems.

- Polystrate fossils show that the layers they span must have been deposited quickly, before the organism had time to decay (see ch. 7).

- Flat gaps: smooth boundary lines between layers shows that there has been no time for significant erosion between geological layers (see ch. 7).

- Humans accumulate 100–300 slightly harmful mutations every generation, and natural selection can't remove them. This would have resulted in genetic meltdown after even hundreds of thousands of years. Supercomputer modelling of observed mutation rates and genetic load match the exponential decrease of human lifespans after the Flood and Babel (see ch. 3).

—∞—

Chapter 13

ORIGIN OF LIFE

THE origin of first life is a problem for materialists, since natural selection can't explain it. Even the simplest living creatures are extremely complex, and this complexity largely involves informational 'software'. Many enzymes are needed for the vital processes of life, including the nano-motor ATP synthase to supply the energy units.

Darwin proposed a protein origin for life, but in reality proteins would be destroyed in a primordial soup, and can't reproduce, as Dawkins admits. Dawkins' favoured alternative (at least in the current book), the RNA World, has huge problems, in that RNA is even more unstable than proteins and harder to produce, and even ribozymes (RNA-based enzymes) are poor enzymes compared to many protein enzymes that are essential for life.

Some recent claims purporting to support the RNA World, which Dawkins alludes to, are addressed. Like most chemical evolution 'simulations', they involve unacceptable levels of interference from an intelligent investigator—something not available in the alleged primordial soup.

Darwinian processes can't explain *first* life

The origin of *first* life is a big problem for materialists such as Dawkins: if evolution by natural selection could not have started in the first place, it's dead in the water. *It's pointless to talk about selection between two runners if both are dead on the starting line!*

The famous philosopher Antony Flew (1923–), until recently known as a leading proponent of atheism, recently abandoned this belief, to the consternation of the atheistic community.[1] One major factor was the enormous complexity of even the simplest self-reproducing cell. He explains, directly addressing Dawkins' own materialistic claims:

"It seems to me that Richard Dawkins constantly overlooks the fact that Darwin himself, in the fourteenth chapter of *The Origin of Species*, pointed out that his whole argument began with a being which already possessed reproductive powers. This is the creature the evolution of which a truly comprehensive theory of evolution must give some account.

"Darwin himself was well aware that he had not produced such an account. It now seems to me that the findings of more than fifty years of DNA research have provided materials for a new and enormously powerful argument to design."[2]

The simple cell?

In Darwin's day, many people swallowed the theory of spontaneous generation—that life arose from non-living matter. It was somewhat easier to believe then because the cell's structure was almost unknown. Ernst Haeckel, Darwin's popularizer in Germany, claimed that a cell was a "simple lump of albuminous combination of carbon."[3,4]

The molecular biological revolution of the last half century has shown how the cell requires both high *information content* and a means to pass this information on to the next generation (*reproduction*).

The cell's information content

All the cell's machinery is programmed on the famous double-helix molecule, DNA (deoxyribonucleic acid). This recipe has an enormous *information content*, which is transmitted from one generation to the next, so that living things reproduce 'after their kinds' (cf. Genesis 1, 10 times). Dawkins stated in a previous work:

1. See Flew, A. with Varghese, R., *There is no a God: How the world's most notorious atheist changed his mind*, Harper Collins, New York, 2007; and detailed review by Cosner, L., *J. Creation* 22(3):21–24, 2008; creation.com/flew.
2. My Pilgrimage from Atheism to Theism: an exclusive interview with former British atheist Professor Antony Flew by Gary Habermas, *Philosophia Christi*, Winter 2005; www.illustramedia.com/IDArticles/flew-interview.pdf.
3. Behe, M.J., *Darwin's Black Box: The Biochemical Challenge to Evolution*, p. 24, The Free Press, New York, 1996.
4. Haeckel was also a notorious fraudster—he forged embryonic diagrams to bolster the erroneous idea that the embryo's development recapitulated (re-traced) its alleged evolutionary ancestry. See Grigg, R., Ernst Haeckel: Evangelist for evolution and apostle of deceit, *Creation* 18(2):33–36, 1996; creation.com/haeckel.

"[T]here is enough information capacity in a single human cell to store the *Encyclopaedia Britannica*, all 30 volumes of it, three or four times over."[5]

In *Greatest Show,* Dawkins says:

"The difference between life and non-life is a matter not of substance but information. Living things contain prodigious quantities of information. Most of the information is coded in DNA ..." (p. 405)

Coded linguistic information

Dawkins' statements above are most apt, since the information is analogous to *language*, with its own language convention, the *genetic code.* Another way of putting it is: the secret of life lies not with the chemical ingredients, but with the *organizational arrangement* of the molecules.

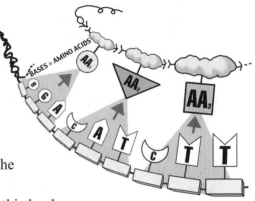

To explain: the information in this book is not based on the properties of the ink molecules on the paper, but on the way they are arranged into letters, words, phrases, sentences, paragraphs—an ink spill will not generate the plays of Shakespeare. And the letters are meaningless unless one understands the language they are in. For example, 'gift' in English means a present, in German it means poison. The wrong convention can mean the wrong message. One German friend told me that the first time he came to an English-speaking country, he thought we were stark raving mad for having poison shops everywhere.

In DNA, the information is stored as sequences of four types of DNA bases, A,C,G and T. These could be called chemical 'letters' because they store information in an analogous way to printed letters.[6] There are huge problems for evolutionists explaining how just the 'letters' alone could come from a primordial soup. But even if this were solved, it would be as meaningless as getting a bowl of alphabet soup, because the letters would not spell anything. This must be decoded accurately, otherwise, like the German gift, the wrong protein will result.

---

5. Dawkins, R., *The Blind Watchmaker*, p. 115, W.W. Norton, New York, 1986.
6. Adenine, cytosine, guanine and thymine. They are part of building blocks called nucleotides, which comprise the sugar deoxyribose, a phosphate and a base. In RNA, uracil (U) substitutes for thymine and ribose substitutes for deoxyribose.

In living organisms, three DNA 'letters' code for one protein 'letter' or amino acid. There is an astronomical number of possible genetic codes, i.e. ways of matching the 64 possible DNA triplets to the 20 amino acids plus one stop codon—1.51×10^{84}, so why is ours *almost*[7] universal in living things? It turns out that ours, or something almost like it, is optimal for protecting against errors. That is, a point mutation, or single-letter typo, in the DNA will often not change the amino acid coded for, or will code for one chemically similar. [8]

A message requires a message sender, a book requires an author, and a program requires a programmer. So the DNA message and its accompanying language system are strong evidence that they too had an original message sender, consistent with the Genesis creation of the original kinds, programmed to be able to pass on their programs.

Cell's 'software' a problem to naturalism

Renowned physicist Paul Davies, certainly no friend to creationists or Christians in general, has pointed out that the living cell would be more meaningfully equated to an incredibly powerful supercomputer. In Davies' words, the living cell is "an information processing and replicating system of astonishing complexity."[9] Davies continued:

> "DNA is not a special life-giving molecule, but a genetic databank that transmits its information using a mathematical code. Most of the workings of the cell are best described, not in terms of material stuff—hardware—but as information, or software. Trying to make life by mixing chemicals in a test tube is like soldering switches and wires in an attempt to produce Windows 98. It won't work because it addresses the problem at the wrong conceptual level."[9]

But as Davies recognized, explaining life's information content from a naturalistic origin-of-life perspective ...

> " ... leaves us with a curious conundrum. How did nature fabricate the world's first digital information processor—the original living cell—from the blind chaos of blundering molecules? How did molecular hardware get to write its own software?"[9]

---

7. There are exceptions, some known since the 1970s. An example is *Paramecium*, where a few of the 64 (4^3 or 4x4x4) possible codons code for different amino acids. More examples are being found constantly. Certain archaea and eubacteria code for 21st or 22nd amino acids, selenocysteine and pyrrolysine—see Atkins, J.F. and Gesteland, R., The 22nd amino acid, *Science* **296**(5572):1409–10, 2002; commentary on technical papers on pp. 1459–62 and 1462–66. This is another problem for common ancestry evolution: evolving from one code to another would scramble messages, just like switching keys on a keyboard.
8. Knight, J., Top translator, *New Scientist* **158**(2130):15, 1998.
9. Davies, P., How we could create life—The key to existence will be found not in primordial sludge, but in the nanotechnology of the living cell, *The Guardian*, 11 December 2002, www.guardian.co.uk/education/2002/dec/11/highereducation.uk.

Simplest possible life?

As above, *information*, rather than chemistry, is the main problem for origin of *first* life. E*ven the simplest life has enormous information content*. *Mycoplasma genitalium* has the smallest known genome of any free-living organism—a virus doesn't count because it can't reproduce without hijacking the machinery of cells[10] which are more complex. *Mycoplasma* contains 482 genes comprising 580,000 bases.[11] Of course, these genes are only functional with pre-existing translational and replicating machinery, a cell membrane, etc. But *Mycoplasma* has no cell walls, and can only survive by parasitizing more complex organisms (e.g. the respiratory system and urogenital tract of humans) that provide many of the nutrients it cannot manufacture for itself. Indeed, this organism seems to have arisen by *loss* of genetic information, making it dependent on its host.[12]

But could anything simpler have arisen? A decade ago, Eugene Koonin, a researcher interested in making artificial biological organisms, tried to calculate the bare minimum required for a living cell. He based this on mycoplasmas, and estimating how many genes even these simple cells could do without. His team came up with a result of 256 genes.[13]

But they doubted whether such a hypothetical bug could survive for long, because such an organism could barely repair DNA damage, could no longer fine-tune the ability of its remaining genes, would lack the ability to digest complex compounds, and would need a comprehensive supply of organic nutrients in its environment.

So it is not surprising that follow-up research has revised this number significantly upwards. This new minimum genome consists of 387 protein-coding and 43 RNA-coding genes.[14]

A recent *New Scientist* article stated:

"There is no doubt that the common ancestor possessed DNA, RNA and proteins, a universal genetic code, ribosomes (the protein-building factories), ATP and a proton-powered enzyme for making ATP [see p. 242].

---

10. Yet a virus has a powerful nano-motor to wind up DNA for packaging; Sarfati, J., Virus has powerful mini-motor to pack up its DNA, *J. Creation* **22**(1):15–16, 2008; creation.com/virusmotor; Fuller, D.N., *et al.*, Single phage T4 DNA packaging motors exhibit large force generation, high velocity, and dynamic variability, *Proc. Nat. Acad. Sci. USA* **104**(43):16868–16873, 2007.
11. Fraser, C.M. *et al.*, The minimal gene complement of *Mycoplasma genitalium*, *Science* **270**(5235):397–403, 1995; perspective by Goffeau, A., Life with 482 Genes, same issue, pp. 445–446. Other reports have a different number, but all within the same ball park.
12. Wood, T.C., Genome decay in the Mycoplasmas, *Impact* 340, 2001; www.icr.org/pubs/imp/imp-340.htm.
13. Wells, W., Taking life to bits, *New Scientist* **155**(2095):30–33, 1997.
14. Glass, J.I. *et al.*, Essential genes of a minimal bacterium, *Proc. Nat. Acad. Sci. USA* **103**(2):425–430, 2006 | doi:10.1073/pnas.0510013103.

The detailed mechanisms for reading off DNA and converting genes into proteins were also in place. In short, then, the last common ancestor of all life looks pretty much like a modern cell."[15]

Much more information on the complexity of even the 'simplest' life can be found in my book *By Design,* ch. 11, "Origin of Life". So the following will address the major difficulties in Dawkins' ideas, as well as some widely publicized recent chemical evolution experiments which Dawkins seems to allude to.

Natural selection can't work without life

Certainly Dawkins' books defending atheistic evolution included origin-of-life scenarios, but they were mutually incompatible (though he doesn't seem to realize that, possibly because he is not a chemist). But as Flew recognized, natural selection could not have been responsible. Theodosius Dobzhansky (1900–1975), one of the leading evolutionists of the 20th century and an ardent materialist (despite a Russian Orthodox upbringing) realized the same thing.[16] In commenting on the origin of life, he firmly rejected theorists who invoked natural selection as an explanation, because *this requires pre-existing life*:

> "In reading some other literature on the origin of life, I am afraid that not all authors have used the term [natural selection] carefully. *Natural selection is differential reproduction, organism perpetuation. In order to have natural selection, you have to have self-reproduction or self-replication and at least two distinct self-replicating units or entities. ...* I would like to plead with you, simply, please realize you cannot use the words 'natural selection' loosely. *Prebiological natural selection is a contradiction of terms.*"[17]

Chemical evolution

Many evolutionists now claim that origin of life from non-living chemicals has nothing to do with evolution, and claim that 'abiogenesis' is the correct term for the former. But their fellow evolutionist Gordy Slack rebukes them for that:

---

15. Lane, Nick, Was our oldest ancestor a proton-powered rock? *New Scientist* **204** (2730):38–42 17 October 2009.
16. See documentation by O'Leary, D., Darwinist Theodosius Dobzhansky was *not* an orthodox Christian believer! post-darwinist.blogspot.com/2006/09/darwinist-theodosius-dobzhansky-was.html, 8 September 2006.
17. Dobzhansky, T.G., Discussion of Synthesis of Nucleosides and Polynucleotides with Metaphoric Esters, by George Schramm, in Fox, S.W., ed., *The Origins of Prebiological Systems and of Their Molecular Matrices*, Proc. Conference at Wakulla Springs, Florida, pp. 309–310, 27–30 October 1963, Academic Press, NY, 1965.

"I think it is disingenuous to argue that the origin of life is irrelevant to evolution. It is no less relevant than the Big Bang is to physics or cosmology. Evolution should be able to explain, in theory at least, all the way back to the very first organism that could replicate itself through biological or chemical processes. And to understand that organism fully, we would simply have to know what came before it. And right now we are nowhere close."[18]

Slack is right—as stated in ch. 1, the "General Theory of Evolution" has been defined as "the theory that all the living forms in the world have arisen from a single source which itself came from an inorganic form."[19] Certainly, this part of evolution can't be *Darwinian*, as stated, but it is often called 'chemical evolution'. For example, the September 1978 issue of *Scientific American* was specially devoted to evolution, and one major article was "Chemical Evolution and the Origin of Life".[20] This stated:

"J.B.S. Haldane, the British biochemist, seems to have been the first to appreciate that a reducing atmosphere, one with no free oxygen, was a requirement for the *evolution of life from non-living organic matter*." [Emphasis added]

And an old stalwart of origin-of-life theories, Cyril Ponnamperuma, co-authored a paper with the same title, and his affiliation was the Laboratory of Chemical Evolution, Chemistry Department, University of Maryland.[21]

Dawkins must realize that chemical evolution is an issue, given his many forays into the area.

Darwin's views

Flew is right that Darwin had not developed an account of the origin of first life. None other than Darwin's great admirer Ernst Haeckel agreed:

"The chief defect of the Darwinian theory is that it throws no light on the origin of the primitive organism—probably a simple cell—from which all the others have descended. When Darwin assumes a special creative act for this first species, he is not consistent, and, I think, not quite sincere."[22]

---

18. Slack, G., What neo-creationists get right—an evolutionist shares lessons he's learned from the Intelligent Design camp, *The Scientist*, 20 June 2008; www.the-scientist.com/.
19. Kerkut, G.A., *Implications of Evolution*, Pergamon, Oxford, UK, p. 157, 1960.
20. Dickerson, R.E., Chemical Evolution and the Origin of Life, *Scientific American* **239**(3):62–102, September 1978.
21. Pleasant, L.G. and Ponnamperuma, C., Chemical evolution and the origin of life, *Origins of Life and Evolution of Biospheres* **10**(1), 1980; www.springerlink.com/content/m185944813n42138/.
22. Haeckel E., *Die Radiolarien (Rhizopoda Radiaria). Eine Monographie*, Druck und Verlag Von Georg Reimer, Berlin, 1862; cited in Peretó et al., Ref. 23.

And when Haeckel's compatriot, geologist Heinrich Georg Bronn (1800–1862), translated *Origin* in 1860, he added a chapter of his own with ideas on spontaneous generation. That year, Bronn wrote an essay strongly maintaining that Darwin's theory was incomplete without an explanation of the origin of *first* life.[23]

Did Darwin believe in a Creator?

In the final chapter of *Origin,* Darwin wrote:

"I believe that animals have descended from at most only four or five progenitors, and plants from an equal or lesser number.

"Analogy would lead me one step further, namely, to the belief that all animals and plants have descended from some one prototype."[24]

In the last paragraph of all, which Dawkins reproduces on p. 399 of *Greatest Show,* Darwin said:

"Thus, from the war of nature, from famine and death, the most exalted object which we are capable of conceiving, namely, the production of the higher animals, directly follows. There is grandeur in this view of life, with its several powers, having been originally breathed into a few forms or into one; and that, whilst this planet has gone cycling on according to the fixed law of gravity, from so simple a beginning endless forms most beautiful and most wonderful have been, and are being, evolved."[25]

Some naïve Christian evolutionists object that Darwin wrote "… breathed by the Creator …". However, Dawkins says:

"Presumably bowing to pressure from the religious lobby, Darwin inserted 'by the Creator' to second and all subsequent editions. …

"It seems that Darwin regretted this sop to religious opinion. In a letter of 1863 to his friend the botanist Joseph Hooker, he said, '[It will be some time before we see "slime, protoplasm, &c." generating a new animal.] But I have long regretted that I truckled to public opinion, and used the Pentateuchal term of creation, by which I really meant "appeared" by some wholly unknown process.'[26] The 'Pentateuchal

23. Peretó, J., Bada, J.L. and Lazcano, A., Charles Darwin and the Origin of Life, *Orig Life Evol Biosph* 39:395–406, 2009 | doi 10.1007/s11084-009-9172-7.
24. Darwin, Charles, *On the origin of species*, pp. 484, 1st edition, John Murray, London, 1859; available online from darwin-online.org.uk/.
25. Darwin, Ref. 24, p. 490.
26. *The Life and Letters of Charles Darwin*, edited by his son Francis Darwin, London: John Murray, 1887, Vol. 3, p. 18; darwin-online.org.uk.

term' Darwin is referring to is the word 'creation'. ... Nowadays, we should dispense even with the 'originally breathed'." (pp. 403–4)

However, Dawkins overlooked passages in the 1st edition of *Origin*, such as (emphases added):

"It makes *the works of God* a mere mockery and deception; ..."[27]

"Let this process go on for millions on millions of years; and during each year on millions of individuals of many kinds; and may we not believe that a living optical instrument might thus be formed as superior to one of glass, as the *works of the Creator* are to those of man?"[28]

"Authors of the highest eminence seem to be fully satisfied with the view that each species has been independently created. To my mind it accords better with what we know of the laws impressed on matter *by the Creator*, that the production and extinction of the past and present inhabitants of the world should have been due to secondary causes, like those determining the birth and death of the individual."[29]

It's likely that Darwin was "truckling to public opinion" even in Dawkins' precious first edition!

Darwin and spontaneous generation

Dawkins goes on to say:

"[Darwin] thought that the problem was beyond the science of his day. In the letter to Hooker ... Darwin went on to say, 'It is mere rubbish thinking at present of the origin of life; one might as well think of the origin of matter.'[26,30] He didn't rule out the possibility that the problem would eventually be solved (indeed, the problem of matter has largely been solved [*ipse dixit*[31]]) but only in the distant future: 'It will be some time before we see "slime, protoplasm, etc.," generating a new animal.'" (p. 417)

However, in 1871, just eight years later, consistent with his drive to explain origins entirely materialistically, Darwin speculated:

27. Darwin, Ref. 24, p. 167.
28. Darwin, Ref. 24, p. 189.
29. Darwin, Ref. 24, p. 488.
30. Or as he expressed it elsewhere, "our ignorance is as profound on the origin of life as on the origin of force or matter." Darwin, C., The doctrine of heterogeny and modification of species, *Athenaeum* 1852:554–555, 1863.
31. Latin for 'he himself said it', i.e. an unsupported assertion; Dawkins probably believes that the big bang explains the origin of matter. But see for example Williams, A. and Hartnett, J.G., *Dismantling the Big Bang*, Master books, Green Forest, AR, 2005.

" ... if (and Oh! what a big if!) we could conceive in some warm little pond, with all sorts of ammonia and phosphoric salts, light, heat, electricity, etc., present, that a proteine [*sic*] compound was chemically formed ready to undergo still more complex changes, at the present day such matter would be instantly devoured or absorbed, which would not have been the case before living creatures were formed."(cited also by Dawkins, p. 417)

Then Darwin read a book, *The Beginnings of Life* (1872), by Henry Charlton Bastian (1837–1915), which defended "archebiosis" or the "origin of living things from not-living materials". Darwin's letter to his co-discoverer A.R. Wallace showed that he found the arguments for it unconvincing, but accepted it anyway—much like many evolutionists today (cf. p. 246):

"My Dear Wallace,—I have at last finished the gigantic job of reading Dr. Bastian's book and have been deeply interested by it. You wished to hear my impression, but it is not worth sending. He seems to me an extremely able man, as, indeed, I thought when I read his first essay. His general argument in favour of Archebiosis is wonderfully strong, though I cannot think much of some few of his arguments. The result is that I am bewildered and astonished by his statements, but am not convinced, though, on the whole, it seems to me probable that Archebiosis is true."[32]

In an 1887 letter to Haeckel, thanking him for his book, Darwin made it clear that spontaneous generation was important, but was still unconvinced that it had been solved:

"... I will at the same time send a paper which has interested me; it need not be returned. It contains a singular statement bearing on so-called Spontaneous Generation. I much wish that this latter question could be settled, but I see no prospect of it. If it could be proved true this would be most important to us ...." (Ref. 26, p. 18)

Darwin's views remained consistent till the end of his life: he *believed* that life came from non-life, but beyond the *science* of his day.[23]

But as shown above (p. 224), Darwin's 'warm pond' idea was futile, because he was thinking only of a mere assemblage of chemicals, instead of information-processing machines. In today's terminology, cf. Davies, Darwin seems to have been thinking of life only as hardware, not software.

---

32. Letter 8488; cited in Peretó *et al.*, Ref. 23.

Destruction of building blocks

Darwin's famous 'warm little pond' letter (above, p. 232) was trying to explain away why such has not been seen today—because other living creatures would destroy any spontaneously generated proteins (cf. Dawkins' explanation, p. 418)

Yet proteins would be destroyed *anyway,* because they are still subject to the second law of thermodynamics, so they will eventually break up because of random motion of the atoms and background radiation. For example, water tends to break proteins down into their constituent amino acids (hydrolysis),[33] and they would undergo destructive cross reactions with other chemicals[34] in the alleged primordial soup.[35]

The most recent estimates place an *upper limit* of 2.7 Ma (million years) on collagen and 110 Ma for the bone protein osteocalcin at freezing point (0°C). At a still cool 10°C, the upper limits are much less—180,000 years for collagen and 7.5 Ma for osteocalcin. At 20°C, the maximum lifetimes are even shorter: 15,000 and 580,000 years.[36,37] Since, in general, reaction rate increases *exponentially* with temperature,[38] this problem becomes insoluble for a 'warm' pond. Furthermore, as will be shown below (p. 235), the problem is even more acute for Dawkins' favoured scenario.

Proteins can't reproduce

However, how do you get a living cell capable of self-reproduction from a "protein compound … ready to undergo still more complex changes"? Dawkins has to admit:

"Darwin, in his 'warm little pond' paragraph, speculated that the key event in the origin of life might have been the spontaneous arising of a protein, but this turns out to be less promising than most of Darwin's ideas. … But there is something that proteins are outstandingly bad at, and this Darwin overlooked. They are completely hopeless

33. Sarfati, J., Origin of life: the polymerization problem, *J. Creation* 12(3):281–284, 1998; creation.com/polymer.
34. E.g. the amino group (–NH₂) in the amino acid reacts readily with the carbonyl group (O=C<) in the sugar, releasing a water molecule (H₂0) to form an imine (HN=C<), which is useless for life. See Bergman, J., Why the Miller–Urey research argues against abiogenesis, *J. Creation* 18(2):74–84, 2002; creation.com/urey.
35. If such a soup produced all the nitrogenous compounds required for life, why is there no trace of them in the 'earliest' rocks? Cf. Brooks, J., and Shaw, G., *Origins and Development of Living Systems*, Academic Press, London and New York, 1973.
36. Nielsen-Marsh, C., Biomolecules in fossil remains: Multidisciplinary approach to endurance, *The Biochemist* 24(3):12–14, June 2002; www.biochemist.org/bio/02403/0012/024030012.pdf.
37. Doyle, S., The Real Jurassic Park, *Creation* 30(3):12–15, 2008.
38. This is the simple Arrhenius rate equation $k = A \exp(-E_a/RT)$, where k is the rate constant, A is a temperature-independent constant (often called the frequency factor), exp is the exponential function, E_a is the activation energy, R is the universal gas constant, and T is the absolute temperature.

at replication. They can't make copies of themselves. This means that the key step in the origin of life cannot have been the spontaneous arising of a protein." (pp. 419–20)

Yet the best known experiments on the origin of life start by making a few very dilute and grossly contaminated amino acids, the components of proteins, by sparking a sealed mixture of gases. These experiments were pioneered by Stanley Miller (1930–2007), a graduate student of Harold Urey (1893–1981), who had won the 1934 Nobel Prize for Chemistry for discovering deuterium (heavy hydrogen).[39] But the Miller–Urey experiments, by Dawkins' own admission, lead to a dead end since even their hoped-for end-product, a protein, would not be adequate for life. But a protein would never form from their mixture anyway, since the chemical processes move in the wrong direction, as per the previous section.

Self-replicating molecules?[40]

Dawkins says:

"The 'Catch-22' of the origin of life is this: DNA can replicate, but it needs enzymes in order to catalyse the process. Proteins can catalyse DNA formation, but they need DNA to specify the correct sequence of amino acids." (p. 420)

Indeed, the origin of the genetic code is a vicious circle: protein machines are needed to read the DNA, but these protein machines are themselves encoded on the DNA. Furthermore, they use energy, which requires ATP, made by the nano-motor ATP synthase. Yet this is encoded on the DNA, decoded by machines needing ATP. The proteins are the machinery, and the DNA is the reproductive material, yet both are needed at the same time for the cell to function at all. And of course, this would be useless without any *information* to reproduce (see p. 224).

To try to grasp both horns of the dilemma, some evolutionists have theorized that one type of molecule could perform both catalytic and reproductive roles. The solution Dawkins proposes is: "Enter RNA".

The RNA World

This idea goes back to 1967, when Carl Woese suggested that RNA was not only reproductive, but could also act as a catalyst, and thus perform both roles.[41] Thomas Cech and Sidney Altman independently demonstrated

---

39. http://nobelprize.org/nobel_prizes/chemistry/laureates/1934/urey-bio.html.
40. After Sarfati, J., Self-replicating enzymes? A critique of some current evolutionary origin-of-life models, *J. Creation* 11(1):4–6, 1997; creation.com/replicating.
41. Woese, C., *The Genetic Code*, Harper and Row, NY, 1967.

that some sequences of RNA had catalytic effects. For "discovery of catalytic properties of RNA", they received the Nobel Prize in chemistry in 1989.[42]

The discovery of such *ribozymes* has led many evolutionists to postulate an 'RNA World'. They propose that the first life consisted mainly of RNA, which could not only reproduce but also carry out many of the functions now carried out by enzymes. Dawkins says:

> "Now this is the key point of the 'RNA World' theory of the origin of life. In addition to stretching out in a form suitable for passing on sequence information, RNA is also capable of self-assembling . . . into three-dimensional shapes, which have enzymatic activity. RNA enzymes do exist. They are not as efficient as protein enzymes, but they do work. The RNA World theory suggests that RNA was a good enough enzyme to hold the fort until proteins evolved to take over the enzyme role, and that RNA was a good enough replicator to muddle along in that role until DNA evolved.

> "I find the RNA World theory plausible, and I think it quite likely that chemists will, within the next few decades, simulate in the laboratory a full reconstruction of the events that launched natural selection on its momentous way four billion years ago. Fascinating steps in that direction have already been taken." (p. 421)

Some problems for the RNA World hypotheses[43]

- RNA is actually a very complex molecule, and it's a flight of fantasy to claim that it could have arisen in a primordial soup.

- RNA is even less stable than DNA, which is much less stable than proteins. Recent estimates of DNA stability put its upper limit of survival at 125,000 years at 0°C, 17,500 at 10°C and 2,500 at 20°C.[36]

- Even the RNA building blocks, nucleotides, are themselves quite complex molecules, and have not been produced in a primordial soup.

- Spark discharge experiments, like the Miller-Urey ones, do not produce the RNA/DNA base cytosine. Cytosine itself, even if it could be made, is too unstable to accumulate sufficiently to be useful, even over alleged geological 'deep time', as its half life for decomposition is 340 years at 25°C.[44]

42. http://nobelprize.org/nobel_prizes/chemistry/laureates/1989/press.html.
43. See also Mills, G.C. and Kenyon, D.H., The RNA World: A Critique, *Origins and Design* **17**(1): 9–16, 1996; www.arn.org/docs/odesign/od171/rnaworld171.htm.
44. Shapiro, R., Prebiotic cytosine synthesis: A critical analysis and implications for the origin of life, *Proc. Nat. Acad. Sci. USA* **96**(8):4396–4401, 1999.

- Even the simpler 'building blocks' of RNA are unstable in abiotic environments. The half life $(t_{1/2})$ of ribose is only 44 years at pH 7.0 (neutral) and 0°C. It's even worse at high temperatures—73 minutes at 100°C.[45] And RNA bases are destroyed very quickly in water at 100°C, a problem for 'warm ponds' or hydrothermal theories[46]—adenine and guanine having half lives of about a year, uracil about 12 years, and cytosine only 19 days.[47]

- Nucleotides do not spontaneously polymerize; they need to be *activated*. Furthermore, "buffer and ionic conditions optimal for polymerization [ref.] also promote ribozyme and template degradation,"[48] because chemical reactions are reversible.

- Building blocks must be exclusively 'one-handed', otherwise the information-storing helix would not form. But a primordial soup would generate a 50-50 mix of 'left-' and 'right-handed' forms.[49] Even a small fraction of wrong-handed molecules terminates RNA replication.[50]

- Even if such polymers *could* form, which first must have been without a pre-existing template, they would then have to be able to *replicate* themselves. This replication must be accurate, otherwise it would lose any information it managed to acquire by chance. Even 96.7% accuracy, as per one highly touted case,[51] would be nowhere near accurate enough. Human replication has an accuracy much higher even than one mistake every *million*, thanks to sophisticated error correction machinery.

- Such self-replicating RNA molecules would have to have all the functions needed to sustain (maintain) an organism.

- How could such an RNA organism possibly give rise to a modern organism, with protein catalysts, coded on reproducing DNA? This requires a whole new layer of decoding machinery.[52]

---

45. Larralde, R., Robertson, M.P. and Miller, S.L., Rates of decomposition of ribose and other sugars: Implications for chemical evolution, *Proc. Nat. Acad. Sci. USA* 92:8158–8160, 1995.
46. Sarfati, J., Hydrothermal origin of life? *J. Creation* 13(2):5–6, 1999; creation.com/hydrothermal.
47. Levy, M and Miller, S.L., The stability of the RNA bases: Implications for the origin of life, *Proc. Nat. Acad. Sci. USA* 95(14):7933–38, 1998.
48. Johnston W.K., *et al.*, RNA-catalyzed RNA polymerization: accurate and general RNA-templated primer extension, *Science* 292(5520):131925, 18 May 2001 | doi: 10.1126/science.1060786.
49. Sarfati, J., Origin of Life: The chirality problem, *J. Creation* 12(3):263–266, 1998; creation.com/chirality.
50. Joyce, G.F., *et al.*, Chiral selection in poly(C)-directed synthesis of oligo(G), *Nature* 310:602–4, 1984.
51. Johnston, Ref. 48, admits that their ribozyme's copying accuracy is "still lower than the ≥0.996 fidelity seen with viral polymerases that replicate RNA by using RNA templates,[refs] and it is much lower than that seen for polymerases that replicate DNA."
52. Further chemical problems are found in Cairns-Smith, A.G., *Genetic Takeover: And the Mineral Origins of Life*, Cambridge University Press, 1982; see extract at creation.com/rna.

It is no wonder that one of the leading researchers into 'RNA World' models, Gerald Joyce, wrote:

"The most reasonable assumption is that life did not start with RNA. ... The transition to an RNA world, like the origins of life in general, is fraught with uncertainty and is plagued by a lack of experimental data."[53]

Another chemical evolutionist, Robert Shapiro, stated after showing that one of the building blocks of RNA was an implausible component of a primordial soup, said:

"the evidence that is available at the present time does not support the idea that RNA, or an alternative replicator that uses the current set of RNA bases, was present at the start of life."[44]

Further problems are explained in *By Design*, ch. 11, "The Origin of Life". But I will address a couple of widely touted experiments that have been conducted since I wrote that.

Does RNA really self-replicate?

A paper in *Science* by the abovementioned Gerald Joyce and his Ph.D. student Tracey Lincoln was entitled "Self-sustained replication of an RNA enzyme."[54] Quite often, the media hype just doesn't match what was actually discovered. To be fair, Joyce, a well-known chemical evolutionist, made it clear that he and Lincoln had not produced life, despite the headlines that claimed this.[55]

Joyce and Lincoln started off with a fairly long RNA molecule. Given that nothing like RNA appears in Miller-Urey experiments, as shown above, this already shows unjustified interference from an intelligent investigator. Furthermore, this paper didn't demonstrate replication but ligation—the joining of two small RNA pieces. So this research already assumed not just one but *three* RNA strands. For this to be relevant to chemical evolution, the two pieces just *by chance* had to have pretty close to the complementary base pairs of the first piece—natural selection could not be invoked before reproduction was occurring.

Furthermore, as shown, polymerization is unfavourable, so the RNA pieces must be chemically activated in some way. Note that a catalyst merely accelerates the approach to equilibrium; it doesn't change it.[56] The paper

53. Joyce, G. F., RNA evolution and the origins of life, *Nature* 338:217–224, 1989.
54. Lincoln, T. and Joyce, G., Self-sustained replication of an RNA enzyme, *Science* **323**(5918):1229–1232, 2009.
55. Britt, R., Life as we know it nearly created in lab, *LiveScience*, 11 January 2009.
56. See diagram and explanation in Wieland, C. and Sarfati, J., Dino proteins and blood vessels: are they a big deal? creation.com/dino-proteins-and-blood-vessels-are-they-a-big-deal, 9 May 2009.

states that one of the two joining RNA strands has a triphosphate group on the end. This is very reactive, so would be an even more unlikely component of a primordial soup, and would not last long even if it appeared. So a supply of matching activated RNA pieces likewise shows unacceptable investigator interference.

Can nucleotides be formed in a primordial soup after all?

A 2009 paper claimed to solve the problem of synthesizing the monomers that string together to make RNA[57]—a problem one would never know existed from reading Dawkins. This paper admitted a major problem: no plausible method had yet been found to join the pyrimidine (single-ring) bases to ribose to form nucleosides. This was a major roadblock to RNA World ideas. The authors admit in the abstract:

"… it is far from obvious how such ribonucleotides could have formed from their constituent parts (ribose and nucleobases). Ribose is difficult to form selectively [refs.] and the addition of nucleobases to ribose is inefficient in the case of purines [ref.] and does not occur at all in the case of the canonical pyrimidines [ref.]."[57]

So, as *Science News* reported team member John Sutherland of the University of Manchester as saying, to describe a process which their own diagram showed as having 13 steps:[58]

"'Basically, we took half a base, added that to half a sugar, added the other piece of base, and so on,' Sutherland says. 'The key turned out to be the order that the ingredients are added and the way you put them together—like making a soufflé.'"

"Another difference is that Sutherland and his team added the phosphate to the mix earlier than in past experiments. Having the phosphate around so early helped the later stages of the reaction happen more quickly and efficiently, the scientists say."[59]

57. Powner, M.W., Gerland, B. and Sutherland J.D., Synthesis of activated pyrimidine ribonucleotides in prebiotically plausible conditions, *Nature* 459(7244): 239–242, 14 May 2009 | doi:10.1038/nature08013.

58. To demonstrate the unacceptable level of investigator interference in the alleged prebiotic simulation, Ref. 57's abstract continues: "Here we show that activated pyrimidine ribonucleotides can be formed in a short sequence that bypasses free ribose and the nucleobases, and instead proceeds through arabinose amino-oxazoline and anhydronucleoside intermediates. The starting materials for the synthesis—cyanamide, cyanoacetylene, glycolaldehyde, glyceraldehyde and inorganic phosphate—are plausible prebiotic feedstock molecules [refs.] and the conditions of the synthesis are consistent with potential early-Earth geochemical models. Although inorganic phosphate is only incorporated into the nucleotides at a late stage of the sequence, its presence from the start is essential as it controls three reactions in the earlier stages by acting as a general acid/base catalyst, a nucleophilic catalyst, a pH buffer and a chemical buffer. For prebiotic reaction sequences, our results highlight the importance of working with mixed chemical systems in which reactants for a particular reaction step can also control other steps."

59. *Science News*, p. 6, 6 June 2009.

Unacceptable investigator interference (again)

Sutherland actually gave a clue as to the problems: they reacted in such a way because the chemists forced them to react in a particular order. The chemicals would not have been so cooperative on the primordial earth. Some chemical evolutionists affirm this:

> "However, Robert Shapiro, professor emeritus of chemistry at New York University disagrees. 'Although as an exercise in chemistry this represents some very elegant work, this has nothing to do with the origin of life on Earth whatsoever,' he says. According to Shapiro, it is hard to imagine RNA forming in a prebiotic world along the lines of Sutherland's synthesis.

> "'The chances that blind, undirected, inanimate chemistry would go out of its way in multiple steps and use of reagents in just the right sequence to form RNA is highly unlikely,' argues Shapiro. Instead, he advocates the metabolism-first argument: that early self-sustaining autocatalytic chemosynthetic systems associated with amino acids predated RNA."[60]

This is just another example in a long line of chemical evolutionary research that in effect argues along the following lines: find a trace of compound A in a spark discharge experiment, and compound B in another simulation (sometimes with mutually incompatible conditions), then claim, "See, A and B can be produced under realistic primitive-earth conditions." Then they obtain pure, homochiral, concentrated A and B from an industrial synthetic chemicals company, react them to form traces of the more complex compound C.[61] Then the news is trumpeted that C will form under primitive earth conditions. But doesn't show that *dilute* A and B can react that way, or that they won't react with contaminants D, E or F that were also formed in the first experiments. In short, the evolutionists' simulations have an unacceptable level of intelligent interference.[62]

Much of the evolutionary propaganda resembles the following hypothetical theory for the origin of a car:

> "Design is an unscientific explanation, so we must find a naturalistic explanation instead. Now, experiments have shown that one of the important building blocks of the car—iron—can be produced by heating naturally occurring minerals like hematite to temperatures

60. Urquhart, J., Insight into RNA origins, *Chemistry World*, www.rsc.org/, 13 May 2009.
61. The evolutionist Cairns-Smith has raised the same objections against the typical 'origin of life' simulation experiments in Ref. 52.
62. Thaxton, C.B., Bradley, W.L. and Olsen, R.L., *The Mystery of Life's Origin*, ch. 6, Philosophical Library Inc., New York, 1984.

which are found in some locations on Earth. What's more, iron can be shown to form thin sheets under pressures which are known to occur in certain geological formations. ..."

If this seems far-fetched, then note that even the simplest self-reproducing cell, which has 482 genes,[63] has a vastly higher information content than a car, yet self reproduction is a pre-requisite for neo-Darwinian evolution.

Where did such pure chemicals come from?

Recent Nobel Laureate[64] Jack Szostak (1952–) wrote a favourable perspective in the same issue of *Nature*, but realizes the problems of obtaining those chemicals in such favourable forms:

> "Of course, much remains to be done. We must now try to determine how the various starting materials could have accumulated in a relatively pure and concentrated form in local environments on early Earth. Furthermore, although Powner and colleagues' synthetic sequence yields the pyrimidine ribonucleotides, it cannot explain how purine ribonucleotides (which incorporate guanine and adenine) might have formed."[65]

Indeed, Powner, Gerland and Sutherland performed excellent organic synthesis, but this was something the primordial soup just could not provide. Organic chemist Dr Charles Garner points out:

> "As far as being relevant to OOL [Origin of Life], the chemistry has all of the usual problems. The starting materials are 'plausibly' obtainable by abiotic means, but need to be kept isolated from one another until the right step, as Sutherland admits. One of the starting materials is a single mirror image for which there is no plausible way to get it that way abiotically. Then Sutherland ran these reactions as any organic chemist would, with pure materials under carefully controlled conditions. In general, he purified the desired products after each step, and adjusted the conditions (pH, temperature, etc.) to maximum advantage along the way. Not at all what one would expect from a lagoon of organic soup. He recognized that making of a lot of biologically problematic side products was inevitable, but found that UV light applied at the right time and for the right duration could destroy much of the junk

63. Fraser, C.M., *et al.*, The minimal gene complement of *Mycoplasma genitalium*, *Science* **270**(5235):397–403, 1995; Perspective by Goffeau, A., Life with 482 genes, same issue, pp. 445–6.
64. nobelprize.org/nobel_prizes/medicine/laureates/2009/ "for the discovery of how chromosomes are protected by telomeres and the enzyme telomerase".
65. Szostak, J.W., Origins of life: Systems chemistry on early Earth, *Nature* **459**(7244):171–172, 14 May 2009 | doi:10.1038/459171a.

without too much damage to the desired material. Meaning, of course, that without great care little of the desired chemistry would plausibly occur. But it is more than enough for true believers in OOL to rejoice over, and, predictably, to way overstate in the press."[66]

Furthermore, phosphate was essential for this synthesis—but the researchers used about a million times the concentration found in the sea today.

Enzymes

To return to Dawkins' hope that "RNA was a good enough enzyme" (p. 421), there are some enzymes that must be *extremely good indeed* for life to survive. Without them, many reactions essential for life would be far too slow for life to exist.[67]

Super-catalysts

For example, enzyme expert Richard Wolfenden showed in 1998[68] that a reaction "'absolutely essential' in creating the building blocks of DNA and RNA would take 78 million years in water", but was speeded up 10^{18} times[69] by an enzyme.[70] This enzyme needed a special shape to work.[71]

In 2003, Wolfenden found another enzyme that exceeded even this vast rate enhancement. A *phosphatase*, which catalyzes the hydrolysis (splitting) of phosphate bonds, magnified the reaction rate by a thousand times more than even that previous enzyme—10^{21} times. This enzyme allows reactions vital for cell signalling and regulation to take place in a hundredth of a second. Without the enzyme, this essential reaction would take a trillion years— almost a hundred times even the supposed evolutionary age of the universe (about 15 billion years)![72]

66. Garner; cited in Luskin, Casey, Scientists say intelligent designer needed for origin of life chemistry, www.evolutionnews.org, 7 July 2009.
67. Catalysts do not affect the equilibrium, but only the *rate* at which equilibrium is reached. They work by lowering the activation energy, which means decreasing the energy of a transitional state or reaction intermediate.
68. Miller, B.G., Hassell, A.M., Wolfenden, R., Milburn, M.V., and Short, S.A., Anatomy of a proficient enzyme: The structure of orotidine 5′-monophosphate decarboxylase in the presence and absence of a potential transition state analog, *Proc. Nat. Acad. Sci. USA* **97**(5):2011–2016, 2000; www.pnas.org.
69. Cited in Lang, L.H., Without enzyme catalyst, slowest known biological reaction takes 1 trillion years, *Biocompare Life Science News*, news.biocompare.com, 2003.
70. This was orotidine 5′-monophosphate decarboxylase, responsible for *de novo* synthesis of uridine 5′-phosphate, an essential precursor of RNA and DNA, by decarboxylating orotidine 5′-monophosphate (OMP).
71. More detail can be found in Sarfati, J., *J. Creation* **19**(2):13–14, 2005; creation.com/enzymes, and in *By Design* ch. 11.
72. Lad, C., Williams, N.H. and Wolfenden, R., The rate of hydrolysis of phosphomonoester dianions and the exceptional catalytic proficiencies of protein and inositol phosphatases, *Proc. Nat. Acad. Sci. USA* **100**(10):5607–5610, 2003; www.pnas.org/cgi/content/full/100/10/5607.

Implications

Wolfenden said:

> "Without catalysts, there would be no life at all, from microbes to humans. It makes you wonder how natural selection operated in such a way as to produce a protein that got off the ground as a primitive catalyst for such an extraordinarily slow reaction."[69]

Of course, as pointed out on p. 223, natural selection could not have been operational until there was life, while as he says, life could not have functioned without these enzymes to speed up vital reactions enormously.

Evolutionists admit that ribozymes are not efficient enzymes; they could never achieve the efficiencies of these enzymes that are necessary for life.

The world's tiniest motor: ATP synthase

Another vital enzyme for life is ATP synthase (see diagram, right), that makes the energy currency of the body, ATP. ATP stands for **a**denosine **tri**phosphate. It is a high energy compound, and releases this energy by losing a phosphate group to give ADP, **a**denosine **di**phosphate. Energy is essential for life, and all life uses ATP as its energy currency.[73] Yet all living things, even bacteria and archaea, have ATP synthase motors. This probably makes ATP synthase the most ubiquitous protein assembly on Earth.

In fact, the human body generates about its own weight of ATP every day, generated by many trillions of these motors. And it is consumed very quickly to power vital biochemical reactions, including DNA and protein synthesis, muscle contraction, transport of nutrients and nerve impulses. An organism without ATP is like a car without gasoline; cyanide is so toxic precisely because it stops ATP production.

This motor is unique in that it uses electricity to turn a rotor, which squeezes two components of ATP (ADP and phosphate) at high enough energy to form ATP. Then it throws off the ATP and prepares to accept new ADP and phosphate. This motor turns at about 10,000 rpm, and each rotation produces three ATP molecules.

It's actually two motors in one. The top half (called F_1-*ATPase*) has three parts that are each ATP factories as described above. The bottom half, F_O,[74] is the one directly powered by the electric current, which is positively charged (proton flow) instead of the negatively charged (electron flow) current that

73. Bergman, J., ATP: The perfect energy currency for the cell, *Creation Res. Soc. Q.* **36**(1):2–10, 1999; www.creationresearch.org/crsq/articles/36/36_1/atp.html.

74. Note that it is a subscript letter O *not* the number zero, for historical reasons: from 'oligomycin binding fraction'.

drives the motors designed by people. The antibiotic oligomycin specifically inhibits the F_O half of ATP synthase with deadly effect. More details can be found in *By Design*, ch. 10, "Motors".[75] But one more detail has since been discovered, concerning the way these motors are connected.

Elastic power transmission: ~100% efficiency

Ten protons are used for every rotation, which means there must be *exactly* ten 'c' subunits in the rotor of the F_O unit (bottom of diagram) or it won't work.[76] This 10:3 ratio turns out to be important: this 'mismatch' means that "their coupled operation is smoothed and speeded by elastic power transmission, which accounts for its high kinetic efficiency and robust function."[77]

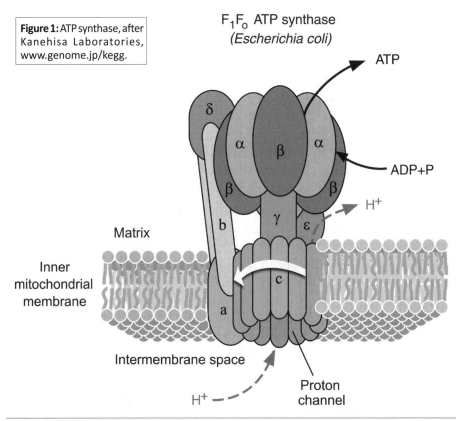

Figure 1: ATP synthase, after Kanehisa Laboratories, www.genome.jp/kegg.

F_1F_O ATP synthase
(Escherichia coli)

75. Updated from Sarfati, J., Design in living organisms (motors), *J. Creation* **12**(1):3–5, 1998; creation.com/motor, written not long after the original work on the motor was published, and the Nobel Prize was awarded to the discoverers of the motor operation. A more up-to-date layman's article is Thomas, B., ATP synthase: Majestic molecular machine made by a Mastermind, *Creation* **31**(4):21–23, 2009.

76. Mitome, N. *et al.*, Thermophilic ATP synthase has a decamer c-ring: Indication of noninteger 10:3 H+/ATP ratio and permissive elastic coupling, *Proc. Nat. Acad. Sci. USA* **101**(33):12159–12164 | 10.1073/pnas.0403545101.

77. Junge, W., Sielaff, H., & Engelbrecht, S., Review Article: Torque generation and elastic power transmission in the rotary FOF1-ATPase, *Nature* **459**(7245):364–370, 21 May 2009 | doi:10.1038/nature08145.

How efficient? "The match implies 100% efficiency for the conversion of the Gibbs free energy of ATP hydrolysis into mechanical work performed on the elastically strained filament."[77,78]

Evolution of ATP synthase?

This motor has many components that need to be fully together before it can work at all. In particular, the 10-fold symmetry of the F_O carousel has no function by itself. And the three-fold symmetry of the F_1 'mushroom cap', with just the right molecular arrangements to give the three possible conformations, would be useless without the rotating stalk to change the conformations. And the motor would not run without the proton channel in the right place. The motor works only because the correct components are *organized correctly*. Similarly, the existence of electrical wiring, brushes and magnets does not explain how these were organized specifically to form a functional electric motor.

Some evolutionists have speculated that the F_1 sector could have arisen via a certain helicase, the enzyme that unwinds/separates the two DNA strands. They try to justify this by pointing out some degree of similarity and the fact that helicase "is an active unwinding motor",[79] where supposedly the DNA chain is analogous to the γ-subunit of the ATP synthase. However, the operation of helicase *itself* uses ATP copiously, *currently supplied by ATP synthase,* so how could these supposed precursors operate at all?

Also, because energy is vital for life, life could not have evolved before this motor was fully functional. But as pointed out in this chapter, natural selection by definition is differential reproduction, so it requires self-reproducing entities at the start. Yet self-reproduction requires ATP to supply the energy! So does the expression of the information that is selected. So even if a series of gradual steps could be imagined up this peak of Dawkins' "Mount Improbable", there would be no natural selection to enable that climb. This is because all the hypothetical intermediates would be lacking energy and thus *dead*.

Furthermore, helicase itself is probably essential for life and so had to be present at the formation of the first life, before natural selection could even get started. So ATP synthase and helicase had to *both* pop into existence at the formation of the first life. Believing in the flying spaghetti monster might be more reasonable.

---

78. This was actually for the enzyme running *in reverse*. That is, using the energy of ATP to make an isolated motor spin. This has been used to power the tiniest man-made motor by attaching a nano-propeller to the ATP synthase: Soong, R.K. *et al.,* Powering an Inorganic Nanodevice with a Biomolecular Motor, *Science* **290**(5496)1555–1558, 24 November 2000 | doi: 10.1126/science.290.5496.1555.

79. Researchers solve mystery of how DNA strands separate, *Physorg.com*, www.physorg.com/news102663442. html, 2007.

Danger of enzymes

Enzymes are catalysts: they accelerate the desired reaction, but also the *reverse* reaction; all they do is speed up the approach to equilibrium. And this equilibrium tends to be away *from* life. For example, ATP synthase *makes* ATP only if it is in a complex membrane system with a pH gradient generated by respiration involving many other enzymes. But on its own, it would *destroy* any ATP molecules present—and the energy release would power the rotation of the motor.[79]

The same applies to other enzymes; they would destroy life unless they were made at the right time and sent to the right place. E.g. if a protease arose by chance, it would destroy the other proteins. A ribonuclease (RNase) would spell the end of an incipient RNA world.

It's also important to note that many metabolic processes require a chain of enzymes operating at the right time and in the right place, for biochemical multi-step reactions. In many cases, the intermediate products of these reactions have no biological use, and function only as precursors to the next stage. Just one of many examples was pointed out by Dr Larry Thaete, a medical research scientist at Northwestern University Feinberg School of Medicine:

"The hormone endothelin, a vasoconstrictor (a chemical that narrows blood vessels), is not coded directly by DNA. It originates as a much larger molecule (212 amino acids long) and that molecule does absolutely nothing! An enzyme has to be there to cut a portion of it off and make a smaller molecule—which also does absolutely nothing! Yet another enzyme reduces the molecular size of the protein producing another inactive molecule. A different and very specialized enzyme has to be present to reduce the size of this third molecule even further to its final size (only 21 amino acids long)—the active form of the molecule."[80]

Natural selection would tend to eliminate the inactive forms of the molecule before the appropriate enzymes arose to transform the molecule into its active form. And this is not nearly as complex as the miniature motors of the bacterial flagellum or ATP synthase which is vital for all living creatures.

In fact, some of these intermediates would become toxic if allowed to build up. This can happen if there is not the proper balance in the expression

80. Saving the other patient: Lita Cosner chats with prenatal medical researcher Dr Larry Thaete, *Creation* **32**(1):47–49, 2010.

of genes to produce the different enzymes. This is a major reason for Down's Syndrome, because sufferers have an extra 21st chromosome, i.e., instead of a pair of chromosome 21, they have a triple, hence the other term for this syndrome, *trisomy 21*. This gives them an extra copy of a number of genes, which are thus over-expressed. One proposed candidate for the problem gene is the superoxide dismutase which breaks down the very reactive superoxide ion (O_2^-). Its product is peroxide (O_2^{2-}), also a strong oxidizer, which is normally broken down by the next enzyme, glutathione peroxidase. But the imbalance of superoxide dismutase can result in peroxide build-up which damages the cell.

We should be satisfied with an *implausible* theory?

Dawkins admits about chemical evolutionary scenarios for the origin of first life:

> "The truth is that there is no overwhelming consensus. Several promising ideas have been suggested, but there is no decisive evidence pointing unmistakeably to any one." (p. 419)

He further tacitly admits that chemical evolution is a problem, but tries to twist this in his favour, because of the Fermi Paradox—if there are aliens, then why haven't we heard from them?

> "The theory we seek, of the origin of life on this planet, should therefore positively not be a plausible theory! If it were, then life should be common in the galaxy. Maybe it is common, in which case a plausible theory is what we want. But we have no evidence that life exists outside this planet, and at very least we are entitled to be satisfied with an implausible theory." (p. 422)

Similarly, in his earlier book, *Climbing Mount Improbable* (p. 259), Dawkins repeated the idea that he proposed in his first book, *The Selfish Gene:*

> "Nobody knows how it happened but, somehow, without violating the laws of physics and chemistry, a molecule arose that just happened to have the property of self-copying—a replicator."

But notice the admission of ignorance, which is consistent:

> "'I would have to be more of a chemist than I am to know how likely it is that you are going to get such molecules,' says Dawkins, 'I don't know how difficult it would be to achieve that chemically.'"[81]

---

81. Miele, F., Darwin's dangerous disciple: An Interview with Richard Dawkins, *Skeptic* **3**(4):80–85, 1995.

Chemical evolution: evidence or blind faith?

The non-creationist information theorist Hubert Yockey made a very revealing comment 30 years ago, which certainly describes Dawkins' own credulity as being strong enough to accept an implausible theory:

"Research on the origin of life seems to be unique in that the conclusion has already been authoritatively accepted ... . What remains to be done is to find the scenarios which describe the detailed mechanisms and processes by which this happened."[82]

This is important to keep in mind when reading popular accounts of evolution, or in response to those who claim that believers in design are 'biased'.

Dr Yockey finished his paper with:

"One must conclude that, contrary to the established and current wisdom a scenario describing the genesis of life on Earth by chance and natural causes which can be accepted on the basis of fact and not faith has not yet been written."[82]

The Origin-of-Life Foundation, Inc. currently offers a $1 million prize to anyone providing a chemically plausible naturalistic solution for the origin of the genetic code and life. The website states:

"'The Origin-of-Life Prize'® (hereafter called "the Prize") will be awarded for proposing a highly plausible *mechanism* for the spontaneous rise of *genetic instructions* in nature sufficient to give rise to life. To win, the explanation must be consistent with empirical biochemical, kinetic, and thermodynamic concepts as further delineated herein, and be published in a well-respected, peer-reviewed science journal(s)."[83]

Thus far, there have been no awards and the more we know of the minimum requirements for life, the more unlikely it seems that any even remotely plausible materialistic explanation for the origin of life will be found. The problem is further from being solved than ever, quite contrary to the impression someone might get from Dawkins' bluffing.[84]

Summary

- Origin of life from non-living chemicals has been an article of blind faith, not science— and has been so from Darwin to Dawkins.

82. Yockey, H.P., A calculation of the probability of spontaneous biogenesis by information theory, *J. Theoretical Biol.* 67:377–398, 1977; quotes from pp. 379, 396.
83. www.us.net/life/.
84. Smith, Calvin, Who wants to be a millionaire? $1 million prize offered for scientific proof of 'natural-process' origin of life, creation.com/lifeprize, 2007.

- Darwin's main error, repeated in much chemical evolutionary literature, was considering life as an assembly of chemicals rather than an *information-processing* machine.

- How did molecular hardware get to write its own software? Natural selection can't explain origin of *first* life.

- Machines are required to process this information. But this information includes instructions to build these machines. A chicken and egg problem.

- These machines need energy, made by the ATP synthase motor. But this can't be built without the instructions or reading machinery.

- Other enzymes are essential to speed up vital reactions that would take millions of years without them.

- Yet enzymes alone would be destructive, e.g. an isolated ATP synthase would destroy ATP, not make it.

- Proteins can't reproduce and would break down; RNA is a weak enzyme and is even more unstable.

- Some RNA building blocks have not been formed in chemical evolution 'simulation' experiments, and would be dilute, contaminated and unstable. Further, they would not be in the 'one-handed' form required for life.

—∞—

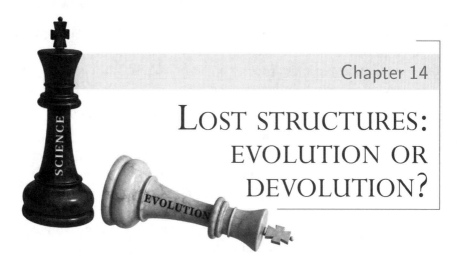

Chapter 14

LOST STRUCTURES: EVOLUTION OR DEVOLUTION?

In his Chapter 11, "History written all over us", Dawkins claims that our own evolutionary history is also shown by the features that have degenerated or even been lost from our assumed evolutionary ancestors. But much of this ignores what biblical creationists actually teach: that this creation is cursed, so degeneration is to be expected. What would be more impressive is organs *improving*—there are many more ways to get worse than to get better.

Goosebumps

Dawkins's first example is goosebumps. He claims:

"Even we naked apes still have the machinery to raise non-existent (or barely existent) hairs, and we call it goosebumps. The hair-erection machinery is a vestige, a non-functional relic of something that did a useful job in our long-dead ancestors. Vestigial hairs are among the many instances of history written all over us. They contain persuasive evidence that evolution has occurred, and again it comes not from fossils but from modern animals." (p. 340)

However, goosebumps are not functionless; they *do* make a difference even with our small hairs, in trapping a layer of air. Also, the muscles help squeeze oil on to the skin. The hairs help stop the oil glands being clogged. The muscle contractions themselves generate heat, of which more can be generated by shivering. The whole process is called *piloerection*. Body hairs provide extra sensitivity to touch, and also help in the cooling process by keeping perspiration in an even layer rather than dripping off. The fact that men tend to perspire more (due to higher metabolic rate) is one reason that men have more body hair than women.

Lost eyes in cave-dwelling creatures

In a favourite example, Dawkins blatantly knocks down a straw man:

"… numerous different kinds of animals that live in the depths of dark caves where there is no light have reduced or lost their eyes, and are, as Darwin himself noted, more or less completely blind. The word 'troglobite'[1] has been coined for an animal that lives only in the darkest parts of caves and is so specialized that it can live nowhere else. Troglobites include some salamanders, fish, shrimps, crayfish, millipedes, spiders, crickets, and many other animals. They are often white, having lost all pigment, and blind. They usually, however, retain vestiges of eyes, and that is the point of mentioning them here. Vestigial eyes are evidence of evolution. Given that a cave salamander living in perpetual darkness has no use for eyes, why would a divine creator nevertheless furnish it with dummy eyes, clearly related to eyes, but non-functional?" (p. 351)

Dawkins also covered this in "The Blind Cave Fish's Tale" in his collection of essays, *The Ancestor's Tale*.

However, creationists have long pointed out that this last question is highly leading—we don't believe that any creator made dummy eyes, and have explained it on much the same lines as Dawkins. For example, I addressed atheist Christopher Hitchens' 'eureka moment' argument from blind salamanders against creation in 2008,[2] and this was merely the latest among several articles by my colleagues on the topic.[3,4] Bottom line: creationists have long agreed that blind cave creatures are descended from sighted surface creatures, and used it as a good example of post-Fall deterioration of a "very good" creation—**de**volution, not evolution.

Compare Dawkins with what we have said:

---

1. Dawkins' own footnote: "Yes, troglobite, not troglodyte, which means something less extreme." Creationist cave expert Dr Emil Silvestru, formerly head scientist at the world's first Speleological Institute (speleology = the study of caves) in Cluj, Romania, uses the term "troglobiont", *Geology & Cave Formation: A Post-Flood Story*, DVD, 2004.
2. Sarfati, J., Christopher Hitchens—blind to salamander reality, A well-known atheist's 'eureka moment' shows the desperation of evolutionists, creation.com/hitchens, 26 July 2008.
3. E.g., Wieland, C., Blind fish, island immigrants and hairy babies, *Creation* 23(1):46–49, 2000; creation.com/blind-island; answering Dawkins' fellow antitheistic evolutionist and ally Jerry Coyne.
4. Wieland, C., Let the blind see…breeding blind fish with blind fish restores sight, *Creation* 30(4):54–55, 2008; creation.com/blindsee.

Dawkins: "Evolutionists on the other hand, need to come up with an explanation for the loss of eyes where they are no longer needed. ... How does losing its eyes benefit an individual cave salamander so that it is more likely to survive and reproduce than a rival salamander that keeps a perfect pair of eyes, even though it never uses them?

"Well, eyes are almost certainly not cost free. Setting aside the arguably modest costs of making an eye, a moist eye socket, which has to be open to the world to accommodate the swivelling eyeball with its transparent surface, might be vulnerable to infection. So a cave salamander that sealed up its eyes behind tough body skin might survive better than a rival salamander that kept its eyes.

"But there is another way to answer this question ... most mutations are disadvantageous, if only because they are random and there are many more ways of getting worse than getting better. Natural selection promptly penalizes the bad mutations. Individuals possessing them are more likely to die and less likely to reproduce, and this automatically removes the mutations from the gene pool. Every animal and plant is subject to a constant bombardment of deleterious mutations: a hailstorm of attrition. It is a bit like the moon's surface, which becomes increasingly pitted with craters due to the steady bombardment of meteorites. With rare exceptions, every time a gene concerned with an eye, for example, is hit by a marauding mutation, the eye becomes a little less functional, a little less capable of seeing, a little less worthy of the name of eye. In an animal that lives in the light and uses the sense of sight, such deleterious mutations (the majority) are quickly removed from the gene pool by natural selection.

"But in total darkness the deleterious mutations that bombard the genes for making eyes are not penalized. Vision is impossible anyway. The eye of a cave salamander is like the moon, pitted with mutational craters that are never removed. The eye of a daylight-dwelling salamander is like the earth, hit by mutations at the same rate as cave-dwellers' eyes, but with each deleterious mutation (crater) being removed by natural selection (erosion)." (pp. 351–3)

CMI (2000):[3] "Consider a fish, one of many swept into an underground waterway, which inherits a defective gene for eye development (because of a mutation—an error in copying the DNA code during reproduction). Should the fish survive to reproduce, this defect will be passed on to all of its descendants. Above ground, such a mutation would be very quickly 'selected against', as any fish inheriting it would be less likely to find food and evade predators, so would be less likely to survive and pass on the mutational defect. But in a totally dark environment, any blind fish are not at a disadvantage to their sighted fellows—in fact the opposite. Without light, there are no visual warnings when cave fish are about to scrape into a sharp rock, for instance. Eyes are delicate and thus easily injured in darkness, allowing the entry of potentially lethal bacteria. So, in total darkness, eyes are no longer an asset, but a handicap. On average, the eyeless fish will be more likely to survive and reproduce. It would not need many generations before all the fish in that environment were of the 'eyeless' type."[3]

CMI (2008): "This is easily explainable: there are many ways to *break* something, but not many ways to *make* something in the first place. So it's not surprising that it would be relatively easy for a mutation, or copying mistake in the genes, to ruin the eyes. In the light, natural selection would eliminate such mutations, since blind creatures could see neither prey nor predators.

"But in a pitch-black cave, there would be no natural selection against blind creatures, so they could proliferate. They might even have an advantage, because a shrivelled eye is less likely to be damaged.[5]"[2]

So, Dawkins is once again shooting at phantoms; creationists don't propose that God created animals with rudimentary eyes at all.

Pleiotropy

Dawkins continues:

"Of course, the story of the cave-dweller's eye isn't only a negative one: positive selection comes in too, to favour the growth of protective skin over the vulnerable sockets of the optically deteriorating eyes." (p. 353)

There is another positive selective effect Dawkins doesn't mention here, proposed by evolutionists but also compatible with the biblical creation model. As I pointed out:

"In one of the best known blind cave fish, *Astyanax mexicanus*, there is another reason why the blind fish can have an advantage in caves. This is *pleiotropy*, where a single gene has more than one effect on an organism. It turns out that a control gene, *hedgehog*, which affects a number of processes including development of the jaws and tastebuds, also inhibits another control gene, *pax6*, which controls development of the eyes. A fish with bigger jaws and more sensitive tastebuds would have an advantage in finding food, but this must be traded off with the loss of eye development. In the light, loss of eyes is a big disadvantage, so natural selection would eliminate a fish that over-expresses *hedgehog*, despite its better jaws and taste. But in the dark caves, a fish with highly expressed *hedgehog* would have a big advantage, since the loss of eyes would be irrelevant.[5]"2

Unless Dawkins can show that the growth of skin over the eye sockets of eyeless fish involves the creation of new genes by natural processes, it does not qualify as 'proving evolution'. It is likely a pre-programmed response to having an unfilled hole in the skeleton of the fish, or a pleiotropic effect resulting from the damaging of the genes for eye formation—the genes for normal eyes some way or other prevent the skin from growing over the eyes, so damaging those genes would likely allow the growth of the skin over the eye sockets.

Recent loss of sight

Studying blind cave fish provides strong evidence that this loss of sight need not take long, and indeed, could not have been long ago, contrary to evolutionary claims. As I wrote:

"Also, to underscore the point that there are many ways to break things, there are actually a number of ways to produce blindness, even in *Astyanax*. This is shown by breeding different populations of blind fish, and resulting in a number of sighted progeny. This is explained because the sight loss in the different populations is caused by different mutations, so 'when you cross them, the genetic deficiencies in one lineage are compensated for by strengths in the other, and vice-versa.'[6]"2

But if the sight loss had occurred millions of years ago, then other genes involved with sight would have had time to be "cratered" by mutations, not removed by natural selection. Then crossing such mutated genes would not restore sight.

"We have also pointed this out [in Ref. 4], so Hitchens [and Dawkins] has even less excuse—exactly the same principles apply to blind salamanders and other blind troglobionts.

5. Jeffrey, W.R., Adaptive evolution of eye degeneration in the Mexican blind cavefish, *Journal of Heredity* **96**(3):185–196, 2005.
6. New York University, Progeny of blind fish can regain their sight, ScienceDaily.com, 8 Jan 2008; the work was formally published in an issue of *Current Biology*.

"When it comes to breaking something, it need not take very long either. Breaking is often quicker than making, just as it's often much quicker to fall off a mountain than to climb it. We can see this in humans, when sighted parents have blind children due to a genetic defect—*this can happen in only one generation.* Yet Hitchens gushed:

'Even as I was grasping the implications of this, the fine voice of Sir David Attenborough was telling me how many millions of years it had taken for these denizens of the underworld to *lose* the eyes they had once possessed.'

"He of course provides no proof. Indeed, the fact that sight can be regained in one generation shows that there has been little time for mutations to further degenerate the genes—note that natural selection would not preserve genes connected to eyes and the visual parts of the brain if there were no selection for eyesight. [I.e. to use Dawkins' helpful analogy, these genes would be heavily cratered.]"[2]

Loss of wings

Flightless birds

The flightless cormorant most impressed Darwin, and impresses Dawkins today. Dawkins claims:

"But all flightless birds including ostriches and their kind, which lost their wings a very long time ago, are clearly descended from ancestors that used them to fly. No reasonable observer should doubt the truth of that, which means that anyone who thinks about it should find it very hard—why not impossible—to doubt the fact of evolution." (p. 345)

However, once again, this is no problem for the *biblical* creation model, which includes the Fall. That is, we agree with Darwin and Dawkins that flightless birds (at least most of them) descended from flying birds, losing their ability to fly. Once again, this is post-Fall *de*volution, not evolution. If Dawkins could show creatures *acquiring* the power of flight (or sight), then this might count as evidence for evolution; but *loss* of flight (or sight) does not. The argument might impress Dawkins' gullible choir in the Church of Saint Darwin, but it should not convince anyone who does not already have a religious commitment to naturalism (materialism) and who cares to think about it.

Flightless cormorants

Here is CMI's June 2009 comment (incorporating its 2005 explanation) on that bird that so fascinated Darwin and Dawkins:

"This is the only variety of cormorant that lives on the Galápagos Islands, and is the only variety of cormorant that cannot fly. It has even been classified as a different genus; it is in the genus *Nannopterum* while all other cormorants belong to the genus *Phalacrocorax*. The changes that the flightless cormorant underwent are similar to that of other flightless birds; the keel on the breast bone which supports the muscles used for flight is much smaller, and its legs are much stronger than those of other cormorants. Since it does not need to use its wings for flight, over time they have deteriorated in ways that would have been eliminated in flying birds; its feathers are softer and more hair-like, much like the feathers of other flightless birds.[7]

"Since the flightless cormorants could not have swum from the mainland to the islands (it never ventures more than 100 metres from shore while fishing), how did it arise? Darwin proposed that it developed from cormorants that had flown to the island, but whose descendants had lost this ability. Now we realize that this loss occurred through a mutation, or genetic copying mistakes. Such a mutation would normally be *harmful* for a bird species, but may have been *beneficial* to the cormorants on that particular island.[8]

"This would be similar to the case of flightless beetles on windy islands that are more likely to survive, while the beetles that can fly are more likely to be swept away.[9] Or else it may simply have been a case of *reduced selection pressure*—with none of the mainland predators and plentiful food in the sea, loss of flight would be a less serious disadvantage, much like cave creatures that lose their sight over generations [see p. 250 ff.]. However, this would not be an example of evolution; the mutation that caused the flightless cormorant to lose the ability to fly is an example of a *loss* of genetic information. Goo-to-you evolution would require changes that result in *new* genetic information."[10]

Once again, creationists had published[8] on how the flightless cormorant fits the biblical model of creation well before Dawkins published his latest book, so it seems that Dawkins has just assumed from his own imagination what he thinks creationists believe, rather than actually checking. Alternatively,

7. Flightless Cormorant, people.rit.edu/rhrsbi/GalápagosPages/Cormorant.html, accessed 21 October 2008.
8. Wieland, C., Darwin's Eden, *Creation* 27(3):10–15, 2005; creation.com/darwin_eden.
9. Wieland, C., Beetle Bloopers: Even a defect can be an advantage sometimes, *Creation* 19(3):30–35, 1997; creation.com/beetle.
10. Cosner, L. and Sarfati, J., The Birds of the Galápagos, *Creation* 31(3):28–31, 2009.

he knew and ignored it, in order to be able to include this 'knock-down' argument in his book.

Kakapo

Dawkins describes this bird as follows:

"… kakapos, New Zealand's flightless parrots, whose flying ancestors apparently lived so recently that kakapos still try to fly although they lack the equipment to succeed." (p. 345)

Once again, this is hardly news to creationists[11]—a deterioration due to mutations, which natural selection did not 'punish' in the absence of predators. Yet this is a problem for long-age ideas: New Zealand was supposedly isolated many millions of years ago, and its fauna isolated from predators for that time, yet this flightlessness is clearly recent.

Penguins

As Dawkins says, "… penguins … use their wings to 'fly underwater' …" This is compatible with a design explanation—that penguins were designed to do what they do, rather than being an example of loss of flight. The point is that the principles of flight are the same regardless of the fluid used—a fluid is a material that flows, i.e. a liquid or a gas. Merely the optimal dimensions must be changed. This is why flight simulations often use a different fluid and dimensions and are still accurate.[12]

Halteres: lost/evolved wings on insects?

Dawkins then discusses certain features of flies (diptera), with only two wings instead of four, like most insects. Instead of hindwings, they have little stalks with knobs called halteres. They have long been known to act as a gyroscope, because they beat in antiphase to the wings, i.e. in reverse direction. The base of the haltere has mechanical sensors called *campaniform* (bell-shaped) *sensilla* that quickly pass on flight information to the wing-steering muscles, so they can respond fast enough to stabilize the fly. Thus halteres are the equivalent of an aircraft's *attitude indicator*.[13]

---

11. See Bates, A., Parrot of the night—NZ's kakapo, *Creation* **30**(4):28–30, 2008.
12. It doesn't matter what fluid is used for a simulation, as long the *Reynold's Number* is constant (providing *dynamic similitude*). This number is a ratio of inertial to viscous forces named after the British engineer Osborne Reynolds (1842–1912), given by $Re = {}^{\rho v l}/_{\mu}$, where ρ is density, v is mean velocity, l is a characteristic length and μ is viscosity.
13. Wieland, C., Why a fly can fly like a fly, *J. Creation* **12**(3):260–261, 1998; creation.com/fly.

Stability vs maneuvrability

Dawkins explains this as part of the trade-off between stability and maneuvrability as all flying machines have, and puts the following evolutionary slant on it:

> "The great John Maynard Smith, who worked as an aircraft designer before returning to the university to read zoology ... pointed out that flying animals can move in evolutionary time, back and forth along the spectrum of this trade-off, sometimes losing inherent stability in the interests of increased manœvrability, but paying for it in the form of increased instrumentation and computation capability—brain power." (p. 348)

Then there is a diversion to illustrate his point with pterosaurs.

Pterosaurs

Dawkins illustrates a supposedly early pterosaur, *Rhamphorhynchus*, with a long tail "with the ping-pong bat at the end", so it was very stable, so "would not have needed sophisticated gyroscopic control". But it was not very maneuvrable, he says. But *Anhanguera*, allegedly 60 million years later, had almost no tail, so "it would surely have been an unstable aircraft, reliant on instrumentation and computation to exercise subtle, moment-to-moment control over its flight surfaces." (pp. 347–8)

In this case, the controls were most likely provided by orientational information from the semicircular canals (balance organs in the inner ear). Indeed, they were very large. But Dawkins grudgingly admits, "although, a touch disappointingly for the Maynard Smith hypothesis, they were large in *Rhamphorhynchus* as well as *Anhanguera*." (p. 348)

A new pterosaur fossil, published after I wrote most of this chapter, provides an even bigger problem: *Darwinopterus modularis*.[14] First of all, it was 'dated' at 160 million years old, which is on the younger end of the evolutionary age range of *Rhamphorhynchus* (165 to 150 million years[15]). But far more important, it is evidence against the Maynard Smith theory, since it had *both* a long tail *and* 'advanced' features in the head and neck. I.e. the latter features arose *without* being driven by selection for compensation for loss of stability. We can see this from the comments of one of the discoverers,

14. Lü, J., *et al.*, Evidence for modular evolution in a long-tailed pterosaur with a pterodactyloid skull, *Proc. R. Soc. B*; 14 October 2009 | doi: 10.1098/rspb.2009.1603.
15. *Walking with Dinosaurs*, Fact file: *Rhamphorynchus*, www.abc.net.au.

Dr David Unwin from the University of Leicester, UK, who had expected an intermediate along the Maynard-Smith lines:

> "*Darwinopterus* came as quite a shock to us. We had always expected a gap-filler with typically intermediate features such as a moderately elongate tail—neither long nor short.

> "But the strange thing about *Darwinopterus* is that it has a head and neck just like that of advanced pterosaurs, while the rest of the skeleton, including a very long tail, is identical to that of primitive forms."[16]

Instead, the researchers propose a novel idea, which goes against Dawkins' Darwinian gradualism: that natural selection selected whole 'modules'; hence the species name (*modularis*):

> "This pattern supports the idea that modules, tightly integrated complexes of characters with discrete, semi-independent and temporally persistent histories, were the principal focus of natural selection and played a leading role in evolutionary transitions."[13]

But this evidence is better explained by *biotic message theory*, as proposed by creationist Walter ReMine in *The Biotic Message*.[17] That is, the evidence from nature points to a *single* designer, but with a pattern which thwarts evolutionary explanations. In this case, the common modules point to *one* common designer—one who worked with various modules, creating different creatures with different modules that fit no consistent evolutionary pattern. Also, in most cultures around the world, such a *pattern of commonality would bring honour to a Designer*, and would also indicate the Designer's authority over and mastery of His designs.[18] More is explained in chapters 6 and 8.

Origin of Pterosaurs

A far bigger problem is that the fossil record sheds no light on the alleged evolution of pterosaurs from non-flying creatures, a far bigger jump than between different types of pterosaur, which doesn't fit Dawkins' favourite evolutionary story anyway, as he and Unwin admitted. For example, researchers including Dr Unwin recently discovered that pterosaurs used their tiny pteroid bone as a support for a wing flap, without which they likely could

---

16. Unwin, D., cited in McGrath, M., New flying reptile fossils found, http://news.bbc.co.uk/, 14 October 2009.
17. ReMine, W.J., *The Biotic Message: Evolution Versus Message Theory*, Saint Paul Science, Saint Paul, Minnesota, USA, 1993; see review: Batten, D., *J. Creation* 11(3):292–298, 1997; creation.com/biotic.
18. Holding, J.P., 'Not to Be Used Again': Homologous Structures and the Presumption of Originality as a Critical Value, *J. Creation* 21(1):13–14, 2007; creation.com/homologous.

not have risen off the ground in the first place.[19,20] So they had sophisticated design concepts that enabled them to fly.

And the fossil record shows that pterosaurs, and bats for that matter, have always been pterosaurs and bats, with no evidence of intermediates with partial wings. For more, see ch. 8, p. 127.

Pringle on halteres

Returning to halteres, Dawkins cites the work of J.W.S. Pringle (1912–1982), one of his own Oxford professors from his student days, one of the first to work out the gyroscopic function of the halteres. But after this good science, Pringle speculated on their origin, as Dawkins relates:

"Pringle suggested that the four-winged ancestors of flies probably had long abdomens, which would have made them stable. All four wings would have acted as rudimentary gyroscopes. Then, he suggests, the ancestors of flies started to move along the stability continuum, becoming more manœvrable and less stable as the abdomens got shorter. The hind wings started to shift more towards the gyroscopic function (which they had always performed [due to tiny sense organs in the base, p. 347] becoming smaller, and heavier for their size, while the forewings enlarged to take over more of the flying. There would have been a gradual continuum of change, as the forewings assumed ever more of the burden of aviation, while the hind wings shrank to take over the avionics." (pp. 348–9)

Dragonflies in the ointment

One problem with the Pringle story is that the allegedly primitive insects in the Odonata (dragonflies and damselflies) have both long abdomens and sophisticated flying methods, so efficient that engineers are trying to copy them.[21] They have "unusual musculature" that allows them to move each of their four wings *independently*. Robotic simulations showed that their out-of-phase flapping allows the hind wings to extract extra energy from the wake of the front wings, improving energy efficiency by 22%.[22]

19. Wilkinson, M.T., Unwin, D.M. and Ellington, C.P., High lift function of the pteroid bone and forewing of pterosaurs, *Proc. R. Soc.* **273**(1582):119–126, 2006 | doi: 10.1098/rspb.2005.3278.
20. Sarfati, J., Pterosaurs flew like modern aeroplanes, *Creation* **28**(3):53, 2006; creation.com/pterosaur.
21. See also Catchpoole, D., Dragonfly design tips, creation.com/dragonfly-design, 20 October 2009; *Creation* **32**(2):51, 2010.
22. Usherwood, J. and Lehmann, F., Phasing of dragonfly wings can improve aerodynamic efficiency by removing swirl, *Journal of the Royal Society Interface*, doi:10.1098/rsif.2008.0124, 13 May 2008.

Indeed, the researchers realized that this was a problem for Pringle-type scenarios:

"Caution must be applied when interpreting the biological significance of the above observations. Suggesting an evolutionary advantage to either two-winged or four-winged forms is unwise, considering the success and diversity of the true flies (Diptera), and yet the maintenance of the four-winged form by dragonflies since the Carboniferous."

A better idea is that they were designed by an intelligence far greater than our own, so it's not surprising that we can learn from them. Creationist Prof. Stuart Burgess, leader of the Design Engineering Research Group at the University of Bristol (UK), informs us:

"Flying insects like dragonflies are another strong evidence for design because their flight mechanisms (and navigation systems[23]) are incredibly sophisticated although evolutionists regard dragonflies as 'primitive' insects that appeared many millions of years ago. My own research group at Bristol University is developing micro air vehicles based on the wings of dragonflies. We have filmed dragonflies with high speed cameras and recorded the exact flapping and twisting motion of their wings. We have then produced linkage mechanisms that can copy that motion in made-made micro air vehicles."[24,25,26]

Furthermore, not only do dragonflies have sophisticated flying, they also have sophisticated instrumentation. They can track other insects with incredibly intricate maneuvring that makes the dragonfly appear stationary to its target.[27] Insects' compound eyes are good at detecting the slightest motion by optic flow,[28] so the flight patterns must have amazing control systems. Appearing stationary would be very useful for sneaking up on other insects or for eluding a predator.

A brief report in *New Scientist* said, "Dragonflies overshadow their enemies in complex manoeuvres that military fighter pilots can only dream of. ... It demands exquisite position sensing and control."[29] The researcher,

23. Sarfati, J., Astonishing acrobatics—dragonflies, *Creation* 25(4):56, 2003; creation.com/dragonfly; after Mizutani, A., *et al.*, Motion camouflage in dragonflies, *Nature* 423:604, 2003.
24. Expert engineer eschews "evolutionary design": Philip Bell interviews creationist and Professor of Engineering Design, Stuart Burgess, *Creation* 32(1):35–37, 2010.
25. Conn, A.T., Burgess, S.C., Ling, C.S. and Vaidyanathan, R., The design optimisation of an insect-inspired micro air vehicle, *Int. J. of Design & Nature and Ecodynamics* 3(1):12–27, 2008.
26. Conn, A.T., Burgess, S.C. & Ling, C.S., Design of a parallel crank-rocker flapping mechanism for insect-inspired micro air vehicles, *Proc. Institution of Mechanical Engineers, Part C: J. Mechanical Engineering Science (Special Issue)* 221(10):1211–1222, 2007.
27. Mizutani, A. *et al.*, Motion camouflage in dragonflies, *Nature* 423:604, 2003.
28. Sarfati, J., Can it bee? *Creation* 25(2):44–45, 2003; creation.com/can-it-bee.
29. Anon., How stealthy insects outsmart their foe, *New Scientist* 178(2398):26, 2003.

Akiko Mizutani, of the Centre for Visual Science at the Australian National University in Canberra, said, "This sort of performance is extremely hard to achieve without very expensive and bulky measurement systems."[28]

Yet somehow, what the most ingenious human designers can't achieve with bulky systems was supposedly programmed into the tiny dragonfly brain without any intelligence involved at all!

Dragonfly navigation adds to the *Rhamphorhynchus* semicircular canals, and even more, *Darwinopterus,* as counter-examples to the evolutionary Maynard Smith hypothesis, upon which the Pringle hypothesis for haltere origin depends.[30] Once again predictions made on the basis of evolutionary conjecture prove to be wrong.

Origin of insect flight

Of course, the above deals with creatures that can *already* fly. But how did insects evolve flight in the first place? At such small scales, flying through air would be like us swimming through treacle.[31] But modern research has shown that they use very intricate wing motions to exploit aerodynamic phenomena.

One experiment used a 'robot insect', but this had to be programmed to flap like a living insect. By copying the intricate changes of wing rotation and camber, a leading-edge vortex (LEV) was generated, which lowers pressure thus generating lift. We can see LEVs in ordinary folded paper planes—they explain why there can be a final 'boost' before the plane lands. But the LEVs can't keep the dart upright for long because it becomes unstable and falls away from the wing's surface. But in insects, LEVs generate the extra lift needed because the vortex stays 'stuck' to the leading edge of the wing for long enough.[32,33]

Such vortices are not the only feature of insect flight. Two researchers from Oxford University trained red admiral butterflies (*Vanessa atalanta*) to fly freely between artificial flowers in a wind tunnel. Thus they could analyze the flow with smoke trails and a high-speed digital camera. They found:

"The images show that free-flying butterflies use a variety of unconventional aerodynamic mechanisms to generate force: wake capture, two different types of leading-edge vortex, active and inactive upstrokes, in addition to the use of rotational mechanisms and the Weis-Fogh 'clap-and-fling' mechanism. Free-flying butterflies often used different aerodynamic mechanisms in successive strokes. There

30. More information on haltere design, and refuting evolutionary stories, can be found in *By Design* ch. 4.
31. The viscosity term of the Reynold's Number dominates—see Ref. 11.
32. On a wing and a vortex, *New Scientist* **156**(2103):24–27, 1997.
33. Insects—defying the laws of aerodynamics? *Creation* **20**(2):31, 1998; creation.com/insects.

seems to be no one 'key' to insect flight, instead insects rely on a wide array of aerodynamic mechanisms to take off, manoeuvre, maintain steady flight, and for landing."[34]

Furthermore, the fossil record sheds no light on the origin of insect flight. Rather, the earliest (by evolutionary 'dating') winged insects were already capable fliers, just as with the first pterosaurs (see p. 258). Evolutionary entomologist Ellington admits:

"The origins of insect flight are shrouded in the past, and studies of the fossil record and extant insects have provided few answers. Speculations abound with no hard facts to check them, and we are left in a rather unconvincing muddle."[35]

Vestigial leg bones in whales?

Dawkins claims:

"Whales have no hind limbs, but there are tiny bones, buried deep inside them, which are the remnants of the pelvic girdle and hind legs of their long-gone walking ancestors." (p. 342)

However, these so-called 'remnants' are not useless at all, but help anchor the reproductive organs—the bones are different in males and females, which reinforces this conclusion.[36] As for the extinct long and thin whale *Basilosaurus*, this did have small hind limbs (certainly too small for walking). But they were probably used for grasping during copulation, according even to other evolutionists. For example, the evolutionary whale specialist Philip Gingerich said, "It seems to me that they could only have been some kind of sexual and reproductive clasper."[37]

One myth promulgated by some evolutionists says that some whales have been found with hind legs, complete with thigh and knee muscles. However, this story probably grew by legendary accretion from a true account of a real sperm whale with a 14 cm (5.5 inch) bump with a 12 cm (5 inch) piece of bone inside. Sperm whales are typically about 19 m (62 feet) long, so this abnormal piece of bone is minute in comparison with the whale—this hardly qualifies as a "leg"![38]

34. Srygley, R.B. and Thomas, A.L., Unconventional lift-generating mechanisms in free-flying butterflies, *Nature* **420**(6916):660–664, 2002.
35. Ellington, C.P. Aerodynamics and the Origin of Insect Flight, *Advances in Insect Physiology* 23, 1991.
36. Bergman, J. and Howe, G., "Vestigial Organs" are Fully Functional (Creation Research Society Monograph No. 4).
37. As quoted in *The Press Enterprise*, 1 July 1990, p. A–15.
38. Wieland, C., The strange tale of a leg on a whale', *Creation* **20**(3):10–13, 1998.

Even if these whale bones were the result of degeneration of previous structures, once again *(ad nauseum!)*, *loss* of features gives no support to the belief system that Dawkins is trying to 'prove': that all of the diversity of life came about by natural selection. Dawkins needs to show that natural processes can *create* eyes, wings and limbs not *destroy* them.

Summary

- At best, Dawkins' examples would show devolution, i.e. the opposite process of goo-to-you evolution.

- Goosebumps are not vestigial, since the small hairs trap some insulating air, and help prevent oil glands from clogging, and the muscles generate heat.

- Contrary to Dawkins' straw man, creationists do NOT believe that God created blind eyes in cave-dwelling creatures. Rather, we have long taught much the same explanation as his: that these eyes degenerated through mutation, since a light-free cave would have no selection pressure to eliminate the mutants. Indeed, shrivelled eyes would be less vulnerable to injury in the dark, so there would be selection *for* such shrivelling. Also, the sight loss must have occurred *recently*, since breeding can produce sighted fish, showing that mutations in genes involved with sight have not had time to accumulate.

- Flightless birds are another example of devolution, where selection pressure no longer eliminates mutants with defective wings.

- Dawkins uses halteres (on flies) and pterosaurs to illustrate the common evolutionary theory of how flying creatures evolved. That is, first fliers were stable, long-bodied creatures; they shortened to become more manoeuvrable, and evolved compensating machinery to compensate for the lower stability. Yet recent discoveries on allegedly 'primitive' dragonflies show that they have the sophisticated flying and navigation equipment, even though they have the long body that provided stability. And Dawkins admits that the stable 'early' pterosaur *Rhamphorynchus* had large semicircular canals, which spoils the theory. And the 'early' pterosaur *Darwinopterus*, discovered after Dawkins wrote, knocks over the theory. That is, it had *both* a long tail *and* 'advanced' features in the head and neck, so the latter features arose *without* being driven by selection for compensation for loss of stability.

—∞—

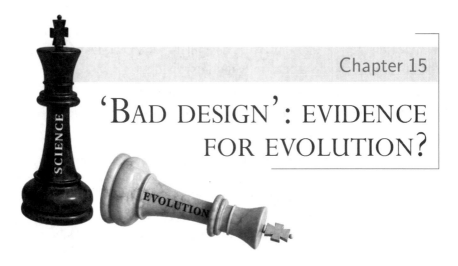

Chapter 15

'Bad design': evidence for evolution?

In Ch. 11 of *Greatest Show*, "History written all over us", Dawkins claims that our own evolutionary history is written over us. This is mainly in structures which he claims would be bad or nasty design, if a Designer created them, but make sense if they are relics of evolution. Such claims are theological, not scientific. Many of his claims show ignorance of the reasons for the apparent bad design, which with proper understanding is actually vital.

Roman Empire

On p. 349, Dawkins returns to his analogy of the Roman Empire. Once again, the best evidence is the historical written records. But Dawkins tells us of the Roman remains in his own country of Britain: Hadrian's Wall, the Roman flint fort of Old Sarum, and:

> "Unfold an Ordinance Survey map of England. Whenever you see a long, dead straight country road, especially when there are green field gaps between stretches of road or cart track that you can line up exactly with a ruler, you'll almost always find a Roman label beside it. Vestiges of the Roman Empire are all around us.

> "Living bodies, too, have their evolutionary history written all over them. They bristle with the biological equivalent of Roman roads, walls, monuments, potsherds, even ancient inscriptions carved into the living DNA, ready to be deciphered by scholars."

Ironically, the Roman roads were a product of intelligent design, as are the vestiges that tell us that they were designed in the past. Dawkins apparently did not see the inconsistency in using this analogy.

It's worth summarizing the principal arguments against his case of supposed bad design, before dealing with his specific examples:

Badly designed structures?[1]

- In using this argument, evolutionists are tacitly supporting the two-model approach—that an argument against creation is an argument for evolution. This form of argument is known as a *disjunctive syllogism*, and works only if these are the only two possibilities. Yet evolutionists often rail against creationists for using an identical form of argument, i.e. using arguments against evolution to support creation!

- An assertion about what a designer would or would not do is actually a *pseudo-theological* argument, *not* a scientific argument that mutations and natural selection could produce a particular complex design.

- Similarly, a claim that a designer might have designed something badly at best proves that the designer is less than perfect, not that there is no designer. This is not my belief, as will be shown, but it still demonstrates a hole in the critics' logic and that they are making *theological* assumptions about the nature of the designer.

- And a complaint about all the nasty things in nature can at best suggest that the designer is mean, not that there is none. (Again, this is not my own belief—the next chapter elaborates on a cogent explanation that the 'Intelligent Design' (ID) movement cannot offer.)

- A single *feature* may not be optimal, but the *combination* of features may be. E.g. a thicker shell, considered only for its protective properties, might work better against predators and environmental damage. But if it is too thick, its manufacture wastes resources, and even worse, it could weigh down the creature, so as a whole, the creature is worse off. Dawkins himself understands this much: "We can't know all the details but we do know (it is an unbreakable law of economics) that it is possible to spend too much on one department of life, thereby taking resources away from some other department of life. An individual that puts more than the ideal resources into running may save its own skin. But in the Darwinian stakes it will be out-competed by a rival individual of the same species, who skimps a little on running speed and hence incurs a greater risk of being eaten, but who

---

1. From *By Design*, ch. 12.

gets the balance right and ends up with more descendants to pass on the genes for getting the balance right. ... Legs that are long and thin are good at running fast. Inevitably they are also good at breaking." (p. 385)

- It's important to remember that multi-cellular life forms begin from a single cell, and there is a continuous development into the adult form. Yet for the adult even to exist, these younger stages must be viable. Thus there are some features in the adult that are genuine vestigial organs, but they are *vestiges of ontogeny (development) not phylogeny (evolutionary history)*. I.e. the adult could not exist if the embryo didn't have the features that have since degenerated in the adult. For example, the adult mammal has vestiges of the circulatory system that connected with its mother's placenta, and the shunt that re-routed the blood to the lungs at birth.

- Similarly, the designer must work from the materials available.

- Some accusations of poor design reflect ignorance, the evolutionist's own version of Dawkins' own term, "the argument from personal incredulity" ("I can't see why it was designed that way, so it must be badly designed"). In many cases, when more information comes to hand, the 'poor design' turns out to be excellent.

- An organ may not be *necessary*, but it may still be *nice* to have. Such organs can be removed, but this doesn't prove they are functionless. Many designed systems have back-up features that make the system as a whole less likely to break down. This would explain the two kidneys and two lungs we have, although we can get by on one of each. Indeed, such redundancy is a problem for evolution because the selective advantage (increased fitness) for an individual having the redundancy freshly evolved (assuming this could even happen) would be so small under normal circumstances as to be not selectable by natural selection. It would be lost by what is known as genetic drift.

- It is impossible to prove that an organ is useless, and thus a "vestige" of evolution. The function may simply be unknown and its use may be discovered in future. This has happened with more than 100 organs in humans that we now know are essential but which evolutionists formerly deemed were useless leftovers of evolution (vestigial organs). This is a clear case where evolution has impeded the development of science.

- Under the biblical framework, a particular biological system that appears poorly designed may not have been originally designed that way, but has gone downhill since the Fall. Thus many organs that are claimed to be vestiges of evolution would really prove 'devolution' not evolution. However, the particles-to-people evolution model needs to find examples of *nascent* organs, i.e. those which are beginning to appear and *increasing* in complexity.

Badly designed vertebrate eyes?

Helmholtz: the eye has faulty optics?

Dawkins argues that vertebrate eyes are poorly designed:

"Among the most interesting of historical relics are those features that are being used for something (and so are not vestiges in the sense of having outlived their purpose), but seem badly designed for that purpose. The vertebrate eye, at its best—say the eye of a hawk or a human—is a superb precision instrument, capable of feats of fine resolution to rival the best that Zeiss or Nikon can deliver. If it were not so, Zeiss and Nikon would be wasting their time producing high-resolution images for them to look at. On the other hand, Hermann von Helmholtz, the great German scientist (you might call him a physicist, but his contributions to biology and psychology were greater), said, of the eye, 'If an optician wanted to sell me an instrument which had all these defects, I should think myself justified in blaming his carelessness in the strongest terms, and giving him back his instrument.'

"One reason why the eye seems better than Helmholtz, the physicist, judged it to be is that the brain does an amazing job of cleaning the images afterwards, a sort of ultra-sophisticated Photoshop. As far as the optics are concerned, the human eye achieves its Zeiss/Nikon quality only in the fovea, the central part of the retina that we use for reading. When we scan a scene, we move the fovea over different parts, seeing each one in utmost detail and precision, and the brain's 'Photoshop' fools us into thinking we are seeing the whole scene with the same precision. A top quality Zeiss and Nikon lens really *does* show the whole scene with almost equal clarity.

"So what the eye lacks in optics the brain makes up for with its sophisticated image-simulating software." (p. 353)

Yet in my book *By Design*, ch. 12 (2008), I answered this objection by Helmholtz (showing also that Dawkins had partially answered it himself without realizing it):

"[Helmholtz] didn't actually find an optician who had sold a better instrument, of course, considering all the eye's features. And his main error was treating the eye as a *static* instrument, like a camera, which needs to focus all areas finely to generate a picture. But he ignored the key feature of the eye—that it is a *dynamic* instrument that would be useless without *processing its information in the brain.*

"If he had understood the *fovea/saccade* system [see below], he might have realised that the system has at least two advantages over a hypothetical eye that focused perfectly in the periphery:

1. The lack of focus in the periphery has a certain advantage, in that we can concentrate more easily on the objects finely focused in our central vision.

2. A perfect focus in the periphery would be wasted unless our brains could process this information, and that would require heads too big to fit through a doorway. [2]"

Earlier on, I had explained (*By Design*, ch. 1):

Fovea and saccades[3]

Only a small (<1%) part of the eye in the centre, called the *fovea*, has very high resolution for fine detail. It sees only the central 2° of the visual field, or about twice the width of your thumbnail at arm's length. The fovea has a higher density of receptors, and needs a much larger area of our brain to process its information—over 50% of the visual cortex.[2]

But most of the eye's area is used for the peripheral (non-central) vision, which has much lower resolution, and therefore needs less brain processing power. You can understand this for yourself by trying to read this page without moving your eyes. Rather, normally the low-resolution parts of the eye detect objects of interest, and our eyes have unconscious motions (*saccades*) to aim our foveas at these objects.[4] This way we can see the details of a wide area with minimal brain computing power.

So why not simply have the whole retina in sharp focus? Because there is no point having much detail unless the brain can process it, and ours would need to be 50 times larger to process such information! This would give only a minute advantage over our current system, where the peripheral area can pick out possible areas of interest, then zoom in the fovea to analyze more closely—with much less brain processing power. But the 'superior' design would have a major disadvantage in our head being unable to fit through doorways.[2]

2. Catania, K.C., The nose takes a starring role, *Scientific American* **287**(1):40, 2002.
3. After Weston, P. and Wieland, C., The Mole, and Sarfati, J., Superb sense organ sheds light on alleged eye imperfection, *Creation* **25**(2):46–50, 2003; creation.com/mole.
4. There are other vital motions of the eye—see Wagner, T., Darwin vs the Eye, *Creation* **16**(4):10–13, 1994; creation.com/eye.

Also, there would actually be a *disadvantage* to seeing too well in the periphery. For example, it would also make it impossible to read, because if every word was in equal focus, they would all be attracting the reader's attention—"pick me, pick me!"—instead of the reader being able to concentrate on a few words at a time.[5] So the lack of clear focus in the periphery is consistent with an *intentional* design of the eye-brain system, quite aside from the much more efficient information processing.

The fovea-saccade method also has applications in other senses: fovea/saccade combination occurs in the tactile (touch) and auditory (hearing) senses in some creatures [in the star-nosed mole and bat, respectively].[6]

Why eyes 'jitter'[7]

When a person fixes their gaze on something, their eyes 'jitter', i.e. they make small, involuntary movements. These movements wiggle the image on the retina. In the 1950s, researchers using mirrors to negate the jitter when volunteers looked at an object discovered that the volunteers began to lose sight of the object (disappearing into a featureless grey), so the researchers concluded that jittering kept the image from fading.

Decades later, Boston University neuroscientist Michele Rucci and his colleagues, using computer technology to track the eye's movements, discovered that the jitters are in fact crucial to helping the brain discern the finer details of an image.[8] Negating the jitters resulted in a 16% reduction in volunteers' ability to pick out the details in fine-lined patterns—the same ability needed to locate a single tree in a forest, or a berry on a bush.

"Vision isn't like a camera, where you take a picture and the brain processes it,' explains Rucci. 'The actual process of looking ... affects what you see."[9]

Thus the jitters are crucial to picking out the details of what we see. The fact that we have such 'an eye for detail' points to design, not evolution.

Backwardly-wired retina?

Dawkins repeats a claim he has been making for over 20 years:

"But I haven't mentioned the most glaring example of imperfection in the optics. The retina is back to front.

5.   Menton, D., *The Hearing Ear and the Seeing Eye* (DVD).
6.   See also the article by a creationist ophthalmologist, Gurney, P.W., Our eye movements and their control, *J. Creation*: part 1 in **16**(3):111–115, 2002; Part 2 in **17**(1):103–110, 2003.
7.   After Catchpoole, D., An eye for detail—why your eyes 'jitter', creation.com/jitter, 2007.
8.   Rucci, M., *et al.*, Miniature eye movements enhance fine spatial detail, *Nature* **447**(7146):852–855, 2007.
9.   Telis, G., Shifty eyes see finer details, *ScienceNOW Daily News*, sciencenow.sciencemag.org/cgi/content/full/2007/613/2, 2007.

"Imagine a latter-day Helmholtz presented by an engineer with a digital camera, with its screen of tiny photocells, set up to capture images projected directly on to the surface of the screen. That makes good sense, and obviously each photocell has a wire connecting it to a computing device of some kind where images are collated. Makes sense again. Helmholtz wouldn't send it back.

"But now, suppose I tell you that the eye's 'photocells' are pointing backwards, away from the scene being looked at. The 'wires' connecting the photocells to the brain run over all the surface of the retina, so the light rays have to pass through a carpet of massed wires before they hit the photocells. That doesn't make sense …" (pp. 353–4)

Actually it *does* make sense, as ophthalmologists know, and have explained for years, so Dawkins has no excuse for repeating such discredited arguments. Dawkins' analogy fails because photocells don't have to be chemically regenerated, while the eye's photoreceptors are chemically active, and need a rich blood supply for regeneration. As I wrote in *By Design*, ch. 12:

Regenerating photoreceptors

Someone who *does* know about eye design is the ophthalmologist Dr George Marshall, who said:

"The idea that the eye is wired backward comes from a lack of knowledge of eye function and anatomy."[10]

He explained that the nerves could not go behind the eye, because the choroid occupies that space. This provides the rich blood supply needed for the very metabolically active retinal pigment epithelium (RPE). This is necessary to regenerate the photoreceptors, and to absorb excess heat from the light. So it is necessary for the nerves to go in front rather than behind. But as will be shown below, the eye's design overcomes even this slight drawback.

In fact, what limits the eye's resolution is the *diffraction* of light waves at the pupil (proportional to the wavelength and inversely proportional to the pupil's size); so alleged improvements of the retina would make no difference to the eye's performance.

It's important to note that the 'superior' design of Dawkins with the (virtually transparent) nerves behind the photoreceptors would require either:

10. Marshall, G. (interviewee), An eye for creation. *Creation* **18**(4):20–21, 1996; creation.com/marshall.

- The choroid in front of the retina—but the choroid is opaque because of all the red blood cells, so this design would be as useless as an eye with a hemorrhage!

- Photoreceptors not in contact with the RPE and choroid at all—but without a rich blood supply to regenerate, then it would probably take months before we could see properly after we were photographed with a flashbulb or we glanced at some bright object.

Are squid eyes 'properly' wired?

Some evolutionists [including Dawkins in *The Blind Watchmaker*] claim that the cephalopod (e.g. squid and octopus) eye is somehow 'right', i.e. with nerves behind the receptor. They use this as a counter-argument to the points in the previous section about the need for the 'backward' wiring. But no-one who has actually bothered to study cephalopod eyes could make such claims with integrity. In fact, cephalopods don't see as well as humans, e.g. no colour vision, and the octopus eye structure is totally different and much simpler. It's more like 'a compound eye with a single lens'. And it is no accident that we say 'eyes like a hawk/eagle' rather than 'eyes like a squid', because the former really are sharper, despite their alleged 'backward' wiring.

Fibre optic plate

The above section explains why the vertebrate retina must be wired the way it is. But scientists at Leipzig University have recently shown that the vertebrate eye has an ingenious feature that overcomes even the slight disadvantage of the transparent nerves in front of the light receptors [the "carpet of massed wires" that Dawkins complains about].[11]

The light is collected and funnelled through the nerve net to the receptors by the *Müller glial cells*, which act as

Müller cells in the eye work as optical fibres

11. Franze, K. *et al.,* Müller cells are living optical fibers in the vertebrate retina, *Proc. Nat. Acad. Sci. USA*, 10.1073/pnas.0611180104, 7 May 2007; www.pnas.org/cgi/content/abstract/0611180104v1.

optical fibres. Each cone cell has one Müller cell guiding the light to it, while several rods can share the same Müller cell.

The Müller cells work almost exactly like a *fibre optic plate* that optical engineers can use to transmit an image with low distortion without using a lens. The cells even have the right variation in refractive index for "image transfer through the vertebrate retina with minimal distortion and low loss."[11]

Indeed, Müller cells are even better than optical fibres, because they are funnel-shaped, which collects more light for the receptors. The wide entrances to Müller cells cover the entire surface of the retina, so collect the maximum amount of light.

One of the research team, Andreas Reichenbach, commented:

"Nature is so clever. This means there is enough room in the eye for all the neurons and synapses and so on, but still the Müller cells can capture and transmit as much light as possible."[12]

Blind spot

Dawkins complains further:

"... it gets even worse. One consequence of the photocells pointing backwards is that the wires that carry their data somehow have to pass through the retina and back to the brain. What they do, in the vertebrate eye, is all converge on a particular hole in the retina, where they dive through it. The hole filled with nerves is called the blind spot, because it is blind, but 'spot' is too flattering, for it is quite large, more like a blind patch, which again doesn't inconvenience us much because of the 'automatic Photoshop' software in the brain. Once again, send it back, it's not just bad design, it's the design of a complete idiot.

"Or is it? If it were, the eye would be terrible at seeing, and it is not. It is actually very good. It is good because natural selection, working as a sweeper-up of countless little details, came along after the big original error of installing the retina backwards, and restored it to a high-quality precision instrument." (pp. 354–5)

Once more, Dawkins shows no understanding of the need to regenerate the photocells, which necessitates this 'backward wiring'. He also begs the question of how mutations and natural selection could create the sophisticated software, which rather speaks of intelligent programming (as does the real Photoshop). Some of this programming was explained in *By Design*, ch. 1.

12. Sheriff, L., Living optical fibres found in the eye: Moving light past all those synapses, *The Register*, 20007; www.theregister.co.uk/2007/05/01/eye_eye/.

Signal processing

Another amazing design feature of the retina is the signal processing that occurs even before the information is transmitted to the brain. This occurs in the retinal layers between the ganglion cells and the photoreceptors. For example, a process called *edge extraction* enhances the recognition of edges of objects. John Stevens, an associate professor of physiology and biomedical engineering, pointed out that it would take "a minimum of a hundred years of Cray [supercomputer] time to simulate what takes place in your eye many times each second."[13] And the retina's analog computing needs far less power than the digital supercomputers and is elegant in its simplicity. Once again, the eye outstrips any human technology, this time in another area.

Indeed, research into the retina shows that the 12 different types of ganglion cells send 12 different 'movies', i.e. distinct representations of a visual scene, to the brain for final interpretation. One movie is mainly a line drawing of the edges of objects, and others deal only in motion in a specific direction, and still others transmit information about shadows and highlights. How the brain integrates these movies into the final picture is still a subject of intense investigation. Understanding this would help researchers trying to design artificial light sensors to help the blind to see.[14]

Ophthalmologist Peter Gurney, in his detailed response to the question, "Is the inverted retina really 'bad design'?",[15] also addresses the blind spot. He points out that the blind spot occupies only 0.25% of the visual field, so Dawkins is exaggerating to try to call it a patch rather than a spot. Furthermore, it is far (15°) from the visual axis, so that the normal visual acuity of the region is only about 15% of the acuity of the foveola, the most sensitive area of the retina right on the visual axis. And having two eyes effectively means there is no blind spot. So the alleged defect is only theoretical, not practical. The blind spot is not considered handicap enough to stop a one-eyed person from driving a private motor vehicle. The main problem with only one eye is the lack of stereoscopic vision.

Problem for Dawkins' own just-so story of eye evolution

In Dawkins' earlier book *Climbing Mt Improbable*, he cited a computer simulation by Dan Nilsson and Susanne Pelger from a widely publicized

---

13. *Byte*, April 1985.
14. Roska, B., Molnar, A., Werblin, F.S., Parallel processing in retinal ganglion cells: How integration of space-time patterns of excitation and inhibition form the spiking output, *J. Neurophys.* 95:3810–3822, 2006. The lead researchers wrote a semi-popular article: Werblin, F. and Roska, B., The movies in our eyes, *Scientific Amer.* **296**(4):54–61, 2007.
15. Gurney, P.W., Is our 'inverted' retina really 'bad design'? *J. Creation* **13**(1):37–44, 1999; creation.com/retina.

paper.[16] Taking their cue from Darwin, who started with a light-sensitive spot when 'explaining' the origin of the eye, their simulation starts with a light-sensitive layer, with a transparent coating in front and a light-absorbing layer behind. But the hypothetical ancestor starts with the nerve *behind* the light-sensitive spot, rather than from in front, as in the vertebrate eye. Yet the evolutionary just-so story can *provide no transition from having the nerves behind to in front*, with all the other complex coordinated changes that would have to occur as well.[17]

Indeed, Dawkins has no plausible explanation for the origin of the integrated components that work together to account for vision, such as that seen in vertebrates. Claiming that it is poorly designed because he has not carefully researched the matter does not explain how evolution created it.

Recurrent laryngeal nerve

Dawkins complains about the recurrent laryngeal nerve (RLN):

"It is a branch of one of the cranial nerves, those nerves that lead directly from the brain rather than from the spinal cord. One of the cranial nerves, the vagus (the name means 'wandering' and is apt), has various branches, two of which go to the heart, and two on each side to the larynx (voice box in mammals). On each side of the neck, one of the branches of the laryngeal nerve goes straight to the larynx, following a direct route such as a designer might have chosen. The other one goes to the larynx via an astonishing detour. It dives right down into the chest, loops around one of the main arteries leaving the heart (a different artery on the left and right sides, but the principle is the same), and then heads back up the neck to its destination.

"If you think of it as the product of design, the recurrent laryngeal nerve is a disgrace. Helmholz would have had even more cause to send it back than the eye. But, like the eye, it makes perfect sense the moment you forget design and think history instead." (p. 356)

Dawkins then argues that it makes better sense if we evolved from fish, and touching on something akin to Haeckel's discredited embryonic recapitulation theory,[18] concludes:

16. Nilsson, D.E. and Pelger, S., A pessimistic estimate of the time required for an eye to evolve. *Proc. R. Soc. Lond.* B 256:53–58, 1994.
17. Sodera, V., *One Small Speck to Man: The Evolution Myth*, pp. 292–302, Vij Sodera Publications, Bognor Regis, UK, 2003; the author is a surgeon.
18. Grigg, R., Ernst Haeckel: Evangelist for evolution and apostle of deceit, *Creation* **18**(2):33–36, 1996; creation.com/haeckel.

"All that we need to know, to understand the history of our recurrent laryngeal nerve, is that in the fish the vagus nerve has branches that supply the last three of the six gills, and it is natural for them, therefore, to pass behind the appropriate gill arteries. There is nothing recurrent about these branches: they seek out their end organs, the gills, by the most direct and logical route.

"During the evolution of the mammals, however, the neck stretched (fish don't have necks) and the gills disappeared, some of them turning into useful things such as the thyroid and parathyroid glands, and the various other bits and pieces that combine to form the larynx. Those other useful things, including parts of the larynx, received their blood supply and their nerve connections from the evolutionary descendants of the blood vessels and nerves that, once upon a time, served the gills in orderly sequence. As the ancestors of mammals evolved further and further away from their fish ancestors, nerves and blood vessels found themselves pulled and stretched in puzzling directions, which distorted their spatial relations one to another. The vertebrate chest and neck became a mess, unlike the tidily symmetrical, serial repetitiveness of fish gills. And the recurrent laryngeal nerves became more than ordinarily exaggerated casualties of this distortion." (pp. 359–360)

Richard Owen and opponents of Darwin

Dawkins goes on to describe how the RLN's detour could be 15 feet long in a large giraffe. He relates witnessing the dissection of such a nerve in a young giraffe that had died in a zoo. He expressed admiration of the skill of the team of anatomists performing the dissection, which increased his respect for the creationist opponent of Darwin, Richard Owen, who had achieved this feat in 1837. Yet, says Dawkins, Owen failed to reject the idea of a designer.

This should tell us something. It's notable that much of the opposition to Darwin came from scientists[19] like Owen, as well as Professor Johann H. Blasius, director of the Ducal[20] Natural History Museum of Braunschweig (Brunswick), Germany, who stated in a review of Darwin's *Origin*:[21]

"I have also seldom read a scientific book which makes such wide-ranging conclusions with so few facts supporting them. ... Darwin wants to show that *Arten* [types, kinds, species] come from other *Arten*. I regard this as somewhat of a highhanded hypothesis, because

---

19. Foard, J., Holy war? Who really opposed Darwin? Popular belief has it back to front ..., *Creation* 21(4):26–27, 1999; creation.com/holy-war
20. German *herzoglich*, presumably established under the auspices of the local duke (*Herzog*).
21. Wieland, C., Blast from the past, creation.com/blasius, 16 June 2006.

he argues using unproven possibilities, without even naming a single example of the origin of a particular species."[22]

Design features of the recurrent laryngeal nerve

As for good reasons Owen did not draw evolutionary conclusions, there are several. The well-known textbook *Gray's Anatomy* states:

"As the recurrent nerve hooks around the subclavian artery or aorta, it gives off several cardiac filaments to the deep part of the cardiac plexus. As it ascends in the neck it gives off branches, more numerous on the left than on the right side, to the mucous membrane and muscular coat of the esophagus; branches to the mucous membrane and muscular fibers of the trachea; and some pharyngeal filaments to the Constrictor pharyngis inferior."[23]

That is, Dawkins considers only its main destination, the larynx. In reality, the nerve also has a role in servicing parts of the heart, windpipe muscles and mucous membranes, and the esophagus, which could explain its route.

Even apart from this function, there are features that are the result of embryonic development—not because of evolution, but because the embryo develops from a single cell in a certain order. For example, the embryo needs a functioning simple heart early on; this later descends to its position in the chest, dragging the nerve bundle with it.

Also, would a circuitous route necessarily be bad design? There could be reasons for this (and in the case of the RLN we have a good idea, as per *Gray's*). Biologist and geologist John Woodmorappe's review of Jerry Coyne's book *Why Evolution is True* (which Dawkins recommends for its section on the RLN (note, p. 356)) points out:

"Human-designed machines and structures are full of such things as circuitous wiring and plumbing, but that hardly means that they are not the products of intelligent design.

"Now let us consider situations in which a circuitous route is actually harmful to its bearer. The automobile with its engine in front requires a long, tortuous exhaust system perched underneath the car. This clearly makes it more vulnerable to injury from obstructions than the short exhaust system of engine-in-back cars (I speak from personal experience). Following Coyne's logic, should we suppose that engine-in-front cars are not the products of intelligent design? No. We realize

22. Director Blasius interview: "Evolution is only a Hypothesis", 1859, cited in *Braunschweiger Zeitung,* 29 March 2004.
23. Available online at www.theodora.com/anatomy/the_vagus_nerve.html/.

that there is an engineering trade-off between the advantages of the car with its front-situated engine and the concomitant disadvantage of its more easily-damaged long, circuitous exhaust system."[24]

Messy design?

Dawkins claims:

"When we look at animals from the outside, we are overwhelmingly impressed by the elegant illusion of design. ... When we look at the inside, the impression is opposite. Admittedly, the impression of elegant design is conveyed by simplified diagrams in textbooks, neatly laid out and colour-coded like an engineer's blueprint. But the reality that hits you when you see an animal opened up on a dissecting table is very different. I think it would be an instructive exercise to ask an engineer to draw an improved version of, say, the arteries leaving the heart. I imagine the result would be something like the exhaust manifold of the car, with a neat line of pipes coming off in an orderly fashion, instead of the haphazard mess that we actually see when we open a real chest." (pp. 370–1)

OK, I'll ask a *real* engineer, and a top one at that, Prof. Stuart Burgess, leader of the Design Engineering Research Group at the University of Bristol (UK). He states that he sees a perfect *concept* of design in the human body—the skeleton and joints and so on, but one which has been subsequently marred.[25] So maybe this allegedly haphazard mess is not so messy after all. Also, the insides of many man-made things, including cars that Dawkins mentions, and computers, look most haphazard to the naïve.

Wonderful nets

Dawkins continues in this vein of apparently knowing what a designer would do.

"But the overwhelming impression you get from surveying the innards of a large animal is that it is a mess! Not only would a designer never have made a mistake like that nervous detour; a decent designer would never have perpetuated *anything* of the shambles that is the criss-crossing maze of arteries, veins, nerves, intestines, wads of fat and muscle, mesenteries and more. To quote the American biologist Colin Pittendrigh, the whole thing is nothing but 'a patchwork of makeshifts pieced together, as it were, from what was available when opportunity

24. Woodmorappe, J., Why evolution need not be true, *J. Creation* **24**(1):24–29, 2010.
25. Burgess, S., interviewed on CMI's Darwin bicentennial documentary, *The Voyage that Shook the World,* 2009.

knocked, and accepted in the hindsight, not foresight, of natural selection.'" (p. 371)

Furthermore, the apparently messy appearance of a dissected animal largely results from the actions of the dissector in trying to separate out the various parts and lay out what was a three dimensional structure in two dimensions. Yet the insides are not meant to impress Dawkins' sense of aesthetics, but to benefit the animal, and they seem to do this rather well. One obvious benefit of criss-crossing veins and arteries is the *counter-current heat exchange*, a principle well known to engineers. That is, transferring heat from the outgoing (hot) blood in the arteries to the incoming (cold) blood in the veins. This minimizes heat loss from the extremities. In some cases, this network is very pronounced and known as a *rete mirabile* (Latin for "wonderful net"; plural *retia mirabilia*). Such nets occur in penguin feet, flippers and nasal passages to stop heat loss in frigid Antarctic waters; the neck of the dog to prevent the brain from overheating; in mammalian testes to keep them cooler than body temperature.

Another important use is in the giraffe neck. This creature needs a very powerful heart to pump the blood up such a height to its brain. But when it bends down to drink, this massive pressure would blow its brain—were it not for pressure sensors which automatically cause arterial blood to be shunted off to a *rete*.[26]

Testes tubing

Dawkins grumbles about another supposedly circuitous route:

"The vas deferens is the pipe that carries sperm from the testis to the penis. ... It takes a ridiculous detour around the ureter, the pipe that carries urine from the kidney to the bladder. If this were designed, nobody could seriously deny that the designer had made a bad error. But just as with the recurrent laryngeal nerve, all becomes clear when we look at evolutionary history. ... When, in the evolution of the mammals, the testes descended to their present position in the scrotum (for reasons that are unclear, but are often thought to be associated with temperature), the *vas deferens* unfortunately got hooked the wrong way over the ureter."

Once again, we see a quasi-theological argument, since the actual evolutionary explanations are vague. Once more, Coyne uses this argument, and Woodmorappe shows the fallacy:

---

26. See also Hofland, L., Giraffes ... animals that stand out in a crowd, *Creation* **18**(4):10–13, 1996; creation. com/giraffe.

"Let us examine another 'bad design' argument more closely—the human testicles. Coyne points out that human sperm requires relatively cool temperatures. Males are ostensibly stuck with the preexisting fish-ancestry body-build that now requires the embryonic testicles to migrate down the inguinal canals to outside the body, a process which eventually leads to weak spots that can develop into hernias (p. 13). By his own admission, Coyne cannot explain why evolution favoured the placement of testicles in an easily-injured position, and the fact that some mammals (e.g., the platypus and elephant) do just fine with internal testicles (p. 235). The heat-intolerance of sperm may be secondary—a consequence, not cause, of the externally-situated human testicles (p. 236). Obviously, the 'whats', let alone the 'whys', of this subject are not well understood. If nothing else, external testicles are a problem for evolutionists."

Bad back

Problems with bad backs have often been blamed on a design flaw in our spines, supposedly because we imperfectly evolved from four-legged creatures. Dawkins is no exception. He cites the atheistic Welsh-born Australian TV journalist Robyn Williams[27] (1944–):

"After complaining of the agony his own back gives him … Williams goes on, 'nearly all backs could make an instant claim on the warranty, if there were one. If [God] *were* responsible for back design, you'll have to concede that it wasn't one of His best moments and must have been a deadline rush at the end of the Six Days.'

"The problem, of course, is that our ancestors walked for hundreds of millions of years on all fours with the backbone held more-or-less horizontally, and it doesn't take kindly to the sudden readjustment imposed by the last few million. And the point, once again, is that a real designer of an upright-walking primate would have gone back to the drawing board and done the job properly, instead of starting with a quadruped and tinkering." (p. 369)

27. Williams is a man who has carried Dawkins' dismissal of objective ethics to its logical conclusion: he has even bragged about breaking an agreement with a creationist, albeit one defending an argument CMI doesn't hold. This is documented in Cameron Horn's book *Science v Truth* which cites Williams' book *The Science Show:* "The speed of light brigade were more determined. The ideas were to be presented by a GP from Adelaide. I was required to agree that no critical comment would follow his exposition." Then: "As soon as the interview finished, I called a friend at the physics department at the University of Sydney to ask: 'What do you make of this?' [He] gave me clear and damning refutations of the creationist claim which I duly put to air. In the same program." Horn comments quite fairly:"So Williams is quite open about not honouring the verbal commitment. 'Dr Conjunction' [Cameron's pseudonym for the Adelaide GP], unused to dealing with media folk, was naïve not to get the commitment in writing."

Once again, Dawkins is out of touch with real experts of the spine who disagree, preferring the opinions of non-scientists like Williams, and his own quasi-theological opinion on what a designer might do. For example, Prof. Richard Porter (1935–2005) was Director of Education and Training for the Royal College of Surgeons of Edinburgh (1995–97), published over 60 papers in peer-reviewed journals on spinal disorders alone, and was awarded the first Volvo Award in 1979 for work on spinal stenosis.[28] As stated in *By Design*, ch. 12:

Lordosis: essential curvature for upright creatures

Prof. Porter explains the common evolutionary claim:

"For example, the inward curve of the lumbar spine—the lordosis—was thought by evolutionists to be a problem, the result of man standing upright. Therefore some researchers may look at a patient with back pain and say it's because mankind has recently stood upright, and the spine has not yet evolved satisfactorily. If therapists have the wrong starting assumption, then it's not surprising that they have advocated treatments to reduce the lordosis, which made the problem worse."[29]

However, he explains how the design perspective has been much more helpful to his research than evolutionary assumptions:

"I start from quite a different position and say—from my understanding of human anatomy and physiology and my understanding of God, the form of God's creation always matches its function. So you can be sure that the form of the spine is perfectly designed for its function. God has made a wonderful spine. It you start with that premise, it gives you a head start when trying to understand the mechanism of the spine.

"When you start to examine the biomechanics of the curved spine asking why it's that shape, and what's good about it, you find that the arch of the spine has a beautiful purpose, it's like the arch of a bridge, it adds strength. Because of that arch in the lumbar spine, a man with a lumbar lordosis can lift proportionally more weight than a Gorilla with its kyphotic (outwardly curving) spine!

"Thus it's not surprising that treating back pain with postures and exercises that *restore* the lordosis work exceedingly well."[30]

---

28. His obituary in the *British Medical Journal* noted his scientific achievements, as well as his strong Christian faith and generosity to overseas doctors and refugees www.bmj.com/cgi/content/full/332/7534/182-e/DC1.
29. See also Bergman, J., Back problems: how Darwinism misled researchers, *J. Creation* **15**(3):79–84, 2001; creation.com/backproblem.
30. Smail, R., Oh my aching back! *Creation* **12**(4):20–21, September 1990; creation.com/backache. The therapist Robin McKenzie, from New Zealand, discovered this lordosis-restoring treatment by chance in 1956. While not a Design advocate, McKenzie's work lends considerable support to the Design model.

Spine design

Furthermore, according to Prof. Porter, the human spine exhibits very good design features:

> "My inaugural lecture in Aberdeen [as Professor of Orthopaedic Surgery at the University of Aberdeen, Scotland] was 'Upright man' and I tried to explain how the wonderful human spine is a perfect match between form and function. Things go wrong with the spine when we abuse it (if we fail to keep ourselves fit, or overload it, or have an accident). We are learning to use 'foam filling' in building, (a sandwich of honeycomb material between two plates) to make something that is both light and strong, but the bones of the spine have been 'foam filled' with cancellous bone (with an open, latticed, or porous structure) surrounded by harder cortical bone since creation.

> "The vertebral bodies increase in cross sectional area as you go further down the spine, because in the upright position the lower ones have to take more load. The bones are not denser, they are just bigger. By contrast, animals that walk on all fours have a roughly horizontal spine that has a roughly equal load all the way. So they have vertebrae of similar cross sectional area all down the spine. Form matches function. We would have expected our vertebral bodies to be like quadrupeds if we had only recently stood upright, but that is not the case.'

> "We designed radial-ply tyres for motor cars, and then find God had constructed the rim of the intervertebral disc with radial-ply fibres from the beginning. That construction makes a healthy disc stronger than the bones. When you examine the way the human body is formed and how it works, you are constantly amazed. It's like looking at a piece of beautiful bone china and seeing the maker's mark beneath."

Evolutionary notions of bad design in the human spine have impeded the development of appropriate treatments for injured backs.[30]

Koala pouch

Another alleged bad design example also comes from Williams:

> "Williams next mentions the pouch of that iconic Australian animal the koala, which—not a great idea in an animal that spends its time clinging to tree trunks—opens downwards, instead of upwards, as in a kangaroo. Once again, the reason is a legacy of history. Koalas are descended from a wombat-like ancestor. Wombats are champion diggers:

"Flinging great paws full of soil backwards like an excavator digging out a tunnel, its babies would have had eyes and teeth permanently filled with grit. So backwards it was, and when one day the creature moved up a tree, perhaps to exploit a fresh food source, the 'design' came with it, too complicated to change."

"As with the recurrent laryngeal nerve, it might be theoretically possible to change the embryology of the koala to turn its pouch the other way up. But—I'm guessing—the embryological upheaval attendant on such a major change would render the intermediates even worse off than the koalas coping with the existing state of affairs."

First, notice the self-professed guesswork in this just-so story: "I'm guessing", "might be", "perhaps" …

Second, this alleged change must have happened in reverse, given that evolutionists believe that wombats descended from a marsupial with a forward-facing pouch. For a wombat, the explanation for its backward pouch makes good design sense; but one must wonder how the babies of the intermediates survived before the pouch pointed backwards.

Third, the backward-facing pouch has a good reason in a koala.[31] For a jumper like a kangaroo, a forward-facing pouch is best so the joey doesn't fall out the bottom. The same likely applies to a nimble opossum, which jumps quickly from branch to branch. But the koala moves much more sedately and more closely to the trunk and branch, with its belly rubbing against the bark and would likely accumulate debris in a pouch that opened forward. As it is, the backward pouch has a sphincter in the backwardly facing opening to hold the young ones in.

Furthermore, the koala has another good design feature: since she can't lick clean the backward opening pouch for her offspring, the pouch has a remarkable self-cleaning antiseptic system. During the non-breeding season, crusty "wads of brown stuff" accumulate, but when she is ready to breed, this muck disappears as "the pouch becomes a completely different place", according to Professor Elizabeth Deane of Macquarie University, Australia.[32]

"'It becomes glistening, pristine and almost translucent. You can go in and the back of it is almost see-through and you can see droplets of clear material on the pouch,' she said. The secret to the pouch becoming

---

31. See also Catchpoole, D., creation.com/practical-pouches, 13 March 2007
32. Salleh, A., Koala pouch may have its own bug buster, *ABC Science Online*, 31 July 2006.

squeaky-clean is in these clear droplets oozing into the pouch—the liquid contains powerful proteins, that kill microbes."[33]

This means that the koala's pouch does the job it was designed to do, and is thus no evidence for an evolutionary mistake.

Summary

- The argument from 'bad design' is flawed from the start, since it is basically theological—'no designer would do this'; and is often an appeal to ignorance—we don't understand the function, so it must be an evolutionary vestige.

- Some designs that appear suboptimal when considering one feature may be best when the *combination* of features is considered. Similarly, thicker armour might protect better, but if it's too thick, it would waste resources and add too much weight.

- Dawkins regurgitates Helmholtz's charges against the eye's defects, but these treat the eye as a static rather than dynamic instrument. A high-resolution image across the whole retina would need 50 times the brain size to process, otherwise it's pointless. It is far more efficient to have a small central area of the retina, the fovea, for high resolution, and the low-resolution peripheral area can pick out possible areas of interest, then zoom in the fovea to analyze more closely.

- Dawkins once more brings up the tired old 'backwardly wired retina' canard. But leading eye experts point out that Dawkins' 'superior' front-wired retina could not be supplied with the copious blood it needs to regenerate the photoreceptors and remove excess heat. Furthermore, the Müller cells are now known to form a fibre-optic plate, which transmits the image through the nerve network without distortion.

- Like a number of modern evolutionists, Dawkins asserts that the recurrent laryngeal nerve is a pointless detour, and a relic of evolution from fish. But the nerve also has a role in servicing parts of the heart, windpipe muscles and mucous membranes, and the esophagus, which could explain its route.

- Bad backs are allegedly the relic of our evolution from four-legged creatures. But leading spine experts point out that the human spine's inward curve (lordosis) makes it stronger than a gorilla's spine, pound-for-

---

33. Deane's team of researchers is analyzing koala pouch secretions prior to birth to identify which of the proteins are responsible for the antimicrobial action. Bobek, G., and Deane, E., Possible antimicrobial compounds from the pouch of the koala, *Phascolarctos cinereus*, *Letters in Peptide Science* **8**(3–5):133–137, 2001.

pound. Restoring this curve has helped treat bad backs, while evolutionary assumptions have worsened them.

- The koala's backwardly-opening pouch is not bad design, but rather good for a creature that crawls through trees and branches, since it stops debris coming in. The pouch also secretes antimicrobial proteins before it's due to carry young, which makes the pouch "squeaky-clean".

—∞—

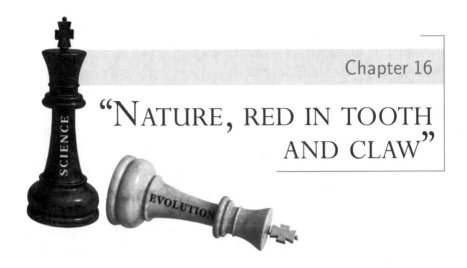

Chapter 16

"NATURE, RED IN TOOTH AND CLAW"

DAWKINS argues that evolutionary theory explains the death, bloodshed, suffering, disease and wastage in the living world. Yet much of that can be explained by the biblical model of the Fall. For example, a number of 'carnivorous' features can be used for a vegetarian diet. Insects are not regarded as 'living' in the biblical sense, and appear not to feel pain. Many disease germs seem to be degenerated forms of benign ones. And in the plant kingdom, trees are not just wasteful results of competition for light, but constitute three-dimensional communities with good biodiversity.

In ch. 12 of *Greatest Show*, "Arms Race and Evolutionary Theodicy", Dawkins points out the tremendous amount of death and suffering in this world, and designs of creatures clearly intended to harm other creatures. Like many evolutionary apologists, he likes to emphasize the bloodshed and violence that drives these biological changes. They see "Nature, red in tooth and claw," in the memorable phrase from the very long 1850 poem *In Memoriam, A.H.H.* by Alfred Lord Tennyson (1809–1892). This is supposed to be 'knock-down' evidence against creation, believing it disproves the possibility of a benevolent, wise Creator—following Darwin. The fact that Tennyson's poem predates Darwin's *Origin* indicates that Darwin was greatly influenced by philosophical ideas of his day.

> Once again, this is a quasi-theological argument rather than a scientific argument—it is about what God supposedly would or would not do rather than about the scientific evidence. But a major answer lies in the biblical teaching of the Fall,[1,2] as I've explained in *By Design* ch. 13 (with some updates for this book).

Origin of carnivory

The Bible doesn't specifically explain how carnivory originated, but since creation was finished after Day 6 (Genesis 2:1–3), there is no possibility that God later created new carnivorous animals. The Bible is, however, clear that the current situation was not the way God originally created things (Genesis 1:31), and will not be the way in the restored future (Isaiah 11 and 65). Instead, biblical creationists have three explanations in general, although the specific explanation depends on the particular case.[3]

1. *The Bible appears not to regard insects and other invertebrates as 'living', in the same sense as humans and vertebrate animals.*

   The Hebrew never refers to them as *nephesh chayyāh* (נֶפֶשׁ חַיָּה 'living soul/creature'), unlike humans and even fish (Genesis 1:20, 2:7). This is consistent with the Bible saying that "the life of the flesh is in the blood" (Leviticus 17:11) and the fact that insects don't have the same sort of 'blood' that vertebrates do. Therefore, the pre-Fall diet of animals did not necessarily exclude invertebrates. Interestingly, insects apparently do not have a complex enough brain to register a stimulus as 'pain':

   Some insects normally show no signs of painful experience at all. A dragonfly, for example, may eat much of its own abdomen if its tail end is brought into the mouthparts. Removal of part of the abdomen of a honeybee does not stop the animal's feeding. If the head of a blow-fly (*Phormia*) is cut off, it nevertheless stretches its tubular feeding organ (proboscis) and begins to suck if its chemoreceptors (labellae) are brought in touch with a sugar solution; the ingested solution simply flows out at the severed neck.[4]

2. *Before the Fall, many attack/defence structures could have been used in a vegetarian lifestyle.*

---

1. The theological implications of the Fall, what was affected, are discussed in Sarfati, *Refuting Compromise*, ch. 6, Creation Book Publishers, Atlanta, GA, 2004.
2. For a thorough treatment of the implications of the Fall taught by Romans ch. 8, see Smith, H.B., Cosmic and universal death from Adam's Fall: An exegesis of Romans 8:19–23a, *J. Creation* **21**(1):75–85, 2007; creation.com/romans8.
3. Batten, D., Catchpoole, D., Sarfati, J. and Wieland, C., *The Creation Answers Book*, ch. 6., Creation Book Publishers, 2007; creation.com/cab.
4. 'Sensory Reception: Mechanoreception', *Encyclopædia Britannica* (Electronic edition on CD).

For example, spiders normally now use their webs for trapping insects and other prey. But some baby spiders catch pollen for food,[5] providing a possible clue to a pre-Fall function for the spider web.[6] And the small Central American jumping spider *Bagheera kiplingi* is a genuine vegetarian spider, eating mainly specialized leaf tips of acacia shrubs called Beltian Bodies.[7,8]

There are modern examples of lions that didn't eat meat,[9,10] and the converse of 'herbivores' (cow, sheep) eating chickens.[11,12] And a 'seed-eating' bird (finch) has turned to blood-sucking.[13] So some of the behaviour can be learned. That there can be very similar species, clearly derived from the one original created kind, with one a vegetarian and the other a carnivore, shows how animals can adapt to carnivory from vegetarianism. Examples include the vegetarian relative of the piranha called the *pacu*,[14] and the palm-nut vulture,[15] which is largely vegetarian, while a 'bird of prey' (oilbird) is totally vegetarian.[16] The fruit bat has very sharp teeth, and is even classified as a carnivore, despite its diet.

And "Although bears have teeth designed for eating meat, their diet consists mainly of plants."[17] Maybe the teeth are really designed for what they do! And pandas have the sharp teeth and claws of other bears but eat mainly bamboo.

The Fall could have resulted in benign features becoming used for attacking. The *need* to attack may have arisen for several reasons. For some animals, the curse upon them (Genesis 3:14) may have resulted in their losing the ability to synthesize certain essential protein components (amino acids) from ingested plant material, hence their need to eat other animals containing those nutrients. Similarly, with the curse on the ground (Genesis 3:17–18), plants might have lost nutritional value such that some animals, which could no longer survive on the available plants, turned to eating the animals that

5. White, T., Pollen-eating spiders, *Nature Australia* **26**(7):5, Summer 1999–2000.
6. Pollen-eating spiders, *Creation* **22**(3):5, 2000.
7. Meehan, C.J. *et al.*, Exploitation of the *Pseudomyrmex-Acacia* mutualism by a predominantly vegetarian jumping spider (*Bagheera kiplingi*), *93rd ESA [Ecological Ssociety of America] Annual Meeting*, 7 August 2008; *Current Biology*, 13 October 2009.
8. Catchpoole, D., Vegetarian spider, *Creation* **31**(4):46, 2009.
9. Catchpoole, D., The lion that wouldn't eat meat, *Creation* **22**(2):22–23, 2000; creation.com/lion.
10. Catchpoole, D., Lea, the spaghetti lioness, *Creation* **29**(4):44–45, 2007; creation.com/spag.
11. Carnivorous cow, *Creation* **29**(4):7, 2007.
12. Wild and woolly, *Creation* **21**(4):9, 1999.
13. Catchpoole, D., Vampire finches of the Galápagos, *Creation* **29**(3):52–53, 2007.
14. Catchpoole, D., Piranha, *Creation* **22**(4):20–23, 2000; creation.com/piranha.
15. Catchpoole, D., The 'bird of prey' that's not, *Creation* **23**(1):24–25, 2000; creation.com/vulture.
16. Bell, B., The super-senses of oilbirds: *Bizarre birds elude an evolutionary explanation*, *Creation* **28**(1):38–41, 2005; creation.com/oilbird.
17. Taronga Zoo, Bear Exhibit, Australia, July 1999.

could. Thus animals with the right conveniently-predesigned features (e.g., claws, venom) could turn to predation to gain their required nutrients.

Poisons

With regard to poisons, the concept of 'poison' depends on amounts—'the dose *makes* the toxin'. Many poisons have benefits in small amounts, e.g. the potent digitalis toxin in foxglove plants in tiny amounts stabilizes arrhythmias in heart patients. Conversely, even 'good' things like oxygen and water can act as poisons in large amounts.[18] Before the Fall, the levels of toxins would have been low enough for them not to be toxic. Following the Fall, plants could, through mutational loss of information, lose control of the synthesis of substances that then accumulate to toxic levels, or lose enzymes in metabolic pathways such that the substrates for those enzymes accumulate to toxic levels.

3. *God foreknew the Fall, so He programmed creatures with the information for attack and defence features, which they would need in a cursed world. This information was 'switched on' at the Fall.*

It's notable that the development of every individual multi-celled creature involves a programmed switching off of genetic information. Each individual begins as a single cell—a *zygote* or an ovum fertilized by a spermatozoon. This fertilized ovum has all the instructions coded in the DNA to make us what we are physically (given the right environmental conditions).

But as the embryo grows, different cells in different places have to specialize, so that only certain instructions are executed—the cells become *differentiated*. The instructions are there, but turned off somehow. There are complicated genetic switches involved, and also a process called *methylation*—attaching methyl groups to the chemical 'letters' of DNA that code for instructions that need to be 'turned off'.

All the on/off switching must occur in the right sequence; the information for this sequencing is partly encoded in the DNA, but there are also controls outside the genes, hence the term *epigenetic*. This is why it would be impossible to clone dinosaurs and mammoths even if we found intact DNA—we would need the ovum (mother's egg) too.

The result of these elaborately designed switching sequences is that bone cells execute only instructions pertaining to bone—the instructions for blood, nerves, skin, etc. are still in the cells' DNA, but turned off. Similarly for blood, skin and other types of cells.

---

18. Bergman, J., Understanding Poisons from a Creationist Perspective, *J. Creation* **11**(3):353–360, 1997; creation.com/poison.

Thus if one can believe that this switching-off information was programmed by a Master Genetic Programmer, it is plausible that this Programmer could also have switched on information at the Fall.

This seems to be the best explanation for the clearly designed features such as the jellyfish sting, another type of catapult mechanism. Evolutionary notions of its origin are contradicted by the evolutionary time frame. One evolutionist admitted:

> "It is inconceivable that large predatory organisms like jellyfish could have existed at a time when there was nothing else around for them to feed on!"[19]

This applies to stinging for defence, too, because large predators had not evolved yet. But the evidence is consistent with the Fall affecting all creatures at the same time.[20]

Pathogens and creation

Some people wonder where disease germs fit into the biblical framework, if God created everything 'very good'. Under this framework, obviously the Fall was responsible for disease, but how, if God had finished creating at the end of Creation Week?

Genome decay

However, even something usually known as a deadly germ can have a mild variant that causes no illness. Presumably, something like this was created during Creation Week—even today, *Vibrio cholerae*, the germ that causes cholera, has a non-virulent form. This also has a role in the ecosystems of brackish waters and estuaries, and the original may have had a role living symbiotically with some people. Even its toxin may have a beneficial function in small amounts, like many poisons. The virulence arose after the Fall, by natural selection of varieties producing more and more toxin as contaminated water became more plentiful. This process would need no new genetic information. Also, recent evidence shows that the *loss* of *chemotaxis*—the ability to move in response to changes in chemical concentrations—will 'markedly increase infectivity in an infant mouse model of cholera.'[21]

19. Phylum Cnidaria, www.palaeos.com/Invertebrates/Coelenterates/Cnidaria.htm, 2003.
20. Catchpoole, D., Skeptics challenge: a 'God of love' created a killer jellyfish? Crush, kill, destroy—why do creatures have equipment to attack, kill and eat other animals? *Creation* **25**(4):34–35, 2003; creation.com/jellyfish.
21. Merrell, D.S. *et al.*, Host-induced epidemic spread of the cholera bacterium, *Nature* **417**(6889):642–644, 2002.

The leprosy germ is another good example. The form that causes disease, *Mycobacterium leprae,* has lost more than 2,000 genes, about a quarter of its total genome.[22]

Another likely example of virulence arising by information loss is the *mycoplasmas*, the smallest known self-reproducing organisms (parasitic bacteria with no cell walls and fewer than 1,000 genes, which are found in the respiratory system and urogenital tracts of humans). Loss of genetic information, e.g. for amino acid synthesis, could have resulted in the mycoplasmas' becoming increasingly dependent on their hosts for survival.[23,24]

Devolution of flagellum motor

One recent evolutionary paper explicitly discussed how information loss is common among disease-causing germs, including the loss of motility (ability to *initiate* movement rather than being carried along):

"Genome shrinkage is a common feature of most intra-cellular pathogens and symbionts. Reduction of genome sizes is among the best-characterised natural strategies adopted by intra-cellular organisms to save and avoid maintaining expensive redundant biological processes. Endosymbiotic bacteria of insects are examples of biological economy taken to completion because their genomes are dramatically reduced. These bacteria are non-motile and their biochemical processes are intimately related to those of their host. Because of this relationship, many of the processes in these bacteria have been either lost or have suffered massive re-modelling to adapt to the intra-cellular symbiotic lifestyle."[25]

Then it discussed the main point of the paper, which is actually relevant to one of Dawkins' earlier claims, i.e. the degeneration of the flagellum motor that normally propels germs:

"An example of such changes is the flagellum structure that is essential for bacterial motility and infectivity. Our analysis indicates that genes responsible for flagellar assembly have been partially or totally lost in most intra-cellular symbionts of gamma-Proteobacteria. Comparative genomic analyses show that flagellar genes have been differentially lost in endosymbiotic bacteria of insects. Only proteins involved in protein

22. Eiglmeier, K. The decaying genome of *Mycobacterium leprae, Lepr. Rev.,* 72:387–398, 2001.
23. Wood, T.C., Genome decay in the Mycoplasmas, *Impact* 340, October 2001; www.icr.org/pubs/imp/imp-340.htm.
24. Wieland, C., Diseases on the Ark (Answering the critics), *J. Creation* 8(1):16–18, 1994, creation.com/diseases, explains important related concepts.
25. Toft, C., and Fares, M., The evolution of the flagellar assembly pathway in endosymbiotic bacterial genomes, *Molecular Biology and Evolution,* 17 July 2008 | doi:10.1093/molbev/msn153.

export within the flagella assembly pathway (type III secretion system and the basal-body) have been kept in most of the endosymbionts whereas those involved in building the filament and hook of flagella have only in few instances been kept, indicating a change in the functional purpose of this pathway. In some endosymbionts, genes controlling protein-export switch and hook length have undergone functional divergence as shown through an analysis of their evolutionary dynamics. Based on our results we suggest that genes of the flagellum have diverged functionally as to specialise in the export of proteins from the bacterium to the host."

Dawkins had earlier endorsed the claim of theistic evolutionist Kenneth Miller[26] that the electric rotary motor of the flagellum evolved from such a secretion system.[27] But as the above, and several other evolutionary papers show,[28,29] the secretion system *devolved* from the flagellum. Thus the origin of that amazing motor remains unexplained by evolution (see *By Design*, ch. 10, "Motors").

Viruses

Similarly, too, with viruses: the most harmful viruses seem to have *de*volved, e.g. the most pathogenic HIV strains are also the least fit (they don't survive as well as less virulent strains).[30]

Some clues to possible benign pre-Fall roles for viruses can be gleaned from functions they have even today. Viruses are non-living entities, because they can't reproduce on their own, but need the copying machinery of more complex cells. But they have a number of useful functions even now, including transporting genes among plants and animals, keeping soil fertile, keeping water clean and regulating gases in the atmosphere.[31] So, once again, some alleged evidence for evolution actually provides support for the Creation/Fall model.

26. A more recent version of Miller's argument is Miller, K.R., The Flagellum Unspun: The Collapse of 'Irreducible Complexity'; in: Dembski, W.A. and Ruse, M., eds., *Debating Design: From Darwin to DNA*, Cambridge University Press, 2004.
27. Dawkins, R., Inferior Design, *New York Times,* 1 July 2007; see refutation, Sarfati, J., Misotheist's misology: Dawkins attacks Behe but digs himself into logical potholes, creation.com/dawkbehe, 13 July 2007.
28. Mecsas, J., and Strauss, E.J., Molecular Mechanisms of Bacterial Virulence: Type III Secretion and Pathogenicity Islands, *Emerging Infectious Diseases* 2(4), October–December 1996; www.cdc.gov/ncidod/EID/vol2no4/mecsas.htm.
29. Nguyen L. *et al.*, Phylogenetic analyses of the constituents of Type III protein secretion systems, *J. Mol. Microbiol. Biotechnol.* 2(2):125–44, April 2000.
30. Wodarz, D. and Levy, D.N., Human immunodeficiency virus evolution towards reduced replicative fitness *in vivo* and the development of AIDS, *Proc. Royal Soc. B*, 31 July 2007 | doi:10.1098/rspb.2007.0413.
31. See also Bergman, J., Did God make pathogenic viruses? *J. Creation* 13(1):115–125, 1999, creation.com/viruses; Kim, M., Biological view of viruses: creation vs evolution, *J. Creation* 20(3):12–13, 2006.

Priming the immune system

We should also note that microbes 'help prime the immune system' and many allergies might be due to a living environment that's too clean. Note that the immune system would be important even before the Fall, to distinguish between 'self' and 'non-self'.

So with some of these general principles explained, let's look at some of Dawkins' examples.

Animal pain

Dawkins once more raises a theological issue of the *benevolence* or otherwise of a designer, which is irrelevant to the scientific issue of *whether* something has been designed:

> "We shall stay with the idea of a planner, a designer, but our planner will be a moral philosopher rather than an economist. A beneficent designer might—you'd idealistically think—seek to minimize suffering. … it unfortunately doesn't happen in nature. Why should it? Terrible but true, the suffering among wild animals is so appalling that sensitive souls would best not contemplate it. Darwin knew whereof he spoke when he said, in a letter to his friend Hooker, 'What a book a devil's chaplain might write on the clumsy, wasteful, blundering low and horribly cruel works of nature.' The memorable phrase 'devil's chaplain' gave me my title for one of my previous books, and in another [*River out of Eden*] I put it like this:
>
> > [N]ature is neither kind nor wasteful. She is neither against suffering, nor for it, Nature is not interested in suffering one way or another unless it affects the survival of the DNA. It is easy to imagine a gene that, say, tranquillises gazelles when they are about to suffer a killing bite. Would such a gene be favoured by natural selection? Not unless the act of tranquillising a gazelle improved that gene's chances of being propagated into future generations. It is hard to see why this should be so and we may therefore guess that gazelles suffer horrible pain and fear when they are pursued to death—as most of them eventually are. The total amount of suffering per year is beyond all decent comprehension." (pp. 390–1)

As shown above (p. 288), insects appear not to feel pain. But what about sufferings of *nephesh chayyāh*, the vertebrates?

Some try to downplay the extent, and to a point they are right. Many animals go into acute stress reaction or psychological shock, which can cause fainting, a daze or minimization of pain. An example in humans occurred when Elisabeth of Bavaria was stabbed with a sharpened file in 1898 by an assassin called Luigi Lucheni, while she was boarding the steamship Genève on Lake Geneva. She got to her feet and boarded the ship, not realising that the file had punctured her heart. She later collapsed and bled to death from the wound; her last words were, "What happened to me?"

Theologian John Wenham argues that "there is reason to think that extreme sensations of pain and experiences of suffering may be rare or even non-existent among animals" in the wild state. Yet he apparently accepts that there is some pain and suffering in the wild state.[32]

Philosopher Michael Murray invokes recent biological research and studies on the philosophy of mind to propose three levels in an ascending pain hierarchy:

Level 1: information-bearing neural states produced by noxious stimuli resulting in aversive behaviour.

Level 2: a first order, subjective experience of pain.

Level 3: a second order awareness that one is oneself experiencing (2).[33]

As stated above (p. 288), invertebrates, the most common examples invoked by Darwin, experience response to noxious stimuli (1), without any evidence of experience of pain (2). Vertebrates seem to experience pain (2), but possibly not actual awareness of experiencing pain (3). To be aware that one is oneself in pain requires self-awareness, which is centred in the pre-frontal cortex of the brain—this is lacking in all animals except for the humanoid primates. So it's possible that the Creator was merciful enough to spare most animals the awareness of pain.

It seems that Darwin and his followers like Dawkins who use nature's so-called cruelties to attack God are guilty of the fallacy of anthropopathism, i.e. ascribing human feelings to non-human entities. Even Dawkins himself has admitted that he once found himself cursing at his bicycle because it wasn't working properly.[34]

---

32. Wenham, J.W., *The Goodness of God,* pp. 196–205, IVP, Leicester, UK, 1974.
33. Murray, M.J., *Nature Red in Tooth and Claw: Theism and the Problem of Animal Suffering,* Oxford University Press, 2008. Murray agrees that the traditional Christian response is the Fall of Adam, but he is convinced of an old earth that rules this out. He instead argues that atheists lack proof that there is gratuitous evil in the world.
34. See discussion by Christian philosopher and apologist William Lane Craig, *Question 134: Nature's Flaws and Cruelties,* www.reasonablefaith.org, 2009. Craig likewise neglects the Fall, likely because the big bang has long been part of his apologetics arsenal. See Kulikovsky, A.S., *Argumentum ad nihilum*: argument amounting to nothing: A review of *Creation out of Nothing* by Paul Copan and William Lane Craig, *J. Creation* **21**(1):20–26, 2007.

However, it seems indisputable that animals do experience some suffering and pain. Christian medical doctor Robert Gurney writes:

"As it happens, my son Matthew is a conservation biologist, wildlife consultant and safari guide who has worked for many years in Southern and Eastern Africa, closely observing animals in the wild. I discussed this question with him, and he was emphatic in his dismissal of the idea that animals in the wild do not suffer. To be precise, he said, 'That is absolute rubbish!' He has no doubt at all that animals in the wild do indeed suffer. He says, for example, that adult elephants are intelligent animals who show signs of severe grief and distress when their young are killed by predators."[35]

For such reasons, Gurney argues that the Fall must be a major explanation of such suffering. This of course requires that there was no animal death and suffering before the Fall, which in turn requires that the earth is not as old as Dawkins claims (wrongly, as shown in chs. 11 and 12).

Is 'God used evolution' a reasonable defence?

But without the Fall, Christians face a cognitive dissonance to reconcile all these problems with Christianity. Arguing that goo-to-you evolution was God's means of creation not only twists Scripture past its breaking point, but fails to impress evolutionists. For example, David Hull (a non-Christian philosopher of science), wrote:

"The problem that biological evolution poses for natural theologians is the sort of God that a darwinian version of evolution implies ... . The evolutionary process is rife with happenstance, contingency, incredible waste, death, pain and horror ... . Whatever the God implied by evolutionary theory and the data of natural history may be like, He is not the Protestant God of waste not, want not. He is also not a loving God who cares about His productions. He is not even the awful God portrayed in the book of Job. The God of the Galápagos is careless, wasteful, indifferent, almost diabolical. He is certainly not the sort of God to whom anyone would be inclined to pray."[36]

The atheist Jacques Monod was even more direct:

---

35. Gurney, R. J., The carnivorous nature and suffering of animals, *J. Creation* **18**(3): 70–75, 2004; creation. com/carniv.
36. Hull, D., The God of the Galápagos, *Nature* 352:485–86, 8 August 1991. Of course, as shown in ch. 3, we deny that Galápagos implies evolution.

"The more cruel because it is a process of elimination, of destruction. The struggle for life and elimination of the weakest is a horrible process, against which our whole modern ethics revolts. An ideal society is a non-selective society, is one where the weak is protected; which is exactly the reverse of the so-called natural law. I am surprised that a Christian would defend the idea that this is the process which God more or less set up in order to have evolution."[37]

Is evolution really such a great explanation?

Indeed, why should Christians jump on the evolutionary bandwagon anyway? A century before Dawkins' book *Greatest Show*, Christian apologist and novelist G.K. Chesterton argued that evolution doesn't provide a basis for dealing with animals:

"Darwinism can be used to back up two mad moralities, but it cannot be used to back up a single sane one. The kinship and competition of all living creatures can be used as a reason for being insanely cruel or insanely sentimental; but not for a healthy love of animals … That you and a tiger are one may be a reason for being tender to a tiger. Or it may be a reason for being cruel as the tiger. It is one way to train the tiger to imitate you, it is a shorter way to imitate the tiger. But in neither case does evolution tell you how to treat a tiger reasonably, that is, to admire his stripes while avoiding his claws.

"If you want to treat a tiger reasonably, you must go back to the garden of Eden. For the obstinate reminder continues to recur: only the supernaturalist has taken a sane view of Nature. The essence of all pantheism, evolutionism and modern cosmic religion is really in this proposition: that Nature is our mother. Unfortunately, if you regard Nature as a mother, you discover that she is a stepmother. The main point of Christianity was this: that Nature is not our mother: Nature is our sister. We can be proud of her beauty, since we have the same father; but she has no authority over us; we have to admire, but not to imitate."[38,39]

This is consistent with the *Dominion Mandate* of Genesis 1: God called the creation "good" before man arrived, so there is intrinsic worth; but man has authority over the rest of creation.[40]

37. Monod, Jacques, *The Secret of Life*, ABC interview, Australia, 1976.
38. Chesterton, G.K., *Orthodoxy*, ch. 7, "The eternal revolution", 1908; www.leaderu.com/cyber/books/orthodoxy/ch7.html.
39. Cosner, L., "G.K. Chesterton: Darwinism is 'an attack upon thought itself'", *J. Creation* **23**(1):119–112, 2009; creation.com/chesterton.
40. See for example Wieland, C. and Sarfati, J., Earth Day: Is Christianity to blame for environment problems? creation.com/earth_day, 20 March 2002.

Wasteful trees?

Dawkins doesn't stop with the animal kingdom, he also sees waste in gigantic trees. He argues that they need to grow so tall only to compete with each other in capturing solar energy for photosynthesis:

> "And this brings us face to face with the difference between a designed economy and an evolutionary economy. In a designed economy, there would be no trees, or certainly no very tall trees: no forests, no canopy. Trees are a waste. Trees are extravagant. Tree trunks are standing monuments to futile competition—futile if we think in terms of a planned economy. But a natural economy is not planned. Individual plants compete with other plants, of the same and other species, and the result is that they grow taller and taller, far taller than any planner would recommend. Not indefinitely taller, however. There comes a point when growing another foot taller, although it confers a competitive advantage, costs so much that the individual tree doing it actually ends up worse than its rivals that forego the extra foot. It is the balance of costs and benefits to the individual trees that finally determines the height to which trees are pressed to grow, not the benefits that a rational planner could calculate for the trees as a group. And of course the balance ends up at a different maximum in different forests. The Pacific Coast redwoods (see them before you die[41]) have probably never been exceeded."[42] (p. 379)

This is simplistic. First, according to the biblical model today's forests were not planned as such, but re-grew after the Flood. This still requires that the Creator programmed genes for great height so that they could grow (which of course is compatible with foreknowledge of the Fall and the Flood, as explained above—ch. 2). And evolution-based ideas about ecological succession/colonization are having to be revised in light of the evidence. For example, the supposed long periods of time required for 'mature' ecological forest communities to have formed has been shown to be unnecessary. We have seen in modern times indications of how the earth would have rapidly 're-greened' after the Flood of 4,500 years ago, with ecosystems quickly bouncing back from a localized devastation, e.g. after the Mt St Helens

---

41. Many times I have visited Redwood Grove in Whakarewarewa Forest, Rotorua, in the central North Island of New Zealand. These redwoods were planted in 1901; one has reached a height of 67 m and diameter of 169 centimetres. In California, they can grow over 110 m tall and the average lifespan is 600 years, and they may even be able to live as long as 2,000 years. See www.redwoods.co.nz.

42. See also Bates, G., Patriarchs of the forest, *Creation* **25**(1):10–13, 2002; creation.com/talltrees.

eruption in north-west USA,[43] and the colonization of brand new islands such as Surtsey.[44]

There are good ecological reasons for trees, and I am fortunate in having two colleagues who are Ph.D. plant physiologists and tree experts (cf. Dawkins is an animal behaviour specialist), Drs Don Batten and David Catchpoole. They point out that there is a huge ecological benefit provided by tall trees because they make the land biomass three dimensional instead of two. Lifting the photosynthesizers to great height frees the forest floor for animals, otherwise it would be an impenetrable jungle. Many plants and animals thrive in the space between the canopy and floor, e.g. in the branches. Also, not all plants need bright light; there are many species, called understorey plants, which grow well in the shade of the tall trees, e.g. coffee, Cordyline spp., ginger, various lilies and palms. Many of them don't grow well in full sun, so the tall trees provide a habitat for such understory plants.

Furthermore, deep-rooted trees stabilize the soil and hinder erosion, and recycle nutrients that are out of reach of other plants with shallower root systems. They also recycle deep water and humidify the air, helping to increase rainfall.[45] In fact, the desertification of the once-lush Sahara is thought to have been substantially contributed to by the removal of trees. Except for a relatively small part of the world, which according to UN (FAO) studies consists of naturally hyperarid deserts, desertification is often a man-induced process caused by the removal of trees.

The deep roots of tall trees also contribute to the health of the soil by lowering the water table, which helps avoid the development of salinity problems in the less humid parts of the world (excessive tree clearing has caused salinification in many regions).

Of course a caring Creator would have created organisms that had usefulness for humans. Trees, and particularly the ones that grow tall and straight, are supremely useful to mankind as a source of all kinds of timber suited to various purposes. Evolution can have no teleological explanation for such things; it is just luck that they are useful to us.

43. See Swenson, K. and Catchpoole, D., After devastation ... the recovery: An amazing bounce-back after catastrophe gives us insights into how the world recovered from the Flood, *Creation* **22**(2):33–37, 2000.
44. Catchpoole, D., Surtsey still surprises, *Creation* **30**(1):32–34, 2007; creation.com/surtsey-still-surprises.
45. Engineer Adrian Bejan of Duke University argues, "We believe that the main function of the tree is to facilitate the flow of water from the ground and into the atmosphere. To achieve that function, the tree is ideally designed to not only maximize the flow of water, but in order to be successful in the real world, it must also be able to withstand the stresses of the wind. It is exquisitely designed to do just that." Trees, forests and the Eiffel tower reveal theory of design in nature, *Physorg.com*, 14 August 2008. Bejan, without evidence of course, credits evolution as the designer.

There is also valuable biodiversity in the understorey.[46] Creationist botanist Dr Henry Zuill, curator of the Joshua C. Turner Arboretum (a systematic collection of growing trees), which is an affiliate of the Nebraska Statewide Arboretum, explains:

"'Biodiversity' obviously refers to plants, animals and microbes, from bacteria to fungi, that collectively make up living systems—ecosystems. What are not so obvious are other meanings that have become attached to the word. It also refers to different populations of species, with their unique sets of genes and gene products.[47] Even more importantly, it includes the collective ecological services provided by those different species and populations working together for each other, keeping our planet healthy and suitable for life. Baskin describes the relationship this way: 'It is the lavish array of organisms that we call "biodiversity," an intricately linked web of living things whose activities work in concert to make the earth a uniquely habitable planet.'"[48] ...

"I believe there is a connection between biodiversity and creation, although I have seen no such connection made by other authors. All of the attention that I have seen has been directed toward the immediate problem of conservation. Without biodiversity and its ecochemical and ecophysical services, it is doubtful that ecosystems, or possibly even life itself, could exist. This much seems clear.

"Behe noted complex biochemical relationships in cells and suggested design to explain their origin. We tend to see the world through the 'lenses' of our scientific disciplines. Thus Behe, a biochemist, understood cell complexity to result from design. If we jump to the ecological level, at the other end of the spectrum of life, our 'ecology glasses' reveal unimaginable complexity there as well.

"When we look broadly at the panorama of life and ecological relationships, we see that ecological complexity is built on layer upon layer of complexity, going all the way down through different hierarchical structural and organizational levels to the cell and even lower. Thus, if we think cytological complexity is impressive, what must we think when we realize the full scale of ecological complexity?"[49]

46. www.rainforest-australia.com/Rainforest_understorey.htm.
47. Mlot, C. Population diversity crowds the Ark, *Science News* **152**(17):260, October 25, 1997.
48. Baskin, Y., *The Work Of Nature; How the Diversity of Life Sustains Us*, p. 3., Island Press, Washington, DC, 1997.
49. Zuill, H., in Ashton, J., Ed., *In Six Days: Why 50 [Ph.D.] scientists choose to believe in Creation*, New Holland Publishers, Australia, 1999; creation.com/henry-zuill-biology-in-six-days.

Summary

- There is indeed much suffering, pain and waste in nature. But this is ultimately explainable by the biblical Creation/Fall model. Conversely, neither Dawkins nor other atheistic evolutionists are impressed by proposals that God would use such a cruel and inefficient process as mutation/selection over millions of years to create all living things.

- Insects, which most impressed Darwin as examples of cruelty in nature, are not biblical life in the sense of *nephesh chayyāh*. They appear to have no sense of pain as opposed to response to noxious stimuli.

- More advanced animals may possess a first-order, subjective experience of pain, but lack a second-order awareness that one is oneself experiencing this.

- Before the Fall, many attack/defence structures could have been used in a vegetarian lifestyle. This is shown by the pacu, oilbird, vegetarian lions and spiders.

- Whether something is poisonous depends on the amount.

- Many disease-causing bacteria and viruses are degenerated forms of benign ones. E.g. the machinery for the motor driving the flagellum is disabled; this shows that Dawkins' earlier claims about the origin of this motor are back-to-front, and do not undermine the use of the flagellum as an example of irreducible complexity.

- Tall trees are not a wasteful result of competition. They are a key component of an ecological community, providing a third dimension to the land biomass, allowing other plants and animals to live between the floor and canopy, and they recycle nutrients and water. They are also very important for biodiversity and soil stability.

- Common-ancestry evolution provides a basis for being insanely cruel or insanely sentimental towards animals, while only the biblical view provides a healthy assessment of the environment: to be respected but under man's dominion.

—∞—

Chapter 17

EVOLUTION, SCIENCE, HISTORY AND RELIGION

D awkins resorts to guilt-by-association by comparing evolution-deniers with Holocaust deniers and deniers of the reality of the Roman Empire. Yet the Romans and the Holocaust are supported by eyewitness accounts and ample written records, unlike evolution.

Dawkins and many other evolutionists fret that doubt of evolution will be the end of science, but most science works perfectly well without it, including biological. Indeed, most of the branches of modern science were founded by believers in biblical creation, including biological science. In reality, science flourished in the Middle Ages in a Christianized Europe, and increased further after biblical authority was rediscovered in the Reformation. This should not be surprising, since science requires certain presuppositions, and they are all provided by the Bible, but not by Dawkins' materialism or, for example, by mystical religions.

Dawkins demonstrates duplicity in his lecturing of preachers. He demands that they teach that Adam was not historical, yet in his previous book *The God Delusion* he had called a symbolic Adam "barking mad". In *Greatest Show*, he says he respects theistic evolutionists, but in *God Delusion,* he condemned that view.

Does science need evolution?

Dawkins acts as though "history deniers" are a threat to science in general. Even the title of his book, "The Greatest Show on Earth", suggests the overwhelming importance of evolution.

History deniers?

Dawkins begins chapter 1 with:

> "Imagine that you are a teacher of Roman history and the Latin language, anxious to impart your enthusiasm for the ancient world … Yet you find your precious time continually preyed upon, and your class's attention distracted, by a baying pack of ignoramuses … who, with strong political and especially financial support, scurry about tirelessly attempting to persuade your unfortunate pupils that the Romans never existed. There never was a Roman Empire. The entire world came into existence only just beyond living memory. Spanish, Italian, French, Portuguese, Catalan, Occitan, Romansh: all these languages and their constituent dialects sprang spontaneously and separately into being, and owe nothing to any predecessor such as Latin.

> "Instead of devoting your full attention to the noble vocation of classical scholar and teacher, you are forced to divert your time and energy to a rearguard defence of the proposition that the Romans existed at all: a defence against an exhibition of ignorant prejudice that would make you weep if you weren't too busy fighting it." (p. 3)

Of course, here, unlike evolution, there are written records by eyewitnesses of the Romans, and surviving documents in Latin. And all Dawkins' complaints about history denial are hypocritical, since he gives tacit endorsement to a fringe view which is a *real* history denial—the so-called 'Christ myth' that Jesus did not even exist *at all*, not even as a person walking the earth (much less as the incarnate Son of God).[1] In his overtly atheopathic book *The God Delusion*, Dawkins says that it is "possible to mount a serious, though not widely supported, historical case that Jesus never lived at all".[2] However, no historian accepts this.[3] Instead, Dawkins appeals to G.A. Wells, a professor of *German*, not a historian.

Dawkins also appeared in a film by apostate Brian Flemming called *The God Who Wasn't There*. This film stridently defended the 'Christ myth',

1. Holding, J.P., Dawkins' Ironic Hypocrisy, creation.com/dawk-hyp, 21 November 2008.
2. Dawkins, R., *The God Delusion*, p. 97, Transworld Publishers, London, 2006.
3. For extensive documentation of the historical evidence that Jesus existed, see Holding, J.P., *Shattering the Christ Myth*, Xulon Press, 2008.

including the even more absurd proposition that Jesus' life story was derived from accounts of pagan deities.[4] While Dawkins did not address the existence of Jesus in the film, his voluntary appearance—and warm praise for it in *The God Delusion*—amounts to an endorsement of its historical nonsense.

Dawkins continues:

"If my fantasy of the Latin teacher seems too wayward, here's a more realistic example. Imagine you are a teacher of more recent history, and your lessons on 20th-century Europe are boycotted, heckled or otherwise disrupted by well-organised, well-financed and politically muscular groups of Holocaust-deniers. Unlike my hypothetical Rome-deniers, Holocaust deniers really exist. They are vocal, superficially plausible and adept at seeming learned. They are supported by the president of at least one currently powerful state, and they include at least one bishop of the Roman Catholic Church. Imagine that, as a teacher of European history, you are continually faced with belligerent demands to 'teach the controversy', and to give 'equal time' to the 'alternative theory' that the Holocaust never happened but was invented by a bunch of Zionist fabricators." (pp. 3–4)

Here is a classic guilt-by-association ploy. In reality, the Holocaust deniers[5] are doing just what Dawkins (or at least those he endorses) does with Jesus: ignores the eyewitness reports. And of course, there are living witnesses to the Holocaust, census records showing a vast drop in the European Jewish population, hardly any surviving European Jewish families who have not lost members in that tragic time and death camp records helpfully kept by the perpetrators, who were convicted in the Nuremberg trials. Evolution has nothing like this.

Evolution: central principle of biology?

After this rhetorical flourish, Dawkins laments the problem, as he sees it:

"The plight of many science teachers today is not less dire. When they attempt to expound the central and guiding principle of biology; when they honestly place the living world in its historical context—which means evolution; when they explore and explain the very nature of life

---

4. Either the parallels evaporate under even moderate analysis, or they post-date Christianity. See Sarfati, J., Was Christianity plagiarized from pagan myths? Refuting the copycat thesis, creation.com/copycat, 10 January 2009.

5. What really is often denied is the overtly evolutionary basis of the Nazi Holocaust and eugenics programs. See Weikart, R., *From Darwin to Hitler, Evolutionary Ethics, Eugenics and Racism in Germany*, Palgrave MacMillan, NY, 2004; *Hitler's Ethic: The Nazi Pursuit of Evolutionary Progress*, Palgrave Macmillan, NY, 2009. See also Sarfati, J., Refutation of *New Scientist's* "Evolution: 24 myths and misconceptions": The Darwin–Hitler connection, which also refutes the 'Hitler was a Christian' mendacity seen on some gutter atheopathic sites; creation.com/hitler-darwin, 19 November 2008.

itself, they are harried and stymied, hassled and bullied, even threatened with loss of their jobs. At the very least their time is wasted at every turn." (p. 4)

Yet the ones who are threatened with loss of jobs are usually those who dare to dissent from goo-to-you evolution.[6,7] Dawkins provides no evidence for this assertion that science teachers today are threatened with loss of jobs for teaching evolution. This seems like a classic case of *projection* on Dawkins' part.

The alleged centrality of evolution is echoed by the US National Academy of Science's book *Science, Evolution and Creationism*[8] (2008), and even extended, by implication, to other branches of science:

"Scientific and technological advances have had profound effects on human life. In the 19th century, most families could expect to lose one or more children to disease. Today, in the United States and other developed countries, the death of a child from disease is uncommon. Every day we rely on technologies made possible through the application of scientific knowledge and processes. The computers and cell phones which we use, the cars and airplanes in which we travel, the medicines that we take, and many of the foods that we eat were developed in part through insights obtained from scientific research. Science has boosted living standards, has enabled humans to travel into Earth's orbit and to the Moon, and has given us new ways of thinking about ourselves and the universe.

"Evolutionary biology has been and continues to be a cornerstone of modern science."

But it is not hard to notice that most of the scientific advances listed haven't the slightest thing to do with evolution. Computers, cell phones, airplanes, and the moon landings certainly don't! Indeed, they largely depended on the foundations laid by creationist scientists:

- The creationist Robert Boyle (1627–1691) fathered modern chemistry and demolished the faulty Aristotelian four-elements theory. He also funded

---

6.   See documentation in Bergman, J., *Slaughter of the Dissidents: Shocking Truth about Killing the Careers of Darwin Doubters,* Leafcutter Press, 2008; If you can't beat them, ban them, review by Lloyd To, *J. Creation* **23**(2):37–40, 2009.

7.   An entertaining documentary with a very serious message is Ben Stein's *Expelled: No Intelligence Allowed,* Premise Media:, 2008, which features an interview with Dawkins among others. It also documents the evolutionary basis of the Holocaust, including some of the Nazi propaganda films that proclaimed, "We have sinned against natural selection" for allowing the 'unfit' to live and reproduce.

8.   For refutation, see Sarfati., J., Science, Creation and Evolutionism: Response to the latest anti-creationist agitprop from the US National Academy of Sciences (NAS), *Science, Evolution and Creationism*, creation.com/nas, 8 February 2008.

lectures to defend Christianity and sponsored missionaries and Bible translation work.

- Cell phones depend on electromagnetic radiation theory, which was pioneered by creationist James Clerk Maxwell (1831–1879).

- Computing machines were invented by Charles Babbage (1791–1871), who was not a biblical creationist but was a creationist in the broad sense. He "believed that the study of the works of nature with scientific precision, was a necessary and indispensable preparation to the understanding and interpreting their testimony of the wisdom and goodness of their Divine Author."[9]

- The creationist brothers Orville (1871–1948) and Wilbur Wright (1867–1912) invented the airplane after studying God's design of birds.

- The theory of planetary orbits was invented by Johannes Kepler (1571–1630), famous for claiming that his discoveries were "thinking God's thoughts after him". Kepler also calculated a creation date of 3992 BC, close to Ussher's.

- The theory of gravity and the laws of motion, essential for the moon landings, were discovered by the creationist Isaac Newton (1642/3–1727), who also discovered the spectrum of light (so was the forerunner of my own speciality, spectroscopy), invented the reflecting telescope, discovered the exponential law of cooling, and co-invented calculus.

- The moon landing program was headed by Wernher von Braun (1912–1977), who believed in a designer and opposed evolution. And a biblical creationist, James Irwin (1930–1991), walked on the moon.

- America led the world in the number of Nobel prizes awarded, including in biology, before evolution was part of the school curriculum. And the Apollo moon landings were achieved by scientists and engineers educated under the same curriculum.

- Furthermore, these great scientists had precedents in the Middle Ages, often wrongly called the 'Dark Ages'. Science historian Dr James Hannam writes:

"Popular opinion, journalistic cliché and misinformed historians notwithstanding, recent research has shown that the Middle Ages were a period of enormous advances in science, technology and culture.

---

9. Buxton, H.W., *Memoir of the Life and Labours of the Late Charles Babbage Esq.*, unpublished, p. 1986. Cited in: Dubbey, J.M., *The Mathematical Work of Charles Babbage,* Cambridge University Press, Cambridge, 1978, p. 227.

The compass, paper, printing, stirrups and gunpowder all appeared in Western Europe between AD 500 and AD 1500."[10]

These 'dark ages' also saw the development of water and wind power, agricultural advances that enabled huge population growth, spectacles, magnificent architecture, the blast furnace, and much more.[10] It was also the time when universities were founded—including Dawkins' own Oxford—and these were modelled on theological colleges.

Some have claimed that most of these scientists would have been evolutionists had they known about Darwin. This is hypothetical and question-begging; it doesn't explain the creationists who were contemporaneous with Darwin or lived after him, and ignores the fact that evolutionary ideas had long predated Darwin.[11]

Does biology need evolution?

Some might argue, the above have nothing to do with biology, so we should not expect evolution to be relevant. However, an extremely common first point of attack on anti-evolutionists is that they are 'anti-science' and that science in general would collapse if evolution were not taught, yet the above shows how much science has little to do with evolution. So evolutionists have no just cause for complaint when all these branches of science are used as a rebuttal to their exaggerated accusation.

Furthermore, even in biology, some prominent academics have recently queried its *usefulness*. A.S. Wilkins, editor of the journal *BioEssays*, commented: "Evolution would appear to be the indispensable unifying idea and, at the same time, a highly superfluous one."[12] The leading chemist Philip Skell, a member of the National Academy of Sciences, echoed similar thoughts in a column he wrote for *The Scientist*:

> "Further, Darwinian explanations for such things are often too supple: Natural selection makes humans self-centered and aggressive—except when it makes them altruistic and peaceable. Or natural selection produces virile men who eagerly spread their seed—except when it prefers men who are faithful protectors and providers. When an explanation is so supple that it can explain any behavior, it is difficult

10. See Hannam, J., *God's Philosophers: How the Medieval World Laid the Foundations of Modern Science*, p. 5, Icon Books, 2009.
11. See Sarfati, J., Newton was a creationist only because there was no alternative? (response to critic) creation.com/newt-alt, 29 July 2002. The critic I was replying to later wrote thanking CMI for the response, and to say that he no longer agreed with the sentiments of his original letter. He was happy for his original letter and response to remain as a teaching point for others who might need correcting.
12. Wilkins, A.S., Evolutionary processes: a special issue, *BioEssays* 22:1051–1052, 2000.

to test it experimentally, much less use it as a catalyst for scientific discovery."[13]

Dr Marc Kirschner, founding chair of the Department of Systems Biology at Harvard Medical School stated:

"In fact, over the last 100 years, almost all of biology has proceeded independent of evolution, except evolutionary biology itself. Molecular biology, biochemistry, physiology, have not taken evolution into account at all."[14]

Does medicine need evolution?

Then what about medicine? Dawkins touched on this with antibiotic resistance (pp. 132–3), as refuted in ch. 4. I noted that even antibiotics were developed by the creationist Jew, Ernst Chain. What about other advances in science that are rightly credited with the vast drop in deaths of children due to disease and elimination of many scourges like smallpox and polio? No joy here for the evolutionists either. Many of the most important medical advances were made without the slightest use being made of evolution:

* Vaccination was discovered by Edward Jenner (1749–1823—note that Darwin published *Origin* in 1859).

* Aseptic surgery by Joseph Lister, creationist (1827–1912).

* Anaesthesia by James Young Simpson (1811–1870), who believed that God was the first anaesthetist, citing Genesis 2:21.

* Germ theory of disease by Louis Pasteur, creationist (1822–1895), who disproved spontaneous generation, still an evolutionary belief, as shown in ch. 13.

* In modern times, we have the outspoken biblical creationist Raymond Damadian (1936–), inventor of the Magnetic Resonance Imaging (MRI) scanner,[15,16] and John Sanford (1950–), the inventor of the gene gun.

See more in "Darwinian medicine?", ch. 4, p. 77.

---

13. Skell, P.S., Why Do We Invoke Darwin? Evolutionary theory contributes little to experimental biology, *The Scientist* **19**(16):10, 29 August 2005. Skell wrote a similar article: The Dangers Of Overselling Evolution: Focusing on Darwin and his theory doesn't further scientific progress, *Forbes magazine,* www.forbes.com, 23 Feb., 2009.
14. Quoted in the *Boston Globe*, 23 October 2005.
15. Mattson, J. and Simon, M., *The Pioneers of NMR and Magnetic Resonance in Medicine: The Story of MRI*, Bar-Ilan University Press, Jericho, New York, 1996; chapter 8: "Raymond V. Damadian: Originator of the Concept of Whole-Body NMR Scanning (MRI) and Discoverer of the NMR Tissue Relaxation Differences That Made It Possible."
16. See also Sarfati, J., Dr Damadian's vital contribution to MRI: Nobel prize controversy returns, 21–22 October 2006, creation.com/damadian. This documents Dr Damadian's vital contribution: showing that healthy and diseased tissue could be differentiated. Without this discovery, there would be nothing for MRI to 'image'.

The Christian roots of science[17]

Many anti-Christians claim that Christianity and science have been enemies for centuries. This is the opposite of the truth, as already shown above with all the Christian founders of modern science. Informed historians of science, including non-Christians, have pointed out that modern science first flourished under a Christian world view while it was *stillborn* in other cultures such as ancient Greece, China and Arabia.[18]

This should be no surprise when we ask why science works at all. There are certain essential features that make science possible, and they simply did not exist in non-Christian cultures.[19]

1. There is such a thing as *objective truth*. Jesus said, "I am the way, and the truth, and the life. No one comes to the Father except through me" (John 14:6). But postmodernism, for example, denies objective truth. One example is, "What's true for you is not true for me." So maybe they should try jumping off a cliff to see if the Law of Gravity is true for them. Another postmodern claim is, "There is no truth"—so is *that* statement true?; or, "We can't know truth"—so how do they *know* that?

2. The universe is *real*, because God created the heavens and the earth (Genesis 1). This sounds obvious, but many eastern philosophies believe that everything is an illusion (so is *that* belief an illusion as well?). There is no point in trying to investigate an illusion by experimenting on it.

3. The universe is *orderly*, because God is a God of order not of confusion—1 Corinthians 14:33. But if there is no creator, or if Zeus and his gang were in charge, why should there be any order at all? If some Eastern religions were right that the universe is a great Thought, then it could change its mind any moment.

   It is impossible to prove from nature that it is orderly, because the proofs would have to presuppose this very order to try to prove it. Also, in this *fallen* world with natural disasters and thunderstorms and general chaos, it is not so obvious that it was made by an orderly Creator. This is a major message of the book of Ecclesiastes—if we try to live our lives only according to what is under the sun, the result is futility. Hence our chief end is to "Fear God and keep his commandments" (Ecclesiastes 12:13).

17. Based on my articles Why does science work at all? *Creation* **31**(3):12–14, 2009; and The biblical roots of modern science, *Creation* **32**(4), 2010; creation.com/roots.
18. Stark, R., *For the Glory of God: How monotheism led to reformations, science, witch-hunts and the end of slavery,* Princeton University Press, 2003; see also review by Williams A., The biblical origins of science, *J. Creation* **18**(2):49–52, 2004; creation.com/stark.
19. I acknowledge Sean Wieland's input into such a list.

A fundamental facet of science is deriving laws that provide for predictable outcomes. This is only possible because the universe is orderly.

4. Since God is sovereign, He was free to create as He pleased. So the only way to find out how His creation works is to *investigate* and *experiment*, not rely on man-made philosophies as did the ancient Greeks.

This is illustrated with Galileo Galilei (1564–1642). He showed by experiment that weights fall at the same speed (apart from air resistance), which refuted the Greek philosophy that heavy objects fall faster. He also showed by *observation* that the sun had spots, refuting the Greek idea that the heavenly bodies are perfect.

Another example is Johannes Kepler (1571–1630), who discovered that planets moved in ellipses around the sun. This refuted the Greek philosophies that insisted on circles because they are the most 'perfect' shapes, which then needed the addition of an increasingly cumbersome system of circles upon circles called *epicycles* to try to accommodate the observations.

But when it comes to origins as opposed to understanding how things work, God has revealed that He created about 6,000 years ago over six normal-length days, and judged the earth with a globe-covering flood about 4,500 years ago. It's thus no accident that Kepler calculated a Creation date of 3992 BC, and Isaac Newton (1643–1727), probably the greatest scientist of all time, also strongly defended biblical chronology.

5. Man *can and should investigate* the world, because God gave us *dominion* over His creation (Genesis 1:28); creation is not divine. So we don't need to sacrifice to the forest god to cut down a tree, or appease the water spirits to measure its boiling point. On the contrary, many other founders of modern science saw their scientific research as bringing glory to God. Newton said:

> "This most beautiful system of the sun, planets, and comets, could only proceed from the counsel and dominion of an intelligent Being. ... This Being governs all things, not as the soul of the world, but as Lord over all; and on account of his dominion he is wont to be called 'Lord God' Παντωκράτωρ [*Pantōkrator*], or 'Universal Ruler'. ... The Supreme God is a Being eternal, infinite, absolutely perfect."[20]

---

20. *Principia*, Book III; cited in; *Newton's Philosophy of Nature: Selections from his writings*, p. 42, ed. H.S. Thayer, Hafner Library of Classics, NY, 1953.

Also: "Opposition to godliness is atheism in profession and idolatry in practice. Atheism is so senseless and odious to mankind that it never had many professors."[21]

6. Man can *initiate* thoughts and actions; they are not fully determined by deterministic laws of brain chemistry. This is a deduction from the biblical teaching that man has both a material and immaterial aspect (e.g. Genesis 35:18, 1 Kings 17:21–22, Matthew 10:28). This immaterial aspect of man means that he is more than matter, so his thoughts are likewise not bound by the material makeup of his brain.

But if materialism were true, then 'thought' is just an epiphenomenon of the brain, and the results of the laws of chemistry. Thus, *given their own presuppositions*, materialists have not freely arrived at their conclusion that materialism is true, because their conclusion was *predetermined by brain chemistry*. But then, why should their brain chemistry be trusted over mine, since both obey the same infallible laws of chemistry? So in reality, if materialists were right, then they can't even help what they believe (including their belief in materialism!). Yet they often call themselves 'freethinkers', overlooking the glaring irony. Genuine initiation of thought is an insuperable problem for materialism, as is consciousness itself (see also ch. 9, p. 147).[22]

Even a non-Christian social commentator, Dr Theodore Dalrymple, showed up the flaws in this evolutionary reasoning, as promoted by the atheist philosopher Daniel Dennett:

"Dennett argues that religion is explicable in evolutionary terms—for example, by our inborn human propensity, at one time valuable for our survival on the African savannahs, to attribute animate agency to threatening events.

"For Dennett, to prove the biological origin of belief in God is to show its irrationality, to break its spell. But of course it is a necessary part of the argument that all possible human beliefs, including belief in evolution, must be explicable in precisely the same way; or else why single out religion for this treatment? Either we test ideas according to arguments in their favour, independent of their origins, thus making the argument from evolution

---

21. *A Short Scheme of the True Religion*, manuscript quoted in *Memoirs of the Life, Writings and Discoveries of Sir Isaac Newton* by Sir David Brewster, Edinburgh, 1850; cited in; *Newton's Philosophy of Nature*, p. 65, Ref. 20.

22. Thompson, B. and Harrub, B., Consciousness: the king of evolutionary problems, *CRSQ* **41**(2):113–130, 2004; see review by Tate, D., Consciousness: a problem for naturalism, *J. Creation* **21**(1):29–32, 2007.

irrelevant, or all possible beliefs come under the same suspicion of being only evolutionary adaptations—and thus biologically contingent rather than true or false. We find ourselves facing a version of the paradox of the Cretan liar: all beliefs, including this one, are the products of evolution, and all beliefs that are products of evolution cannot be known to be true."[23]

7. Man can think rationally and logically, and that logic itself is objective. This is a deduction from the fact that he was created in God's image (Genesis 1:26–27), and from the fact that Jesus, the Second Person of the Trinity, is the *logos* (John 1:1–3). This ability to think logically has been impaired *but not eliminated* by the Fall of man into sinful rebellion against his Creator. (The Fall means that sometimes the reasoning is flawed, and sometimes the reasoning is valid but from the wrong premises. So it is folly to elevate man's reasoning above what God has revealed in Scripture.[24]) But if evolution were true, then there would be selection only for survival advantage, not rationality.

8. Results should be reported *honestly*, because God has forbidden false witness (Exodus 20:16). But if evolution were true, then why not lie? It is not that surprising that scientific fraud[25] is now "a serious, deeply rooted problem."[26] "[T]he dozen or so proven cases of falsification that have cropped up in the past five years have occurred in some of the world's most distinguished research institutions—Cornell, Harvard, Sloan-Kettering, Yale and so on."[27] This was said in 1981 and evolution has even more of a stranglehold on thinking today.

Note, it's important to understand the point here—*not* that atheists can't be moral but that they have *no objective basis for this morality from within their own system*. Dawkins himself admits that our "best impulses have no basis in nature,"[28] and his fellow anti-theistic evolutionary biologist William Provine said that evolution means, "There is no ultimate foundation for ethics, no ultimate meaning in life, and no free will for humans, either."[29]

23. Dalrymple, T., What the new atheists don't see: to regret religion is to regret Western civilization, *City Journal*, www.city-journal.org, Autumn 2007.
24. Sarfati, J., Loving God with all your mind: Logic and creation, *J. Creation* 12(2):142–151, 1998; creation.com/logic.
25. Bergman, J., Why the epidemic of fraud exists in science today, *J. Creation* 18(3):104–109, 2005.
26. Roman, M., When good scientists turn bad, *Discover* 9(4):50–58; 1986; p. 58.
27. Editorial: Is science really a pack of lies? *Nature* 303:361–362, 1981; p. 361.
28. Evolution: The dissent of Darwin, *Psychology Today*, January/February 1997, p. 62.
29. Provine, W.B. (Professor of Biological Sciences, Cornell University, USA), *Origins Research* 16(1/2):9, 1994.

Scientific jump after the Reformation

Europe in the Middle Ages had a Judeo-Christian worldview, what Oxford don C.S. Lewis[30] (1898–1963) called "Mere Christianity" in a famous book of that name. So it's not surprising that there were very significant advances in science at that time, as documented above (p. 306). But it took the Reformation to recover specific biblical authority. With this came the recovery of a plain or historical-grammatical understanding of the Bible,[31] recovering the understanding of the New Testament authors[32] and most of the early Church Fathers.[33] This turned out to have a huge positive impact on the development of modern science. This is so counter to common (mis)understanding, yet it is well documented by Peter Harrison, then a professor of history and philosophy at Bond University in Queensland, Australia (and now Andreas Idreos Professor of Science and Religion at the University of Oxford):

"It is commonly supposed that when in the early modern period individuals began to look at the world in a different way, they could no longer believe what they read in the Bible. In this book I shall suggest that the reverse is the case: that when in the sixteenth century people began to read the Bible in a different way, they found themselves forced to jettison traditional conceptions of the world."[34]

As Prof. Harrison explained:

"Strange as it may seem, the Bible played a positive role in the development of science. ... Had it not been for the rise of the literal interpretation of the Bible and the subsequent appropriation of biblical narratives by early modern scientists, modern science may not have arisen at all. In sum, the Bible and its literal interpretation have played a vital role in the development of Western science."[35]

Stephen Snobelen, Assistant Professor of History of Science and Technology, University of King's College, Halifax, Canada, writes in a similar vein, and also explains the somewhat misleading term 'literal interpretation'[36]:

"Here is a final paradox. Recent work on early modern science has demonstrated a direct (and positive) relationship between the

30. See also Bergman, J., C.S. Lewis: creationist and anti-evolutionist, *J. Creation* **23**(3): 110–115, 3009.
31. Kulikovsky, A., The Bible and hermeneutics, *J. Creation* **19**(3):14–20, 2005; creation.com/hermeneutics.
32. Sarfati, J., Genesis: Bible authors believed it to be history, *Creation* **28**(2):21–23, 2006; creation.com/gen-hist.
33. Q&A: Genesis: Early Church Fathers; creation.com/fathers.
34. Harrison, P., *The Bible, Protestantism and the rise of natural science*, Cambridge University Press, 2001; see review by Weinberger, L., *J. Creation* **23**(3):21–24, 2009.
35 Harrison, P., The Bible and the rise of science, *Australasian Science* **23**(3):14–15, 2002.
36. Grigg, R., Should Genesis be taken literally? *Creation* **16**(1):38–41, 1993; creation.com/literal.

resurgence of the Hebraic, literal exegesis of the Bible in the Protestant Reformation, and the rise of the empirical method in modern science. I'm not referring to wooden literalism, but the sophisticated literal-historical hermeneutics that Martin Luther and others (including Newton) championed."[37]

Prof. Snobelen explains the reason why: scientists started to study nature in the same way they studied the Bible. Just as they studied what the Bible really said, rather than imposing outside philosophies and traditions upon it, they likewise studied how nature really did work, rather than accept philosophical ideas about how it should work (extending their allegorizing readings of Scripture to the natural world).

"It was, in part, when this method was transferred to science, when students of nature moved on from studying nature as symbols, allegories and metaphors to observing nature directly in an inductive and empirical way, that modern science was born. In this, Newton also played a pivotal role. As strange as it may sound, science will forever be in the debt of millenarians and biblical literalists."[37]

It is thus no accident that science has flowered since the Reformation, where the Bible's authority was rediscovered. And it is no accident that the country with the strongest remnants of Bible-based Christian faith, the USA, the one Dawkins disparages because 40% of its population believe in creation, leads the world by a mile in the output of useful science.

Belief in the Fall of Adam: how it inspired science

Prof. Harrison has researched another commonly overlooked factor in the development of science: belief in a literal Fall of a literal first man Adam. These founding modern scientists, including Francis Bacon,[38] reasoned that the Fall not only destroyed man's innocence, but also greatly impaired his knowledge. The first problem was remedied by the innocent Last Adam, Jesus Christ[39]—His sacrifice enabled our sin to be imputed (credited) to Him (Isaiah 53:6), and His perfect life enabled His righteousness to be imputed to believers in Him (2 Corinthians 5:21). But as for recovering what they believed to be Adam's encyclopedic knowledge, they looked to science.

Harrison explains:

37. Snobelen, S., "Isaac Newton and Apocalypse Now: a response to Tom Harpur's 'Newton's strange bedfellows'; A longer version of the letter published in the Toronto Star, 26 February 2004; isaacnewton. ca/media/Reply_to_Tom_Harpur-Feb_26.pdf.

38. Wieland, C. and Sarfati, J., Culture wars Part 1: Bacon vs Ham—*The story behind the modern-day separation of faith and science, Creation* **25**(1):46–48, 2002; creation.com/bacon.

39. Cosner, L., The Resurrection and Genesis, *Creation* **32**(2):48–50, 2010; creation.com/res-gen.

"New [*sic*] literal readings of the creation narratives in Genesis provided 17th Century thinkers with powerful motivating images for pursuing the natural sciences.

"Adam was thought to have possessed a perfect knowledge of all sciences, a knowledge lost to posterity when he fell from grace and was expelled from the Garden of Eden. The goal of 17th Century scientists such as Francis Bacon and his successors in the Royal Society of London was to regain the scientific knowledge of the first man. Indeed, for these individuals, the whole scientific enterprise was an integral part of a redemptive enterprise that, along with the Christian religion, was to help restore the original race to its original perfection. The biblical account of the creation thus provided these scientists with an important source of motivation, and in an age still thoroughly committed to traditional Christianity, the new science was to gain social legitimacy on account of these religious associations."[35]

"For many champions of the new learning in the seventeenth century, the encyclopaedic knowledge of Adam was the benchmark against which their own aspirations were gauged. ...

"The experimental approach, I shall argue, was deeply indebted to Augustinian views about the limitations of human knowledge in the wake of the Fall, and thus inductive experimentalism can also lay claim to a filial relationship with the tradition of Augustinianism."[40]

Objection

Some atheists admit that science was in effect a child of Christianity, but now claim that it's time science grew up and cut the apron strings. However, none other than former UK Prime Minister Margaret Thatcher answered that type of claim:

"I think back to many discussions in my early life when we all agreed that if you try to take the fruits of Christianity without its roots, the fruits will wither. And they will not come again unless you nurture the roots.

"But we must not profess the Christian faith and go to Church simply because we want social reforms and benefits or a better standard of behaviour; but because we accept the sanctity of life, the responsibility that comes with freedom and the supreme sacrifice of Christ expressed so well in the hymn:

---

40. Harrison, P., *The Fall of Man and the Foundations of Science*, Cambridge University Press, 2007, introduction.

'When I survey the wondrous Cross, On which the Prince of glory died, My richest gain I count but loss, And pour contempt on all my pride.'"[41]

So Dawkins' decades-long campaign against Christian faith is undermining the roots of the science he professes to love.

Will the real Clinton Richard Dawkins please stand up?

Dawkins asserts that his book is not anti-religious, although it attacks the foundational belief of God as creator. In doing this, he invokes the 'churchians' who support evolution.

"It is frequently, and rightly, said that senior clergy and theologians have no problem with evolution and, in many cases, actively support scientists in this respect. This is often true, as I know from the agreeable experience of collaborating with the Bishop of Oxford, now Lord Harries, on two separate occasions. In 2004 we wrote a joint article in *The Sunday Times* whose concluding words were: 'Nowadays there is nothing to debate. Evolution is a fact and, from a Christian perspective, one of the greatest of God's works.' The last sentence was written by Richard Harries, but we agreed about all the rest of our article. …

"The Archbishop of Canterbury has no problem with evolution, nor does the Pope (give or take the odd wobble over the precise palaeontological juncture when the human soul was injected), nor do educated priests and professors of theology. *The Greatest Show on Earth* is a book about the positive evidence that evolution is a fact. It is not intended as an antireligious book. I've done that, it's another T-shirt, this is not the place to wear it again. Bishops and theologians who have attended to the evidence for evolution have given up the struggle against it. Some may do so reluctantly, some, like Richard Harries, enthusiastically, but all except the woefully uninformed are forced to accept the fact of evolution. …

"They may think God had a hand in starting the process off, and perhaps didn't stay his hand in guiding its future progress. They probably think God cranked the Universe up in the first place, and solemnised its birth with a harmonious set of laws and physical constants calculated to fulfil some inscrutable purpose in which we were eventually to play a role. But, grudgingly in some cases, happily in others, thoughtful

41. Thatcher, M., *Christianity and Wealth*, Speech to the Church of Scotland General Assembly, 21 May 1988; www.margaretthatcher.org.

and rational churchmen and women accept the evidence for evolution." (pp. 4–6)

Yet in *The God Delusion,* Dawkins had nothing but contempt for the idea of God using evolution as His means of creation. For example,

"I am continually astonished by those theists who, far from having their consciousness raised in the way that I propose, seem to rejoice in natural selection as 'God's way of achieving his creation'."[42]

This suggests that Dawkins regards these churchian evolutionists as 'useful idiots', to use Lenin's term for his dupes in the West who couldn't see that they were cutting off the branches on which they sat. See also ch. 16 for why this is indeed an untenable view.

Dawkins continues (in *Greatest Show*):

"To return to the enlightened bishops and theologians, it would be nice if they'd put a bit more effort into combating the anti-scientific nonsense that they deplore. All too many preachers, while agreeing that evolution is true and Adam and Eve never existed, will then blithely go into the pulpit and make some moral or theological point about Adam and Eve in their sermons without once mentioning that, of course, Adam and Eve never actually existed! If challenged, they will protest that they intended a purely 'symbolic' meaning, perhaps something to do with 'original sin', or the virtues of innocence. They may add witheringly that, obviously, nobody would be so foolish as to take their words literally. But do their congregations know that? How is the person in the pew, or on the prayer-mat, supposed to know which bits of scripture to take literally, which symbolically? Is it really so easy for an uneducated churchgoer to guess? In all too many cases the answer is clearly no, and anybody could be forgiven for feeling confused." (pp. 7–8)

Yet in *The God Delusion*, Dawkins was withering about ministers who do exactly that, including his buddy Harries:

"Oh, but of course, the story of Adam and Eve was only ever *symbolic*, wasn't it? *Symbolic*? So, in order to impress himself, Jesus had himself tortured and executed, in vicarious punishment for a *symbolic* sin committed by a *non-existent* individual? As I said, barking mad, as well as viciously unpleasant."[43]

42. Dawkins, *The God Delusion*, p. 118.
43. Dawkins, *The God Delusion*, p. 253, emphasis in original.

It doesn't bother him that belief in a historical Adam and historical Fall was instrumental in the beginnings of modern science, as documented above (p. 315). Then Dawkins preaches (*Greatest Show* again):

"Think about it, Bishop. Be careful, Vicar. You are playing with dynamite, fooling around with a misunderstanding that's waiting to happen—one might even say almost bound to happen if not forestalled. Shouldn't you take greater care, when speaking in public, to let your yea be yea and your nay be nay? Lest ye fall into condemnation, shouldn't you be going out of your way to counter that already extremely widespread popular misunderstanding and lend active and enthusiastic support to scientists and science teachers? The history-deniers themselves are among those who I am trying to reach. But, perhaps more importantly, I aspire to arm those who are not history-deniers but know some—perhaps members of their own family or church—and find themselves inadequately prepared to argue the case." (p. 8)

This is ironic, because a frequent mantra of evolutionists is 'Leave creation out of the schools; teach it in church only.' But now Dawkins wants church leaders to teach evolution in church! In America, this putsch to get creation (God) out of schools is augmented with the mantra 'Separation of Church and State', which is nowhere found in the US Constitution.[44] And at the start of his book, Dawkins complained about people telling biology teachers what to teach. Yet Dawkins now objects to creation being taught in churches as well, and is telling pastors what to teach!

Summary

- Dawkins' attempt at guilt-by-association rebounds: the Holocaust and Roman Empire have ample written records by eyewitnesses in support. And Dawkins himself has given tacit support to a fringe history denial: the claim that Jesus of Nazareth never existed.

- While denial of evolution is often equated to denial of science, most science functions perfectly well without belief in evolution. This includes biology. Many scientific advances were made before Darwin.

44. In the case, *ACLU vs Mercer County* (KY, 2005), circuit judge Richard Suhrheinrich ruled: "[T]he ACLU makes repeated reference to 'the separation of church and state.' This extra-constitutional construct grows tiresome. The First Amendment does not demand a wall of separation between church and state ... our Nation's history is replete with governmental acknowledgment and in some cases, accommodation of religion. ... ('There is an unbroken history of official acknowledgment by all three branches of government of the role of religion in American life from at least 1789.') After all, '[w]e are a religious people whose institutions presuppose a Supreme Being.' ... Thus, state recognition of religion that falls short of endorsement is constitutionally permissible. [Cited court cases omitted]"...

- The Bible provides presuppositions essential for science to work, such as objective reality of nature, freedom of the Creator to create, so that only experiments and observation would find out how; that the Creator was a God of Order so the universe would be orderly; the right to investigate it and that this investigation would honour the Creator; that man can initiate thoughts and think logically, and that results should be reported honestly. Evolution can't provide any basis for these presuppositions.

- Most branches of modern science were founded by creationists. The misnamed 'Dark Ages' in Christianized Europe was a period of much invention and scientific advance.

- After the Reformation, an objective understanding of Scripture was rediscovered, which scientists carried over to nature, leading to huge advances.

- Belief in a real historical Fall of a historical first man Adam inspired scientists like Bacon to use science to try to rediscover the superior knowledge of an unfallen Adam.

- Trying to use the fruits of Christianity while rejecting the roots will result in withering of the fruits.

- Dawkins allies with churchians who claim that God used evolution, yet he has nothing but contempt for this belief.

- Dawkins demands that preachers tell their congregation that Adam was not a real figure, but also claims that belief in a symbolic Adam is "barking mad".

- Dawkins complains when Christians tell biology teachers what not to teach (evolution), but he tells Christian pastors what not to teach (a historical Adam).

—∞—

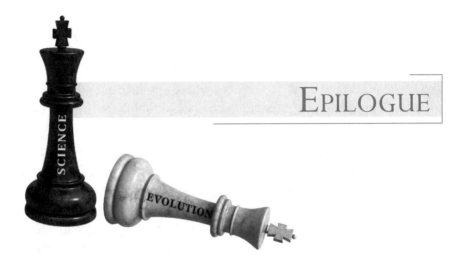

EPILOGUE

To be charitable to Dawkins, it's not likely that (despite the rhetoric hyping *Greatest Show*) any single book on the subject of origins—including this one—can be anything like comprehensive. This is a huge subject, with worldview implications, covering not just a vast range of scientific disciplines, but also philosophy, theology, history and more.

Hopefully, however, enough has been presented to show that Dawkins' work is very far from being an 'unanswerable' challenge. And that there is much reason for confidence that the Bible's big picture of history can more than stand, in fair and open debate, against the best that secularism can provide.

Dawkins is irate whenever he feels that evolution is misrepresented by its critics, and hates it when anti-evolutionists fail to deal with the strongest proponents and arguments. But by its very nature, this book can't be guilty of this, since it addresses the strongest arguments he could muster, and he is an acknowledged champion of evolution.

The reader should have gleaned, too, that it is hardly likely that reading the works of anticreationists such as Dawkins will provide a fair insight into what informed creation-believing scientists really do teach and believe. Nor will it likely give a representative picture of the strengths and weaknesses of the current state of the science in support of straightforward Genesis. It's highly recommended to read the core books summarizing what creationists believe and propose, follow up the references where applicable, and use intensively the search engine on, e.g., creation.com with its 7,000+ articles on a huge range of subjects.

It should also be clear that the argument is not so much about the 'facts' but how they are interpreted, especially when it comes to the unobserved past history of our planet and its biota, including humanity. Many of my qualified colleagues in the creation movement have had the opportunity of seeing the evidence through the lens of secular presuppositions—prior to seeing how it looks through a biblical one. And even those who have been creationists throughout are more aware of how the evidence looks through an evolution-lens than most secularists are of the converse—if only because the media today tends to present most 'facts' in a pre-digested, pre-interpreted setting.

The evolutionary 'big picture' is thus going to be a self-reinforcing paradigm, in which most scientists and intellectuals believe it, essentially because most scientists and intellectuals believe it.

One would hope that this work will start a whole new round of truth-seeking in which evolution-believers will be encouraged to try the biblical lens on for size, as it were—to see how the world looks when not interpreting everything through a strictly naturalistic one.

Investigating and resolving the subject of origins will inevitably have deep implications for ultimate meaning and destiny; arguably the most important thing in your life. If (I would say 'since') we are the product of design, it is only rational that a Designer would communicate something of the purpose of that designing to His rational creatures. The Bible claims to be that communication, containing what we need to know for salvation and fulfilled living.[1,2] This includes telling us that He created, when He created, and the sequence of creative acts.[3] And that book defeats all other explanations decisively as an explanation of the world as we find it, with both exquisite design and the present ugliness around.[4] As shown in the last chapter, the Bible also provided

1. Sarfati, J., The Authority of Scripture, *Apologia* 3(2):12–16, 1994; creation.com/authority.
2. Livingston, D., Jesus Christ on the infallibility of Scripture, in: 'A Critique of Dewey Beegle's book titled: *Inspiration of Scripture'*, M.A. Thesis, 2003; www.creation.com/jesus_bible.
3. See also Sarfati, J., Genesis: Bible authors believed it to be history, *Creation* 28(2):21–23, 2006, creation.com/gen_hist.
4. See also Catchpoole. D., Holy books? Which one are you going to trust? *Creation* 26(1):1, 2003; creation.com/holybooks.

the framework for the explosion of science that started in the Middle Ages of Europe, and really took off after the Reformation. The history recorded in the Bible also explains geology (the Flood), languages (evolutionists have no Babel[5]), population distribution, and the origin of agriculture.

The Bible also reveals that the Designer sent an Emissary—his Son, Jesus of Nazareth, who is the exact representation of the Designer.[6] The Son proved His credentials impeccably by His words and deeds, and said, "Then you will know the truth, and the truth will set you free" (John 8:32). Finally, although Jesus' enemies killed Him, historical evidence shows that He conquered death on the third day. James Patrick Holding has shown that there are at least 17 factors that meant Christianity could not have succeeded in the ancient world, unless it were backed up with irrefutable proof of Jesus' Resurrection.[7]

In the Bible, the Designer has also told us what He expects from those whom He made, and how their disobedience resulted in death and cutting off from Himself.[8] But the same book reveals His rescue plan. His Son Jesus Christ came into the world to take upon Himself the penalty for our sins, and endure death and shame in our place. He rose from the dead, proving that He had paid the price and conquered death.[9]

—∞—

5. Languages change rapidly; the dozen or more languages existing after the dispersion diverged and split repeatedly within what are now known as (distinct, unconnected) language families. See creation.com/babel.
6. "… God … has spoken to us by his Son, whom he appointed the heir of all things, through whom also he created the world. He is the radiance of the glory of God and the exact representation of his being, and he upholds the universe by the word of his power" (Hebrews 1:1–3).
7. Holding, J.P., *The Impossible Faith*, Xulon Press, Florida, USA, 2007.
8. For more information, see Sarfati, J., The Fall: a cosmic catastrophe—Hugh Ross's blunders on plant death in the Bible, *J. Creation* **19**(3):60–64, 2005; creation.com/plant_death.
9. See also Good news! creation.com/goodnews.

INDEX

Other books by Jonathan Sarfati

Refuting Evolution

A hard-hitting critique of the most up-to-date arguments for evolution, to challenge educators, students and parents. It is a powerful, yet concise summary of the arguments against evolution and for creation. It will stimulate much discussion and help students and teachers think more critically about origins. This top-selling book has over 500,000 copies in print. 144 p.

Refuting Evolution 2

A sequel that comprehensively refutes arguments to support evolution (as presented in TV documentaries and *Scientific American*). Read world-leading evolutionists in their own words, and then find straightforward answers from science and the Bible. Refuting Evolution 2 will prepare you to answer the best arguments thrown at you by peers, teachers, neighbours and skeptics. 240 p.

Refuting Compromise

A comprehensive and resounding refutation of the position of 'progressive creationist' Hugh Ross, whose views are causing massive confusion about science and the Bible. The most powerful and scientific defense of a straightforward view of Genesis creation ever written. 425 p.

By Design: Evidence for nature's Intelligent Designer—the God of the Bible

Presents case after case for amazing design in the living world, and demolishes theories of chemical evolution of the first life. Yet unlike many in the prominent Intelligent Design Movement, Dr Sarfati is up-front about the truth of the Bible. This enables him to refute many anti-design arguments, and answer the key question: 'Who is the Designer?' 260 p.

Wholesale: www.creationbookpublishers.com
Retail: creation.com or similar creation sites

DVD presentations by Jonathan Sarfati

All these DVDs include English sub-titles for hearing-impaired viewers

Chemicals to Living Cell: Fantasy or Science?

See how 'goo-to-you' evolution is refuted right at the start! In this fascinating illustrated lecture, a Ph.D. chemist shows how the laws of real chemistry prevent non-living chemicals from arranging themselves into living cells. Self-reproducing cells have far more complexity than Darwin imagined. 57 min.

Arguments Creationists Should NOT Use

In this candid presentation before an international conference of nearly 600 creationist speakers and writers, Sarfati reveals the out-of-date, faulty and downright flaky evidences that reputable creationists must avoid. In his trademark style, he challenges some of the most-loved arguments of modern creationists, while encouraging us to focus intensely on God's written Word as the absolute guide to evidence interpretations. 49 min.

Jesus in Genesis: The Messianic Prophecies

See how the whole Bible, right from the beginning, points to Jesus Christ as God and man, and Saviour. The time, place and manner of His birth, and His mission, are just what the prophets foretold. Genesis is foundational to all this teaching. 60 min.

Evolution and the Holocaust

How could such an advanced country descend to unspeakable brutality? Evolutionary ideas permeating Germany undermined the sanctity of innocent human life. See a chilling Nazi propaganda clip, "we have sinned against natural selection" by allowing the "unfit" to live. Learn how the abortion and euthanasia lobbies make the same mistake. 39 min.

Leaving Your Brains at the Church Door?
The power of logic in defending your faith.

Why should Christians defend their faith? How should they do so? See how to spot common fallacies and use correct logic—both to present a positive case for Christianity, and refute objections. Anti-Christian fads such as evolutionism and postmodernism assail Christians, but logic is a powerful weapon to demolish them. 56 min.